SAM AND FRIENDS

Sam and Friends

The Story of Jim Henson's First Television Show

Craig Shemin

Foreword by

Frank Oz

BearManor Media
2022

Front cover: Photo by Del Ankers, *Sam and Friends* logo and television artwork by Jim Henson.

Cover design by Craig Shemin, executed by Dave Hulteen, Jr.

Front and back cover images: The Muppets and associated characters, trademarks, and design elements are owned by Disney Enterprises, Inc. © Disney

© Craig Shemin

Foreword © Frank Oz

Sam and Friends © The Jim Henson Company. JIM HENSON'S mark and logo, SAM AND FRIENDS mark & logo, and certain characters and elements are trademarks of The Jim Henson Company. All Rights Reserved.

The Muppets and associated characters, trademarks, and design elements are owned by Disney Enterprises, Inc. © Disney

Images provided courtesy of The Jim Henson Company (unless otherwise noted).

Additional photography Jack L. Hiller, © 1959

Baltimore American photograph courtesy of Hearst Communications Inc.
Esskay News images courtesy of the Baltimore Museum of Industry.

Additional photos courtesy of:
Special Collections, University of Maryland Libraries.
D.C. Public Library, Star Collection © Washington Post

HUCKLEBERRY HOUND FOR PRESIDENT
Words by Joseph Barbera, William Hanna, and Hoyt Curtin
Copyright © 1962 (Renewed) BARBERA-HANNA MUSIC
Huckleberry Hound is a trademark of and copyrighted by *Hanna-Barbera Productions Inc.*
All Rights Reserved
Used by Permission of ALFRED MUSIC

I COME FOR TO SING
Words and Music by Bob Gibson, Chick Jung, and William Wright
TRO – © Copyright 1960 (Renewed) 1964 (Renewed) Melody Trails, Inc., New York, NY/Robert Josiah Music BMI administered by Wixen Music Publishing, Inc.
International Copyright Secured Made in U.S.A.
All Rights Reserved Including Public Performance for Profit
Used by Permission

GO GO POGO
Words and Music by Walt Kelly, Norman Monath
Copyright © 1956 Walt Kelly
Pogo is a trademark of and copyrighted by Okefenokee Glee & Perloo, Inc.
All Rights Reserved
Used by Permission

Published in the United States of America by:

BearManor Media

4700 Millenia Blvd.
Suite 175 PMB 90497
Orlando, FL 32839

bearmanormedia.com

Printed in the United States.

Typesetting and layout by BearManor Media

ISBN—978-1-62933-620-6

TABLE OF CONTENTS

Foreword by Frank Oz   xi

Introduction   1

Part I – The *Sam and Friends* Story

Chapter 1: The History   11

Chapter 2: This Is WRC-TV Washington   15

Chapter 3: Admiration at First Sight   20

Chapter 4: Sam and His Friends   32

Chapter 5: National Exposure   54

Chapter 6: It's Time to Play the Music   71

Chapter 7: 1958: A Very Major Big Year   84

Chapter 8: Jim and Jane Henson   95

Chapter 9: Brought to You by Esskay   108

Chapter 10: It's Time to Light the Lights   118

Chapter 11: The Surviving Shows   141

Chapter 12: Jerry   160

Chapter 13: Five Scripts   171

Chapter 14: I Come for to Sing   206

Part II – The *Sam and Friends* Episode Guide

Credits	227
Air Schedule History	228
Music List and Partial Episode Guide	233
1961 Esskay Commercials	518
Additional Sam and Friends Music	529
Live Appearances	534
Acknowledgments	539
End Notes	543
Index	560

For Stephanie, who inspires me . . .

And for Jane Henson, who tried to stay out of the spotlight but whose contributions deserve celebration and acknowledgment. She's going to get her share of credit in this book, and there's nothing she can do about it.

Foreword

By

Frank Oz

I never saw *Sam and Friends* when it was on television. I lived in Oakland, California, and *Sam and Friends* was a local Washington, D.C., show.

The first time I actually saw Jim's work was at home in Oakland in 1961. I was seventeen.

Our TV was on, and up popped this very short commercial for Calso Water, a California product. On the screen there was one weird, amorphous-like character behind a cannon aiming it at a weird, triangle-shaped character. The first character asks the second, "Do you like Calso Water?" The triangle-shaped character answers, "No!" The first character then blows him away with the cannon. Then the cannon is turned straight to camera, and, with a tacit threat, the first character asks the viewer, "Now, do *you* like Calso Water?"

That seven-second commercial was revelatory to me. It was like nothing I'd ever seen before. The soft puppets, the abstract design of the characters, the precise lip sync, the absence of a puppet proscenium, the hip humor, the simplicity, the violent punchline, the clarity of the message in only seven seconds. It was astonishing.

At the time, I didn't realize that the characters were Wilkins and Wontkins and that the same structure of that commercial was also used with other products in different regions of the country. ("Do you like Wilkins Coffee?" "Do you like Merita Bread?") And I certainly couldn't know that in a few years I'd be performing Wontkins to Jim's Wilkins, along with some of the characters and bits that had been on *Sam and Friends*.

Jim had seen me perform when I was seventeen at a Puppeteers of America convention in Northern California. Prior to that, I had been performing with my own show. (Since I was twelve, I had puppeteered at birthday parties, fairs, supermarket openings, parking lots, national parks, and school assemblies in the San Francisco Bay Area . . . those were my training grounds.)

He came to see me backstage after I performed at that convention. He said he really liked my show but that my ending was weak. I understood years later why he said that. His bits mostly ended with explosions or monsters eating each other. He then went back to D.C. (after extending a job offer to my older friend Jerry Juhl), and I continued school in Oakland.

I never wanted to be a puppeteer. I wanted to be a journalist. At eighteen, after I graduated high school, I enrolled at Oakland City College to begin my career in journalism. It was 1963, almost a year after Jim had moved the Muppets from Washington, D.C., to New York.

I had been in class for just four months, at which time I turned nineteen. That's when Jim contacted me. After not having seen me for almost two years, Jim asked me if I would come join the Muppets in New York City part time for six months. My parents knew Jim, and they knew he was a good person, so they selflessly supported their nineteen-year-old to go work and live by himself in the NYC of the 1960s, which was exciting but turbulent.

I flew to New York on a rainy August night in 1963 and was picked up at the airport by Jim and Jerry in Jim's station wagon. I stayed with Jim and his wife, Jane, that night.

I spent the first few years learning the Muppet style of performing. During that time, I viewed a lot of old *Sam and Friends* clips on black-and-white kinescopes (as the copies were called then). I loved everything I saw, but I especially loved the very last show.

In it, there is a quiet moment between Harry and Kermit (although he was not a frog at that time). As they are sadly talking about how this is the last show, Kermit quietly and wistfully notes that they won't be using the sets anymore. Harry then says, "So let's blow them up!" And with loud explosions and smoke half-covering the screen, Harry runs around blowing up all the sets.

This was pure Jim. He went against the grain whenever he had the opportunity. And it was the controlled, affectionate anarchy that began with *Sam and Friends* that was at the heart of the Muppets and became part of all of us who worked with Jim.

A frame from a Wilkins commercial outtake: Frank Oz watches Jim Henson's work on the monitor as Jerry Juhl looks on. Frank Oz's six-month stint with the Muppets turned into several decades, and along the way, he originated many beloved iconic Muppet characters, including Grover, Bert, Cookie Monster, Fozzie Bear, Sam the Eagle, Animal, and the incomparable Miss Piggy. He began his long film directing career with the Muppets, as co-director of *The Dark Crystal* (1981) with Jim Henson, and as director of *The Muppets Take Manhattan* (1984).

Introduction

In the early 1990s, I was working for The Jim Henson Company (then known as Henson Associates or ha!) as the public relations assistant and part-time archivist. This was after the Henson archives had been established by Bob Payne, whom you'll soon be reading about, and before the hiring of the amazing longtime Jim Henson Company Archives Director Karen Falk. At the time, the company's off-site storage was at a warehouse near the George Washington Bridge. Unseen by most employees, it was referred to simply as "The Bridge," as in, "We don't need those files—send them to The Bridge." Rarely would anything our department sent to The Bridge ever be seen again.

Word came down that the company was moving its off-site storage to a warehouse in Brooklyn and every department had to send someone to The Bridge to weed out unnecessary items. For our department, that person was me.

On the day of my journey, someone from the production department handed me a piece of paper with a list of box numbers labeled as "old production files." I was told that the production department didn't need these boxes anymore, and if I wanted them for the archives, I could have them. At the time, the production boxes were the least of my concerns. I had a couple hundred public relations department boxes to go through.

I hailed a taxi and headed uptown. Way uptown.

The sign read SOFIA BROTHERS FIREPROOF WAREHOUSE, but once I arrived, it occurred to me that while the building may be fireproof, most everything stored inside it was certainly not. If you've seen the last scene from *Raiders of the Lost Ark,* that should give you an idea of what it looked like.

Once I was finished sorting the P.R. boxes, I walked over to the production department storage area and located the five or six boxes on the list I had been given. As soon as I opened the first one, I knew this material could be important. I recognized the handwriting on the folder tabs. It belonged to Jim Henson, who had passed away just a year or so earlier.

Inside the folders were storyboards, sketches, notes, scripts—all from the beginning of *Sesame Street* or earlier.

Each box contained a different batch of amazing finds—storyboards from Jim's commercials and *Sesame Street* counting films, the first sketches of Rowlf the Dog. While the archive that I was entrusted with preserving contained some amazing things, I had never seen this volume of original material from the earliest days of Jim Henson's career.

One file was labeled *Sam and Friends* and contained Jim's handwritten scripts and some typed ones. I knew *Sam and Friends* from the handful of kinescopes I had watched on my lunch hour—it was Jim's first televised creation from the 1950s—and in my hands, I was holding a direct connection to the original production. I went to the warehouse office, called a car service, and took these newfound treasures back to the Henson townhouse on Manhattan's Upper East Side, which at that time was the New York headquarters for the company.

When work started on *Jim Henson: The Works,* the coffee-table book published in 1993, these files and sketches were shared with the editorial and design team, and by this time, Karen Falk had begun her career at Henson and was able to properly catalog and preserve them. In the years since, the items found in these boxes have been shared with the public in various books and exhibitions.

Not long after my discovery, my work at Henson had changed. I still was very interested in the history of the company, but I became a staff writer and was working to create new work and not look back at the old stuff.

In 2002, after fourteen years, I left the Henson Company to devote my time to freelance work (with the occasional Muppet gig in the mix). But while I left the company, I didn't leave the Henson family. Jane Henson invited me to join the Board of Trustees of The Jim Henson Legacy, the nonprofit organization she founded to celebrate her husband's career and share it with the public. Jane knew that the Henson Company, Sesame Workshop, and Disney would keep Jim's characters alive, but she wanted to make sure that Jim was identified as the artist behind the characters.

The Legacy organization has since created exhibitions, special events, panels, and screenings all to serve its mission of celebrating Jim's work.

My passion project has always been the screenings, especially those of Jim's earliest work. In 2004, we first presented *Muppets, Music & Magic*. The project began as a weekend film and television retrospective at the Brooklyn Academy of Music (BAM)—eighteen screenings in all four of its movie theaters jammed into two days. Each day culminated with brand-new compilations of some of Jim Henson's rarest work. I assembled these in consultation with Jane Henson and Jerry Juhl, the longtime head writer (and early performer) of the Muppets.

In putting together these programs, I was able to see material that the public had never seen, and I was thrilled to share it with as many people as possible, but would there be any interest? The folks at BAM were concerned. In the week leading up to the event, advance ticket sales were much lower than expected. Our fears were allayed when the crowds did indeed materialize (BAM later learned that a computer glitch prevented many advance sales from taking place). We knew we were doing well when the head of BAM told us we were breaking records for popcorn sales at the concession stands. This weekend laid the groundwork for a long-running screening tour that would take me from Detroit, Michigan, to Melbourne, Australia, and many cities in between.

I had a real fascination for Jim's early work—*Sam and Friends* in particular—and I would discuss it with Jane Henson at every opportunity. In 2009, Jane sat down for a few interviews with me to talk about those early days. In those interviews, Jane's deep fondness for the show emerged—it was the Muppet project in which she was most directly involved and one that she remained close to, both figuratively and literally. In fact, for many years, the show's original acetate audio transcription discs sat in her garage. When they came to the archives, Jane asked me to put some of them on a CD so she could use them in puppetry workshops.

While Jane once said she believed that some lost television shows should remain lost, I certainly don't think she felt *Sam and Friends* was one of them. She remembered word for word many of the songs she had lip-synced to fifty years earlier, and she enjoyed watching the clips when we screened them, always asking me to include the full episodes so audiences could see the beginning, middle, and ending that Jim devised.

Sadly, there weren't that many episodes to show, but every so often, there would be a new discovery in The Jim Henson Company Archives. When a reel of assorted Henson commercials was transferred to video in the early 2000s, the lost *Sam and Friends* episode "Weather Warehouse" happened to be on it. In 2015, while planning the permanent Henson exhibitions at the Center for Puppetry Arts and the Museum of the Moving Image, a Legacy project to create new high-definition transfers from the surviving prints and elements of Jim's short films and commercials turned up all sorts of goodies we had never seen before—including another lost *Sam and Friends* episode ("Glow Worm") and a couple of Esskay commercials from the show. One more episode, "Miss Cone," was uncovered as I was finishing work on this book.

In 2015, Henson Archives Director Karen Falk and Media Archivist Carla DellaVedova discovered another treasure in the collection: forty-four reel-to-reel tapes containing more than four hundred audio recordings made during *Sam and Friends* broadcasts, starting in late 1958 and running until the end of the series in 1961.

When I had interviewed Jane Henson in 2009, I had thought about the possibility of writing a book about *Sam and Friends,* but I didn't know whether there would be enough material to work with. However, with the discovery of these tapes, I realized we had found the missing link to really breaking down what the show was about.

An examination of *Sam and Friends* allows us to appreciate Jim Henson's unfiltered art, work created before he had dozens of artists working with him. In 1990, I was working on location during the production of *The Muppets at Walt Disney World* in Orlando, Florida, when I overheard a discussion between Jim and a very young fan during a break between scenes:

YOUNG FAN:	Do you do Gonzo?
JIM:	No, I don't do Gonzo.
YOUNG FAN:	Do you do Animal?
JIM:	No, I don't do Animal.
YOUNG FAN:	Do you do Miss Piggy?
JIM:	No, I don't do Miss Piggy.
YOUNG FAN:	Don't you do anything anymore?

Jim smiled and laughed as he was called back to the set. While the young fan wasn't quite accurate—Jim certainly still did quite a lot as an executive producer, a director, a performer, and President of Henson Associates—this book is a visit to a time when he was more actively engaged and hands-on with all the tasks associated with bringing the Muppets to the airwaves. It's about how he executed his vision alongside his partner (who would become his wife), Jane Nebel, who brought along her own sense of humor and creative play to the equation.

When considering Jim's earlier work, it's important to understand the technological environment in which he was operating; these were the days of *live* television. *Sam and Friends* premiered in 1955, only eight years after the station on which it aired—WRC, the NBC affiliate in Washington, D.C.—was first licensed to broadcast. To call the technology primitive would be an understatement. While the dialogue and music were prerecorded, almost every episode's puppetry performance was broadcast live. Jim, who was writing and co-performing in the show while also juggling his courses at the University of Maryland, was often at the studio for two five-minute broadcasts each day—taking place about five hours apart—in addition to appearing in other WRC broadcasts and working in the studio scene shop.

By the time the run of *Sam and Friends* ended in 1961, it was broadcasting in living color and the era of videotape had begun, although the show continued to air live. If something went wrong, viewers saw it happen.

At this time, most areas in the country had access to only a handful of television channels. There were three major broadcast networks (plus the smaller DuMont network in a few areas), and the lucky markets also had one or two independent stations. But even with these limitations, television was a sensation with an audience growing from 35,000 television sets throughout the country in 1948 to more than thirty million sets in 1955 when *Sam and Friends* began. With only a few channels, programs could reach large numbers of people. Stars were made overnight, and even a five-minute show could become a hit among viewers.

It's unfortunate that *Sam and Friends* was seen in only one—and sometimes two—local markets and that most of the country couldn't experience Jim's brilliance and the genesis of the Muppets. It's even more unfortunate that so few episodes survive. My hope is that this book will help spread the word about this little-known yet very important first chapter in Jim Henson's professional story and perhaps inspire a new generation of creators.

This is the story of how a young college student turned a five-minute program into thirty-five years of television and film creativity. We'll begin this book in earnest just as most episodes of the show began. . . .

Sam and Friends . . .
Buh-duh-dum-dum-dum . . .

Is brought to you by . . .
Buh-duh-dum-dum-dum . . .

Esskay . . .
Buh-bup-bup-buh-bup-buh-bum.

PART I

The *Sam and Friends* Story

CHAPTER 1

The History

"For everybody else in the world, puppets are a magical part of our childhood, and here is a man who never gave them a thought and his name is Jim Henson, the most famous name in the whole history of puppetry," said Orson Welles, dumbstruck, after Henson explained that he had never played with puppets as a child and never so much as saw a puppet show before he decided to use the form as a means to break into television.

It was 1979, and Jim Henson and Frank Oz were guests on a talk show pilot hosted by the legendary film director, likely as thanks for Welles's cameo in *The Muppet Movie,* which was released that year. Henson and Oz sat in large, imposing armchairs opposite their equally imposing inquisitor. Welles, a self-described "puppetstruck" lover of the ancient art form, couldn't get past the idea that Henson had never played with puppets as a child.

"I just heard about a television station that was looking for puppeteers, and so I made puppets and auditioned because I really wanted to work in television," Henson said.

"Puppets are very ancient entertainers," said Welles, as he turned the interview into a soliloquy. "They don't just go back to the crib. They go back to the cave. I'm afraid they were beginning to show their age a little until you came along and dragged that whole squeaking box of dolls into the twentieth century and into the mainstream, big time."

Welles spoke direct to the camera in that distinct tone that could only be described as Wellesian. But this time, he was not selling wine or frozen peas; he was selling Jim Henson. The man who made *Citizen Kane* (1941) closed the interview by proclaiming the Muppets to be "for my money, the most original thing that ever happened on the box." It was high praise coming from a man who had reimagined cinema when he was twenty-five years old.

In June of 1954, Jim Henson's career working on "the box," which was less than a month old, looked as if it was coming to an end. WTOP, Washington, D.C.'s CBS affiliate, had pulled *The Junior Morning Show* off the air after only three once-weekly broadcasts, leaving Pierre the French Rat and his puppeteer, high school student Jimmy Henson, out of a job.

The short-lived *Junior Morning Show* had been the brainchild of Roy Meachum—a pivot after his own cancellation months earlier. Meachum had been hosting *Meet Roy Meachum* in the 7 to 9 a.m. weekday time slot on WTOP when, in early 1954, CBS decided to launch their own counterprogramming to NBC's *Today*. The daily national broadcast, *The Morning Show,* featured Walter Cronkite in the anchor chair and Bil Baird's puppets providing comic relief. Out of a job, Meachum found inspiration from *The Morning Show* and its puppet segments and decided to create his own weekend version for WTOP—*The Junior Morning Show*—with children filling all the roles, right down to a young puppeteer occupying the role the Bairds played on *The Morning Show*.

WTOP believed that recently revised child labor regulations that relaxed rules for young performers would allow them to hire children under fourteen for the new show, so a casting call was placed in Lawrence Laurent's *Washington Post* column: "Roy Meachum of WTOP-TV has started a search for youngsters 12 to 14 years of age who can manipulate marionettes."

The producers also paid a visit to the puppetry club at Northwestern High School in Hyattsville, Maryland, in which Jim was a member—albeit as a set builder, not a puppeteer.

Jim saw the opportunity as his ticket into the television industry.

"I absolutely loved television," Jim said in a 1982 interview retrieved from The Jim Henson Company Archives. "I was tremendously excited by the medium. I loved the idea that it was taking place at the same time; I mean it was one of those absolutely wonderful things."

The only thing holding Jim back from this possible TV puppetry gig was his complete lack of knowledge about puppetry. He checked out a couple of library books (*The Puppet Theatre Handbook* by Marjorie Batchelder and *My Profession* by Sergei Vladimirovich Obraztsov), built some puppets, and auditioned. He got the job.

Jim wasn't an expert by any means, but he more than compensated for his rudimentary puppetry skills with a keen sense of humor. Joe Irwin, a friend from Jim's days at Northwestern High School, recalled Jim's impish and creative take on daily life. When the pair were on the Northwestern tennis team, players were required to run laps around the school, but on each lap, Jim and Joe took a novel shortcut through the building.

"We would go into the school on the far side and come back out the front door, way down the way where no one would notice... it shortened the trip." That may be one of the few instances when Jim Henson ever cut corners.

With his hands full—both figuratively and literally—Jim enlisted the assistance of Russell Wall, a friend from the Northwestern High School drama club, to join him at WTOP to perform the puppets during the live broadcasts.

Rehearsals began in early June 1954, and for a high school student who wanted to work in television, *The Junior Morning Show* was a dream come true... until it went away.

Unfortunately, the producers at WTOP had misinterpreted the relaxed child labor regulations, and the sad result of their error was announced in *The* (Washington, D.C.) *Evening Star*'s June 25, 1954, issue. "OOPS, SORRY—That 'Junior Morning Show' which WTOP-TV launched last Saturday will go back into drydock after tomorrow's telecast. Reason: Discovery that the revision of the child labor law permitting children to appear on stage here applies to the stage and not to television. Three of the program's key participants were under 14 and consequently couldn't get work permits."

In the three weeks the show did air, Jim Henson's puppetry must have made an impression. While *The Junior Morning Show* was history, Jim and his high school classmate Russell Wall, who were both well over fourteen years old and thus permitted to work, stayed on at the station to do lip-sync segments for Roy Meachum's new *Saturday* show—until it, too, was canceled in August. Jim and Russell parted ways—after all, they had graduated high school and were moving on. Jim planned to enter the University of Maryland in the fall.

In a 1969 interview in Washington, D.C.'s *Sunday Star TV Magazine*, Roy Meachum said that when his show ended, he called Jim Kovach, the program director at WRC at the time, and asked him to find a spot for Jim's puppets. "They were just too talented to forget about."

CHAPTER 2

This Is WRC-TV Washington

Jim Kovach would indeed find a spot for Jim Henson and his puppets, and in the fall of 1954, the program director put the recent high school graduate to work at NBC's Washington, D.C., station, WRC—on the air as a puppeteer and behind the scenes as a set builder.

"He told me he was up there working on sets," said Joe Irwin, Jim's high school friend. "You know, I didn't know about puppets with him initially. I knew that he was up there working on designing backgrounds for the show and things like that. . . . One day he told me about how he was working with different colors on the sets to see how it looked in black and white." This was important experimentation for Jim, as WRC was still a few years away from color broadcasting.

Jim was thrilled to learn about the medium he loved. And one of the first things he learned, as he revealed in a 1982 interview later published online, was that "there wasn't much money in television in those days." When he first started, he received just $5 a show—but he didn't mind: "I was a kid and it was fun," he said in the interview. Jim would eventually make more money at WRC, but he still had to pay for the puppet and set materials out of pocket. Still, within a few months, he confided to Sharon Doran of *The Evening Star*'s "Teen Scene" column, "I'm making GREAT MONEY—in three figures, yet!"

Crafting his own puppets was a big part of Jim's work at the WRC, though he was still learning puppetry techniques through trial and error. His earliest puppets—like Pierre the French Rat from WTOP—were crafted from hard materials like plastic-wood and had very little flexibility. Even with his limited puppetry experience, Jim realized that he needed softer, more pliable puppets to create a more dynamic relationship with the close-up medium of television. While some of his new characters would continue to be made from plastic-wood, more and more of his puppets would take form in fabric, fleece, and foam.

Not long after he started puppet building, Jim dubbed his troupe of characters "The Muppets." "For a long time, I would tell people it was a combination of marionettes and puppets," Jim said in the 1982 interview. "But basically, it was really just a word that we coined. We have done very few things connected with marionettes."

While working at WRC, Jim also began classes at the University of Maryland—where he would have his first so-called formal training as a puppeteer. He enrolled in the university's puppetry class, which was taught by Ed Longley, a recent Columbia University Teachers College graduate with little experience in the art form.

In fact, Longley's specialty was crafts. "I think his main craft was jewelry," Jim's wife, Jane Henson, who was also a student in the puppetry class at the time, recalled in 2009. "When Ed Longley was hired, he was mostly jewelry and metallurgy, but the University of Maryland told him that they wanted him to teach a puppetry class. I felt like he knew ahead of time that he was going to be asked to do it, so he was prepared to teach the class, but in an academic sort of way—because he had no background in puppetry at all himself."

Longley soon realized that Jim Henson's puppetry experience, limited as it was, outweighed his own, and according to Jane, Longley was more than happy to take advantage. It wasn't long before Jim was helping to teach the class.

"Jim was extremely capable of doing puppets, obviously," said Longley at a 2006 panel discussion at the University of Maryland. "He had learned a lot in high school. When he came to the class, though, I was very rigid. I had thirty projects for them to do. I had a project of hand puppets . . . there was another one with stick puppets, and then the famous marionette. However, Jim didn't go with that, he went with a combination of the stick puppet with the hand puppet. And you've seen the result. He was extremely interested in making those puppets work." In the classroom, Jim explored live puppet theater for the first time while also constructing a new cast of Muppets for WRC.

Local TV stations of the 1950s had a patchwork schedule to fill, with empty blocks of time between network broadcasts that had to be programmed throughout the day. While today's local television news can fill up to six hours a day, back then, fifteen minutes seemed like plenty, and most of the local TV time was divided between shows for housewives and shows for children. With budgets thin to nonexistent, old movies became fodder for kids shows.

On WRC, *Circle 4 Ranch* was the daily outpost where Cowboy Joe Campbell presented the day's Western flick to a home audience of little buckaroos. Shortly after Jim Henson joined WRC, *Circle 4*'s director, Bob Porter, introduced Cowboy Joe to the station's new scenic artist/puppeteer. Two new Muppets, Longhorn and Shorthorn, soon joined the ranch, with their prerecorded voices provided by Joe Campbell.

Jim Henson's voice would eventually become instantly recognizable to generations, but in 1954, he was not yet voicing his characters. Instead, he preferred to perform to recordings, just as Bil and Cora Baird had done on *The Morning Show*. "They were just doing novelty records and little, tiny, short bits and pieces," Jim said in 1982. "I guess that was kind of how I started off into doing the record lip-sync stuff." When he got the WTOP gig to do his own version of the Bairds' CBS *Morning Show* spots, he just followed their lead. Although *The Junior Morning Show* and Jim's time at WTOP was over, he continued to do the same lip-sync style of performances at WRC.

WRC's *Circle 4 Ranch*, behind the scenes. Photo by Jim Henson

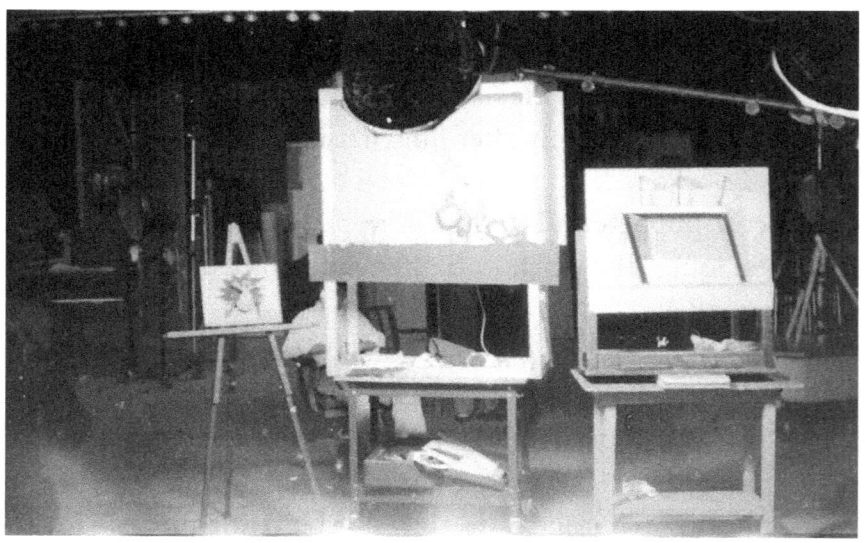

Jim's puppet setup for *Circle 4 Ranch*. Photo by Jim Henson

While *The Junior Morning Show* and Cowboy Joe's *Circle 4 Ranch* were aimed at children, Jim was not specifically focused on that audience. He would soon find that WRC would bring him opportunities to reach a broader audience.

Jim Henson at WRC-TV in 1956. Photo by Philip Geraci,
Courtesy of Special Collections, University of Maryland Libraries.
©1956 University of Maryland

CHAPTER 3

Admiration at First Sight

Jane Nebel was planning on a career in art education. Born in Queens, New York, and six years later transplanted to Salisbury, Maryland, Jane enrolled in the University of Maryland as an art education major. When she was a senior, she was in Ed Longley's puppetry class because she had to be—it was required for her major.

"It was a senior class—a seniors course for art education majors," Jane said in 2009. "It wasn't a very big class—about eight people. But everybody else in the class were people who had been together for a few years, and then Jim came in as this young . . . dude," she said with a laugh.

When asked if it was love at first sight, she smiled.

"It was admiration at first sight."

Although he was just a freshman, Jim soon displayed his natural leadership qualities. "Jim was great in that class," Jane said. "He never . . . pushed himself forward. It's just that he took over everything." Even then, Jane recalled, he was "a totally natural leader. . . . He doesn't want to be pushy about it, but he just assumes he's going to be the leader." Jane, on the other hand, described herself as a follower.

Jim put his own creative spin on the projects Ed Longley assigned. He brought in James Thurber's *The 13 Clocks* for the marionette group to adapt—even though Jim himself wasn't in the group. Jane Nebel played the Golux, the brave prince's sidekick who joins the prince on a quest to gather a thousand jewels in ninety-nine hours and restart thirteen frozen clocks. Jim played the good knight.

While Jane worked in the marionette group, Jim led the hand-puppet team.

"He really helped make all the puppets," Jane said. "He wrote it . . . he did the scenery for it. He didn't *do* everything, but he sort of directed it all."

She compared the project to a Monty Python piece—made almost fifteen years before Monty Python. "The basic story was good versus evil. . . . Good wins, but evil sort of has a comedy part. Not exactly a vicious part—more of a comedy part."

It was a stage performance, but Jim's work in television influenced the design in a very specific way.

"He was working mostly in no color—white, values of gray," Jane said. "And I know now—looking back on it—that's because what he was doing on television, everything was black and white, so he liked working in grays. So the puppets and the scenery were all in black and white. There may have been an accent of color here and there, but mostly it was black and white."

The class concluded the fall semester with a public performance of their work. Jane vividly remembered having fun performing as the Golux—and she must have made a good impression on Jim. After working solo at WRC for months, Jim was about to start doing a segment on a new daily show called *Afternoon,* and while working out his first bit—set to Georgia Gibbs's 1954 record, "Tweedle Dee"—he realized he needed another hand . . . or two. He turned to Jane.

Jane explained how she became involved with the show to Jim's biographer, Brian Jay Jones, in 2010: "It was all planned, and then he needed somebody to work with . . . so he asked me to come in and work with him on that piece and I enjoyed it, and I think I just kept doing it because I enjoyed it. It's not like I went, 'Oh, wow, this is just wonderful.' You know, it was very . . . it was enjoyable."

Afternoon was a mix of a "home show" and variety show targeted at housewives—an amalgam of recipes, fashion, news, and music all presided over by masters of ceremonies Mac McGarry and Willard Scott. The show featured performer Jack Maggio, weathercaster (and fellow University of Maryland student) Tippy Stringer, beauty and fashion expert Inga Rundvold, and music from the Mel Clement Quartet. Starting with the show's initial broadcast on March 7, 1955, the Muppets were a part of this daily block of local television, contributing their own music-based performances.

Tippy Stringer rehearses for *Afternoon* with Mel Clement at the piano and director Carl Degen. Photo by Jim Henson

Inga Rundvold on the *Afternoon* set. Born in Norway, Inga was a model before beginning her long television career. Photo by Jim Henson.

Onscreen, the Muppets never interacted with the other presenters—they just lip-synced to a record. For Jim, who was relatively new to puppetry, using records was, as he explained in a 1982 interview, "a way that one could do entertaining pieces rather safely and easily. And so for years, we did that and built up slightly."

"We would pick a record. . . . He would build puppets that would go with it and I would help perform," Jane said in 2009.

For that first performance of "Tweedle Dee," Jim constructed two bird puppets with articulated beaks. "I think one of them had wings, one didn't . . . and they sang it and that was pretty much it. It's not a complicated piece . . . the complications came later," Jane said, alluding to the more elaborate routines Jim eventually created. From the beginning, Jane had a good time, she told biographer Brian Jay Jones. "It was enjoyable, and I liked the way Jim went about working. [I was] totally impressed with the way he was working." But, as impressed with Jim as she was, Jane saw this new extracurricular activity only as something that was fun to do while she was student teaching and interviewing for teaching jobs.

Jane Nebel enjoys a break on the *Afternoon* set. Photo by Jim Henson.

Sam watches himself during an *Afternoon* broadcast.

With a regular daily broadcast, *Afternoon* is where Jim received a good deal of his on-the-job training, and he impressed the staff and crew with his imaginative approach. *Afternoon*'s director Carl Degen told *The Washington Post and Times–Herald*, "the kid is positively a genius. He's absolutely amazing."

"You know, in Washington, D.C., the television stations were mostly about news shows," Jane said. "And, really, Jim went to play. It was very playful and very imaginative and so . . . the crews—the engineers—were more than happy to work with him, and he was really smart about learning that. They would be more than happy to have him around the control room and such and learn the different things. And then he took a job in the scene shop, so he did sets for other shows, too. He mostly wanted to be around television, so he spent a lot of time at WRC. I think he always took two courses at University of Maryland. He went full time, I guess for maybe a year, but then after that, he went part time."

Management of WRC took notice of the positive viewer response to the Muppets, and they decided to give Jim his own daily five-minute show—called *Sam and Friends*—while also keeping the characters on *Afternoon*.

"I think Joe Goodfellow was the one who chose to put us on," Jane Henson said. Goodfellow, a station executive, must have thought there was something appealing about the Muppets because he gave them a prime spot on TV— leading right into *The Tonight Show*, and eventually, a slot at the tail end of the news/sports/weather strip during the dinner hour.

Not everyone at WRC was convinced. One executive expressed concern about whether it was even appropriate to program a puppet show like *Sam and Friends* as part of a block of news programming.

"In those days, we did a range of things," Jim recalled in a 1982 interview. "They went from silly and lightweight pieces, and then we would do some slightly . . . I always enjoyed doing slightly strange and surrealistic kinds of things that nobody would understand what we were doing. And it was this nice little show that was on late at night, it was only five minutes long. Nobody really cared, so you could do almost anything."

While the show was considered daring, Jane didn't see any harm in what they were putting out over the air. "We didn't do questionable material. Just sort of goofy," she said.

As *Sam and Friends* launched in May of 1955, Jane was in the process of graduating from the University of Maryland with her bachelor's degree and planning her future as an art teacher. Jim, however, wanted her to stick around and continue working with him on the new show, Jane said. He insisted it was a short-term arrangement, suggesting, "Why don't you just do it for the summer?"

So she did. Jane and two friends took an apartment in Washington, D.C., near Dupont Circle with the idea that she would continue to interview for teaching positions while working with Jim on the various Muppet performances.

Sam and Friends was warmly received by its audience and by newspaper columnists. Lawrence Laurent of *The Washington Post and Times–Herald* and Bernie Harrison of *The Evening Star* were always effusive in their praise. Harrison proclaimed Sam to be the most brilliant newcomer to the Washington scene. "His friends are all right, too."

Jim and Jane had not realized how popular the show had become until station management suddenly decided to pull it off the air after just three months. Bernie Harrison broke the news in his column on August 19, 1955: "Write an angry letter right now to the head man at WRC—Benedict Arnold," Harrison wrote. *Sam and Friends* left the airwaves after its Friday, August 26, 1955, broadcast, but Harrison's call for letters succeeded. After only one Muppetless Monday, WRC relented and returned the show to its 11:25 p.m. slot the next day, August 30.

Bernie Harrison relayed the good news in *The Evening Star* the next day: "Sam came back last night to WRC-4 at 11:25, in fact, being off only one night, which must be a Washington and world's record for the distance. And if you're wondering how it was done, that's easy. Your letters and phone calls."

Harrison then printed a dispatch he had received the previous day—a response to his column about the removal of *Sam and Friends* from the schedule:

Dear Bernie:

My boss took your column to his boss and before he finished reading it, the mailman had jammed the office with mailbags.

Well, his jaw dropped even lower than mine (and that's hard to do) and the next thing I know, I was being carried to the music library to plan some more programs.

So, between you and my TV friends and the boss, we're hoping to be with you as long as we're really wanted. Thank you for laughing with me and writing about me.

SAM

P.S. Jim Henson and Jane Nebel would like to thank the people, too.

Jane had a big decision to make in the summer of 1955. She had applied for a teaching position and was offered the opportunity to begin her new career as an art educator. "I had to make a decision whether or not I was staying with him or taking that job." She decided to postpone her teaching plans and instead continue to work with Jim on the various Muppet commitments while pursuing a master's degree at Catholic University. For her master's dissertation, Jane created a large ceramic nativity scene—a project she would reinvent for a live puppet production decades later.

"Mom was a serious artist, a painter and ceramicist," said Cheryl Henson, Jim and Jane's daughter. "She was a studio assistant to abstract expressionist painter Kenneth Noland when she was a graduate student at Catholic University. Her work was different from Jim's. It had a depth and spiritual aspect but also a rebellious antiestablishment, anarchic side that complemented his humor well."

In a 1959 "Career Girl" profile in *The Sunday Star,* Jane described throwing pottery as one of her most relaxing pastimes, "next to making Muppets. . . . It's fascinating; I never tire of it because I learn something new each time." She confessed to being "a beginner" at the potter's wheel, though reporter Ruth Dean wrote that "she appears to handle it like an expert."

To refine that expertise, Jane usually took two morning classes at the university before joining Jim at WRC.

She told TV columnist Lawrence Laurent that Jim was "the boss" of the team. In the same article, Jim said that he and Jane were partners, but he conceded that he may be the boss "just a little bit."

In the years and decades to come, Jane tried to keep the public focus on Jim, but some of the spotlight couldn't help but shine on this young woman who was working in an unusual job in the entertainment business. Even *Glamour* magazine featured a photo of Jane at work.

Katherine Elson profiled Jane in *The Washington Post and Times-Herald* in early 1957 when *Sam and Friends* aired twice a day on WRC. "One of the brightest young talents in local TV is never seen on camera," the article began. Typical in an era when women were often defined by their appearance, Elson takes care to say that Jane is a meticulous dresser, designing and making many of her own clothes. And although her work often had her kneeling on the studio floor, Jane wore a skirt with her bright red knee socks, sneakers, and sweater.

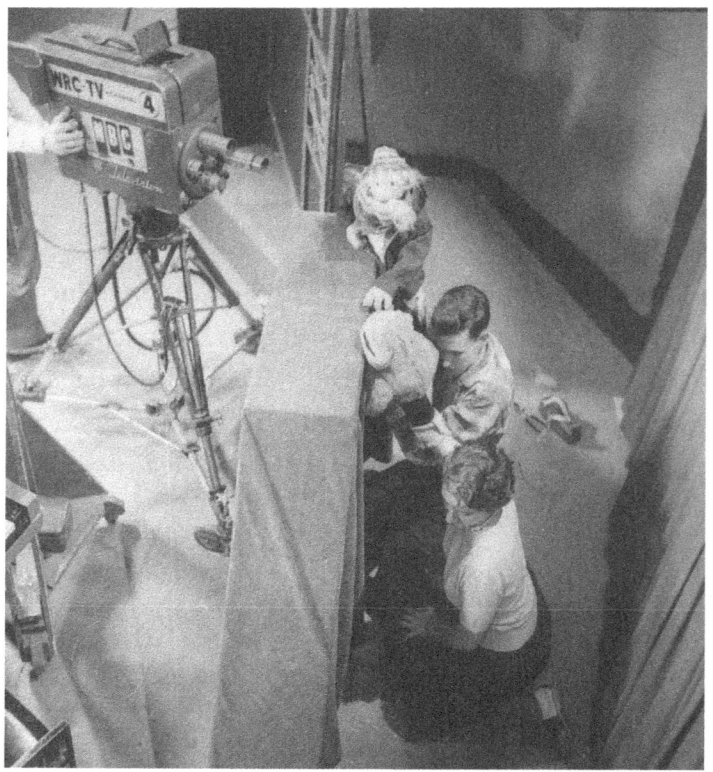

Jane and Jim at work at WRC in 1956. Note Jane's skirt and saddle shoes. Photo by Philip Geraci, Courtesy of Special Collections, University of Maryland Libraries. ©1956 University of Maryland

"Jane lives in an apartment over near CU with a fellow art student who has never seen Jane's shows," the article continued. "They have no TV set."

In the piece, Elson described a typical day in Jane's life: "Up every morning for her graduate classes in art at Catholic University, Jane usually has a quick lunch before meeting Jim for 'ideas' sessions on the show at his family's house. Then the pair head for the studio at the Sheraton-Park Hotel in Jim's snazzy white Thunderbird (a present from Sam).

"After the 6:30 p.m. show... Jane and Jim are free for dinner and homework until about 10:30 or so. They're back at the studio after that for their 11:25 p.m. program."

Jim and Sam in Jim's Thunderbird.

With his hectic schedule, Jim spent a lot of time in the Thunderbird that "Sam" bought for him. It was only about two miles from Jim's parents' house to the University of Maryland and then ten miles from the university to the WRC studio at the Sheraton-Park Hotel in Washington, D.C. The Rodel studio, where Jim and Jane would soon be working on a series of commercials, was in Georgetown, about three miles from the hotel. Jane's apartment near Catholic University was about midway between Jim's parents' house and WRC. Even in the mid-1950s, traffic in Washington, D.C., could add time to Jim's various commutes. As if Jim wasn't busy enough with classes and the Muppets, he had started a silk-screen poster business operating out of the University of Maryland's Student Union. (A statue of Jim and Kermit can be found outside of the building today.)

The poster for Jim's silk-screen poster business.

Jim was always working on something or on his way to work on something, occasionally stopping for a meal—often a hamburger and milkshake with Jane at a Hot Shoppes restaurant. He put a lot of mileage on the Thunderbird, but Jim really enjoyed being behind the wheel, according to friend Joe Irwin, who spent three weeks with Jim on a cross-country road trip shortly after Jim purchased the car in 1956.

In October of 1955, only weeks after the viewing audience had saved *Sam and Friends,* the show was once again removed from the schedule, replaced by *The Les Paul and Mary Ford Show*. Sponsored by Listerine, the nationally syndicated five-minute show featured the well-known husband and wife duo doing various chores around the house, yet always finding excuses to stop what they were doing to perform a song.

Needless to say, despite the high production value of Les Paul and Mary Ford's filmed series, WRC viewers were not pleased.

"Many remarks could be made about the absurdity of replacing clever Sam with the guitar-flaying Listerine battle [could be a newspaper typo meant to be "guitar-playing Listerine bottle"] (not that I don't appreciate the talents of Les Paul and Mary Ford); but five minutes viewing of channel four at 11:25 p.m. these nights is worth a million remarks. All summed up—phooey! Bring back our Sam," wrote Mrs. K to *The Evening Star*'s "TV and Radio Mailbag."

Losing the 11:25 time slot made Jim and Jane only slightly less busy, as their work continued on *Afternoon* as well as other occasional appearances on WRC.

Jim and Jane were spending a lot of time together, but Elson's Jane Nebel profile insisted that the relationship was strictly business; the article even mentioned that Jane was dating a philosophy student. This business-only arrangement would soon evolve.

CHAPTER 4

Sam and His Friends

Jim's first puppet-building effort, Pierre the French Rat, based on a cartoon he drew in high school, was pretty primitive. Because Pierre's head was constructed from hard plastic wood, the puppet had little expressiveness and only minor capability of lip-sync movements. Jim had learned the construction technique from two books written about puppetry for the stage, not television.

Pierre the French Rat

"Most puppeteers at that point worked with absolutely rigid faces and generally no expression at all in the character because puppets in general, before television, were meant to be seen at a distance," Jim said in a 1982 interview. "They were usually small figures . . . without moving mouths . . . meant to be seen at a distance of fifteen to fifty feet."

Jim soon realized he could take advantage of the close-up nature of television by using materials that would allow for more subtle movements in the puppets. "I think we were one of the first people to design puppets for use on television where you're looking at it very close, so you're working with what you can do with that face seen very close and relating to the camera," he said.

Plastic wood and similar techniques would still be used for some characters—including Sam and his friend Yorick—but, as Jim explained in 1982, he "immediately started working in soft things and fabric. And at that point, urethane foam, foam rubber, all of that stuff was really new. When we first started working, there was only foam rubber, and that was available in sheets. One could take that and do wonderful things with it. But I don't think puppeteers had figured out what you could do with different kinds of materials."

Jim and Jane make an adjustment to Sam on the set. Photo by Philip Geraci, Courtesy of Special Collections, University of Maryland Libraries. ©1956 University of Maryland

As his cast of characters grew, Jim took more and more care in their design and construction, with his new partner, Jane, a skilled artist, contributing her talents to the process. When looking back on those early days, Jane would always direct the focus to Jim, saying that "it was clearly Jim's vision and Jim built the great puppets and . . . visualized the whole thing." But Jane would eventually concede that for every three puppets he built, she built one.

When it came to performances, the decision on who performed which puppet varied based on the puppet's role in the individual piece. Jane described the process in 2009:

"Basically, [Jim] would take the main character, and I took the secondary character. He would prefer that the secondary character not be Kermit, because he would prefer I not work Kermit, but very often, it was." For example, in "That Old Black Magic," Jim opted to perform Sam and handed off Kermit to Jane so Jim could make the most of Sam's unique shoulder movements.

Here is a closer look at the *Sam and Friends* cast of characters:

Sam

SAM

Sam was bald and silent—except when singing with someone else's voice. "He's easy going . . . not too brilliant, the most human and least animalistic of the lot," Jim Henson said of Sam in a 1956 newspaper article. The other characters were more abstract, and while they evoked some animalistic features and traits, they weren't designed to represent any specific species. According to Jane Henson, "[Sam] was the only human because the whole thing was about how a human, a simple human, reacts to life. And all the other characters were like things going on in his head. That's the design of it. The friends are within him, within Sam. And they're abstractions." While *Sam and Friends* is a very whimsical approach to the idea of inner self, Jim explored the concepts a little more seriously with his later experimental work.

Like Jim's very first puppets, Sam was constructed from hard materials and had a face incapable of subtle expressions. Sam's deadpan appearance allowed the viewer to assign any emotion to his blank look. To one viewer, he might have appeared frightened; to another, excited. It all depended on the other characters in the scene and the audio track being used. Sam was essentially a blank slate, but in Jim Henson's hands, Sam's body movement could speak volumes.

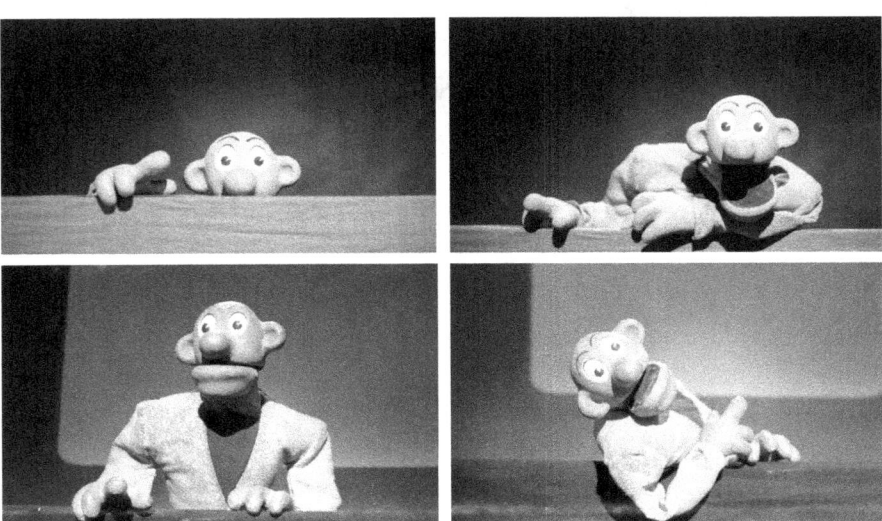

The many faces of Sam.

"I made him originally to use with Phil Harris records," Jim said in a 1957 *Sunday Star Magazine* article. "But he proved the most popular Muppet of all. That gave us the idea for *Sam and Friends*."

There wasn't much political content in *Sam and Friends,* but when the 1960 presidential election came along, following in the footsteps of Walt Kelly's comic strip character Pogo Possum, Sam ran unsuccessfully for the presidency of the United States on the "Republicratic Party" ticket. Though he usually did not speak, he made an exception for the campaign, but only delivering the same prerecorded speech over and over: "Friends, I say when the world situation is hopelessly confused, you need a president who fits the situation."

Sam was born in October 1954 shortly after Jim started work at WRC. His copyright certificate, #Gu 27449, was issued on October 9, 1956.

Kermit

KERMIT

The tale of Kermit's origin has been told many times—about as many times as Spider-Man's origin has been depicted on film. And it's true: Jim Henson built Kermit from a Ping-Pong ball and an old coat that his mother had tossed into the household rag bag. But, as Jim often reminded people while telling the story, the original Kermit was not the color we identify with him now. "It was sort of more a turquoise—sort of a milky turquoise," he said in a 1982 interview. As long as we're setting the record straight, while Jim did know a boy named T. Kermit Scott when he was a child in Mississippi, the Kermit character was not named for him; as with all of his characters, Jim just picked a name that he thought was appropriate. In other words, the Muppet looked like a Kermit.

Jim built Kermit while his family was going through a very difficult time—the illness and eventual passing of Jim's grandfather Maury Heady Brown (known to Jim as Pop). While waiting to take his turn at Pop's bedside, Jim would sit at his grandparents' round dining table and stitch pieces of his mother's old coat into a puppet that would eventually become the most famous puppet character in the world. Jim seemed able to channel sadness and grief into creative energy. About a year after Kermit's creation, on April 15, 1956, Jim's brother, Paul, an ensign in the U.S. Navy, was killed in an auto accident in Florida. This tragedy seemed to spur Jim to work even harder.

Kermit joined the Muppets in March 1955, shortly before *Sam and Friends* premiered. Over time, he became more and more central to the show, appearing in sketches, songs, and commercials. He was a very versatile guy.

The one thing he was not, however, was a frog. With the exception of the eponymous Sam, the Muppets of WRC-TV were abstract characters, not intended to replicate any specific species but able to lend themselves to any need created by song or story. "All the characters in those days were abstract because that was part of the principle that I was working under—that you wanted abstract things," Jim said in 1982.

"If you take a character and you call him a frog . . . or a dog, you immediately give the audience a handle," Jim said. "You're assisting the audience to understand; you're giving them a bridge or an access. And if you don't give them that, if you keep it more abstract, it's almost more pure. It's a cooler thing. It's a difference of sort of warmth and cool."

Kermit poses on a log, foreshadowing his later career as a frog.

So Kermit was not a frog back then. Appearing more reptilian than amphibian, his skinny body resembled a lizard more than a frog. In fact, he was occasionally referred to as a tree lizard. Kermit could also be described as gender-fluid, with a wig quickly added to turn Kermit into Kermeena—Jim's spelling—as needed.

Kermit as Kermeena

One major similarity between the original Kermit and the frog he would become was his expressiveness. Jim's 1982 evaluation of the character could easily apply to the 1950s version: "The nice thing about Kermit is there's nothing in that head. I mean, the whole shape is merely just a cloth pattern, and so it takes the shape of your hand inside, and so the whole thing is really created by your hand, which is why he's a delightful character to operate, too. He's so flexible and very responsive. One of the things we've always tried to do with any of our puppets is to try and get them flexible enough so that you have a wide range of emotions possible."

Jane said Jim designed Kermit to take advantage of the close-ups on camera. "We didn't know it then, but very possibly, Kermit was the first puppet . . . designed specifically for what the camera does, because everybody else [performing] puppets that were on television had started out in the live venue, the live theater," Jane said in 2010.

"From the very beginning, though, Kermit had a special place for Jim," she said. "I think it was because of the way he was made, he had nothing inside of him, so no matter what Jim did, it was Jim's hand doing it. . . . In close-ups, the manipulation was so subtle, and Jim just loved that subtlety, and he never really did any other character like that afterward."

Even in 1957, Jim declared Kermit to be his favorite among the Muppet characters. "Kermit can do everything but talk . . . and the records make him do that," Jim said in a *Sunday Star Magazine* interview. Very soon after that statement, Jim gave voice to Kermit and no longer needed records to make the character speak.

Kermit was created in March 1955; his copyright certificate, #Gu 27448, was issued on October 9, 1956.

Harry

HARRY

Harry—sometimes referred to as Harry the Hipster—was the cool dude behind the dark shades. Constructed from a brown nubby-textured fabric and never seen without his trademark sunglasses, he was the first in a long line of Muppet hipsters. In addition to his reputation as a jazz musician, Harry was among the major proponents of "The Poet's Corner," a recurring segment of *Sam and Friends*. In it, cast members would take turns reciting poems—some made up by Jim, some classics by the likes of Lewis Carroll, and some submitted by viewers.

From a contact sheet: Jane manipulates Harry for a photo shoot.

Harry always spoke in slang, referring to jobs as "gigs" and people as "cats"—it's unsure what he called actual cats.

Born in September 1954, Harry was one of the earliest Muppets constructed by Jim Henson. His copyright certificate, #Gu 27450, was issued on October 9, 1956.

Moldy Hay

MOLDY HAY

Moldy was a Southern boy—no doubt inspired by Jim Henson's own Mississippi roots. According to various mentions on the show and integrated commercials, Moldy grew up on a farm with his sister, Doozey May. As such, he was usually the cast member who delivered the commercials for Esskay Hickory Smoked Bacon, mentioning his homesickness for a genuine farm-style breakfast. With his hair flopped over his forehead, he was one of the Muppets whose eyes you never saw. Moldy also has the distinction, along with Kermit, of introducing one of the most often-used pieces of Muppet comedy material, as seen in this December 5, 1958, Esskay commercial:

MOLDY HAY: I used to take care of a bunch of cows my daddy had.
KERMIT: Not bunch, Moldy. Herd.
MOLDY HAY: Herd of what?

KERMIT: Herd of cows.
MOLDY HAY: Well, sure I've heard of cows.
KERMIT: No! I mean the cows' herd!
MOLDY HAY: Well, I don't care if they heard. I haven't said anything to be ashamed of.

"It's a beautifully made puppet," Jane said of Moldy, whose abstract features are more or less humanoid. "It was one of Jim's really beautiful puppets, I think." Moldy Hay was created in May 1956, which would coincide with the premiere of *Footlight Theater*, the Muppets' next WRC project following their October 1955 cancellation.

Omar

OMAR

Omar was a hard-faced puppet who holds the distinction of being the first of Jim's live-hands puppets—where Jim manipulated the character's head and used his own left hand as Omar's left hand, while Jane provided Omar's right hand. This technique, which Jim later employed with the Swedish Chef, was depicted in the Sergei Obraztsov book Jim referred to when building his first puppets for WTOP. (While Yorick was sometimes seen with a gloved hand, it was a disembodied one; the puppet was not designed as a true live-hands puppet.)

Omar joined the Muppets in 1956 at the launch of *Footlight Theater* with Paul Arnold and was initially voiced by Arnold. Press photos show him dressed as a pirate, but that persona faded away with *Footlight Theater*. Since he had live hands and could manipulate the ingredients, Omar starred in the first wild Muppet cooking sketch, laying the groundwork for the Swedish Chef two decades later.

The Omar puppet was constructed by Jane Henson, who built him as a camel, but as with most *Sam and Friends* characters, Omar was really an abstract form who could fit any need that might arise in the script.

Professor Madcliffe

PROFESSOR MADCLIFFE

Professor Orin E. Madcliffe (or, as mentioned in one episode, Herman Finnius Madcliffe) was a mad scientist who, when not inventing machines like a laugh meter, quite often acted as an energetic pitchman for Esskay. Jane Henson compared his hyperactive, frantic voice to Guy Smiley. "Jim liked doing those. It was easy for him to do those because they are not like Jim at all."

When Kermit interviewed Madcliffe in an episode, we learned that the professor had received the Birdwell-Frisby Memorial Citation and the Rodel Prize for Accomplishment (Rodel was the name of the studio run by Fritz Roland and Del Ankers where Jim and Jane shot Wilkins Coffee commercials).

Madcliffe's inventions were occasionally featured on the show, none functioning as designed, but in Kermit's on-air interview with the professor, Madcliffe explained that his machines not working as designed was actually by design. "I invent failures," Madcliffe said. "Most inventors try to invent successes, but the world isn't all peaches and cream, you know. You have to have failures in life, too. You don't think things go wrong by themselves, do you?"

Professor Madcliffe, Kermit, and Harry with one of Madcliffe's inventions.

Jim with Professor Madcliffe in the WRC offices.

Judging by his inventions shown on *Sam and Friends*, Madcliffe did an excellent job of doing a rotten job. He constructed a robot named Fisby, which was supposed to have an aptitude for mathematics but instead electrocuted Kermit and ran off to make love to the television camera. In another bit, Madcliffe installed a sense of humor into Fisby so he could tell jokes on "The Jokebook Nook," a recurring segment of *Sam and Friends*. When it came time for Fisby to tell a joke, he emitted a series of beeps (a foreshadowing of R2-D2?). While none of the cast members could understand Fisby's joke, it went over big with the laugh meter, another one of Madcliffe's creations.

While his inventions were failures, Professor Madcliffe's energy and enthusiasm were put to excellent use in the Esskay commercials, usually imploring the other cast members to do a better job selling the product. Professor Madcliffe made his *Sam and Friends* debut in the summer of 1957.

Bernice

BERNICE

Added to the cast in 1959, Bernice was the first little girl Muppet character—a precursor to the little girl from *The Ed Sullivan Show*'s "Beautiful Day" segment and Prairie Dawn from *Sesame Street*. Bernice was also the first Muppet not built by either Jim or Jane or voiced by Jim. Bob Payne built Bernice and performed the character.

Yorick

YORICK

One of the earliest Muppets, Yorick was born in June 1954.

Yorick—whose name was inspired by the skull found in *Hamlet*—was indeed of similar form to a human skull but in a deep shade of purple. His main trait was an insatiable hunger, and he ate anything not nailed down (and probably some things that were). Yorick spoke in a guttural grunt noise, a sound that Jim created by inhaling while speaking, rather than exhaling. Yorick was initially unintelligible, but over time, occasional words and phrases were inserted among his grunts so he could be understood by his many fans.

Yorick was immensely popular with audiences. In a 1957 poll, viewers named him as their favorite *Sam and Friends* character, with 2,007 votes. (Mushmellon—described below—nabbed second place with 1,378 votes; Sam came in third with 1,242; and future worldwide superstar Kermit finished fourth with 953 votes.) Jane Henson recalled that Yorick also received an honorary membership in the Alpha Tau Omega fraternity.

In various episodes, audiences learned that Yorick hailed from Yoricktown (Yorktown), New Yorick, and had a family that shared his culinary voraciousness; in one installment, his mother was identified as having devoured a missing station wagon.

From a technical point of view, even though Yorick had no body, he was the first puppet that Jim used a live hand with, most notably when Yorick fed himself in segments like "Hunger Is From."

Icky Gunk

ICKY GUNK

Icky Gunk, a snakelike creature, made his *Sam and Friends* debut on August 4, 1959. His first performance was a bit of typecasting: He lip-synced to the novelty record "S-S-S'Wonderful," portraying the reptile mentioned within the song, a nearsighted rattlesnake named Hector. His next appearance was believed to be in the "Drain Dweller" sketch as Orwell Filchmouth, the dweller of the drain in question.

In subsequent installments of the series, Icky became a sort of smarmy antagonist. In one episode, he planned to take over as the station's weather forecaster, and in another, he offered payola to the Muppets to *not* perform a record.

Mushmellon

MUSHMELLON

Mushmellon was born in June 1955. A roly-poly blob of a puppet, he was honored with his own day on March 2, 1961, as the show changed its name to *Mushmellon and Friends* and celebrated National Mushmellon Day. On that episode, viewers learned that Mushmellon was born "at a very early age on the Melonesian island of Mush. His talent soon became obvious—he could bounce . . . and who but Mushmellon can squash himself down?"

That day, Mushmellon received testimonials from the other characters. "Mushmellon is one of the bounciest characters I ever met," Kermit said. "Mushmellon is very mushy," said Bernice, who was referred to as Mushmellon's ex-girlfriend. We also learned that jazz musician Harry worked at the same club that Mushmellon worked at as a bouncer. "The cats used to call him the Shake, Rattle, and Roll Kid. When he hit the scene, the floor shook, the windows rattled, and the heads rolled."

In that episode, Arctic Icky (Icky Gunk) made an appearance as an Alaskan dog sledder who used to have Mushmellon on his sled team—but Icky explained that he knew Mush by another name. "We called him Melvin, or Mel for short. Although he wasn't a dog, he bounced very fast across the snow and soon became the leader of my dog sled team. I used to shout to him, 'Onward, Melvin,' or 'On, Mel, on!' or 'Mush, Melvin, onward,' and eventually this became shortened to 'Mush, Mel, on!' and the name stuck."

Popular among fans, Mushmellon was ranked second in the 1957 poll ranking the popularity of *Sam and Friends* characters. Jane built Mushmellon and shared credit on the copyright certificate #Gu 27447, which was issued on October 9, 1956.

Hank and Frank

HANK AND FRANK

Hank and Frank were a pair of matching puppets—twins who usually spoke together, sometimes in unison, and sometimes alternating words between them.

One of their biggest roles (or, to be more accurate, two of their biggest roles) can be seen in one of the surviving shows. In a 1961 episode, Hank and Frank played newscasters Chet Huntley and David Brinkley.

Hank and Frank were born in July 1954.

Chicken Liver

CHICKEN LIVER

So named because Jim and Jane thought he resembled a chicken liver, Chicken Liver's construction by Jane Henson was documented in the *Northern Virginia Sun*. The character was originally introduced on August 12, 1959, as "Theodore," a radio announcer sent to the show by NBC to investigate Professor Madcliffe's faulty laugh meter, a device that was meant to gauge the intensity of the laughter generated by the show. He continued in his role as an announcer for a few days before dropping the name Theodore and settling in as a multifaceted character in the cast.

Jane Henson at work on Chicken Liver. Photo by Jack L. Hiller, © 1959.

Chicken Liver had a serious tone and delivery, always making efforts to improve the content of the program, but he was not above partaking in a little fun, too—like when he performed the classic "Yes! We Have No Bananas" with Harry on the *Today* show and *Sam and Friends*.

While these were the familiar faces of *Sam and Friends,* other characters occasionally popped up, including Henrietta—who was sometimes referred to as Mildred and was possibly an early version of the Mildred character introduced on *The Muppet Show*—as well as a character known simply as Little Girl.

CHAPTER 5

National Exposure

About a year after *Sam and Friends* began (and seven months after it was pulled from the air), the Muppets started performing again in the early evening slot of 6 p.m., only this time they were joined by a human counterpart—a folk singer and disc jockey named Paul Arnold. A native of Denver, Arnold was, by his own admission, kicked out of every fine school in the city before his parents sent him to two military schools and a series of Southern California high schools. (He would finally graduate from the Hollywood Professional School.) Though his publicity boasted that he had memorized more than six hundred folk songs, Arnold began his career in a very different musical genre, performing in opera companies in Los Angeles, Cincinnati, Chicago, and New York.

Arnold's time in New York left him, as TV columnist Lawrence Laurent put it in 1956, "broke, hungry and disgusted with the whole entertainment business." So Arnold took an eight-month trip down the Ohio River on a friend's houseboat, bringing along a $12 guitar for his own entertainment. Switching from operatic music to folk songs and picking up stories and songs in the towns where he stopped along the way, Paul Arnold reinvented himself from an unemployed big-city singer to a possibly employable homespun radio personality.

"Kinda had a hankerin' to try this hyah radio business," Arnold told WBBM's radio program director after walking into his Chicago office, unannounced, in a hickory shirt, work shoes, and a pair of faded dungarees. After working in Chicago, he moved to New York in 1948 for an NBC-TV show called *America Song,* then to CBS-TV for *The Paul Arnold Show* the following year. After a variety of guest shots and announcing gigs, he arrived at WRC in Washington in May 1956.

The Muppets were teamed with Arnold on a show called *Footlight Theater*, which had previously been the station's showcase for old Western movies. In this new incarnation, Arnold would play folk songs on his guitar and introduce the Muppet performances, sometimes providing his own live music and vocals for the characters. "The whole *Footlight Theater* thing—it was so contrived," Jane Henson said in 2010. "They designed the set pieces. It was like a design show that never really worked.... We did it for a little while." It was basically *Sam and Friends* but with a human sidekick.

Some audience members, who had been used to seeing cowboy pictures in that time slot, made their feelings about Paul Arnold known. "I think that *Footlight Theater* is ruined now that Paul Arnold has taken over," wrote one irate viewer in the "TeleVue Mailbag" column in Washington's *Sunday Star TeleVue* supplement. "He thinks that he can sing but to me he sounds terrible." The viewer, identified only as B.L.B., went on to suggest a daily schedule of certain cowboys whose movies should be programmed if *Footlight Theater* were to return to its sagebrush roots.

While some viewers complained about Arnold, the return of the Muppets was welcome news to others, especially *Evening Star* television critic Bernie Harrison, who had encouraged his readers to write to WRC to request that the characters return.

The set for *Footlight Theater* was designed to accommodate the Muppets alongside singer Paul Arnold.

Kermit and Paul Arnold. Photo by Philip Geraci, Courtesy of Special Collections, University of Maryland Libraries. ©1956 University of Maryland

Director Carl Degen, Jim Henson (with Kermit), and Paul Arnold. Photo by Philip Geraci, Courtesy of Special Collections, University of Maryland Libraries. ©1956 University of Maryland

Jim and Kermit watch as Paul Arnold plays guitar. Photo by Philip Geraci, Courtesy of Special Collections, University of Maryland Libraries. ©1956 University of Maryland

Jim and Jane with director Carl Degen on the set of Footlight Theater. Photo by Philip Geraci, Courtesy of Special Collections, University of Maryland Libraries. ©1956 University of Maryland

Kermit and Mushmellon go over the script with
Paul Arnold (with help from Jim and Jane). Photo by
Philip Geraci, Courtesy of Special Collections,
University of Maryland Libraries. ©1956 University of Maryland

WRC was a local station, but it was owned and operated by NBC, so word spread along the coaxial cable all the way up to New York City that there was something special happening at the studio down in Washington. As early as 1955, the Muppets made the national *NBC Chimes* employee newsletter and NBC staffers across the country learned of the popular D.C. show's one-day cancellation and subsequent restoration "after howls of protest from local viewers."

Mentioned more frequently in *Chimes*, of course, was *The Tonight Show*, known simply as *Tonight* when it began in 1953 and hosted by bespectacled comedian Steve Allen. The broadcast was longer than it is now (some stations presented an hour and forty-five minutes of *Tonight* to viewers each weeknight), but it was then, as it is now, a showcase for big-name talent and big talents with smaller names who are ascending the show business ladder.

By 1956, the *Tonight* producers decided to find out more about the puppet troupe that was getting all this attention in D.C. and requested an audition, recalled Jane Henson in a 2009 interview. "They called us and said, 'Would you come up and let us see what you do?' Well, that's a big deal to drive all the way up to New York and to go on a ferry and everything to get there back then. It was a big deal, but on the other hand, we loved the idea of doing the big show."

This was indeed the big show—it was like a major league team calling up a player from the minors. In late August of 1956, Jim and Jane stowed a basket of puppets in Jim's car and made the trip from Washington, D.C., to New York City.

Tonight was broadcast from New York's Hudson Theatre, and Jim and Jane's audition took place in a nondescript room, where a few desks were turned on their sides to give the Muppets a puppet proscenium to hide behind. At the audition, producers Nick Vanoff and William Harbach and director Dwight Hemion were joined by several secretaries and watched as Jim and Jane performed a bit from the *Sam and Friends* repertoire.

"The people in Washington who knew the family of characters know that if you see Yorick, Yorick's going to eat whatever's in sight," said Jane Henson before describing their audition piece, Rosemary Clooney's rendition of "I've Grown Accustomed to Your Face," starring Kermit in his Kermeena persona.

"She's singing, and there's a cloth with a happy face on it next to her, and the happy face gets eaten up, and then Yorick is exposed. Well . . . if you've got a girl puppet singing and Yorick shows up, the Washington audience knows that he will then eat her. . . . They know that. But when we went up to audition, of course, they didn't have any background of the character—the family of characters that we used on *Sam and Friends*. So I'm sure they thought it was totally bizarre to have this character start eating her."

The producers invited more people into the audition room and requested a repeat performance. The small audience may have been a bit surprised by the characters' behaviors, but they were delighted by the originality of the act. "They certainly did let us know that they loved it," Jane said. "They thought it was bizarre and strange, which surprised us because we didn't think it was strange—well, Yorick eats things," she said with a laugh. "Everybody knows that."

Jim and Jane packed up the puppets and went back to Washington to wait for their call up to the big leagues. About six weeks later, that call came, and the two made the trip back to New York.

On October 11, 1956, the Muppets made their network television debut on *Tonight,* introducing audiences around the country to the bizarre and strange presentation of "I've Grown Accustomed to Your Face," as well as Stan Freberg's "The Great Pretender."

The performance has been lost to time, but the next day, TV columnist Bernie Harrison wrote about it in *The Evening Star* under the headline MUPPETS SCORE ON ALLEN SHOW, remarking that the Muppets' appearance late in the broadcast was worth waiting for. "They were so good, it's not inconceivable that this could lead to bigger network things and their departure, sob, from Washington."

Harrison was right about it leading to bigger network things (and eventually he was right about the Muppets' departure from Washington, but that was still a few years off). Jim and Jane were invited back to New York a few weeks later, but this time, it was to join Steve Allen on his Sunday night variety show, which was programmed opposite Ed Sullivan.

In introducing the act on November 4, 1956, Steve briefly summed up the path the Muppets had taken to the stage. "Several years ago in Washington, D.C., there were two young college students, Jim Henson and Jane Nebel. They got together with some little puppets and they formed what people in Washington now know as the Muppets—a little different than a puppet. Folks in Washington, D.C., know them very well. They've been appearing over there on WRC-TV for two and a half years, and they're very big favorites and we can see why. We had them on our *Tonight* show a few weeks ago and they broke it up."

The success on Steve Allen's variety show led to even more network appearances on Will Rogers, Jr.'s *Good Morning* (for a performance of "Cry Me a River"), Arthur Godfrey's show, and a return to Steve Allen's Sunday show in 1957 for a performance of Stan Freberg's "The Yellow Rose of Texas." These coast-to-coast broadcasts started to make an impression on audiences and critics beyond the D.C. beltway, but the ink was not exactly overflowing. *New York Journal-American* columnist Jack O'Brian devoted exactly one sentence to the Henson troupe in December of 1957. "The Baird marionettes are not as funny as The Muffets [sic]."

After Jack Paar replaced Steve Allen on *Tonight*, the Muppets appeared again, with Moldy Hay casually promoting the December 23, 1958, appearance at the start of that evening's *Sam and Friends* broadcast: "Friends, before we start tonight's opus, I'd like to remind you that the Muppets are guestin' on Jack Paar's show later this evenin'. So, if it won't make too long an evenin' for you, why don't you join us on NBC around 11:30 or thereafter and catch the show?"

In addition to giving Jim and Jane their first national exposure, these network gigs introduced the team to some behind-the-scenes personnel whom Jim would end up working with for decades. Dwight Hemion and his producing partner Gary Smith would work with Jim on countless variety show appearances and were consulting producers for the early days of *The Muppet Show*. Producers William Harbach and Nick Vanoff would go on to produce *The Hollywood Palace*, and the Muppets' appearances on that show would introduce Jim to "the other Ray Charles," a music director with whom he would work on *The Muppet Show* and several other specials. Jack Paar's director, Hal Gurnee, would later work with Jim on *The Jimmy Dean Show* before going on to a long run as David Letterman's director. At *The Jimmy Dean*

Show, Jim would meet music coordinator Larry Grossman—who would become the music consultant on *The Muppet Show* before Ray Charles took over in Season 4—and Diana Birkenfield, a producer's assistant who would join Jim's company as a producer and executive.

For Jim Henson, network television was a true networking opportunity, but the downside was that some of the producers and directors who worked with him in those early days continued to see him as that young college student decades later—even after he had become an established media icon. Henson producer Alex Rockwell, who worked as Jim Henson's assistant in the late 1980s, was amused to witness this behavior as she accompanied Jim to various awards shows and variety specials. She recalled that it was not uncommon for Gary Smith or Dwight Hemion to refer to Jim as "Jimmy" as they summoned him to "bring the puppet over here." No one called him Jimmy at the Henson company, and certainly no one barked orders at him.

By the fall of 1956, *Footlight Theater* was back to showing old movies, and *Sam and Friends* was officially back in its own daily slot at 6:30 p.m., but Paul Arnold was still performing with the Muppets. *Sam and Friends* was being promoted by the NBC advertising sales department as *Sam and Friends with Paul Arnold,* positioning Arnold as the "host of this unusual program." His role was basically to introduce the Muppets and either lead into or deliver the commercials.

One of the few surviving visuals of Arnold and the Muppets is a photo from the University of Maryland's *The Old Line* magazine. Future *Muppet Show* guest star Bob Hope is pictured with them in the photo—apparently, Hope made a guest appearance on *Sam and Friends,* but there's no script or recording to document it.

PAUL ARNOLD, the only human who appears on camera with the muppets, laughs with Sam and Yorick as Bob Hope (right) listens intently to all that Kermit has to say.

As published in the University of Maryland's
The *Old Line* magazine. Photo by Morris Semiatin

The Jim Henson Company Archives has the only known
surviving image from that photo shoot, but it does not include
Paul Arnold. Photo by Morris Semiatin

WRC management may have seen teaming Arnold with the Muppets as a way of bringing voice to the characters, who were not yet speaking. In fact, a WRC promotional brochure touting Arnold's arrival at the station referred to him as a "man of many voices."

As a result of the station's publicity efforts, Arnold was sometimes referred to in the press as "the voice" of the Muppets, but Jim Henson did not have any intention of the Muppets being identified with Paul Arnold, and when the Muppets made their network appearances, Arnold was not included. It is uncertain if Arnold's incursion accelerated Jim using his own pipes to voice the Muppets, but it wasn't long before that happened.

There are no kinescopes of Paul Arnold's episodes of *Sam and Friends,* but there are three surviving scripts. In the first one, dated May 27, 1957, Arnold does all the talking—with the silent Sam as his sidekick—before performing his own song and introducing a Muppet lip-sync performance of a Danny Kaye record. The remaining scripts featuring Paul Arnold are dated August 19 and August 20, 1957. By the time those scripts hit the airwaves, the Muppets were speaking—in fact, they may be the first two episodes of *Sam and Friends* in which the Muppets spoke for themselves. The August 18, 1957, edition of *The Sunday Star TeleVue* supplement announced that "Paul Arnold's troupe has added the first talking Muppet—Dr. Madclift [sic], who has a knack for not being able to repair things he's helped put out of working order."

Those two scripts revolved around Paul Arnold's wristwatch and Professor Madcliffe's efforts to repair it. The thin storyline segued in and out of Muppet lip-sync performances. If these scripts are any indication, as the characters began to speak more, Paul Arnold was needed less, and it didn't take long until that became clear to the powers that be. The Muppets soon were flying solo on *Sam and Friends,* and eventually, Arnold left the station, moving to Baltimore's WBAL-TV in October of 1958.

How did the Muppets find their voice? Seven seconds at a time.

* * *

In 1957 Jim was approached by an advertising agency about the possibility of using the Muppets in short television commercials for Wilkins Coffee, a local brand. According to a 1958 interview, company head John H. Wilkins, Jr. happened to see the Muppets on a Sunday night network appearance (most likely *The Steve Allen Show*). "It occurred to me that they were material for commercials," Wilkins told *The Evening Star*. "I brought them together with our advertising agency, M. Belmont VerStandig, Inc."

The husband-and-wife owners of the agency, M. Belmont and Helen VerStandig, made contact with Jim, who was willing to give it a try. So in addition to balancing their existing work and school schedules, Jim and Jane began to work in advertising.

The FCC required broadcasters to identify their station call letters, channel, and air market on the air at the top of every hour, and ten seconds were set aside each hour for this purpose. But it did not take all of ten seconds for an announcer to say "WRC-TV Channel 4, Washington." Stations and ad agencies reasoned that the remaining seven seconds could be sold as commercial time. In June of 1957, the M. Belmont VerStandig advertising agency made an initial agreement with Jim Henson to create three seven-second spots.

Jim conceived two characters for the campaign: Wilkins, the character who *will* drink Wilkins Coffee, and Wontkins, who *won't* drink it. "I built Wilkins," Jane Henson recalled in 2009, adding that she also manipulated the character in the spots. "Jim built Wontkins. The whole thing of Wontkins was Jim. He kind of liked being identified with Wontkins because Jim didn't drink coffee, although he loved the smell of it. In order to go to Washington from where he lived, you go right past the Wilkins factory, so he was very used to smelling the coffee."

The format was simple and allowed for many variations, which was a good thing because the commercials were a hit from the very beginning. Agency creative director and copy chief Jim Young worked with Henson to generate dozens more scripts and storyboards, all of which followed a similar format. Wilkins was the happy spokesman who asked Wontkins if he drank Wilkins Coffee. When Wontkins said "no," something bad would happen to him— he might get pushed out of an airplane, sawed in half, hit on the head with a mallet, or even shot with a pistol (this was a much different time). "It was the basic good guy/bad guy kind of thing that Jim liked," Jane said. "That guy who will do it and the guy who won't do it."

Jim and Jane at work on a Wilkins commercial. Photo by Del Ankers

The John H. Wilkins Company credited the award-winning Muppet spots for a 300 percent increase in their sales of coffee to home consumers. "This is the biggest thing that has ever happened to Wilkins Coffee and to this agency," said M. Belmont VerStandig in 1958.

A grateful company president, John H. Wilkins, Jr. (comically referred to in the commercials as "old man Wilkins" though he was only about fifty-five at the time), entertained Jim and Jane at his home, proudly serving his guests Wilkins Coffee after the meal. "Jim was seated right next to him," Jane said. "I think that's the first time he forced down a cup of coffee. Jim became a coffee drinker later."

In addition to that taste for coffee, Wilkins also gave Jim his first taste of merchandising when the coffee company offered a set of Wilkins and Wontkins vinyl hand puppets as a mail-in premium offer. In one Christmas season, more than 25,000 pairs of puppets were sold for $1 a pair, plus a Wilkins proof-of-purchase.

The commercials were also significant because they gave audiences an opportunity to hear Jim's voice regularly for the first time. "That was almost some of the first voice stuff I did," Jim told an interviewer in 1982. "I had been doing some tiny things on the show until then."

The first three Wilkins spots ("Taxi," "Cannon," and "Jailhouse") did indeed feature Jim's voice, but his itemized bill to the VerStandig agency for the production of the commercials included payments to Paul Arnold and Jane. A close listen to "Taxi" and "Jailhouse" does reveal a non-Jim voice as that of Wilkins, but "Cannon" is all Jim Henson. It is possible that "Cannon"—arguably the most popular Wilkins spot out of the more than 180 commercials created for the campaign—was later rerecorded with Jim doing both voices.

It can be deduced that as Jim gained confidence in his own vocal performances, he no longer needed Paul Arnold's services on other Wilkins spots or *Sam and Friends*. After the Wilkins commercials began airing, the Muppets started speaking more and more. Most of the *Sam and Friends* episodes still heavily featured lip-synced performances to records, but spoken introductions were being added.

The seven-second commercials gave Jim more confidence to use his voice and experiment with different vocalizations, though Jane continued to devote her skills solely to manipulation. She recalled one early *Sam and Friends* segment in which Jim used his own voice. On "Drain Dweller"—about a character who lived in people's drains—Jim spoke while inhaling. "Curiously enough, it was sort of a nonuse of his actual voice because he was breathing in," Jane said.

Around the same time Professor Madcliffe made his debut as the first official Jim Henson-voiced Muppet in the summer of 1957,

Jim developed a voice for Kermit—very similar to the one Kermit would use for the next few decades. Some of his other future characters would end up evoking *Sam and Friends* voices: There is a bit of Dr. Teeth in Harry, and, as Jane noted, the Guy Smiley voice is reminiscent of Professor Madcliffe.

Soon after Jim started using his voice on-air, he was told he had to join the union—essentially get an actor's license. "He thought that was a real hoot," said his high school friend Joe Irwin. "He joked and laughed about that . . . you know . . . he had to be an *actor* now." In fact, Jim and Jane had both joined the American Federation of Television and Radio Artists (AFTRA) in October of 1956 to do *The Steve Allen Show*, but it's possible that WRC had not officially treated Jim as "an actor" until he began speaking for the characters.

Even though *Sam and Friends* ran for only a few minutes a day, the characters were becoming more and more popular, and WRC management decided to capitalize on that. The station printed up postcards featuring Sam and Kermit to respond to viewers' fan mail, and the Muppets were pictured on WRC print ads and program guides.

The postcard WRC used to respond to viewer mail.

The January 1957 WRC Program Schedule, touting the Muppets' network appearances. Note that the show is called *Sam and Friends with Paul Arnold*, but Arnold is nowhere to be seen.

And now that Kermit, Harry, and the others could speak, they could speak on behalf of the station—and they did, making live appearances at promotional events. At one such event, Harry and Kermit presented WRC's schedule of Monday-through-Friday programs (referred to in the television industry as "weekday strip" programming) to advertisers:

HARRY:	Bozo, the world's most famous clown, who is in reality Clark Kent, I mean, Willard Scott, is on the air every weekday in living color. . . . The highest-rated kids strip in the market.
KERMIT:	They do?
HARRY:	Do what? Never mind. A half an hour of clowning around with the studio audience, Bozo cartoons, and . . . like that.
KERMIT:	When do the kids strip?

Though Jim began speaking for the characters, Jane did not.

"Jim never had me do voices, and I'm saying it that way because I don't think it was my choice. I think it was Jim's," Jane told Brian Jay Jones in 2011. Jane acknowledged that she may have been disappointed at Jim's decision, but, at the same time, she didn't have a particularly strong desire to lend her voice to the Muppets. "I'm very ambivalent about that," she said in 2010. "Part of me really wanted to do voices, and then part of me didn't."

While it is true that Jane did not generally perform voices for the Muppets, her voice was heard on the show on very rare occasions—so rare that Jane did not recall them during her interviews. A careful listen to Jim Henson's 424 surviving audio recordings of *Sam and Friends* episodes revealed Jane voiced Bernice in two episodes, substituting for Bob Payne.

CHAPTER 6

It's Time to Play the Music

The Muppets sang before they could speak, lip-syncing to popular (and unpopular) songs. They also spoke their first words thanks to a vast collection of comedy and spoken-word recordings in the WRC record library and Jim's personal record collection.

In 1957, *The Sunday Star Magazine* reported that Jim had five hundred records in his library. "All are either humorous or otherwise suitable for puppeteering. He uses an average 15 numbers a week and never repeats popular ones in a two-month period."

There were two types of recordings Jim selected for his *Sam and Friends* sketches—those that were inherently funny and those that were somewhat serious musical numbers but whose juxtaposition with the Muppets would be comedy gold. For example, there's nothing intrinsically humorous about Rosemary Clooney singing "I've Grown Accustomed to Your Face," but when Kermeena is lip-syncing it while being devoured by the object of her affection—who was just revealed to be a purple skull-like character—well, that's funny. On the other hand, recordings by Stan Freberg and Spike Jones came with built-in comedy. Some songs received multiple treatments: Versions of Cole Porter's "I've Got You Under My Skin" by Peggy Lee, Stan Freberg, and Louis Prima and Keely Smith were all featured on the show.

Selecting the music was one of Jane Henson's favorite parts of the production process, she said in 2009. "It was so fun. You know . . . looking for comedy stuff in the library, and then every time he listened to the radio—in the car or anything—you could just say, 'Oh, that would look good if you did this or that.'" Jim particularly loved barbershop quartets and folk singers like Oscar Brand, Jane said.

"There were all kinds of different things that he just liked, and to have the opportunity to turn those into visual things—it was great."

The library Jane mentioned was the record library at WRC, which served both the television station and AM radio station. While Jim knew what would work musically for his troupe of players, he had help from the record librarian at WRC, Lou Bonelli. "He knew all of the records in the record library at WRC," Jane said. "And there had been so many comedy records in the forties—and then the fifties was just loaded with comedy records."

Jane in the WRC music library with Lou Bonelli. Photo by Jim Henson

Bonelli took his job very seriously even though it involved some of the strangest music ever recorded. And, according to Jane, he was very enthusiastic. "He would constantly be feeding Jim with, 'Oh, did you hear this?' and 'Did you hear that?'"

More help in the selection of records came from a WRC radio personality named Eddie Walker, who had just begun what would become a nineteen-year run as half of "The Joy Boys" (the other half was Willard Scott, who would have his own connection to Muppet history). Eddie Walker had a very keen ear and an excellent memory for records, which Jane Henson credited to his blindness from birth.

Jim and Jane would both spend a lot of time in the record library with Lou and Eddie, listening for possible *Sam and Friends* material.

"The things that they would be laughing so hard at were not necessarily good for us visually—because we had to do visual things to it—so some of them we'd accept and some we wouldn't," Jane Henson said in 2009. "And then, of course, then it would be up to Jim to think of what to do with it."

After it was selected, the record—which would sometimes have to be edited down to fit into the *Sam and Friends* time slot—was dubbed to an acetate (a special lacquer-covered aluminum phonograph disc) that could be played from the control room. According to Jane, there was usually about a week between the record selection and its use on the show, allowing Jim time to create any needed scenery or puppets and a segment that would, as Jim would put it, "work." If the record "worked" on the show, the song or spoken-word piece would be placed in the *Sam and Friends* repertoire and the bit reperformed live on the air from time to time. "If something worked, you did it the same way each time and tried to do it better than you did the time before," Jane said. "But if it wasn't so good, you'd try a different idea. If it didn't look good, we'd drop it." Jim kept track of the

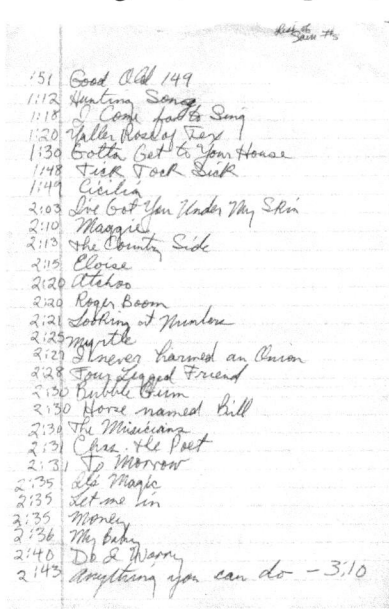

One of Jim's song lists.

records and their timings on handwritten (and, later, typewritten) lists, and from these documents he would make his selections.

In a 1982 interview, Jim Henson recalled one frequently performed *Sam and Friends* song: "We had this puppet that was made from the skull of a squirrel, and we used to take this dumb-looking strange thing . . . and we did this terrible song called 'There's a New Sound.' . . . It's a wonderful song, but it only has one chord. But we used to do that, and it would drive everybody crazy." Crazy, however, is a good thing in the world of the Muppets, and that may explain why Tony Burrello's one-chord wonder would turn up on *The Muppet Show* two decades later and be included on its second original cast album.

Despite the growing repertoire, Jim was always adding new content; many songs performed on *Sam and Friends* were new releases, making their way to the Muppets only weeks after their debut. It was an eclectic mix—standards, novelty songs, Broadway, folk songs, spoken-word comedy—but, oddly, it appears that the biggest name in music at the time, Elvis Presley, never turned up on the show's soundtrack (although he was referenced from time to time and parodied with the help of Stan Freberg's "Heartbreak Hotel").

In 1960, viewers of *Sam and Friends*, who by then were used to hearing Jim speak for the characters in introductions and comedy sketches, heard him sing for the first time as the Muppets lip-synced to Jim's own novelty record. Earlier that year, Signature records released "Tick-Tock Sick" and its B side, "The Countryside." Jim wrote both songs, and the humor of the record was not confined to its grooves. The 45's label jokingly heralded Frank Sinatra as the orchestra conductor. (In 1971, Jim would work for real with Frank's daughter Nancy in her Las Vegas nightclub act.)

Even as the Muppets spoke more and presented more elaborate dialogue sketches, they continued to lip-sync to other people's voices. Some artists were used once or twice, but when examining the list of songs used, it is clear that Jim had his own favorites—a sort of repertory company.

STAN FREBERG

It's not even close. Within the *Sam and Friends* repertoire of involuntary performers, Jim Henson used more Stan Freberg records on the show than any other artist's work. Freberg became famous for his comedy records, but he did so much more. Fans of Warner Bros. cartoons would remember his voice as Pete Puma, Papa Bear, and many other characters (you never saw his name since Mel Blanc's contract secured Blanc's exclusivity as the only voice artist with screen credit). In the waning days of network radio, Freberg created and hosted the last major network prime-time radio series, *The Stan Freberg Show*. For decades, he created radio and television advertising—and, like the Muppets, he didn't think twice about making fun of the sponsor. To promote the CBS series *Hogan's Heroes,* Freberg coined the tagline, "If you liked World War II, you'll love *Hogan's Heroes*." Coincidentally, just before Jim Henson started *Sam and Friends*, Stan Freberg ended his tenure as a puppeteer on the West Coast, providing the voice and manipulation for Cecil the Seasick Sea Serpent on Bob Clampett's series *Time for Beany*.

According to the surviving documentation (which is sparse for the early years of *Sam and Friends*), Jim used twenty-six separate Freberg records—and used them multiple times. Including repeats, there were at least fifty-seven Freberg episodes. His records were a natural fit for *Sam and Friends:* They were often musical (Freberg loved making fun of the latest trends in music, whether the Belafonte calypso sensation or the folk song revolution) and they were always visual. When playing a Freberg record, the listener had to visualize what was happening—and Jim Henson was happy to lend a hand.

Jim and Jane didn't consider getting permission from the recording artists to use their records; they assumed they could do what they wanted since they logged each record with the WRC librarian according to station policy. "We used the records just like somebody playing the record on the radio, so that's what was paid for, just a use on the air. . . . We didn't acknowledge or pay anybody more than that," Jane Henson said.

Stan Freberg eventually heard about the show in Washington that was using his records—it was hard to keep it a secret after Jim and Jane performed to a Freberg record on the nationally broadcast *Steve Allen Show*. At first, by all accounts, he was not pleased. When his travels took him to Washington, D.C., he paid a visit to Jim and Jane at WRC. "I just remember it was the first time I knew the word *entourage*. Stan Freberg came with his entourage!" recalled Jane Henson with a laugh. "And we didn't realize it, but we were a little afraid of it, and a little bit in awe of it. But I think Stan, you know, understandably he thought, 'Hey, wait a minute, guys, you're using this material and it's my material.' But he really enjoyed the show so much, and he became a fan, and [there was] mutual admiration between Jim and Stan."

After the meeting, Stan sent Jim and Jane a telegram, which included the praise, "THIS IS ONE OF THE GREATEST ACTS I HAVE EVER SEEN. AM HONORED TO LET YOU USE MY RECORDS FOR EVER AND LONGER. LOVE AND KISSES TO ALL."

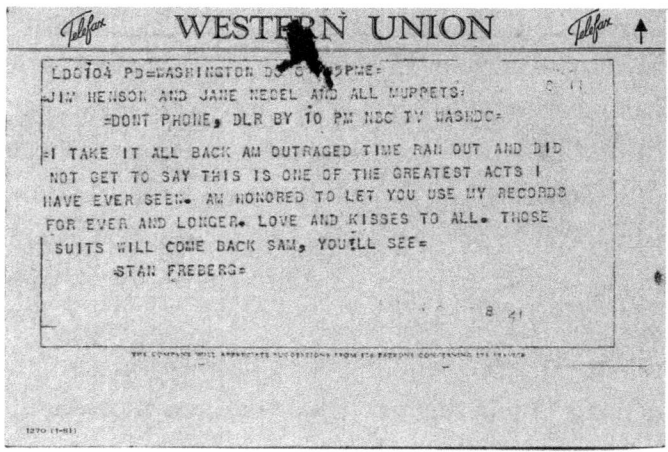

Telegram from Stan Freberg.

Although no film or script exists, Freberg made an appearance on a *Sam and Friends* episode in 1957. Freberg recounted the story in 2008 to puppeteer and podcaster Grant Baciocco.

"I came down to the show and he [Jim] said, 'Just stick your head up there.'" Freberg apparently then entered frame, startling the characters. "'Excuse me, Excuse me . . . My name is Stan Freberg and I'd like a little credit once in a while since you seem to be doing all my records.' . . . Kermit says, 'You want some credit?' I say, 'Yeah,' and he has this big mallet and they're pounding me on the head out of sight."

Despite their collaboration on *Sam and Friends,* Jim and Stan never worked together again, but Freberg took pride in his connection to Henson history.

SPIKE JONES

Before there was Spike Jonze the director, there was Spike Jones the musician. Born in 1911 as Lindley Armstrong Jones, Spike Jones was a bandleader and musician whose comedy records (with his band, the City Slickers) were a popular staple dating back to the 1940s. His early records were usually recordings of standards, which he punctuated with gunshots and other sound effects, as well as nonsensical vocal interludes. His band included Doodles Weaver and Red Ingle, the latter of whom was also heard solo on *Sam and Friends*. Jim's act was not the only one to lip-sync to Spike Jones's records. In his early performances, Dick Van Dyke, as part of a pantomime duo called The Merry Mutes, used Jones's work in his repertoire, as did Jerry Lewis.

Spike's later albums were more Freberg-esque spoken-word comedy recordings and incorporated the talents of a wide range of voice artists. His *Spike Jones in Hi-Fi: A Spooktacular in Screaming Sound* (1959) provided several cuts used on *Sam and Friends,* including "Poison to Poison," a horror-themed parody of Edward R. Murrow's *Person to Person*.

HOMER AND JETHRO

In 1920, Henry Doyle "Junior" Haynes and Kenneth "Dude" Burns were born in Tennessee. Like Jim Henson, they began their careers as teenagers. Actually, they were about twelve when they began playing guitar and mandolin in a country quartet called the String Dusters. In between performances, Haynes and Burns played around with musical satires of standard tunes. The duo eventually moved their comedy routine onstage, and when in 1936 a radio host forgot their stage names during a broadcast, he introduced them as "Homer and Jethro." The name stuck, and while still teens, Homer and Jethro left the String Dusters and became a full-time comedy-music duo.

They enjoyed regional radio and recording success until they both were drafted in 1941. In 1945, they resumed their careers, and in 1949, they hit the Top 10 country chart by teaming with June Carter for a country version of "Baby, It's Cold Outside." The Homer and Jethro version of the Frank Loesser hit would be used several times on *Sam and Friends,* and the song would later show up on *The Muppet Show*. The duo made the Pop Top 20 chart (and won a Grammy for best comedy performance, musical) with "The Battle of Kookamonga," which was featured on *Sam and Friends* as soon as it was released.

Just as Jim would cross paths with many of the artists whose music he used on *Sam and Friends,* he reconnected with Homer and Jethro during their seven appearances on *The Jimmy Dean Show*.

Homer and Jethro were inducted into the Country Music Hall of Fame in 2001, thirty years after Homer Haynes passed away. Jethro Burns continued to work until his death in 1989.

OSCAR BRAND

With dozens of albums to his credit, Oscar Brand spent a seven-decade career as a sort of renaissance man—hosting a radio program, writing books, singing and composing songs, and preserving the music of the past. One of his albums, *Give 'Im the Hook! Songs That Killed Vaudeville* (1958), was the source of several *Sam and Friends* performances. Oscar Brand was one of his generation's preeminent proponents of historical musicology and had a particular flair for finding the humor in folk music. For folk aficionado Jim Henson, Brand's records— which ranged from bawdy sea chanteys to children's music—had strong appeal. Brand and Jim would eventually connect more directly when Brand served on the advisory panel that led to the creation of *Sesame Street*. (While Oscar Brand proudly laid claim to being the inspiration for Oscar the Grouch, a more direct connection can be traced to the surly owner of Oscar's, a restaurant frequented by Jim Henson, Jon Stone, and other members of the creative team.)

KEN NORDINE

Ken Nordine was the creator of "Word Jazz," a technique of spoken-word performance that was almost musical in nature. When used on *Sam and Friends,* Nordine's smooth vocal tones usually emitted from Yorick.

Years after *Sam and Friends,* Jim Henson worked with Ken Nordine on the counting films Henson produced for *Sesame Street. Sesame* graduates may remember Nordine's distinctive voice as the narrator of "Bumble-Ardy."

IRVING TAYLOR

Irving Taylor wasn't a recording artist but a composer with a penchant for creating songs that the Muppets enjoyed working with. His album *Terribly Sophisticated Songs: A Collection of Unpopular Songs for Popular People* (1958) offered several tracks used on *Sam and Friends,* but one that Muppet fans would recognize is "Pachalafaka," a song also used on *The Muppet Show*. Taylor appreciated Jim's work, sending him autographed sheet music as a thank you during the run of *The Muppet Show*. While probably best known for his novelty songs, Taylor also co-wrote Dean Martin's hit "Everybody Loves Somebody" with Ken Lane and Sam Coslow.

WALT KELLY'S SONGS OF THE POGO

Jim was big fan of Walt Kelly's comic strip *Pogo*, the adventures of a possum living in the Okefenokee Swamp. The strip parodied current events and politics, with Pogo as an everyman surrounded by a unique cast of characters (in later years, Jim would describe Kermit as "the Pogo of the group"). Over the years, Kelly wrote songs that were included in *Pogo* book compilations, and in 1956, he released some of these in an album entitled *Songs of the Pogo*, which Jim received as a Christmas gift that year. Jim used several songs from the album on *Sam and Friends*, and "Don't Sugar Me" later showed up on *The Muppet Show*.

Jim, his mother, Betty, and his father, Paul, celebrate Christmas 1956 at the Henson home. Note *Songs of the Pogo* on the shelf at right.

ROSS BAGDASARIAN (DAVID SEVILLE)

Although now best known for his creations Alvin, Simon, and Theodore, Ross Bagdasarian (known professionally as David Seville) had worked in music for a few years before the Chipmunks came along and had been an actor before venturing into songwriting. Despite not being able to read or write music, Bagdasarian co-wrote the Rosemary Clooney hit "Come On-a My House." Bagdasarian—who had been stationed in Seville, Spain, while in the service—took on the stage name David Seville because of record company fears that his real name was too difficult to pronounce. As David Seville, he hit No. 1 with "Witch Doctor," his first experiment with speeding up audiotape. He then used that technique to create Alvin, Simon, and Theodore for their first song, the holiday classic "The Chipmunk Song."

While Jim used a couple of Chipmunks tunes on *Sam and Friends*, he also used some of Bagdasarian's earlier songs like "Cecilia," "The Trouble with Harry," "Little Brass Band," and "Gotta Get to Your House" (which received Seville's own "speed-up" treatment from Henson). Oddly enough, "Witch Doctor" does not appear to have been used by Jim on *Sam and Friends*, but it was performed by Marvin Suggs and his Muppaphone on *The Muppet Show* in 1978.

BOB AND RAY

Bob Elliott and Ray Goulding were a comedy team who began in radio and eventually transitioned to television and records before bringing their act to Broadway. They wrapped up their long career with *The Bob and Ray Public Radio Show* (1984–1987). Their comedy was subtle and dry, targeting radio genres and personality types.

Sam and Friends used several Bob and Ray pieces, including "The Westerners," a sketch that focused on two cowboys who couldn't quite get themselves in the right direction, and "The Voice Coach," about a television voice coach whose monotone delivery belied his life of excitement and danger. In addition to his many recordings with Ray Goulding, Bob Elliott's comedy legacy includes son Chris Elliott and granddaughters Abby and Bridey Elliott.

PHIL HARRIS

Wonga Phillip Harris is probably best remembered today as the voice of Baloo in Disney's animated classic *The Jungle Book*, but Harris was also a big band leader and vocalist whose biggest hit was "That's What I Like About the South." Harris spent sixteen years as Jack Benny's radio bandleader and comedic foil, eventually getting his own show with his wife, film star Alice Faye. Phil Harris's smooth, cool demeanor and syncopated patter songs were an excellent fit for the Muppets – especially, Sam, who Jim had designed with Harris's songs in mind. Harris had a distinctive shoulder movement that Sam, under Jim's masterful manipulation, could imitate.

DANNY KAYE

Danny Kaye, born David Daniel Kaminsky, began his career in New York theater as a Catskills comic and tummler. He developed a flair for patter songs—singing rapidly and scat-singing—and his style was so distinct, it was caricatured in Warner Bros. cartoons, including the short "Book Revue." Kaye eventually became a film superstar, appearing in such classics as *The Court Jester* and *White Christmas*.

He is in the rarified group of *Sam and Friends* artists who would go on to appear on *The Muppet Show,* even performing "Inchworm," a Frank Loesser song from *Hans Christian Andersen* (1952) that was also used on *Sam and Friends*.

***

Several *Muppet Show* numbers were first used on *Sam and Friends,* but probably the most unique one—and a song that would likely be lost to obscurity were it not for Rowlf's frequent performances—was "You and I and George." It was a piece written by Stan Kenton's bass player, Red Kelly, who sang it on the album *Kenton Live from the Las Vegas Tropicana* (1961).

When it came to the pop vocalists of the era, the voices of Perry Como, Jaye P. Morgan, Julie London, and more were borrowed by the Muppets. Were these artists aware that their voices were being commandeered? We may never know, but when Rosemary Clooney performed at an American Society of Composers, Authors, and Publishers (ASCAP) awards ceremony in posthumous honor of Joe Raposo and Jim Henson in the 1990s, a clip of her "performance" as Kermeena's voice in "I've Grown Accustomed to Your Face" was shown before her entrance, and Clooney seemed quite proud of her connection to Muppet posterity.

The list of records used on *Sam and Friends* represents a wide variety of artists and genres—a mid-twentieth-century snapshot of audio culture. While Jim Henson was creating something truly unique with his work, *Sam and Friends* was also a reflection of what was happening around him. The music and spoken-word recordings on *Sam and Friends* present a fascinating survey of Jim's influences and inspirations, some of which would fuel Muppet comedy and music for decades to come.

CHAPTER 7

1958: A Very Major Big Year

Starting in 1965, Jim kept a chronology of significant events in his career (referred to as "The Red Book," since it was written in a red cloth-covered journal). On the page that begins the entries for the year 1979, Jim wrote the subtitle "A Very Major Big Year." Had Jim started The Red Book at the very beginning of his career, it is likely that he would have written a similar subtitle under the year 1958.

At the start of 1958, Jim Henson was just another college student with a part-time job (albeit a fairly unusual one). "It was just stuff that I did as a lark," Jim said in a 1982 interview. "I was going to college and so I was doing this, and it was a way of working my way through school." But, even so, not every University of Maryland student had his own daily TV show and a sideline making coffee commercials. For Jane, this was still just something to do before pursuing an art education career, but she kept delaying that career in favor of working on what was becoming a very popular TV show. In February of 1958, the Federation of Women's Clubs of the District of Columbia named *Sam and Friends* the outstanding local TV show.

By the end of the year, it would become clear that Jim Henson was going to turn this part-time job into a corporation and a career and Jane Nebel would not be teaching any time soon.

1958 was also a very special year for WRC, which moved its studio from the Sheraton-Park Hotel to a new home on Nebraska Avenue—a purpose-built facility constructed not just for television but for the new color broadcasting technology. On May 22, 1958, RCA's David Sarnoff and President Dwight D. Eisenhower dedicated the new studio, and Ike made the first presidential speech recorded in

Jim is honored by the Federation of Women's Clubs of the District of Columbia.

color on videotape (the NBC facility in Burbank, California, actually made the recording via the cross-country coaxial cable since WRC did not yet have the brand-new color videotape machines).

"NBC had established the color television system," Jim said in 1982. "And so they immediately converted their five owned and operated stations to color. Washington was one of those, so we were almost one of the very first people to do color television. NBC was trying to convert all of their local programming to color right away to encourage the sale of the sets."

With the Muppets, WRC had some of the more colorful local TV stars.

Jim and Jane had their own small space at the new WRC studios—a dedicated cubicle with a mirror where they could work out and rehearse the day's shows. Most of the puppets, however, were still constructed in the workspace Jim had at his parents' house; Jim's living situation would not change until the following year.

Henson lore says the turning point for Jim was a trip to Europe he took in 1958 with friend Joe Irwin. "Jim wanted to go away to the Brussels World's Fair in 1958," Jane Henson said in a 2009 interview. "He just wanted to take the show off [the air] and go traveling, because even though it was fun, he was very confined and wasn't able to move around, which is not like Jim."

In a 1982 interview, Jim said he simply wanted to take some time off to paint. "I was an artist, you see, so I was going to take the shows off the air—just quit for a while." But because of *Sam and Friends*' popularity, the station did not want to remove the show from its schedule, even for a six-week period. "The station prevailed upon me; they said, 'Look, we'll pay you money and you can put somebody else doing the show,' and so I realized I can get money and at the same time be off painting," he said in the interview.

Jane could not do the show alone, so Jim turned to another University of Maryland classmate, Bob Payne, whom he had known since they were both students at Northwestern High School. Bob had already graduated from the university (as Jim would have had he not cut back his class schedule to devote time to his television show) but had no immediate plans, so when Jim asked him to work with Jane during Jim's trip, Bob was happy to do so.

"He asked me if I would work on the NBC show . . . and I said, 'I would love to,'" Payne recalled more than sixty years later. "He said, 'I'll introduce you to Jane, and Jane will show you how to do our gimmicks on TV, you'll learn how to do this particular little bit.' And that's what happened."

Bob did not have a background in puppetry, but neither did Jim when he started out. What Bob lacked in experience, he made up for in proximity. Bob lived near Jim in University Park, Maryland, so in the days leading up to the European trip, Jim picked up Bob in his

Thunderbird and drove him to the new WRC studios to learn the puppeteering ropes. It was the first time Bob had witnessed the behind-the-scenes activities at a television studio, and it made a big impression on the young graduate. While he had no way of knowing it, Bob Payne's journey with Jim would continue on and off for many years, taking him to *Sesame Street, The Muppet Show,* and *The Dark Crystal.*

As Jim prepared for his trip, Jane trained Bob in the ways of the Muppets, teaching him the basics of lip sync and how to work with the monitors. "Jim was always doing something, so I just did what Jane showed me to do. . . . She played one of the stories, or, songs, and I had to learn how to do that, and we performed it."

Bob Payne and Jane give Yorick and Kermit a hand.
Photo Jack L. Hiller, © 1959.

On June 19, 1958, Jim and Joe Irwin flew from Washington to Frankfurt, Germany, where they began their European odyssey. The itinerary included Switzerland, France, and Belgium, where Expo 58, the World's Fair, was taking place. Eventually, Jim would find himself traveling solo, as Joe had to cut his trip short to report for Air Force basic training back in the States. But before Joe returned to America, he had a chance to observe Jim starting to see puppetry in a different way.

"In the afternoon, we'd go to the park where they did the Punch and Judy shows," Joe Irwin said. "He was not only watching the Punch and Judy . . . you know, off in the distance there, but he was looking at the people and the children and the whole environment."

When Jim had first picked up a puppet earlier that decade, it was solely a key to unlock the door to a television studio. At this point in his early career, sketching his way through Europe, Jim considered himself an artist but hadn't really thought of puppetry as art—in America, it was more or less regarded as a diversion for children. But in Europe, puppetry had a richer history and reputation, and it was on this trip that Jim was able to appreciate it as an art form for the first time.

"As we watched the show, Jim was . . . marveling at the number of people that were there and the atmosphere," Irwin said. "We'd come back the next day for it, too. It was . . . something he wanted to see again." Jim continued to explore puppet theater throughout his trip.

"I met a puppeteer in Germany—a couple who were working— and those were the first puppeteers I ever met," Jim said in another 1982 interview. "I thought it was really interesting what they were doing. So then, throughout Europe, I would investigate any puppeteers in any city that I went to."

Joe Irwin beside a display of puppets in Germany in the summer of 1958. Photo by Jim Henson

While Jim was in Europe trying to figure out if puppetry was an art form he should continue exploring, Jane and Bob were back in Washington making sure Jim would have a show to return to. During Jim's absence, Jane would plan each day's show, either selecting a record from the repertoire and re-creating Jim's original choreographed bit or picking a new song and creating a new routine.

Jim kept in contact with Jane while he was away. "He would check in to see if we were okay, and he'd be a little disappointed if we said we were," Jane said in 2010 with a laugh. "I think part of him wanted us to say, 'You have to come back, we're a mess.' We may have been a mess, but we were enjoying it. Bobby and I were a funny couple. I didn't know Bobby very well before that, you know, but working together, he was really funny and fun."

Since Jane did not perform voices on *Sam and Friends* and Bob would not do so until after Jim's return, most of the shows presented in Jim's absence either contained the character voices from existing transcription discs or just music and no dialogue at all. One of Jane's favorite episodes that she performed during Jim's absence was set to a record called "Salt" by The Vagabonds.

The song told the story of a storekeeper who has shelves and shelves filled with salt but continues to buy more because of a very skilled salesperson. Fifty years later, Jane still remembered the lyrics: "Salt . . . who sells salt . . . / In a month I ain't sold even a box . . . / Oh but three times a year / There's a salesman comes here, and oy vey! / Could he sell salt!"

While Jane worked out the staging and choreography, Bob, who had majored in fine arts at the University of Maryland, worked on the scenery for "Salt"—along with the other new bits devised in Jim's absence—which he painted on large pieces of paper laid out on the floor of the WRC scene shop. "I did a painting of drawers and drawers and drawers [and] in those, I had . . . salt."

Jane poses in front of the "Salt" backdrop.

"She was delightful to be with," said Payne of his performing partner. "We laughed and had a good time."

After each night's show, Bob and Jane would get in the car to go to their respective homes, still laughing about the show they had done. "We sat and giggled in the car all the time, it was just so much fun," Payne said. "And she had such a sense of humor. We laughed and laughed and laughed, sitting in the parking lot!"

While Jim had the overall creative vision for the *Sam and Friends* Muppets, Jane's work cannot be overlooked. The very fact that she could carry on without him was evidence of her own contributions to the show—and to her own unique sense of humor, which was a marked contrast to Jim's.

"Mom had a smart, subversive sense of humor that complemented my father's lighter, more playful tone," Cheryl Henson said.

Sam, Jane, Yorick, and Bob Payne between Hank and Frank.
Photo by Jack Hiller, © 1959.

Jim left London on August 1, 1958, and arrived back in Washington, D.C., the next day with a renewed enthusiasm—and a beard. The puppet theater productions Jim saw on his trip made it clear to him that a career in puppetry was possible. "I don't think someone would set out to be a puppeteer," Jim said in an interview on the *Henson's Place* TV special in 1984. But even though he didn't set out to find a career in puppetry, the career found him. That fall, Jim decided to not take any classes that semester, and instead concentrate on the Muppets while also working for WRC in the scene shop. "When I came back from that trip . . . I came back all enthused with the idea of what one could do with puppetry," he said in a 1982 interview. Inspired by the puppet theater he saw in Europe, Jim began working on his own production of *Hansel and Gretel,* even building sets and puppets, but he eventually set it aside to concentrate more on his television work. It would be a little while before Jim would produce a puppet fairy tale.

A sample of Jim Henson's Hansel and Gretel design. Photo by Jim Henson.

After the trip, Bob Payne stayed on with *Sam and Friends* as an extra hand (so to speak), and Jim set about turning his part-time job into a real business. Two years earlier in 1956, Jim had done some official paperwork, registering the Muppet characters with the U.S. Copyright Office, but in 1958, the Muppets became a legal entity with the establishment of Muppets Inc.

Incorporated in Washington, D.C., the new company's first organizational meeting was held on November 24, 1958. Jim Henson was elected president, and Jane Nebel became secretary-treasurer. According to the brief minutes of that meeting, Jim explained that the company was established "primarily to carry forward much of the business he has been conducting in the field of creating and producing live and filmed shows for television."

At that same meeting, Jim and Jane voted to establish a business checking account. To fund the account, twenty shares of stock in Muppets Inc. were issued at a price of $100 per share. Jim was allocated twelve shares, and Jane eight. Things were official now. Jim and Jane were both literally invested in the Muppets.

7300 NEVIS ROAD, BETHESDA 14, MD.

Muppets Inc.'s letterhead. In 1967, Henson Associates was incorporated and became the primary Henson business entity, representing Jim's desire to broaden his work beyond Muppets.

That same day, Jim began recording audio of the *Sam and Friends* broadcasts on reel-to-reel tape. These forty-four audio tapes containing more than four hundred episodes—made over the next three years—survived for sixty years; along with several dozen acetate transcription discs and a handful of kinescopes, they are the only remaining representations of the live broadcasts.

The establishment of the legal entity Muppets Inc. also marked the beginning of much of the Henson archival paper trail. From this point on, Jim made a point of saving most everything—from receipts to scripts and all sorts of stuff in between. Official business expenditures were now tracked in a big ledger, and nestled between the very official checks written to AFTRA and the Internal Revenue Service were the everyday expenses necessary to the production of *Sam and Friends*—checks written to gas stations, photo supply stores, film processing labs, art supply stores, hardware stores, toy stores, and several local record stores (including Disc Shop, a well-known Washington, D.C., music store that was frequented by such Beltway celebrities as Jacqueline Kennedy).

The ledger also tracked the growing income to Muppets Inc. WRC's regular payments were augmented by fees for Wilkins-style commercials, which were being licensed by regional advertisers throughout the country.

With more income, Jim and Jane were able to supplement the Muppets' limited workspace at Jim's parents' house and WRC by renting a large room upstairs at the Rodel studio in Georgetown—a convenient place to store the growing collection of sets and props for their commercials.

Muppets Inc.'s studio space at Rodel.
Jane can be seen working near the window.

Starting in 1958, it was clear that Jim thought there was a future with the Muppets, and Jane had no reason to disagree.

"I think Jim's way of operating was extraordinary—and his way of thinking," Jane Henson told Brian Jay Jones in 2010. "I met him when he was eighteen, and it was already in place. I'm telling you. It was in place. . . . Even by eighteen, he was convinced he was going to be successful."

With the establishment of the corporation, Jim and Jane were officially in business together. Another document they would sign the following year would bring them together in a more meaningful way.

CHAPTER 8

Jim and Jane Henson

When Jim and Jane started working together, they were both dating other people. Jane would become engaged to Bill Schmittmann, whom she had been dating since 1955, and Jim's engagement to Anne Marie Hood was announced in December 1957. "We just weren't in the same social realm," Jane said of Jim in a 2010 interview with Brian Jay Jones. "I was like a sorority girl, a senior, and he came in as a freshman. We got together to work, and we enjoyed working together, but it just wasn't a very likely personal relationship at that time."

As they worked together, proximity led to a certain level of familiarity. "We went out on a couple of things that you'd call dates," she told Jones. "He was lovely on a date, but mostly, they weren't dates, they were work situations." Some social engagements, however, were indeed interspersed among the work. "I think we went to see The Kingston Trio," Jane said. "We went to see Harry Belafonte at . . . the amphitheater in the park. We ice-skated a lot on the canal. But I don't know if those were called dates or if that was just something we'd do."

The more time Jim and Jane spent together, the more they realized that their respective significant others were, for the most part, superfluous to the connection that was developing between the two of them. Jane recalled one ride in a WRC elevator that found the two couples—Jim and Anne and Jane and Bill—together. She and Jim looked at each other, and she started thinking, *You know, we're here and that's important, but those two people don't need to be here.* She explained to Jones: "It was that kind of feeling about it. So we had a kind of a permanency about us."

When Jim returned from Europe, he had it in his mind that he and Jane should get married. According to Jane, he explained his plans matter-of-factly: "This is what we're going to do. We're going to do this with the puppets and then we're going to get married."

It wasn't a complete surprise to Jane, and, apparently, other people had recognized the evolving relationship between Jim and Jane before they did themselves. "Later I heard from people in the studio that they just assumed we were going to end up together."

"I think even Bill and Anne knew."

It may have seemed less than romantic, but Jane agreed with Jim's plan.

"We were very fond of being with each other," she said. "There was a love there. I don't—quite honestly, I can't remember a situation of falling in love, it was more like a recognition of, look, this is what's been happening. And then we'd turn around and talk to other people and they'd say, 'Yeah, well, we knew that.'"

Jim and Jane worked side by side into 1959 as a newly engaged couple.

In the weeks before their wedding, there was another ceremony that marked another first for the Muppets. On May 6, 1959, the National Capital Chesapeake Bay Chapter of the National Academy of Television Arts & Sciences presented its eleventh annual local Emmy awards honoring achievement in Washington-area television programming.

Jim's mother didn't go out for many events, but she accompanied Jim, Jane, and Bob Payne to the local Emmy award ceremony.

Sam and Friends, which occupied a relatively small percentage of Washington, D.C.'s television airtime, received the Emmy for best local entertainment. The small trophy, which featured a miniature version of the now-familiar winged Emmy statuette, was presented to Jim by Vice President Richard Nixon as Jane looked on.

"You have to stand there having your picture taken, you have to say something, right?" Jane said in a 2009 interview. "I remember

Jim looking a little baffled in the picture." After he posed for the photograph, Jim told Jane what Nixon had said to him that caused Jim's puzzled look: "I knew a man in the Navy with a beard."

Jim Henson receives his Emmy from
Vice President Richard Nixon. Photo by Jim Curtis

Bob Payne, Kermit, Jim, Sam, and Jane celebrate their Emmy.

Soon after the Emmy win and just before his upcoming nuptials, Jim shaved off his beard. The story goes that Jim's mother felt strongly that "no son of mine is going to get married in a beard." Before the big day, Jane received an envelope containing the hair clippings and a note reading: FROM SAMSON TO DELILAH.

On the May 26, 1959, installment of *Sam and Friends,* Harry told the viewers that the show was taking the summer off. Two days later, on May 28, 1959, Jim and Jane were married, with Jim's Uncle Jinx, an Episcopal minister, officiating. Jim's best man, Joe Irwin, barely made it into town for the wedding.

"I was flying in from St. Louis, and the plane landed and then couldn't take off because of fog," Irwin recalled. The delay caused Irwin's late arrival at Washington's National Airport, and he thought he would certainly miss the wedding, which was being held some 120 miles away at Jane's parents' house in Salisbury, Maryland. Groom Jim Henson would not allow fog to interfere with his wedding. "When I landed at National and got off the plane, my father met me and told me that Jim had arranged for another plane to get me to Salisbury," Irwin said. "So I ran over where my father said to go, and we got on this little plane." Irwin arrived a little late but early enough to see Jane and Jim tie the knot. "As a best man, I was pretty poor; I didn't have a speech ready or anything, but they were happy to see me."

Jim and Jane get married. Jane was not used to seeing Jim without a beard. He would soon regrow it.

That day's *Washington Post and Times–Herald* carried news of the union, but unlike most wedding notices, the blurb was in the television column, not the marriage announcements. TV columnist Lawrence Laurent wrote, "The Muppets are off WRC-TV because Muppeteers Jim Henson and Jane Nebel are becoming Mr. and Mrs. Jim Henson." Their more formal engagement announcement, three weeks earlier, appeared alongside those of six other couples in the *Post*'s "For and About Women" section and made no mention of Muppets at all.

After their honeymoon, Mr. and Mrs. Henson were back in the studio at the beginning of August for their first season of *Sam and Friends* as man and wife.

There were few changes in the way they worked, but one had a big impact: Since Jim and Jane had moved into a new house, they had a new home workshop in which to construct puppets. The Hensons bought a modern house in a new subdivision in Bethesda, Maryland's Flint Hill neighborhood. With homes targeted at young professionals (many in the area worked in government), Jim and Jane's arrival was noticed from the very beginning. Years later, the developer's sales associate recalled that both Jim and Jane were wearing shorts when viewing the house. In 1959, such casual attire would certainly not be worn by serious home buyers and might even raise a red flag regarding their "suitability" for the neighborhood. But Jim and Jane were indeed serious and surprised the developer by paying the $35,000 price of the house in cash, a transaction no doubt made possible by the continuing success of the Wilkins-style commercials across the country. Conveniently located a little more than five miles from the NBC studio, the home's lower level became the first dedicated Muppet workshop, while Jim and Jane lived on the upper level.

Jane waves at her husband the photographer from the balcony of their new home in Bethesda. Photo by Jim Henson

Newlyweds Jim and Jane Henson spend their first Christmas in their new home in 1959.

Jim and Jane at work in their new home workspace.
Photo by Jack L. Hiller, © 1959.

As Jim and Jane continued working together on *Sam and Friends* after the wedding, they also began work on an all-new collaborative production. On May 9, 1960, Harry began the broadcast with a dedication to "Jane Henson; six-pound, ten-ounce Lisa Marie; and her proud new fatherrrrrr—" with the audio grinding to a halt before Jim's name could be uttered on air. The record that followed was, appropriately, Johnny Standley's "Proud New Father."

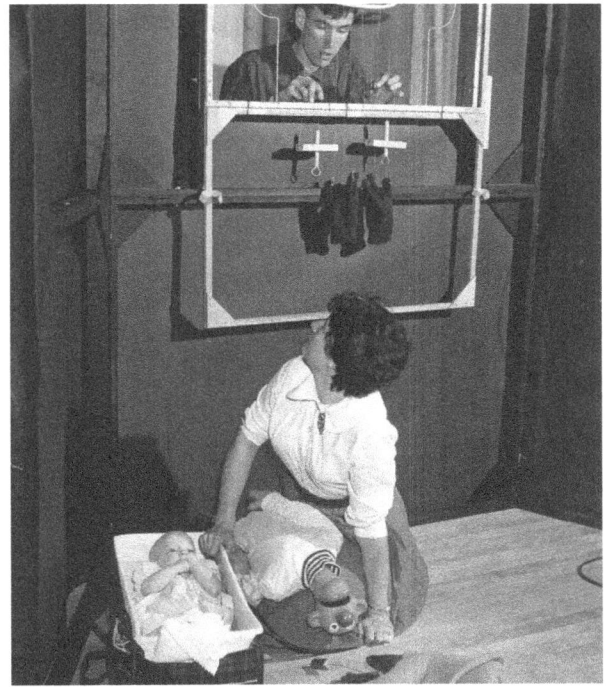

Jim and Jane (and Lisa) prepare for a live performance.

The proud new father was also about to become a college graduate—with a degree in home economics. At that time, as was the case with similar programs throughout the country, the commercial art department at the University of Maryland was located within its school of home economics, creating a distinction between commercial and fine art education. Graduates from commercial art programs would go on to fill creative positions at major advertising agencies, and Jim was already working with some of these real life "Mad Men" of the gray flannel era on *Sam and Friends* and the Wilkins commercials. He was able to speak their visual language in the form of commercial storyboards.

In anticipation of his graduation, Jim visited Rosenthal Chevrolet in Arlington, Virginia, on May 30, 1960, and drove off the lot in a used 1952 Rolls-Royce. Although Jim was a quiet and humble man, he couldn't resist one small exhibition of the success he had already enjoyed while still in college. He drove to his graduation in luxury—second-hand luxury, but luxury, nonetheless. (Later that summer, Jim would splurge on another piece of automotive luxury, selling his Thunderbird and purchasing a Porsche to keep the Rolls company in the Hensons' Bethesda driveway.)

On Graduation Day, Jim poses beside his new Rolls-Royce, joined by the Hensons' cat, George Washington, and their dog, Loki.

Jane told *The Sunday Star TeleVue*'s Bonnie Aikman that the purchase of the Rolls-Royce was "mainly for their infant daughter.... The car provides a most comfortable sleeping area for Lisa Marie during long vacation trips." In August of 1960, with Lisa in her "comfortable sleeping area," Jim and Jane drove the Rolls-Royce to Detroit for a Puppeteers of America festival. The Hensons—who saw the value in connecting with other puppeteers to expand their knowledge of the craft—had joined the Puppeteers of America and become active in the local National Capital Puppetry Guild. The trip to Detroit was their first national puppetry festival, and there they met Burr Tillstrom, the man who at that time was probably the most famous puppeteer in the country. Tillstrom's original *Kukla, Fran and Ollie* program had been broadcast nationally between 1947 and 1957. Like Jim's *Sam and Friends* cast, Tillstrom's characters, accompanied by singer Fran Allison, appealed to adult audiences. Tillstrom immediately took a liking to Jim.

"Burr was a star and enjoyed being a star, so when Jim came in a Rolls-Royce, that made Burr really like Jim," said Jane Henson with a laugh in a 2010 interview. "And we had a sky roof that slid back, and I don't know how Burr could possibly have gotten Jim to do it, but we were driving down downtown Detroit, and Burr got Jim to perform Kermit out the sky roof."

The Muppets were not officially listed in the festival's program, but they did give a performance. A rave review appeared in the September-October 1960 issue of *The Puppetry Journal*, though the act was so new to the Puppeteers of America community that the Henson troupe was referred to throughout as "the Moppets."

"The Moppets a sheer delight," the opening statement of Bill Eubank's review reads. "If you were at the Fest, nothing more need be said. But if you weren't you missed one of the most interesting hours (an all too short hour) of puppets I have witnessed in a long time." According to the review, the Hensons began their festival performance with "That Old Black Magic" and then segued to "I've Grown Accustomed to Your Face." The puppet performance was followed by a brief talk by Jim and Jane and the presentation of a few Wilkins commercials. The review concluded with, "I'm sure we who were there and you who have seen them on your local stations will be eager to hear more about Jim and Jane and those ever fresh creations, the Moppets."

Jim and Jane with Wontkins and Wilkins at
the Detroit Puppeteers of America festival in 1960.

Though most likely not aware of it at the time, Jim Henson was constantly initiating relationships that would lay the foundation for the rest of his career. Also in attendance in Detroit was Don Sahlin, the master puppet builder who had been constructing Tillstrom's Kuklapolitan characters. Within a year or two, Sahlin—a veteran of George Pal's stop-motion Puppetoons shorts—would be building Muppets for Jim.

About five hundred puppeteers converged on the Detroit Institute of Arts for the 1960 festival, and it was the first time Jim and Jane had the chance to meet so many puppeteers in one place. In addition to Tillstrom and Sahlin, the Hensons also met Rufus and Margo Rose (then performing Howdy Doody and the Doodyville cast of characters on NBC) and George Latshaw in Detroit.

"Jim really was anxious to know other puppeteers and also to look for somebody to work with him," Jane said. Now that he was making puppetry a career—and his and Jane's family obligations were increasing—Jim thought it might be time to augment his team.

After the festival, the Hensons drove to Saugatuck, Michigan, for a weekend with Burr at the Oxbow summer art school, where Burr was scheduled to perform a small show. A very lucky live audience got to see the Muppets and the Kuklapolitans appear together for the only time.

From Jim Henson's home movies: Burr Tillstrom.

From Jim Henson's home movies: Ollie puts the bite on Kukla.

"They were having a fundraiser or something," Jane Henson said. "Burr was doing Fletcher Rabbit and he had Kermit come and do it with him, very early Kermit. Fletcher and Kermit really enjoyed each other. And other times after that, Burr and Jim tried to do things together, but it didn't really work because Burr did exactly what he did, really brilliantly well, and there really was not a place where Jim could fit into that. And then he really did not want to work in Jim's kind of area, so they were their own people."

The weekend in Saugatuck was captured in Henson home movies, which show a very relaxed Jim and an infant Lisa, who was along for the ride the whole time—setting a precedent for the Henson children's inclusion in Jim's work. A look at the trip's home movies reveal Jim and Jane enjoying a casual time on the beach with Burr Tillstrom and Don Sahlin and strolling through an outdoor art show.

A frame from Jim Henson's home movies:
Jim and Jane enjoy an art show in Saugatuck.

The Hensons left Michigan refreshed and relaxed and having made the acquaintance of dozens of puppeteers.

As far as finding somebody to work with, delegates from California had talked up a young man named Frank Oznowicz, whose puppeteer parents, Mike and Frances, were in attendance in Detroit. The following year's festival was planned for Asilomar, California, so the Hensons made tentative plans to take the trip then to meet Frank.

One year was about as far as Jim would look ahead. Always thinking of the long-range possibilities, Jim would not commit to WRC for more than a year at a time. As the Hensons drove their new baby back to Washington for a new season of *Sam and Friends,* audiences had no idea how many more one-year deals were ahead for the Muppets and WRC.

CHAPTER 9

Brought to You by Esskay

For about half of its run, *Sam and Friends* was sponsored by The Wm. Schluderberg—T.J. Kurdle Company of Baltimore, Maryland. The venerable local meat packer's roots date to 1858, when William Schluderberg began operations on his own. In 1919, Schluderberg joined forces with Thomas J. Kurdle, and the two combined their initials—"S" and "K"—to form the brand name "Esskay." Schluderberg passed away in 1921 and Kurdle in 1935, neither living to see the invention of television, let alone their products becoming almost synonymous with a cast of Muppet characters. But there were other family members on the job, including the co-founder's descendant Tom Kurdle, the company's field sales manager, who would have the most contact with Jim and Jane.

Esskay had advertised on television before *Sam and Friends*. In 1954, Esskay's *Bobo Newsom's Knothole Gang starring Bobo Newsom* entertained young hot dog and cold cut lovers before every Baltimore Orioles game on both television and radio. Newsom was a retired Major League Baseball pitcher whose career began in 1929 and ended in 1953; he played on more than a dozen teams, but, oddly enough, never for Baltimore.

By 1957, Esskay was spreading some of its advertising dollars into more adult fare, sponsoring *Men of Annapolis*, a WMAR broadcast produced in cooperation with the U.S. Defense Department and the Department of the Navy. The half-hour drama ran on Sunday nights at 10:30 p.m.

The December 1958 issue of *Esskay News*, the company's internal employee newsletter, carried a full-page ad for Esskay's latest advertising sponsorship, *Sam and Friends,* proclaiming, "You and your neighbors will love Esskay's new show."

Back cover ad of *Esskay News*, December 1958.
Courtesy of the Baltimore Museum of Industry Archives

With Baltimore-based Esskay becoming the sponsor, *Sam and Friends* would now be broadcast on Baltimore's WBAL-TV as well as on its originating station, WRC. The November 25, 1958, show began with Omar proudly welcoming Baltimore to the *Sam and Friends* network. "Let's see, how many stations does that make now?" he calls to someone offscreen. "TWO!" is the shouted response.

"Of course, the thing that was so wonderful was the people's names that owned it—Schluderberg and Kurdle—so Jim loved to write things about Schluderberg and Kurdle," Jane Henson said in a 2009 interview.

There is no paper trail for how Esskay got paired up with *Sam and Friends,* but WRC executive Joe Goodfellow and his sales team, as well as Esskay's agency VanSant Dugdale, probably made the match, no doubt influenced by the success of the Muppets' Wilkins Coffee commercials.

Most episodes of *Sam and Friends* featured a commercial performed by the cast (not an unusual occurrence in 1950s television) in which they sang the praises of the various Esskay products in a silly manner. "They were great fun to do because it had to do with, you know, eating hot dogs and things you could make fun of," Jane said. And with the bulk of *Sam and Friends* still devoted mostly to lip-syncing records, the Esskay commercials gave Jim and Jane an opportunity to develop the characters in a meaningful way.

Tom Shaw, a young copywriter for the VanSant Dugdale agency who would go on to a long career as a board game designer and executive, was assigned to the Esskay account and wrote many of the commercials for the show—with plenty of input from Jim—until he left in 1960 to join the Avalon Hill game company.

"It was my job to conceive and write 60-second TV commercials expounding the virtues of eating Esskay meats and I did so in a humorous vein compatible with the ambience of the show," Shaw wrote in a book about his career in board games.

"I delivered the commercials, a bunch at a time, to WRC-TV, by car," he wrote. By his count, Shaw penned about fifty spots for *Sam and Friends,* and the agency even received positive mail from viewers—which was a rarity when it came to television commercials.

One of Shaw's spots raised the ire of fans of Washington's then-quarterback Eddie LeBaron. The Esskay Muppet commercial dated December 9, 1959, featured Omar as football player Eddie LeFumble of the Washington Deadskins, interviewed by sportscaster Kermit:

KERMIT: You called a great game, Eddie. What do you think was the turning point?
OMAR: It was during halftime.
KERMIT: You mean, the coach gave you a pep talk?
OMAR: No . . . he gave us some Esskay franks. Man, those warm, hickory smoked franks sure gave us a pickup on a cold day. They're pure meat, just loaded with protein.

Aside from the name parodies, there was nothing derogatory to LeBaron or the team in the commercial, but fans can get a little sensitive when they've just lost their fourth game in a row. (The team went 3-9 in the 1959 season.)

Often, the commercials were about the commercials themselves. In more than one spot, Professor Madcliffe stopped the action to criticize the quality of the cast's recent work:

KERMIT: Folks, tonight I'd like to talk about—
PROFESSOR: Hold it! Stop the presses!
KERMIT: Excuse me, Professor, but I'm in the middle of a commercial and you shouldn't interrupt me.
PROFESSOR: Nope, I've decided that we're gonna call off the commercial tonight and have a little drilling around here. You're all getting sloppy on your delivery. Come on up here, all of you.
KERMIT: The Esskay people aren't gonna like this, skipping the commercial.
PROFESSOR: All right now, gentlemen, we've got a problem. We're not getting the Esskay quality story out to our

	audience. Here's a company that's been turning out the finest quality products for over one hundred years and what are we doing about it?
KERMIT:	Well, maybe if you'd stop interrup—
PROFESSOR:	Nothing! Those listeners out there are doing an important thing when they shop. They're buying things for the most important people in the world—their family. And that means they shouldn't be buying anything but Esskay quality products. All right then, let's get in there and do a job, now. Try it, Kermit, and give it some gumption!
KERMIT:	I can't. Our time is up.

Each year, the Esskay sales team would meet at the company's Baltimore headquarters, and on January 30, 1959, the *Sam and Friends* cast appeared in person as sales manager T. J. (Tom) Kurdle and Dan Loden of VanSant Dugdale presented an overview of Esskay advertising for the coming year.

Omar and Harry began their report with an announcement of the records that *Sam and Friends* had broken.

OMAR:	On November 23, we broke a record . . . it was called "I've Given Up Hot Dogs Forever" . . . sung by the Cool Cats.
HARRY:	No, Omar, I think you have the wrong idea.
OMAR:	Here's another one we broke, on December the eleventh, sung by Elvis Presley, accompanied by the National Symphony Orchestra. . . "S K stands for Santa Claus at Christmastime in Holland," cha cha cha.
HARRY:	No, that's not the right kind of record.
OMAR:	Oh, we broke many kinds of records . . . a grand total of 472, including such old favorites as, let me

see... here's a version of "The Frantic Frankfurter Frolic," sung by the Hebrew National Kosher Choir.

The live Muppet portion of the meeting ended with Harry emphatically telling the Esskay sales team to "get out there and sell, sell, sell," a refrain that the Muppets would again employ in industrial films for IBM in the 1960s and generic meeting films in the 1970s.

The big news of the 1959 sales meeting was the introduction of the massive "Load O' Loot" promotion that would be advertised on *Sam and Friends* until April 30, 1959. Esskay customers would have the opportunity to win a grand-prize package including a 1959 Chevrolet Impala, a mink stole, a diamond ring, a sterling silver flatware set, a fourteen-foot motorboat, a Hamilton diamond wristwatch, a bedroom set, Encyclopedia Britannica, his and hers sets of golf clubs, power tools, a Lionel train layout, a Philco television set, a Hi-Fi console, a washer-dryer, an upright freezer... and $500 worth of Esskay meats (and that's a lot of meat in 1959). If you didn't win the grand prize, there were still hundreds of Esskay products to win in the contest.

To win the loot, customers simply had to come up with a word that best described the taste of Esskay Hickory Smoked Sliced Bacon and send it in with an entry form found on the back of the package. For three months, *Sam and Friends* commercials featured the "Load O' Loot" contest almost exclusively (with some mentions of Esskay Ham thrown in around Easter). Some spots played it straight with Jim Henson's normal speaking voice reading the copy as images of the prizes flashed onscreen, but most "Load O' Loot" commercials featured the Muppets, who were, themselves, excited about the giveaway.

One ad began with Moldy Hay happily singing, "Oh, I'm gonna enter the contest for the Esskay Load O' Loot..." Yorick joined him and showed Moldy Hay the Esskay Hickory Smoked Sliced Bacon package, silently urging him to read one special part of the contest rules. "*Anyone may enter except employees and their families who work for Esskay, their affiliates, and advertising agency. . . .* Well, so what, Yorick? That just means that people who work for Esskay can't enter the contest. See? If we worked for Esskay, we'd be out of luck. We couldn't have a chance to . . . win . . . those prizes." Moldy slowly realized that he might actually be ineligible to enter; then Professor Madcliffe joined them and imparted some good news. "Pardon me, boys. I couldn't help overreading your discussion. Let me assure you, you can enter. You see, the people down there work for Esskay," he said, gesturing below to the unseen puppeteers. "We don't. As a matter of fact, we don't work at all. So let's get out there and buy that wonderful Esskay new-and-improved Hickory Smoked Sliced Bacon."

Moldy must have been disappointed when Mrs. Henry Renten of Takoma Park, Maryland, won the almost $12,000 in prizes.

The contest boosted sales and "Load O' Loot" was repeated the next year. But before that, *Sam and Friends* presented another contest in 1959: "Name This Steer." The Visking Company, a division of Union Carbide, produced the sausage casings used in making Esskay Franks and sponsored the contest—held through numerous hot dog makers across the country—in which viewers were invited to name their food, or at least a steer that would become their food. The *Sam and Friends* cast dutifully promoted the contest and its grand prize—a new house.

At Esskay's January 29, 1960, annual sales meeting, where the theme was "Super Sales," the company proudly introduced a new three-pound canned ham. After Senior Vice President A. B. Kurdle delivered his address ("The Beef, Veal, and Lamb Outlook for 1960!"), Tom Kurdle introduced the advertising update, which again included a live Muppet presentation, this time with

Kermit as the Esskay Super Salesman visiting a grocery store run by Harry.

HARRY:	Tell me, what kind of advertising is Esskay doing?
KERMIT:	Oh, we're doing lots of advertising . . .
HARRY:	Well? Like what?
KERMIT:	Oh, just very much . . . and uh . . . lots and lots. . . . Like, uh . . . oh, there's . . . well, we sponsor that stupid puppet show, *Somebody and Friends*.
HARRY:	*Sam and Friends* . . . yes, I watch it all the time.

"Super Salesman" Kermit proved to be anything but, as he demonstrated little knowledge of Esskay's print advertising plan and had no copies of the ads with him (he did, however, carry a football schedule and a jokebook). But to be fair, in this sketch, Harry wasn't a very good grocer, either.

HARRY:	How can you help me increase my sales?
KERMIT:	Well, let me see . . . Where do you display the Esskay products?
HARRY:	The bacon is over there underneath the Briggs bacon. Sausage is behind the Swift's and Armour Star. Luncheon meats and chicken is all in the back room.
KERMIT:	Well, that all sounds pretty good. How about that American canned what-cha-ma-call-it I brought you last year?
HARRY:	The American Canned Ham, right? That's in the corner behind the soaps and detergents. I haven't sold it yet.
KERMIT:	Well, you never can tell about something like a canned ham. It's probably spoiled by now. Why don't you throw it away and I'll bring you a new one in the next couple of months or so.

SAM & FRIENDS (JIM AND JANE HENSON) SHOWN WITH
A.B. KURDLE, T.J. KURDLE, T.E. SCHLUDERBERG AND
O.B. SMITH, SINGING PRAISES OF THE ESSKAY AMERICAN CANNED HAM.

The Muppets join the 1960 Esskay sales meeting, as documented in the Esskay News employee newsletter. Courtesy of the Baltimore Museum of Industry Archives

The Muppets became a part of the Esskay family, and the company's employee newsletter proudly touted Jim and Jane's Emmy win in a Summer 1959 issue, reminding readers that the show would return after the summer hiatus. Starting that year, like the major prime-time shows, *Sam and Friends* would leave the air for a summer vacation. This change from year-round programming seemed to coincide with Esskay signing on as sponsor. But before they left, Harry made a heartfelt appeal on the sponsor's behalf. "We've enjoyed doing this show for Esskay. It's a good company, and their products are good. We hope you'll keep buying 'em all summer."

While the Muppets pitched Esskay on television, the VanSant Dugdale agency turned to another comedic mind for the Esskay radio campaign, someone who had a good deal of inadvertent input on *Sam and Friends*—Stan Freberg. Freberg began the Esskay radio spots in 1959 and, like Jim, enjoyed having fun with the founders' names: One spot told the story of "Schluderberg and Kurdle—Song and Dance Team."

Freberg eventually expanded to Esskay television commercials (revenge for all those unauthorized uses of his records on *Sam and Friends*?). The ads featured Jesse White, who was best known as the original lonely Maytag repairman, smoking an Esskay Quality Frank in place of a cigarette. "I'm down to a pack a day."

CHAPTER 10

It's Time to Light the Lights

The six-and-a-half-year run of *Sam and Friends* began in television's infancy and ended when the medium had basically become a toddler. Jim and Jane began broadcasting in black and white from the stage of a repurposed hotel theater, and when the series ended, the show was in color, originating from a state-of-the-art television studio.

The show's first home was the Sheraton-Park, a large resort-style hotel on a sprawling sixteen-acre site in D.C.'s Woodley Park neighborhood, near the National Zoo. Opening in 1918 as the Wardman Park, the hotel had its own pharmacy, post office, butcher shop, grocery store, and dry cleaners; in 1947, it gained its own TV station with the arrival of WNBW, the NBC owned and operated station that had just been licensed to broadcast on Channel 4 in Washington, D.C. In 1952, NBC's Washington radio stations, WRC AM and FM, also moved to the hotel, and two years later, WNBW's call letters were changed to match the radio stations.

The Sheraton-Park Hotel: Note the pharmacy at left. Photo by Jim Henson

A theater in the Wardman Tower—an addition to the hotel built in 1928—became WRC's TV studio. Huge RCA television cameras on the stage blocked the view from the rows of theater seats, which didn't matter because most shows had no audience.

The simple sets for the news, weather, and other segments that made up WRC's daily locally produced content were lined up beside each other on the stage so the cameras could be moved from one setup to the next.

"The floor usually could accommodate two or three [sets] at the same time," Jane Henson said in 2009. "But if you were doing *Afternoon with Inga*, *Afternoon with Inga* would require three or four because they had different kinds of situations; they had the kitchen over there, they'd have the interviewing set over here, and the music over here, and the Muppets over there, and then the cameras were sort of in the center and they'd turn around."

The busy studio floor of WRC's *Afternoon*. Photo by Jim Henson

The cameras could easily pan the stage to go from one set to another, but, according to Jane, in the beginning, they could not pedestal up or down. "They were five feet, six inches. I still remember, five feet, six inches, and so we had to work kneeling."

Jim and Jane working to the fixed-height camera.

On the plus side, Jim and Jane didn't have to worry about making any noise, as all of the audio for the Muppets was prerecorded. When baby Lisa eventually came along, she could visit the studio floor without fear that her happy reactions would be picked up on microphones and broadcast to viewers.

"Everything was burned into acetate [records] . . . and we put, you know, five or six songs on it, or bits, or whatever, and then that would be played from the control room," Jane said. The microphones on the floor were turned off and studio speakers turned up so Jim and Jane could lip-sync their puppets to the audio track. But while the soundtrack was prerecorded, the visual performances were not. "Everything was live, nothing was taped; there was no such thing as tape," Jane said. "Whatever you did went out over the air as you did it."

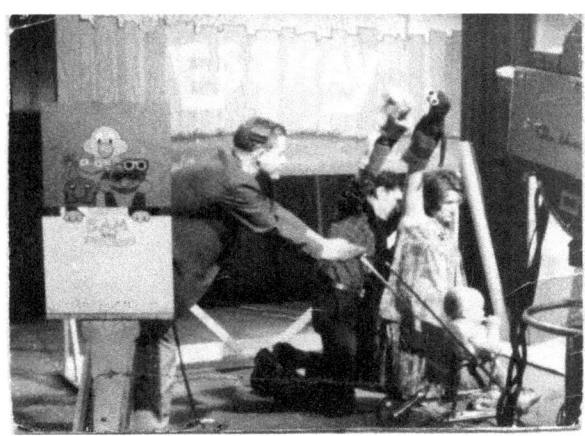

Jim and Jane at work as Lisa watches the monitor from her stroller.

Jim's friend Joe Irwin was an occasional visitor to WRC and recalled the multiset stage at the Sheraton-Park Hotel. "There was a place in there where Tippy Stringer would do the weather in the evening. There was a desk in one area where a newscaster would come in." Irwin, a future National Weather Service meteorologist, noticed that Tippy Stringer's weather forecasts occupied a relatively large amount of studio space, with chalk markings covering the floor. "Someone wrote out what she was going to say, on the floor, which was kind of unusual. I thought that was interesting. But Jim . . . he had a very small area that he would crouch down behind, and he had a monitor."

When WRC moved to its new headquarters, there was more space—and two separate studios to broadcast from. The Muppets usually operated from Studio A, the larger of the two, but they took up relatively little space in the studio. Today, still in operation as an NBC facility, Studio A bears a plaque commemorating the notable broadcasts that originated from within its walls, including *Meet the Press, The Huntley-Brinkley Report,* and, of course, *Sam and Friends.*

At the new building, Jim and Jane had their own workspace down the hall from the studio, an office cubicle they dubbed "Weirdsville."

Bob Payne and Jane in the Muppet cubicle, "Weirdsville." Photo by Jack L. Hiller, © 1959.

In a 2010 interview with Brian Jay Jones, Bob Payne described it: "We had this little cubbyhole at NBC and a cabinet that went high where you could stick all kind of stuff, and then a desk with drawers, and the wigs were in one drawer and the hats were in another drawer—that kind of thing—with a great big mirror on it where we'd sit and rehearse." Bob also recalled that "Weirdsville" was located right next to the desk occupied by weather person (and future bride of newscaster Chet Huntley) Tippy Stringer.

"She could sing," Bob said of Stringer in a 2019 interview. "I was there by myself one time, Tippy was at the next desk, and I was thrilled. I don't know if I was doing anything, I don't think I was doing anything particular, and she stood up and looked over and started singing to me, and I was just in love. It was just absolutely wonderful."

It was here in "Weirdsville" where Jim and Jane would plan and work out their routines and begin to rehearse them.

Jim and Jane rehearse in front of their "Weirdsville" mirror.
Photo by Jack L. Hiller, © 1959.

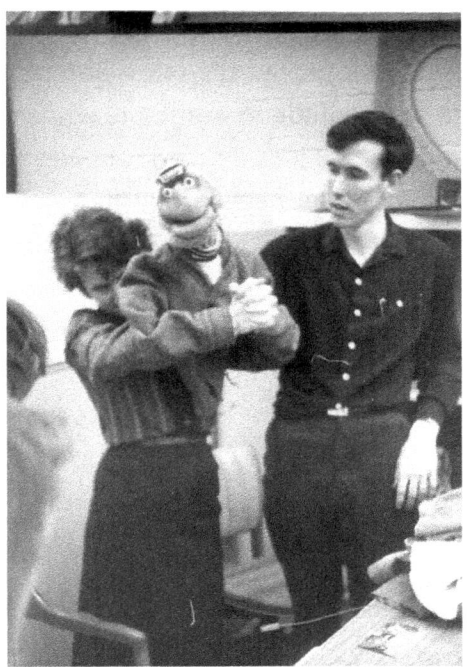

Jim and Jane demonstrate how Omar's hands
work for visitors to "Weirdsville."

Jim documented his daily production process for the Puppeteers of America's *Puppetry Journal* in 1961: "We pre-record the audio of the show at 3:00 in the afternoon, at 5:30 rehearse the show on-camera twice, and the show goes on the air at 6:40. We feel that the camera rehearsal is very important for it is here that the show is smoothed out . . . problems in manipulation as well as technical problems solved. It is here also that the director can see exactly what you're going to do so he can plan the camera shots."

By the time Jim began working at WRC, puppets were, generally speaking, veterans of television. Burr Tillstrom's *Kukla, Fran and Ollie* had been on the air for about seven or eight years, and *Howdy Doody* had been on for nearly as long. The puppeteers working on these shows and most of the other puppeteers working in television at that time had come to the medium from the world of puppet theater. They basically took the same techniques and materials they used in live performances and relocated them to the television studios. Howdy Doody, Kukla, Ollie, and many other characters became beloved by millions, but the television puppetry world was about to be essentially remade by someone whose lack of puppetry experience allowed him to literally work outside the box.

"I think we, as the Muppets, broke new ground because we approached puppetry from a different angle," Jim wrote in 1982. "When I began on television, I really didn't know what I was doing. I'm sure that this was a good thing, because I learned as I tackled each problem of puppetry. I think if you study—if you learn too much of what others have done, you may take the same direction as everybody else."

He may not have intended to lay the groundwork for decades of television puppetry, but Jim brought to the craft several basic innovations that are still being used to this day. The first is the use of the television frame to create a "proscenium" for the action. On *Sam and Friends,* the Muppets were not constrained by a puppet stage like they were in live theater—the characters could move freely about, creating the illusion that they existed in our world and not behind a wall hiding a team of puppeteers. (There were exceptions, of course, when the Muppets would need to work with a wall—for example, when Kermit had to sit and sing "I've Grown Accustomed to Your Face.") By contrast, Kukla and Ollie were always on their little stage with Fran Allison standing in front, the proscenium necessary because the camera had to include Fran in the shot. When the Muppets were working with Paul Arnold, such an artifice was indeed necessary, but on their own, they were free to take up the whole frame, with the deft camerawork of the WRC technicians framing out the world beyond the Muppets.

"We play the puppets in front of a rather large background piece—about six feet wide—using just the frame of the TV picture to keep our arms and head from showing," Jim explained in *The Puppetry Journal*. "With the wide-angle lens (50mm), a short motion toward and then back from the camera will make the puppet very large and then very small. This gives a nice feeling of depth and has many uses in our own work."

A typical performing setup. Note the distance between
Professor Madcliffe and the background.

The use of wide-angle lenses would become a basic technique the Muppets would employ for decades. In *The Puppetry Journal,* Jim even analyzed the importance of lighting as it pertained to his characters: "We have found it best to separate the puppet from the background by at least six to eight feet. This will enable the lighting man to light the puppets separately from the background. There are several reasons for doing this: first, you won't get a shadow or shadows from the puppet on the background—especially annoying on something like a painted sky. Second, the puppets and background can each be lit without spilling light on the other—for instance, the puppets usually look best with some top or side light, rather than all flat front light."

Jim and Jane at work on a backdrop. Photo by Jack L. Hiller, © 1959.

What Jim didn't mention about the backgrounds was that he designed most of them and painted them with assistance from Jane and, eventually, Bob Payne. Jim also designed the cutout elements and props used to augment the set as well as the *Sam and Friends* title cards that opened and closed the show.

In the early days, three panels of this title card flipped in sequence, from left to right, to reveal the show's title and sponsor.

We believe the switch to color prompted a new opening sequence that began with an illustration of the cast, which Sam soon covered with the show's title card. Sam's eyes moved around and his nose flipped to reveal "by" before the screen was filled with the sponsor's name.

This photo of a more abstract title card with several moving parts was found in The Jim Henson Company Archives, but it's unclear when it was used. The photo is dated October 1959.

When Bob Payne joined the team in 1958, he pitched in with the scenic work. "I started right at the beginning painting backdrops," Payne told Jones in 2010. "We had these rolls of scene paper back in the scene dock, and I would go back there and roll out whatever color we wanted—we had all kind of colors for whatever the number was—and then I would do this backdrop." Payne remembered the elaborate setup from a performance of the Danny Kaye song "Inchworm" from the film *Hans Christian Andersen:* "Jim had . . . a machine that he called 'the cut-all' that had a blade underneath, and we would cut out this thick board. You could design something and then cut it out, and then use that as a silhouette or as something to work behind in the scene. And he had done a cutout of a school in silhouette. He painted it black, but the window was cut out." Inside the schoolhouse window were little students in silhouette.

"I don't remember exactly how he had done it, but he had strings where you could pull the strings and [the children] would move their mouths," Payne said. "The inchworm was just a little piece of foam with wires on each end, so you could crawl it out, pump it up, and all that." As Kermit sang the Danny Kaye part, the inchworm would crawl, and the silhouette schoolchildren in the window would sing the children's part on the record.

"I just was so impressed with some of the things that he did," Payne said. "So simple in a sense, but they worked on television. They became dimensional on television."

"Inchworm" as performed by Kermit and Jim's silhouette schoolchildren.

"Inchworm" was performed much the same way twenty years later on *The Muppet Show*, with Charles Aznavour substituting for Kermit.

The sets were saved and reused, as were many of the scripts and recordings that were performed in front of them, but many backdrops would have to be redone as the show made a transition that many television shows of the period would make.

As one of NBC's owned and operated stations, WRC was among the first to upgrade to color broadcasting. While the new color studio had been dedicated in May of 1958, however, the Muppets didn't make the move to color until the following year. The change was teased by the characters at the end of their March 6, 1959, episode, with Harry announcing that they'd be in color the following Monday. The next week, the transition occurred, but no mention of color was made until Thursday, March 12, 1959. The broadcast began not with NBC's colorful peacock logo, but the crow of a rooster. Harry then announced, "The following gig is being laid on you in indefatigable color," a gentle jab at the color broadcasting technology, which was known as "compatible color" because the color transmission was compatible with black and white sets. When Omar asked Harry what happened to the peacock, Harry replied, "For your edification, cat, the only birds on this show will be Esskay chickens."

The switchover wasn't an easy process, Jane Henson said.

"A lot of things that we did that worked in black and white just didn't work in color," she said of the transition. "I think it was exciting and it was also a bother. Jim really loved working sets and stuff in black and white; he loved working in shades of gray. It isn't that Jim didn't like working in color, it's just that he kind of worked out the whole thing in black and white and he liked it that way."

With color broadcasting, Jim was faced with a new set of challenges. When he began, the puppets had to look good only in black and white. Now they had to look good in color—as well as black and white, as most viewers were still watching the show on monochrome sets. Also watching in black and white were Jim and Jane themselves, as the studio monitors they used during their performances hadn't yet been upgraded to color.

This brings us to Jim's second major innovation. While Burr Tillstrom had access to a television monitor, it was secondary to his performance technique. As he had done in his pre-television-era puppetry performances, Tillstrom sat directly behind his puppets with a scrim separating him from the characters. When lit properly, viewers could not see through the scrim, but Tillstrom could see the puppets through it and performed using this direct vision, with an occasional glance to the monitor beside him.

For Jim Henson, the monitor was his entire world, as he manipulated his characters based expressly on what he saw on it. In a 1959 article in the *Northern Virginia Sun,* Jim explained: "On television, you can watch yourself work on the monitor as you do the show. All the motions and gestures can be worked on and improved. This is the first time in history that the puppeteer has been able to see what he is doing while the show is in progress."

And that concept, which was made possible through the wonders of television, is one of the reasons the Muppets became so real to audiences: They appeared to be looking precisely at the viewers and each other. Seasoned television puppeteers call it "eye focus," and its importance cannot be overstated. It's impossible for a performer to know exactly where a puppet is looking without watching the character on a monitor. When a puppet looks directly down the barrel of a lens, it is very powerful and makes a connection with the audience, inviting them to believe this created world and helping suspend disbelief.

From that "home base" of looking directly at the camera, a television puppet can use angles to emote in ways that compensate for its lack of facial muscles. If a puppet is looking slightly above the lens, it gives the character a sense of wonder or thoughtfulness. If a puppet looks down ever so slightly, it may seem sad or pensive. And if a puppet is trying to speak directly to the camera but is not directly focusing on the lens, well, that just looks like bad puppetry.

Knowing where a puppet is looking also helps the characters make connections with each other—they can look *at* each other, as opposed to looking *beyond* each other. That sort of confident connection helps the audience believe that these inanimate objects are living, breathing characters.

And, quite frankly, being able to see exactly what the audience sees also helps the puppeteers keep heads, arms, rods, and other undesirable behind-the-scenes elements out of the frame. While *Sam and Friends* had a WRC staff director in the control room, Jim and Jane could direct the framing and performance using the monitor as their guide.

According to Jane, she and Jim's reliance on the monitor and their fine-tuning of the monitor-performance technique developed gradually. At the very beginning, "We did not work through the monitor. We just worked and the camera took a picture of us," she said. Over time, Jim and Jane realized how the monitor could be used as a tool to guide their performance. At first, they had to work from a monitor stationed across the studio floor. "At that time," Jane said, "it was really a matter of, 'Would you guys please turn the monitor this direction so we can see it?' And it was way over there. Then we were like, 'Okay, the puppet's on the screen, I guess it's okay.' And then as time went by, we brought it closer and closer.

"We learned very quickly to keep our heads out," Jane recalled. "You know, it's not all that hard to learn that." Once in a while, someone would get in the frame, but then Jim and Jane just improvised. "For the most part, then we'd pretend that it was an animal . . . a dog or something. And the puppet would look at it. You know, you make use of it. If it happens, you make use of it."

While transformative to the craft, the monitor technique is challenging—when you move a puppet to your right, on the monitor it appears to move to your left, and vice versa. Jim's friend, Joe Irwin, saw firsthand how challenging the monitor technique was when he lent a hand for a couple of episodes.

"I only did two shows on the same day with Jim, one time. And even that was probably making me nervous," Irwin said. "Jim and Jane were crouched down on the floor, and my job, sort of leaning over behind them, was to work a contraption that Jim made that had three butterflies on it." When Irwin operated the controller—which he compared to a giant spring-loaded clothespin at the end of a string—the butterflies flapped their wings. "And I thought this would be easy, but at one point, Jim sort of looked up and said, 'Go the other direction.' I didn't really realize why I had a problem. . . . I was looking in the monitor, and the directions are opposite in the monitor."

Jim and Jane eventually mastered the monitor, even though their on-camera rehearsal time was limited. In those early days of television, all of WRC's cameras were typically broadcasting or being serviced at any given time, so Jim and Jane had to initially plan their shows in front of a mirror, which offers the opposite view of what a television monitor shows. When the Hensons took their routine from rehearsal in "Weirdsville" to the TV studio, they had the opportunity to run through the show a couple of times before the live broadcast.

When the Muppets were only working in live television, video monitors were always available, but when Jim and Jane started shooting the Wilkins commercials on 16 mm film, they had to resort to the primitive technique of playing to a mirror. A wide mirror was positioned below the camera, directly across from them, so they could see a very rough approximation of their performances, but they could not focus the characters with the precision possible with a video monitor.

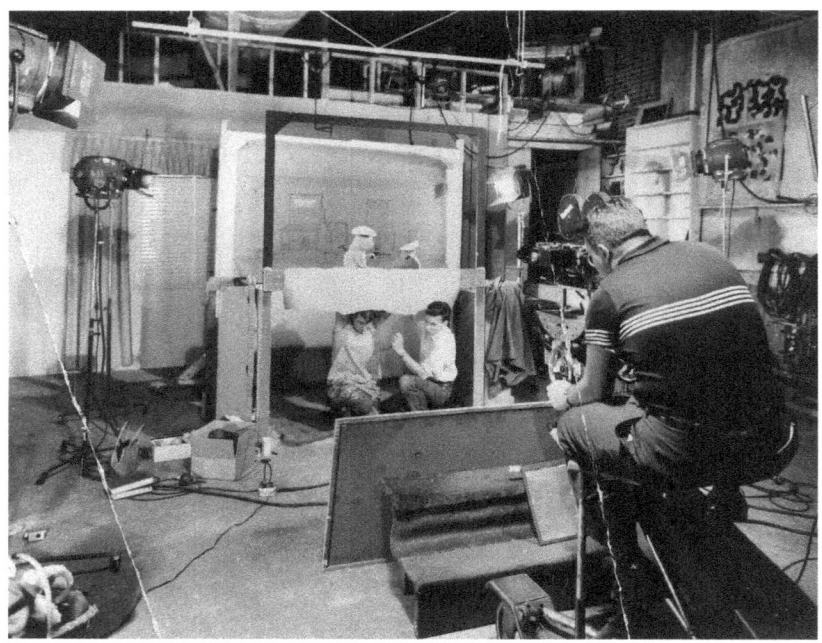

An early commercial shoot—Jim and Jane play to the mirror.

Eventually, a television monitor was added to the filmed commercial shoots—and this was years before the invention of a video assist system that would allow video monitoring of the exact image seen through the film camera's lens.

At a 2006 panel discussion at the University of Maryland, the Wilkins commercials' cinematographer Del Ankers explained how a low-tech workaround was accomplished: "When we were filming the commercials, Jimmy and Jane brought a TV camera and they put it on the same Worrall geared head that my movie camera was on so that they could look at a monitor on the floor and see if there were any imperfections, and if so, Jim would yell, 'Cut.'" This monitor didn't replicate the film camera's frame perfectly, but it was an improvement over the mirror.

Jim and Jane at work on a Wilkins Coffee commercial. Del Ankers and the combined television/film camera setup are visible at left.

The Wilkins setup was essentially a smaller-scale version of Dumont's Electronicam system, which was used to photograph Jackie Gleason's thirty-nine filmed 1955 episodes of *The Honeymooners* just a couple of years earlier. Each of the three massive Electronicam pedestals held a 35 mm film camera beside a television camera. The Electronicam system's television cameras allowed the directors in the control room to position the cameras and call the shots in the same way they would direct a live TV broadcast, while a 16 mm kinescope camera filmed the television image of the director's cut. Simultaneously, 35 mm movie cameras beside each TV camera would film the action. The 16 mm kinescope film would be used as a template to edit the higher-quality 35 mm film master for broadcast. But while the Electronicam was created to aid the director and film editor, Jim's makeshift version was solely for the performer's benefit.

By the time Jim filmed *The Muppet Movie* in 1978, true through-the-lens video assist was possible by using a beam splitter to send the exact image from the film camera lens to a video camera, and, in turn, to a monitor. An engineer named Jim Songer first implemented the technology for Blake Edwards's *The Party* in 1968.

In later decades, when technical advances made it possible to process the monitor's feed so it displayed a mirror image that would be easier to work from, Jim insisted that this not be done. In case there were facilities where the monitor image could not be flipped, he wanted his puppeteers to be able to perform using the more challenging unaltered monitor display. To this day, television puppeteers are trained in Jim's original monitor technique, but, in most cases, they don't have to contend with the pressure of live broadcasting.

While live TV brought with it many challenges, there was no denying that the medium was one of spontaneity and unpredictability. "Live television calls for the idea that you make use of things when they don't go right, and that's part of the charm of it—totally part of the charm of it," Jane Henson said. She explained that when a show is "going out live, you have to assume it isn't all going to work. So we needed to set up a way of working that made it okay if things didn't go all that well, and one of those ways was to not have things perfect." On *Sam and Friends,* the puppets' wigs and hats were placed imperfectly. "If the wig fell off, it would be just part of the material and you'd just use it. . . . If a hat fell off, it just fell off. It isn't like we designed it to fall off, but we liked to keep things kind of rough. I don't want to sound like Jim didn't plan the show, because it was very much planned, but part of the plan was that if it doesn't go right, you make use of it." Over time, the rough edges and imperfections disappeared from both Jim's characters and from the medium of television. In many ways, the medium and the Muppets matured side by side.

Even as videotape became available at WRC in the late 1950s, the Muppets continued to broadcast *Sam and Friends* live, with only an occasional prerecorded broadcast. The main reason was conveyed in a videotaped episode broadcast on June 12, 1961. At the start of the show, Kermit explained that *Sam and Friends* was on videotape that evening, which meant some of the audience would have a different viewing experience. "Tonight, we're on videotape and therefore we're not in color in Washington, and of course we're never in color in Baltimore because the show is telecast there in black and white, but tonight we're especially black and white, even to the people with color sets in Washington or Baltimore, where we always are on in black and white that is . . . and to you people with black and white sets, we're . . . uh . . . just as black and white as usual . . . or perhaps more so."

Apparently, due to the limitations of WRC's equipment and schedule, *Sam and Friends* could broadcast in color *or* on videotape, but not both. That, however, just inspired Jim Henson to turn technical challenges into comic fodder for his program—something he would do throughout his career. "That's very like Jim," Jane Henson said. "Take the situation and turn it into material."

When accepting his induction into the Television Academy Hall of Fame in 1987, Jim Henson looked back on his earliest memories of television, remarking that he considered the TV pictures to be something "quite magical." He loved finding ways to tailor that TV magic to his work, but he was always cautious about using television effects without motivation. "These are all things which are fun to use and very effective if used in the right place, but ineffective if used just for a gimmick," he explained in *The Puppetry Journal.*

In a *Sam and Friends* episode entitled "Visual Thinking," Jim Henson found his motivation in the concept of Kermit giving Harry a lesson in visualizing his thoughts. To bring this to life, Jim created an animated film that could be superimposed over the live television content. As Kermit's lesson went on, images could be seen over the characters' heads until Kermit and Harry's animated thoughts got out of hand and filled the screen, obscuring the characters entirely. If done today, it could be accomplished easily with computer-generated imagery, but back then, Jim painstakingly animated the film by painting under his 16 mm Bolex camera, snapping two frames for every slight movement he made with his brush. The innovation of "Visual Thinking" is probably the reason a rare kinescope of that episode exists, as Jim made an effort to preserve special episodes.

Jim would continue to explore animation throughout the 1960s, but even while still at WRC, he created animated material for the station, including an opening sequence for the long-running high school game show *It's Academic* that would be used for many years. He also used his animation stand and some cutout photos of Kermit to make an on-air promo for his own show.

Jim animated this *Sam and Friends* promo by painting on a black board beneath his animation stand and moving cutout photos of Kermit between exposures.

Some of Jim's innovations were more low-tech, like shooting Kermeena singing "Cry Me a River" through an aquarium as real fish swam across the foreground. A similar technique would be used later on *The Muppet Show* and *Sesame Street*.

Jim could not have accomplished any of this without the technical assistance of the crew at WRC's studios. "They loved working with Jim," Jane Henson said. "Everybody at WRC was so cooperative. They just thought Jim Henson was fun and games." With *Meet the Press*, local news, and half of *The Huntley-Brinkley Report* originating from WRC, for the technical crew, working for the Muppets was their only real chance to do something that wasn't connected to news, weather, or service programming. "*Sam and Friends* was *the* creative show," Jane said of the WRC broadcasts. "And so everybody really wanted to be in on that."

It was a true collaboration between Jim's creativity and the technical crew, as it would be throughout Jim's career. Sometimes an idea would originate with Jim, and the crew would help him find a way to bring it to life, and other times, as Jane Henson recalled, the technicians at WRC would inspire Jim. "They would come up with something that they knew that was technically feasible, and Jim would figure out a way to incorporate it [into the show]."

As excellent as WRC's crew was, sometimes there were, as the phrase goes, "technical difficulties." Viewers tuning in to *Sam and Friends* on Friday, December 19, 1958, were disappointed when the show wasn't transmitted properly; it's hard to determine from the surviving documentation, but there was either no audio or no video. The same episode was re-performed on Monday, with one small addition. Harry addressed the home viewers, offering an explanation for Friday's glitch: "Friends, in case tonight's gig seems a bit repetitious to you cats, leave us say that on Friday, the technicians discovered to their great dismay that chewing gum is not a good conductor of electricity. We hope that we'll be back tomorrow for Esskay—audio and video."

While Jim was definitely interested in technical advancements and continued to develop his television puppetry techniques, the overall look of *Sam and Friends* was deliberately designed to be a little imperfect, a fact that Jane Henson emphasized in 2009.

"We deliberately had the show look like we kind of grabbed a wig from some old box and some piece of clothing from some old box and you painted the scenery . . . you know, it had a very sort of unfinished kind of look . . . that rough-around-the-edges kind of thing, which, very honestly, made it okay to do not very good material. In the beginning, it really was supposed to be like these two kids doing this rough show, and we literally worked out of a basket—a basket of material and a basket of puppets."

Jim Henson and a basket of puppets. *Baltimore American* photo courtesy of Hearst Communications Inc.

CHAPTER 11

The Surviving Shows

When *Sam and Friends* began, the only way to preserve a live television show was through a kinescope. It was a pretty primitive process in which a 16 mm film camera was aimed at a video monitor during the broadcast. The quality was less-than-ideal, and the cost of film and processing made the procedure expensive. Network shows were routinely kinescoped to show advertisers that their sponsorship obligations had been fulfilled by the programs (and, before the transcontinental coaxial cable had been completed, to share East Coast broadcasts with West Coast stations on the network), but local stations often didn't have the budget to preserve their shows, and this is why, out of hundreds of live *Sam and Friends* broadcasts, there are only fifteen episodes known to exist in both audio and visual form. (Not counting a few *Sam and Friends* sketches preserved when the Muppets made guest appearances on other television shows.)

Jim managed to kinescope or film episodes of *Sam and Friends* when he had a particularly ambitious production or special effect. The shows that survive represent a good cross section of what *Sam and Friends* was like.

"That Old Black Magic"

"That Old Black Magic": December 31, 1958; January 26, 1959; February 11, 1960

Louis Prima and Keely Smith began as a Las Vegas act in the mid-1950s. The combination of Prima's swinging rasp and Smith's bold vocal style was a big sensation in a time when rock 'n' roll music was dominating the radio. Their recording of "That Old Black Magic" won the married couple a 1958 Grammy at the first Grammy Awards. The *Sam and Friends* version featured Sam in the Prima role and Kermeena as Smith. The piece begins with Harry watching the duo on a television set. When Sam and Kermeena's audio starts to skip, Harry hits the television set to make the music play as the camera pushes in so we can get a better view of the singers. The rest of the segment is an exhibition of virtuoso puppetry. While Jim usually preferred to perform Kermit, Jane manipulated Kermeena in this segment so Jim could perform the more intricate shoulder movements that Sam was capable of.

When Jim Henson and the Muppets appeared on *The Tonight Show Starring Johnny Carson* in 1974, Jim revived the use of the Prima/Smith record, but instead of Sam and Kermeena, a pig couple (including the then-named Piggy Lee) performed to the song. One year later, Sweetums joined Cher for a duet of the song on her variety show. The song was later used on *The Muppet Show* (sung by guest star Jaye P. Morgan and Dr. Teeth) and on *The Fantastic Miss Piggy Show* (performed by Miss Piggy and Tony Clifton, a.k.a. Andy Kaufman).

"Huntley and Brinkley"

"Huntley and Brinkley": January 6, 1961

In 1956, NBC teamed news anchors Chet Huntley and David Brinkley for *The Huntley-Brinkley Report*, with Huntley broadcasting live from New York City and Brinkley on the air from WRC's Washington, D.C., studio. For quite some time, *Sam and Friends* was the local Washington lead-in for the report, and one day, Jim decided that Chet and David should make a guest appearance alongside Kermit—but without the knowledge of the two newsmen. Employing real audio clips—as Robert Smigel would do years later on *Saturday Night Live*'s "Fun with Real Audio" segments—Jim took snippets from an audio recording of the Huntley-Brinkley broadcast's introduction ("This is Chet Huntley, NBC News, New York" and "David Brinkley, NBC News, Washington") and edited them into responses to Muppet reporter Kermit's questions. For example, Kermit would pose a question, "What's the first name that you think of when it comes to President?" and the puppet representing Brinkley would reply with the carefully edited "Washington."

David Brinkley was watching the live *Sam and Friends* broadcast as he was preparing his show, and only viewers watching in Washington understood why he was laughing when *The Huntley-Brinkley Report* began moments after the Muppets signed off. Chet Huntley in New York couldn't see the bit, but it can be assumed that Brinkley filled him in.

In the original draft of the script, Kermit asks a few more personal questions of Chet Huntley, focusing on his wife, former WRC weather person (and Jim and Jane's former *Afternoon* colleague) Tippy Stringer. "Tell me, what do your friends call you? I mean, do you have any nickname, like, uh, maybe Tippy calls you sweetie pie? Just what do they call you?" The response, of course: "Chet Huntley." Also deleted from the draft script was Kermit asking where Chet and Tippy were living. "Are you commuting from Westport or White Plains or . . ." Huntley's reply: "New York."

"Punsmoke"

"Punsmoke (Powderburn)": August 20, 1959

The most prominent Western television show of the 1950s (and running into the mid-1970s) was *Gunsmoke,* the story of U.S. Marshal Matt Dillon, his sidekick Chester, Miss Kitty, and the goings-on in Dodge City. It was called an "adult Western," to distinguish it from the more kiddie-oriented cowboy fare. *Sam and Friends* brought us a parody, starring Chicken Liver, (when he was still referred to as Theodore) as the cowardly "Matt Dilly, U.S. Marshal, the first man they look for and the last I hope they find."

When his sidekick Pester (Kermit) and girlfriend Miss Doggy (Harry) warn the Marshal about Black Bart's arrival on the next stage, Matt Dilly is found cowering under his desk. He explains that he was down there tying his shoelaces. "You don't have laces on your boots," Miss Doggy says. "Everybody tries to tell me my business," Dilly says. Marshal Dilly is reluctant to a high noon showdown on main street. (Not to be confused with the Bijou Theatre, "the new show down on main street.") But when Bart (Yorick) forces Dilly to make his move, Dilly announces that his next move will be his last. A chess board is revealed and the Marshal takes Black Bart's bishop to achieve checkmate.

The segment is a pun-packed three-minute story reflecting Jim's love of wordplay and verbal humor and the detailed backgrounds, as with most of the sets for the series, were drawn and painted by Jim Henson.

"Poison to Poison"

"Poison to Poison": October 29, 1959

The parody of Edward R. Murrow's *Person to Person* features a Murrow-like interviewer speaking with a Hitchcockian movie director. The recording used is from Spike Jones's 1959 Warner Bros. album *Spike Jones in Hi-Fi: A Spooktacular in Screaming Sound*, with voices provided by the legendary Paul Frees, known as the voice of Bullwinkle's nemesis Boris Badenov. While Jim Henson spelled the title onscreen as "Poison to Poison," the record's liner notes list it as "Poisen to Poisen."

In the bit, Ed Burrow (Harry) remotely joins a very famous motion picture and television director (referred to only as Alfred) at his home, admiring the director's furniture, particularly the armchair Alfred is seated in. Alfred explains the item is very expensive because "it's made out of real arms." Alfred takes Burrow and the audience on a tour of his home, showing off the detailed painted scenery designed and primarily constructed by Jim, and teases his upcoming film, "it's a musical called 'Death Takes a Holiday, Cha-Cha-Cha,' with an all-star cast, Ghoul Brynner, Perry Coma, Red Skeleton, Slab Hunter and Mortician Sahl."

The version of "Poison to Poison" that survives is not a kinescope but a segment filmed for posterity in full color at the Rodel studio by Del Ankers, so Jim's colorful scenic designs can be fully appreciated.

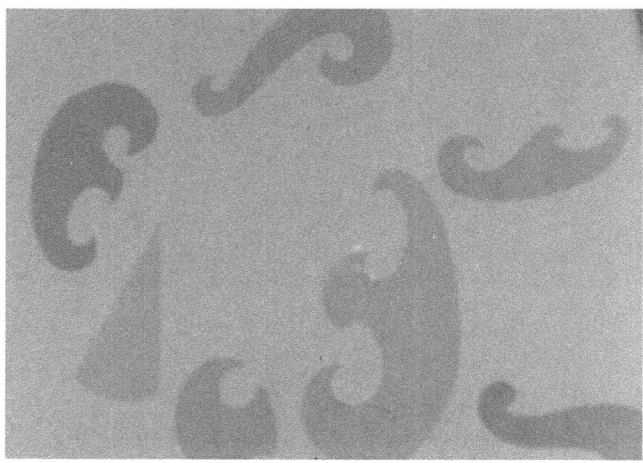

"Miss Cone"

"Miss Cone": December 9, 1960

A rarity among *Sam and Friends* episodes, the recently unearthed "Miss Cone" was a completely animated segment. Jim Henson had long been interested in animation, even contributing occasional title sequences to WRC programs. He bought an animation stand for his 16 mm Bolex camera soon after he was married, Jane Henson recalled.

"He started looking for an animation stand as soon as we had the house, as soon as we got married and had the room for it and everything," she said. "But it took him a little while to locate one that he wanted to have, because he was going to get a new one and they were kind of too expensive. But then he found this one that was for sale that somebody had pretty much hand made." On July 27, 1960, Jim purchased the animation stand for $500, and after picking up a motor for his Bolex camera from Fuller & d'Albert Industrial Photo Supplies for $87.52 on the same day and a few lights and other supplies, Jim's home animation studio was ready.

Jim at his animation stand—a frame from the live-action tag of the segment "Drums West."

For one of his first projects using his new animation equipment, Jim selected Ken Nordine's 1958 record "Miss Cone," the tale of a square's ill-fated romance with a beautiful cone who eventually becomes a star and leaves him for "the littlest guy I've ever known, a point." Doing his painstaking animation work mostly at night when he wouldn't be disturbed, Jim usually employed one of two techniques—painting under the camera or using cut-out pieces of paper—but for "Miss Cone," he also used animation cels to synchronize the brightly colored geometric shapes to Nordine's vocal and accompanying jazz underscore.

Jim hadn't yet perfected the lighting on his setup, so the reflection of his camera is visible on the film image (but was probably too faint to be seen on the broadcast). Both the Nordine recording and Jim's animation of "Miss Cone" share striking similarities with a later story about geometric romance, Norton Juster's book *The Dot and the Line* (1963) and Chuck Jones's subsequent 1965 cartoon adaptation. Coincidentally, *The Dot and the Line* would go on to win the Oscar for best short subject (cartoon) in the same year that Jim Henson's *Time Piece* would be nominated in the best short subject (live action) category.

Despite the absence of the Muppet cast of characters, the episode "came off beautifully," *Evening Star* TV critic Bernie Harrison wrote. "A little more work and I think a network bid is in order." A little more than a month later, on January 19, 1961, the Muppets began making regular remote appearances on NBC's *Today* show, and "Miss Cone" was included on their first broadcast.

"Visual Thinking"

"Visual Thinking": April 1961 (exact date unknown)

Another experiment in animation, "Visual Thinking" combined a film element with live television puppetry. To create this high-concept segment, Jim painted figures under the camera to be superimposed over a conversation between Kermit and Harry.

Kermit begins by explaining the art of "visual thinking," in which he can make his thoughts appear above his head by speaking them. It turns out Harry is experienced in the technique and has used it for years as a tool to visualize his music. Things get dangerous when Harry segues to jazz and his visual images remain onscreen ("jazz tends to linger and you can't get away from it," Harry explains), and the images can only be erased by singing the melody backward. But when Harry and Kermit can't remember their jazz improvisations and try to sing them backward, they instead create a whole new melody and the onscreen jazz imagery continues to build until it covers the entire screen, leaving Kermit and Harry to call for help.

While its initial *Sam and Friends* airdate is unknown, we do know that Jim repeated the bit on the *Today* show on May 5, 1961. Kermit and Harry reprised the sketch on several shows, including *The Mike Douglas Show* (1966). Jim would later reanimate the film element and perform the routine on *The Ed Sullivan Show* (1966), *The Dick Cavett Show* (1971), and *The Tonight Show Starring Johnny Carson* (1974) with Kermit in Harry's role and a character named Grump taking Kermit's old part.

"Weather Warehouse"

"Weather Warehouse": September 29, 1961

As the saying goes, "Everybody talks about the weather, but nobody does anything about it." Well, in this sketch, Harry does something—he sells it, and Kermit is the prospective buyer. "I got a whole warehouse full of nearly new weather to sell at bargain prices," Harry says, showing Kermit a box of bright sunshine he can put away for a rainy day. "A dollar thirty-nine with bird calls, ninety-eight cents without." Harry also has thunderstorms, fog (enough to cover that new swimming pool when the tax assessor comes), and snowstorms. Kermit sees a harmless looking teapot, and Harry warns him against opening it. "Hey, what's so dangerous about a teapot?" Kermit asks as he lifts the lid. Harry replies: "We keep the tempests in there!" As the storm is unleashed, Harry and Kermit head for high ground, but not before Harry signs off with, "That's squall, folks!"

Coincidentally, or perhaps not so much, at the time this sketch aired, Jim's friend Joe Irwin was serving in the Air Force in Germany as a meteorologist. In the seventh season of *Sesame Street*, Kermit is once again targeted by a salesman in the weather business—Grover, who markets a machine capable of creating weather conditions within the home.

"C'est Si Bon"

"C'est Si Bon": January 19, 1959

Eartha Kitt had a hit record with "C'est Si Bon" in 1953. Stan Freberg rushed into action and had his version in record stores the same year. Freberg reached No. 13 on the Billboard chart; Kitt's version made the Top 10.

As with several of Freberg's recordings, "C'est Si Bon" is a song about the making of a song, and on *Sam and Friends,* Moldy Hay takes the role of the lead singer with Hank and Frank as background singers who can't quite hit their cues. Kermit makes a quick appearance, tooting a horn to give the hapless backup vocalists a signal to sing. This surviving segment is another filmed color version and not a kinescope of the live broadcast.

"Chef Omar"

"Chef Omar": November 13, 1961

The character Chef Omar was a precursor to the Swedish Chef, right down to the use of live human hands. In this piece, only part of which survives, Omar, voiced by Jim Henson, prepares an inedible meal that ends with a bang. (Many Muppet sketches of the period ended with either an explosion or one character eating the other.)

In November of 1961, Jim and his new associate Jerry Juhl traveled to Hamburg, Germany, to perform at the U.S. Department of Agriculture's Food Fair, and "Chef Omar" was among the sketches they performed. (This would mark the first Muppet performance on foreign soil.) Just as with the Swedish Chef, Chef Omar used the universal language of silliness and slapstick.

The surviving segment picks up after Chef Omar has assembled his salad and is about to mix the dressing. Though he says he is adding olive oil and wine vinegar, even on a fuzzy kinescope, the viewer can see the bottles are marked as containing the much more volatile liquids, "H_2SO_4" (sulfuric acid) and "Gum Turpentine".

"From this point on," Chef Omar says, "the individuality of the chef comes into great play. One can add a great many things: special oils and condiments, spices and preserves of all kinds, shapes, and varieties." As he speaks, he adds lubricating oil, aerosol spray, toothpaste, and talcum powder into the salad. Finally, after tossing some garlic into the bowl, he is ready for the final touch. "The Omar Salad is served flaming, on a sword," he says, striking a match and dropping it in with the rest of the ingredients. After the ensuing explosion, viewers are invited to request a copy of the recipe by writing to: Chef Omar, 14 Tummy-ache Lane, Indigestion, 3, Ohio.

In Germany, Jim peppered Omar's dialogue with a few fractured German phrases to appeal to the hometown crowd. This may have laid the groundwork for the Swedish Chef's vocal characterization. A version of this sketch, "Chef Bernardi," was performed on *The Mike Douglas Show* in 1966.

"Glow Worm"

"Glow Worm": April 18, 1961 (date estimated)

As Chet Atkins's guitar version of "Glow Worm" plays, Kermit hums along to the tune, observing a small inchworm that's crawling along beside him. As it nears, Kermit leans down and eats the worm. This is repeated several times, with Kermit enjoying his little snacks. The final worm, however, is not a worm at all but a finger, which Kermit learns as he tries to eat it. The finger—and the hand it's attached to—attacks Kermit and wrestles him out of frame.

"Glow Worm" outlasted *Sam and Friends* and was performed on a number of variety shows throughout the 1960s, though the segment changed a bit. In the revised 1960s version, when Kermit tugs at the final worm, he pulls and pulls on the object until it is revealed to be the long nose of a monster. Named Big V (a.k.a. Big Vomit Monster), the monster does not take kindly to the attempt to munch on his nose, and he devours Kermit. By the time the sketch appeared on *The Muppet Show* in 1977, Kermit's role was played by a nondescript lizard character.

"Horse Named Bill"

"Horse Named Bill": March 15, 1960

Historically significant because it marks the first time Kermit is seen playing a banjo, "Horse Named Bill" is a straightforward lip sync to Bob Gibson's interpretation of the traditional folk song, which is known for its silly lyrics:

> In Frisco Bay, there lives a whale
> She eats pork chops by the bale
> By the hogshead
> By the schooner
> Sometimes by the pillbox.
>
> Her name is Luna, she's a peach
> But don't leave food within her reach
> Or babies
> Or nursemaids
> Or chocolate ice cream sodas.
>
> When she's happy, how she smiles
> You see teeth for miles and miles

And tonsils
And spareribs
And things too fierce to mention.

Sadly, only a brief excerpt of this episode survives. Owing to the popularity of folk music during its run, "Folk Song Day" was a regular feature of *Sam and Friends,* and Bob Gibson's music was frequently heard on the show.

A year after this episode aired, Jim's fondness for folk music led him to develop the concept for a folk music series called *Sing-A-Song,* to be hosted by a banjo-playing mountain man and his friendly frog sidekick.

Frames from Jim's storyboard for Sing-A-Song.

Jim's sketch for the Sing-A-Song characters.

While *Sing-A-Song* never made it past the idea stage, *The Muppet Show* presented its own share of folk songs, including "Horse Named Bill," which was sung by Lubbock Lou and His Jughuggers. Another song popularized by Bob Gibson, "To Morrow," was also performed on *The Muppet Show*.

"Hunger Is From"

"Hunger Is From": February 6, 1959; January 12, 1960

Another episode shot in color by Del Ankers, this is a relatively simple routine using Ken Nordine's "Hunger Is From" recording. As Yorick talks about the concept of hunger, he devours a plateful of celery and olives. Although Yorick is usually a disembodied skull, for this piece, he has a gloved hand to help him eat.

"I've Got You Under My Skin"

"I've Got You Under My Skin": March 30, 1959; October 7, 1959
(though it was probably first performed earlier, as the song was transcribed to a *Sam and Friends* disc in August of 1955)

This color film uses a Stan Freberg record as its soundtrack. Freberg was inspired to create its sing-along format by the success of The Weavers' 1951 recording of "On Top of Old Smokey." On that track, Weavers member Pete Seeger encouraged the audience to sing along to the classic folk song, a concept Freberg decided to apply to a Cole Porter classic—with his own comedic spin, of course. On the Muppet version, Kermit lip-syncs to Freberg's increasingly manic leader as he directs choir members Hank and Frank and Icky Gunk, who are echoing their leader's words a little too literally. This

1951 single was only Freberg's second record for Capitol, but the label furnished him with first-class musical talent; the renowned Les Baxter was musical director on the recording.

"Singin' in the Rain"

"Singin' in the Rain": November 19, 1959

Bernice fronts this episode, which is notable for the real water pouring down on her. When she wasn't lip-syncing to someone else's song, Bernice spoke with a high falsetto voice supplied by Bob Payne. In this segment—another color film—Edie Adams (wife of Ernie Kovacs) provides the vocals for "Singin' in the Rain," although you can't really tell as the track is sped up for comic effect. (Yes, we slowed it down to check.) The Arthur Freed/Nacio Herb Brown standard would go on to be used several times in subsequent Henson-related projects, most notably in Gene Kelly's episode of *The Muppet Show*.

"The Westerners"

"The Westerners (Two Face West)": November 4, 1960 (date estimated)

Kermit and Chicken Liver are cowboys trying to maneuver their horses in "The Westerners," a track from Bob and Ray's 1960 RCA album, *Bob and Ray on a Platter*. The cowboys struggle to gain control, and not much else happens as the horses prevent them from both facing in the same direction at the same time. Bob Elliott (father of Chris Elliot) and Ray Goulding were best known as radio comedians in Boston and New York City and later expanded their reach with television and movie appearances.

CHAPTER 12

Jerry

Sam and Friends ended the 1960–61 season on June 13, 1961. In that season finale, the characters mentioned their upcoming trip to the Puppeteers of America festival on the West Coast. For Jim Henson, the trip out west was more than a vacation—it was a scouting mission. With the Henson family growing (by mid-1961, Jim and Jane's second child was on the way), it was decided that Jane should give up some of her performing responsibilities.

"Jim felt I was no longer 'dependable,'" Jane Henson said with a laugh in a 2009 interview. "I never *was* dependable. One evening, I was out at dinner and I just forgot to go to the station. I called after the 11:30 show was over. I said, 'Oh my God! I forgot to go to the station!' and Jim said, 'Don't worry about it. I always keep one ready to do by myself.'" Jim might have been so understanding because it once almost happened to him. In 1956, he told a reporter about the night he had been playing miniature golf, noticed it was 11 p.m., and had to scramble to make it back to the studio in time.

Jane's availability (and dependability) aside, with Bob Payne still on the team, Jim wouldn't have had to work by himself. Even so, with many projects going on, Jim knew he needed additional help—and the festival was an opportunity for him to meet more actual puppeteers. Up to that point, Jim's collaborators were pretty much chosen based first on proximity, second on puppetry experience and ability.

The cross-country trip was an adventure for Jane. "I was very pregnant with Cheryl, our second baby, and I had a . . . fourteen-month-old baby with me, too. We enjoyed that trip very much." The previous year, Jim, Jane, and Lisa had made the trip to Detroit in the

Rolls-Royce, but they decided a more practical vehicle was needed for the voyage to California. In anticipation of the trip, Jim visited the Suburban Cadillac-Oldsmobile Company in Bethesda, Maryland, on May 29, 1961, and bought a new 1961 Oldsmobile station wagon to serve as the Muppets Inc. company car.

The Henson family drove to California in their new station wagon, making a few stops along the way to look up people with whom Jim was interested in working. Singer Bob Gibson, whose records could be heard on *Sam and Friends,* and Chicago puppeteer Robin Reed were among them.

"When we got out to Asilomar, we really loved meeting the West Coast puppeteers—that was great," Jane said. "San Francisco was such a center of puppetry at that point, and a lot [of that was] because of Frank's parents." Mike and Frances Oznowicz, whom Jim and Jane first met at the previous year's festival in Detroit, were widely known in the Bay Area puppetry community. The Hensons were anxious to meet their son Frank, whom they had heard much about in Detroit.

"Frank was, I guess, about seventeen, and we did see him perform," Jane said. "But then we also met Jerry Juhl, who everyone was very high on and said he was a good writer, and he was about four or five years older than Frank. And he was finished with school, so he was ready to move on."

Jerome Ravn Juhl was born in 1938 in St. Paul, Minnesota, and moved to Northern California when he was thirteen. In a 1991 interview from The Jim Henson Company Archives, Jerry said he was "one of those kids who was obsessed with puppets. It just came straight out of the blue."

"I had just always been fascinated by it," he said. "And I started doing shows when I was a teenager." While Jim Henson was attending the University of Maryland and working on *Sam and Friends* in Washington, Jerry Juhl was attending San Jose State College and working on the Channel 11 show *Sylvie and Pup* in San Jose.

In 1958, Juhl and a couple of college friends came up with an idea for a children's show and took it to KNTV, a three-year-old television station owned by a local bread bakery. The station was built right beside the bakery, designed in a way that if the TV station failed, the building could be converted into a garage for bread delivery trucks.

Sylvie and Pup aired every weekday at 4 p.m. with human host Sylvia Cirone interacting with Jerry's Pup puppet character as they presented cartoons from the station's film library. Mel Swope, a name that classic television fans may remember from the credits of *The Partridge Family,* directed the show. "Of course, we were working for *no* money at all," Juhl said. "And it was wonderful. A terrific learning experience, because we were just left alone to do this show. We turned out five hours of this a week. And I'm sure it was not good, but there were probably moments that weren't terrible, either."

During summer breaks from college, Jerry worked for the Oakland Parks and Recreation Department's Vagabond Puppets, and his graduation from college in 1961 happened to coincide with the departure of Vagabond's director, Lettie Schubert. Jerry was invited to take over for the summer, and his assistant was a high school student named Frank Oznowicz.

"That was the summer that the San Francisco puppetry guild hosted the national convention," Juhl said. Jerry and Frank brought their Vagabond show over from Oakland to perform at the festival, which included some very special attendees from Washington, D.C.

While Jerry didn't know Jim Henson personally yet, he was well aware of the Muppets. "I had been amazed by his work on places like the *Today* show, Steve Allen . . . he was doing this completely mad work. I mean, that early stuff is so wonderfully strange and bizarre." Shortly before the puppetry festival, the Bay Area had received a more regular dose of the Muppets thanks to the Wilkins-style commercials that had recently been purchased by Calso Water. "For puppeteers, it was just absolutely startling," Juhl said. "Puppets that didn't look like puppets had ever looked. It was just phenomenal."

At the festival, Jerry and Frank performed their show together, and then Frank performed solo—a pantomime piece featuring a character known only as "The Man." "For many years," Juhl said, "Frank told anyone who would listen to him that he couldn't do voices, so he did this. It was very funny. And that's where we met Jim."

In an interview for PBS's *Great Performances* in 1994, Juhl talked about that historic meeting. "The first impression that I had of Jim personally was so completely different than the image I had from his work that I had seen on television. He was doing this kind of strange, somewhat abstract, and almost, occasionally, almost surrealistic comedy kind of things. And then I met the guy, and he was, he was so straight out of suburbia. He was this kind of soft-spoken guy who showed up. That sort of nice, soft-spoken, slightly Southern way that Jim had about him was at complete odds with the kind of incredible, high-energy, frenetic, frantic, crazed little sketches that you'd see on the television screen."

After the festival, Frank's parents hosted a party at their home for the Bay Area puppeteers, and Jerry noticed that Jim and Jane were also in attendance. "Looking back on it," Juhl said in the 1991 interview, "I realize that Jim had looked over the festival, and he had seen Frank and I and thought those were the people that might be worth working with, and he had come up to talk to us. I didn't really realize it then."

Initially, Jim set his sights on hiring Frank, whose skills in silent manipulation would best serve his needs for the Muppets. But for one big reason, young Oznowicz was not ready to leave town.

"Frank was still in high school," Juhl said. "I may never have worked for the company if Frank had been older, cause Jim needed a puppeteer and Frank was the puppeteer, I wasn't. I was just lucky I was a little older than Frank. I was brought in on an interim basis."

Jerry had doubts about moving to Washington, D.C.—he considered himself a West Coast kid—but he decided to try it for a while. "I said I'd come for a year, as he said he needed somebody while Jane had her infants. I always thought of it as a temporary job," Juhl said.

When Jerry arrived in D.C., he began to wonder if the job might be even more temporary than he had thought. The long run of *Sam and Friends* appeared to be winding down as Esskay was making changes in the sponsorship of the show. "He was in two markets—WRC in Washington and WBAL in Baltimore," Jerry said. "And the day I got there, they dropped the Baltimore market, which meant my salary was considerably less than I expected it to be."

Despite the changes going on with *Sam and Friends,* Jim and Jane did their best to welcome Jerry to Washington. With a couple of suitcases in his hands and a couple hundred dollars in his pocket, Jerry showed up on Jim's doorstep.

"Jim was living in this big, comfortable suburban home in Bethesda, Maryland, and in the driveway, there is this big station wagon, a Porsche, and a Rolls-Royce," Juhl said. "Jim and Jane were very sweet. They put me up in a spare room. We immediately started working, of course, cause that's all you do with Jim. Ever. In those days, he was just in a frenzy, night and day."

Although the work was enjoyable, Jerry felt he needed some time to get set up in his new city. "After a few days, I said, 'Well, listen, I've got to take some time off here 'cause I've got to go rent an apartment and I've got to go buy a car and try to get some sort of life going here 'cause I can't stay in your spare room forever.' Jim said, 'Fine, take the afternoon.'"

Jerry began searching the classified ads for a "really cheap apartment" and a "really cheap second-hand car." He found a few leads on both and asked Jim if he could borrow a car to go check them out. "He said, 'Here, take the Rolls, it hasn't been out of the driveway in two weeks.' I had never been near a car like that. It was one of the old kind, when a Rolls really looked like a Rolls. . . . I drove that all over suburban Washington, looking for a hundred-dollar apartment and a three-hundred-dollar car. And, where I'd go, I'd have to park a half a mile away so the people wouldn't see me getting out of this car."

Initially drawing a take-home salary of $100 a week (the equivalent of about $978 in 2022 dollars), Jerry performed on commercials, the *Today* show, the last weeks of *Sam and Friends,* and anything else that came up. "When I first went to work for Jim, we were all jacks-of-all-trades... you sort of did everything," Jerry said in his *Great Performances* interview. "And, actually, coming from a puppetry background, beginning puppeteers tend to do everything anyway."

Jerry also began to contribute to scripts, a role that would later supersede his performing responsibilities. "Immediately, when I got there, I started writing," Jerry said. "Jim was... hoping to do more written material in *Sam and Friends*... so he was taking advantage of my desire to write, right from the beginning. We were doing everything else, too. I was writing. I was performing. I was helping make props and sets. I was typing up the statements at the end of the month.... sweeping out the shop at the end of the day."

Jerry Juhl joins Jim, Jane, and the Muppets for a group shot.

"He was performing quite nicely," Jane said of Jerry in 2010. "He was helping to build and helping to do the business stuff and everything, but it became pretty obvious between the two of them what they loved doing together was writing, and they would try very hard to spend time writing."

Jerry said that he and Jim had a wonderful time collaborating on scripts from the very beginning. In those early days, much of that was done in Jim's tree-filled backyard in Bethesda. "I remember going out, and one of us would lie on a hammock and the other one would sit in a lawn chair, and the person in the lawn chair would take notes, and you'd swap places. Jim loved to work that way. Jim always liked working [in] very sort of relaxed, casual situations."

Not too long after his arrival, Jerry was given the opportunity to travel far beyond Jim's backyard. In November of 1961, Jerry joined Jim on a trip to Hamburg, Germany, where the Muppets had been invited to perform on behalf of the U.S. Department of Agriculture at its Food Fair. They performed a range of pieces—from their classic "That Old Black Magic" to newer pieces like "Glow Worm" and "Chef Omar."

Joining the more traditional Muppet characters, Limbo the floating face also made the trip overseas. Limbo was an abstract puppet whose outlined facial features are suspended from thin elastic strings attached to a complex rig and manipulated from below with special gloves, the individual fingers of which are connected to various points on the facial features with strings.

Limbo was usually performed against black and television keying effects were used to superimpose the facial features over any background or video source, making the face appear to float in mid-air.

Jim would perform variations of the floating face for many years, but the USDA Food Fair in Germany was one of the few venues where Jim used Limbo in a live setting, without the benefit of television tricks.

THE MUPPETS
Jim and Jane Henson show TV Magazine readers how they manipulate the "floating faces" on their popular WRC—4 show.—Star Staff Photo.

The February 12, 1961, issue of The Sunday Star TV Magazine gave readers a behind-the-scenes look at how the floating face mechanism worked. Reprinted with permission of the D.C. Public Library, Star Collection © Washington Post

From Jim Henson's home movies: A view of the German audience as seen through Limbo.

Jim and Jerry also brought to Germany some newly constructed puppets and experimental routines. One new piece about the machine's superiority to man—performed by a blinking Muppet robot—was based on contributions from Del Close, a pioneering comic performer and writer who began his career with the Compass Players in St. Louis before moving to Chicago's Second City.

They also constructed a complex mechanical military drill team for the shows in Germany. While faux fur, fleece, and foam continued to be the primary tools of the trade, this was the start of the mechanical side of Jim's work as he started to stretch the definition of what a Muppet character could be. The trip to Germany also allowed Jim and Jerry the rare experience of playing to a live audience—and it gave Jim a chance to catch up with his old friend Joe Irwin, who was stationed nearby.

From Jim Henson's home movies: Jerry Juhl
prepares Chef Omar's ingredients.

Sam and Friends • 169

From Jim Henson's home movies: Jim and Jerry are introduced to their Hamburg audience.

The Muppets perform at the U.S. Food Fair in Hamburg, Germany.

Jim's 16 mm Bolex camera (possibly operated by Joe Irwin) found its way backstage during a performance to capture Jim and Jerry at work.]

Jim and Jerry's stint in Germany ended on November 19 and they returned to Washington—but even though Jerry had recently made a big move to D.C. to work with Jim, Jim was about to make a big move of his own.

CHAPTER 13

Five Scripts

As Jim became more comfortable providing voices for the *Sam and Friends* characters, he began to rely more on scripted material as opposed to lip syncs. Content for the show ran the gamut from slapstick comedy to more conceptual pieces. Some scripts were one-off bits, some were serialized stories that would unfold during multiple episodes—similar to what comic strips like Henson favorites *Pogo* and *Peanuts* were doing. Viewers might spend a few days getting to know Yorick's relatives when they came to visit or a week watching Professor Madcliffe tinker with his laugh meter. *Sam and Friends* had several recurring segments, including "The Jokebook Nook," in which characters simply took turns telling jokes, and "The Poet's Corner," in which characters shared poems like this one:

You tell me you love me
You tenderly kiss my finger
But there are things I must tell thee
In case your mood doth linger.

Your handsome mouth I truly love
Your ears are attractive, too
Your attitude is like a dove
Your flatteries choice and few.

But there is one thing I despise
One thing I cannot bear
For where other boys and men have eyes
You have nothing but hair.

Early scripts for *Sam and Friends* were usually handwritten by Jim Henson on steno pads. Some were just brief introductions to round out a short record to the necessary episode length (and sometimes the characters actually made mention of that fact in the dialogue), but as Jim became more comfortable providing voices and more adept with writing for the television medium, he expanded the scripted material to full-length sketches. He continued to write on steno pads, but his later scripts were typed on thin, onionskin paper. In the last weeks of the series, Jerry Juhl contributed to the scripts, but most of the writing was done by Jim.

Here are five scripts from the series, two of which exist in Jim's original handwriting. In those cases, the handwritten script appears next to a more readable transcribed version that contains any changes or revisions reflected in the final recorded audio.

Jim Henson's doodled characters, found on a 1960 *Sam and Friends* script.

"Ghost Interview":
Audio recorded September 26, 1958
(broadcast date unknown)

The inability to photograph ghosts had long been a movie trope—even in 1958. But Jim brought the trope up to date by including television cameras. (Henson always enjoyed dropping technical jargon—like "orthocon [sic] tube"—into his scripts.) The character of Omar is noted in the script with the initial "O," though it seems that only Kermit actually appears in the piece; Omar's voice is heard as the ghost who doesn't come through on TV. Since only one character is seen on camera in the segment, it's possible that this is one episode Jim had at the ready in the event he had to perform the show solo.

announcer — This evening, we are happy to present another on the spot interview with one of the fascinating personalities in our town.

Ⓚ Good Evening, this is Kermit with another fascinating interview with an on the spot personality. I'm sitting beside a tombstone in the Gabriel Park Memorial Cemetary, and this cemetary, if you didn't know it, is the haunt of one of the most famous ghosts in this part of the country. May I present — Lord Randall Worthington.

O Thank you Kermit, its a real pleasure to be here. It's my first time on television.

Ⓚ You look very sporty in your... is that a sort of a chartreuse — shroud?

O Yes, it's called screaming green — It's all the rage this season — Did you notice the ivy-league belt in the back?

GHOST INTERVIEW – PAGE 1

ANNOUNCER: This evening, we are happy to present another on-the-spot interview with one of the fascinating personalities in our town.

KERMIT: Good evening, this is Kermit with another fascinating interview with an on-the-spot personality. I'm sitting beside a tombstone in the Gabriel Park Memorial Cemetery, and this cemetery, if you didn't know it, is the haunt of one of the most famous ghosts in this part of the country. May I present . . . Lord Randall Worthington.

OMAR: Thank you, Kermit, it's a real pleasure to be here. It's my first time on television.

KERMIT: You look very sporty in your . . . is that a sort of chartreuse . . . shroud?

OMAR: Yes, it's called screaming green—it's all the rage this season. Did you notice the Ivy League belt in the back?

②

Ⓚ very stylish ~~th~~ inde... what? excuse me Lord Randall... what? you don't say... not a bit hmmm...

Ⓞ Is there something the matter, Kerm?

Ⓚ well it seems that you're not... uh... coming over so well on television.

Ⓞ Oh horror — did I put on too little makeup?

Ⓚ No — they say that the orthocon tube in the TV kamera doesn't have a frequency response to poltergeists.

Ⓞ Oh the devil! I should have expected something like that.

Ⓚ You mean this has happened before?

Ⓞ Well... I've never taken a good picture....

Ⓚ well gee... I don't what to say, Lord Worthington — after you got all dressed up and all!...

GHOST INTERVIEW – PAGE 2

KERMIT: Very stylish inde— what? Excuse me, Lord Randall . . . what? You don't say . . . not a bit, hmmm.

OMAR: Is there something the matter, Kerm?

KERMIT: Well, it seems that you're not . . . uh . . . coming over so well on television.

OMAR: Oh, horror—did I put on too little makeup?

KERMIT: No—they say that the orthocon [sic] tube in the TV camera doesn't have a frequency response to poltergeists.

OMAR: Oh the devil! I should have expected something like that.

KERMIT: You mean this happened before?

OMAR: Well . . . I've never taken a good picture.

KERMIT: Well, gee . . . I don't know what to say, Lord Worthington—after you got all dressed up and all . . .

Q Does this mean then, that I can't do my tricks?

K well... it would be sort of.. pointless, you know, ... if nobody can see them and all...

Q you might describe them, like a play by play...

K oh... I've never done much of that sort of thing,... I'm afraid I'm not very good at it....

Q I can do a somersault in mid-air, like this!

K very nice... but what can I say? — there was a ghost — turning a somersault in mid-air — you know? it would never make the Steve Allen Show, for instance,... Let me think it over — during this commercial.

GHOST INTERVIEW – PAGE 3

OMAR: Does this mean, then, that I can't do my tricks?

KERMIT: Well . . . it would be sort of . . . pointless, you know . . . if nobody can see them and all . . .

OMAR: You might describe them like a play-by-play . . .

KERMIT: Oh . . . I've never done much of that sort of thing . . . I'm afraid I'm not very good at it . . .

OMAR: I can do a somersault in midair, like this!

KERMIT: Very nice . . . but what can I say? There was a ghost . . . turning a somersault in midair . . . you know? It would never make *The Steve Allen Show*, for instance. . . . Let me think it over during this commercial.

COMMERCIAL

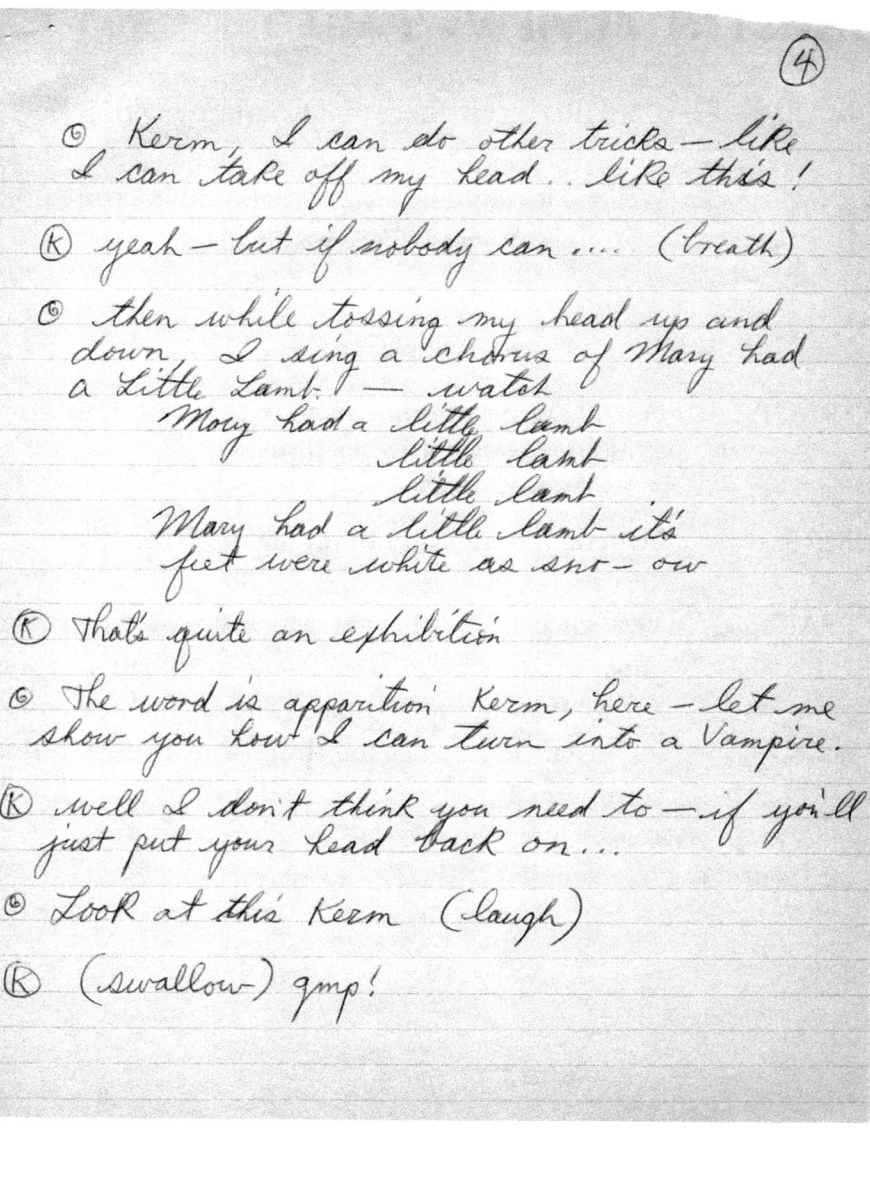

(G) Kerm, I can do other tricks — like I can take off my head.. like this!

(K) yeah — but if nobody can .... (breath)

(G) then while tossing my head up and down, I sing a chorus of Mary had a Little Lamb! — watch
   Mary had a little lamb
        little lamb
        little lamb
   Mary had a little lamb it's
   feet were white as sno—ow

(K) That's quite an exhibition

(G) The word is apparition Kerm, here — let me show you how I can turn into a Vampire.

(K) well I don't think you need to — if you'll just put your head back on...

(G) Look at this Kerm (laugh)

(K) (swallow) gmp!

GHOST INTERVIEW – PAGE 4

OMAR: Kerm, I can do other tricks, like, I can take off my head ... like this!

KERMIT: Yeah, but if nobody can— (breath)

OMAR: Then, while tossing my head up and down, I sing a chorus of "Mary Had a Little Lamb"—watch! Mary had a little lamb, little lamb, little lamb. Mary had a little lamb, its feet were white as sno-ow ...

KERMIT: That's quite an exhibition.

OMAR: The word is apparition, Kerm. Here—let me show you how I can turn into a vampire.

KERMIT: Well, I don't think that you need to. If you'll just put your head back on ...

OMAR: Look at this Kerm! (laugh)

KERMIT: (swallow) Gulp!

⑤

G: It really scares people when I fly around looking like this — watch me!
(yelling & looping)
Hey Kermit woo woo woo woo this makes me sea-sick

K: Thank you very much, Lord W...

G: I'm not finished, Kerm — let me show you my bit that really scares people — just a minute.

K: Well folks — our time is about up so (ahem) goodnight!

G: Look at me now, Kerm! Kermit? Oh there he goes. Hey Kermit — come back sometime when the spirit moves you. (laugh)

GHOST INTERVIEW – PAGE 5

OMAR: It really scares people when I fly around looking like this—watch me! (yelling and looping) Hey, Kermit, woo woo woo woo, this makes me seasick.

KERMIT: Thank you very much, Lord Worthington . . .

OMAR: I'm not finished, Kerm—let me show you my bit that really scares people. Just a minute . . .

KERMIT: Well, folks, our time is about up so, ahem, good night!
(Note: It was recorded as: Well, folks, we're a little late, so, ahem . . . good night!)

OMAR: Look at me now, Kerm! Kermit? Oh, there he goes. Hey, Kermit—come back some time when the spirit moves you! (laughs)
(Note: When recorded, the following was added: I made a funny! Ha-ha-ha-ha-ha-ha!)

"The *Sam and Friends* News Report": Broadcast October 21, 1959

Since Jim and Jane were essentially surrounded by NBC's Washington news organization—*Sam and Friends* aired after the local news and before the national news—it was inevitable for the Muppets to roast the institution of television news. In this script, the Muppets present the *Sam and Friends News Report*.

Jim would continue to lampoon TV news after *Sam and Friends* ended its run—first in a series of spots for Wilkins Coffee featuring characters Scoop and Skip. Later, Kermit became a roving reporter for "*Sesame Street* News," and Jim performed *The Muppet Show*'s newsman who brought viewers "Muppet News" flashes throughout the show's five-year run.

While the humor of *Sam and Friends* is timeless, some aspects of this script place the action firmly in its era. Near the end, when Professor Madcliffe reads some phone numbers, they reflect the location-based telephone exchange system that was in use at the time. Phone numbers consisted of an exchange name followed by five digits, such as KLondike 5-5000. The first two letters of the name of the exchange corresponded to the letters printed alongside each number on the telephone dial. While we're on that subject, back then, telephones had rotary dials . . . and cords . . . and were attached to the wall . . . in your house.

SHOW OPENING

PROFESSOR: In support of our conviction that what this station needs for better programming is more news shows, we present the *Sam and Friends* News Report.

SOUND EFFECT: TELETYPE MACHINES

PROFESSOR: From the four corners of the globe . . .

HARRY: Hold it man, a globe is round, it doesn't have corners.

PROFESSOR: Have you seen our globe?

HARRY: Oh.

PROFESSOR: From the four corners of the globe, top, bottom, left, and right, the *Sam and Friends* News Report.

HARRY: The news is not very bright tonight . . . yes, the news is very dark . . . very, very dark.

PROFESSOR: That's what you get for wearing dark glasses in the studio! Good grief! You're trying to read a sheet of carbon paper.

HARRY: Oh yeah, things are looking brighter already, let's see now, hmmmm, we'll start off the news by taking a look at the film highlights of the day. Roll the film, men. . . . Men? . . . aw, come on, please roll the film. Ah, here we go.

SOUND EFFECT: STATIC APPROX. 6 or 7 SECONDS

HARRY: Well, you wouldn't have been interested in that film anyhow, it was very dull. . . . Nevertheless, we do have our live remote cameras set up at Cape Casserole, where the launching of the first atomic-powered water skis took place about 30 minutes ago. Here's Moldy Hay to describe what happened.

MOLDY HAY: (FILTER) (yawn) My, my, my, my, hi, hi Harry, is this the real thing or is this a rehearsal.

CUT TO SHOT OF HARRY PANTOMIME

MOLDY HAY: I can't hear you, so I guess it's just a rehearsal.

CUT TO HARRY PANTOMIMING NO NO NO NO

MOLDY HAY: Actually, I slept through the whole thing so . . .

CUT TO HARRY BEATING HIS HEAD AGAINST DESK

MOLDY HAY: What's the matter, Harry, you got a headache? Sorry, I can't hear you. Anyhow, when the show goes on the air, I'll make up a good story. . . . I'll sound just like I was there . . . so that's all from me until we get ready to go on the air.

HARRY: . . . Idiotic, blundering, good-for-nothing like an on-the-spot report. Folks, now let's have a check on the weather. Kermit, what's the weather like outside?

KERMIT: I'm sorry, Harry, it's so cloudy outside that I can't see a durn thing. . . . However, today will be fair.

SOUND EFFECT: THUNDER

KERMIT: . . . and warmer . . .

SOUND EFFECT: WIND

KERMIT: . . . with nothing but clear blue skies overhead. Hey, didn't you hear my forecast? I'm going to Florida.

HARRY: What's the matter, man?

KERMIT: This climate doesn't agree with me.

CUT TO PROFESSOR

PROFESSOR: Now here's a quick look at the sports, let's see . . . Sam's a good sport, Yorick is a bad sport when he's hungry, I'm a very good sport, and everybody else is sort of medium. We'll have a peek into the little black notebook after this commercial.

COMMERCIAL

PROFESSOR: In the little black notebook, it says Dolores Smithers, WEdgewood 3-2573, Bermuda Swartz, COlumbine 6-8837 . . . Hey, I guess I picked up somebody else's little black notebook. Good night and good news.

"The Coming Season": Broadcast September 15, 1960

Near the start of the 1960–61 season, *Sam and Friends* gave viewers a preview of what to expect in the shows to come. This script helps provide an idea of what Jim was doing at the start of the 1960s.

KERMIT: Good evening, friends, this evening we thought we'd give you some idea of what's in store for you on *Sam and Friends* this year. First, we want to say how happy we are to be back on the air for Esskay, and if by any chance there's somebody watching the show who doesn't know what Esskay is . . .

HARRY: Are you kidding?

KERMIT: No . . . there may be some people new in town . . . or, I don't know . . . maybe a hermit who, uh . . . just bought a TV set or something.

HARRY: If you just moved here or if you're a hermit, S.K. stands for Sam and Kermit. Bop ba da dee dee, boom boom.

KERMIT: Now, don't be ridiculous, Harry. Esskay stands for the William Schluderberg and T. J. Kurdle Company, that fine Baltimore organization that is known for . . .

HANK & FRANK: (interrupting) We're Schluderberg and Kurdle, the makers of Esskay, Esskay Ka-wality meats, Ka-wality meats . . .

KERMIT:	Hold it, hold it . . . the commercial comes later in the show.
HANK & FRANK:	Yeah, we know, we just thought as long as you mentioned it . . .
	Well, sure, but it never hurts to sing the praises of . . . didn't mean to—sorry.
KERMIT:	Okay, okay, knock it off! Drop it! (clunk) Where was I? Oh yeah . . . this year on our show, we'll be doing a lot of music . . . some poems on "The Poet's Corner" . . . a little politics because the Republicratic Party is thinking of running Sam for president, and . . . uh . . . excuse me . . . uh . . . where was I? Oh—Sam for president, and . . .
RECORD:	TELEPHONE BIT FROM "CHLOE" (11 SECONDS)

(Note: The excerpt from Spike Jones's "Chloe" referred to in this script is a version of the "you don't say/he didn't say" telephone gag: "You don't say. You don't say. You don't say! / Who was it? / He didn't say.")

KERMIT:	(swallow) Ahem, I guess we'll be doing a lot of corny humor on the show, too.
ANNOUNCER:	(filter mike?) Flash! Moldy Hay has just returned from the summer Olympics in Rome where he won the 1,000-meter Hog Calling Contest.
KERMIT:	Wow! And here comes Moldy now!

SOUND EFFECT: CHEERING CROWD

MOLDY HAY: Thank you, thank you.

KERMIT: Wonderful, Moldy . . . we're very proud of you . . . could you maybe demonstrate for us how you won the Olympic Hog Calling Contest?

MOLDY HAY: Sure . . . I just went, sooooo pig . . . here piggy-piggy-piggy, and the pig comes.

KERMIT: That's wonderful, Moldy . . . uh . . . what's that coming?

MOLDY HAY: That's my pig. . . . I'll see you, Kermit.

(PIG RUNS THROUGH: OINK OINK)

KERMIT: I guess that's one of the hazards of the game, and now . . . uh . . . we . . . uh . . . you know, I think I've seen this bit before, so I think I'll go get ready to do the commercial.

RECORD: SECOND TELEPHONE BIT FROM "CHLOE" (11 SECONDS)

COMMERCIAL

CLOSING

"Sam for President: Part 2": Broadcast September 28, 1960

This is the second of a multipart story in which Sam runs for U.S. President. Even though Washington, D.C., was his base of operations, Jim did not normally put a lot of political content in *Sam and Friends,* and when he did, he broadly lampooned entire institutions rather than take aim at specific candidates. All politicians were targets.

In the first part of "Sam for President," which aired the previous day, Kermit prepared Sam for his candidacy: "Remember, *all* candidates are good men, and we're not doubting their motives. We're *all* trying to accomplish the same good things for the nation.... It's just our *methods* that are different. You see, we're using brand-new, tried-and-proven, good methods that won't cost the people any money ... while the other candidates are using selfish, one-sided, inferior, sneaky, egotistical, decadent, pitifully inexcusable, and *wrong* methods that will bankrupt the country in a couple of days."

Sam, usually silent, was ready for his campaign with an all-purpose recorded speech (provided by Jim): "Friends, I say when the world situation is so hopelessly confused, you need a president who fits the situation!" Sam breaks out this speech repeatedly in subsequent election episodes.

As this episode begins, Kermit and Harry are strategizing with the Republicratic candidate, Sam.

KERMIT: Let's hear that speech one more time, Sam.

SAM: (RECORDED) Friends, I say when the world situation is so hopelessly confused, you need a president who fits the situation!

KERMIT: And who is the most hopelessly confused candidate?

HARRY: Sam!

KERMIT: Right! Sam for president, rah rah rah,
Sam isn't hesitant, sis boom bah!

HARRY: Boom a laka, boom a laka, boom a laka bam
Fight team fight and vote for Sam.
Bump ba da dee dee, bip bip.

KERMIT: This is beginning to sound more like a football game than an election. What we need to do is get the issues more into the public eye. You know, to show how Sam feels about the big, major, important, underlying, fundamental principles like . . . uh . . . well, like . . .

HARRY: Outer space! Sam, how do you feel about outer space? You know, the satellites going around the world?

SAM: (RECORDED) Friends, I say when the world situation is so hopelessly confused, you need a president who fits the situation.

KERMIT: And who is that most hopelessly confused candidate?

HARRY: Sam!

KERMIT: Right.

KERMIT/:   Boom get a rat trap bigger than a cat trap,
HARRY   Boom get a chigger digger bigger than ham,
               Boom get a candidate time won't antiquate,
               Don't get your throat smote, vote for Sam!

KERMIT: You know, these campaign cheers are all well and good, but what we really need is a campaign song.

HARRY: A song?

KERMIT: Sure, haven't you heard the campaign songs of the other two candidates? Well, just a second, let me turn on the television set here.

SOUND EFFECT: CLICK . . . SOUND OF STATIC

KERMIT: 'Course, they've got a lot more money than we have . . . you know, big organizations and all . . . here we go.

RECORD: HUCKLEBERRY HOUND CAMPAIGN SONG

(Note: Huckleberry Hound, a popular Hanna-Barbera cartoon character, mounted a campaign for President in 1960 and released the LP *Huckleberry Hound for President*, which contained a campaign song set to the tune of his theme song.)

We proudly now present our next new president,
Meet Huckleberry Hound.

> The only one to run that show in Washington,
> Is Huckleberry Hound.
> He's got a brand-new act to cut your income tax,
> He'll chop it way, way down.
> You're gonna miss that boat unless you cast your vote,
> For Huckleberry Hound.

HARRY: Yeah, I see what you mean . . . what about the other major party?

KERMIT: Well, you know, they're running Pogo again this year, and their campaign song sounds like this . . .

RECORD: GO GO POGO

(Note: Pogo, the possum star of the long-running Walt Kelly comic strip, was a "candidate" for President throughout the 1950s. This song was from the 1956 album *Songs of the Pogo*.)

> As Maine go o so Pogo go Key Largo,
> Otsego to Frisco go to Fargo,
> Okeefenokee playin', possum on a Pogo,
> Stick around and see the show go over
> Land alive a band o' jive will blow go Pogo,
> I go you go who go to go polly voo go,
> From Caravan Diego,
> Waco and Oswego,
> Tweedle de he go she go we go me go Pogo.

KERMIT: 'Course, there are a couple more candidates . . .

HARRY: Really?

SAM AND FRIENDS • 195

KERMIT: Yeah, there's the *Mad* Party that's running Alfred E. Neuman, and there's a little group that's running Kennedy and Nixon . . .

HARRY: I've heard of them . . . they won't give you any trouble.

KERMIT: Nah, they won't give us any trouble. . . . Say, what's Bernice doing over there?

(Note: The last line is a lead-in to the Esskay commercial, which somehow involved Bernice. Neither the script nor the recording includes the commercial.)

"The Great Debate": Broadcast October 7, 1960

At 7:30 p.m. on October 7, 1960, presidential candidates John F. Kennedy and Richard M. Nixon faced off in their second presidential debate at WRC-TV in Washington—in Studio A, which was the usual home of *Sam and Friends*. Amid the excitement, the Muppet team set up in Studio B down the hall and performed their live broadcast less than an hour before the debate. This was a busy day for Jim and Jane (and five-month-old Lisa)—earlier in the day, the Muppets performed a live show at a United Givers Fund (later renamed United Way) fundraising rally at the National Institutes of Health in Bethesda, Maryland.

10/7/60

Boy there's a lot of excitement around WRC-TV this evening.

You know Vice President Nixon and Senator Kennedy are going to do their Great Debate out of Studio A here in Washington in a little less than an hour. They sure are making a lot of noise over there. Hey Dick, John, would you all hold the noise down a little bit...... yeah we're on the air over here. Thank you. That's Dick Koeppel & John Tompkins — our stage crew.

Excuse me Kermit, but we need this background for the Great Debate.

Oh? well okay I guess we don't need it.

THE GREAT DEBATE – PAGE 1

SOUND EFFECT: HAMMERING NOISE

KERMIT: Boy, there's a lot of excitement around WRC-TV this evening. You know, Vice President Nixon and Senator Kennedy are going to do their great debate out of Studio A here in Washington in a little less than an hour. They sure are making a lot of noise over there. Hey Dick, John, would you all hold the noise down a little bit . . . yeah, we're on the air over here. Thank you. That's Dick Koepful and John Tompkins, our stage crew.

OFFSCREEN VOICE: Excuse me, Kermit, but we need this background for the Great Debate.

KERMIT: Oh? Well, okay. I guess we don't need it.

THE BACKGROUND IS MOVED OFF

Say Kermit you're not using these lights over here are you?

Those lights over there? No we're not using them, go ahead & take them.

Say Kermit, we need another television camera you wouldn't mind if we sort of borrow this would you.

OFF hey wait a minute you put that camera baagaack. This is only a five minute show you know! then you can have the whole place. It really is very thrilling though, that they're doing such a big important show from here and ah well uh... excuse me a minute

THE GREAT DEBATE – PAGE 2

OFFSCREEN VOICE: Hey, Kermit, you're not using these lights over here, are you?

KERMIT: Those lights over there? No, we're not using them, go ahead and take them.

THE LIGHTS ARE MOVED OFF

OFFSCREEN VOICE: Hey, Kermit, we need another television camera. You wouldn't mind if we sort of borrow this one, would you?

KERMIT: Hey, wait a minute, come on you guys, bring that camera baaaaack. This is only a five-minute show, you know. Then you can have the whole place. It really is very thrilling, though, that they're doing such an important show from here and, uh, well, uh . . . excuse me a minute.

Kermit this note just came — it's from the Boss.

Let's see... "Dear Kermit, we are getting ready to do the Great Debate, and we have just realized that we don't have enough questions to ask the candidates. I would appreciate it if you would think up some questions and send them over to us. Yours truly, the Boss."

Wow. I think this calls ~~for the~~ ~~brightest intellects~~ of the creative <u>thinking</u> ~~s~~ of the Sam & Friends staff. Here comes one of them now. Hey Professor Madcliff do you have any questions you'd like to ask the presidential candidates? I'm very glad ~~you asked~~ me, because I

Well yes, ~~the first I~~ do ~~(I)~~ happen to have been thinking of a question just now. (ahem)

THE GREAT DEBATE – PAGE 3

OMAR: Kermit, this note just came in. It's from the boss.

KERMIT: Let's see... "Dear Kermit, we are getting ready to do the Great Debate and we have just realized that we don't have enough questions to ask the candidates. I would appreciate it if you would think up some questions and send them over to us. Yours truly, The Boss." Wow. I think this calls for the creative thinking of the whole *Sam and Friends* staff. Let's see, here comes one of them now. Hey, Professor Madcliffe, do you have any questions you'd like to ask the presidential candidates?

PROFESSOR MADCLIFFE ENTERS

PROFESSOR: Well, yes, I'm very glad you asked me, because I do happen to have been thinking of a question just now. Ahem.

"in regard to the applicability & credibility of tangible vulnerability and the affectable & rejectable, expectable of the collectible projectible including the excitable & unwritable of the requitable ignitable and disregarding the fittering, twittering of the glittering bitters; how does this apply to the enormity of conformity in a uniform abnormity of a majority authority?! duh? What do you say to that?

well, would you write up a memo as to what you said there, and I'll consider it.

I can tell you have no feeling for political-type talk.

THE GREAT DEBATE – PAGE 4

PROFESSOR: In regard to the applicability and credibility of tangible vulnerability of the affectable and rejectable expectable of the collectible projectible including the excitable and unwritable of the unrequitable ignitable and disregarding the frittering twittering of the glittering bitters, how does this apply to the enormity of conformity in a uniform abnormity of a majority authority? Hmm? What do you think to that, huh?

KERMIT: What do I think to that? Would you write it down as a memo and I guess I'll consider it?

PROFESSOR: Hmph. I can tell you don't have any feeling for political-type talk at all.

Let's see, maybe Yorick can help out... Yorick, is there anything you'd like to ask the candidates on the Great Debate?

farm surplus.

You want to know how much they would charge for the farm surplus? Why?

Eat it smack smack

You mean you'd eat the whole farm surplus all by yourself?

Oh no

oh I see — your family would help out, huh? Well that's very patriotic of you, but I think they have other plans for the surplus. Sniff sniff — hey I think I smell smoke!

THE GREAT DEBATE – PAGE 5

KERMIT: Let's see. Maybe Yorick can help out. Hey, Yorick, is there anything you'd like to ask the candidates on the Great Debate?

YORICK ENTERS

YORICK: (unintelligible grumbling) . . . farm surplus.

KERMIT: You want to know how much they would charge for the farm surplus? Why?

YORICK: (unintelligible grumbling) . . . eat it. (smack smack)

KERMIT: You mean you'd eat the whole farm surplus all by yourself?

YORICK: Oh no (unintelligible grumbling) . . . fam—

YORICK IS JOINED BY FAMILY MEMBERS

KERMIT: Oh, I see—your family here would help out, huh? Well, that's very patriotic of you, Yorick, but meanwhile, I better think about this on my own. Sniff-sniff—say, I smell something burning!

(Note: The last line about something burning is a lead-in to the Esskay commercial, which apparently involved cooking an Esskay product. Neither the script nor the recording include the commercial.)

CHAPTER 14

I Come for to Sing

One day in the middle of December 1961, viewers saw a sign on the set of *Sam and Friends* that read "X-5." The next day, the sign read "X-4." This countdown continued without comment or explanation until December 15, when Harry finally asked Kermit what the signs meant. Kermit explained that the signs were a countdown—the "X" referred to the final episode of *Sam and Friends,* and with the sign now reading "X-1," the countdown was over.

After their final (for now) Esskay commercial, Kermit—most likely speaking on behalf of Jim Henson—explained that the show had been on for about seven years and it was probably time to move on to something else. Kermit asked Harry to introduce his last song. With the borrowed voice of Bob Gibson, Kermit waxed sentimental with "I Come for to Sing," which seemed to beautifully sum up the whole idea of *Sam and Friends:*

> Some come to dance, and some come to play
> Some merely come to pass time away
> Some come to laugh, their voices do ring
> But as for me, I come for to sing.
>
> Some of you like me, others do not
> Some love to extol on what I ain't got
> But I don't care, it don't mean a thing
> I just keep coming, keep coming to sing.

Could the silly and subversive *Sam and Friends* really end on such a sincere and heartfelt note? Of course not. Since the series was coming to an end, Harry figured that they could not possibly have a need for the costumes, scenery, and equipment they'd accumulated over the years—so why not blow it all up? While Harry executed the explosions, Kermit thanked the viewers and signed off. When Monday, December 18, arrived, viewers of WRC at 11:25 p.m. were greeted with *The 11th Hour Entertainment News* with Gene Archer. As longtime D.C. television columnist Lawrence Laurent put it, "There will be some long, loud and indignant protests over the loss of the Muppets."

While Kermit had said on the air that it was probably time to move on, the impetus to do so did not originate with Jim and Jane. In a letter dated October 30, 1961, VanSant Dugdale Vice President Robert V. Walsh officially informed the Hensons that Esskay was discontinuing its sponsorship of *Sam and Friends,* effective December 15, 1961. "In this business, we often have to stop a show," Walsh wrote. "Generally, it is done with some regret. Seldom, if ever, is it done with the regret we all feel at seeing *Sam and Friends* stop for Esskay."

The cancellation notice read like a fan letter, going on to praise Jim and Jane personally and the quality of the show. "This program has been absolute business pleasure. It has been a delight to watch, it has caused good comment, it has been closely identified with Esskay, and as near as we can determine, it has been a pretty good salesman for us."

Walsh concluded by leaving the door open to future projects and a "hope that we will continue what has been such a warm and pleasant relationship with both of you on a personal basis."

Eleven days before the last episode was broadcast, T.J. Kurdle, Vice President of Esskay, sent his own farewell note. "We at Esskay have become extremely fond of not only the Muppets, but the very nice folks who manipulate them."

Jim "didn't really want it to go off the air," Jane Henson said in 2010. "But he also felt that it was fine for it to go off the air because he had other things he wanted to do."

Fans of *Sam and Friends* had seen the last of the show but certainly not the last of the Muppets, and in some ways, they hadn't seen the last of *Sam and Friends,* either.

With the Hensons' WRC-TV commitment concluded, the Muppets would soon take Manhattan with a regular spot on the *Today* show. The *Today* appearances had begun as live cut-ins from WRC in early 1961 with the Muppets performing their own bits and sometimes interacting remotely with host Dave Garroway. The opportunity to work with the *Today* team in person at the show's Rockefeller Center studio was the carrot that led Jim and Jane to pull up stakes and move to New York in early 1963. "It was totally typical of the way Jim worked," Jerry Juhl said in a 1991 interview. "He was moving his entire family, his entire life, and me from Maryland to the middle of New York City. The moving men were showing up like on a Wednesday in January or February—showing up to pack up all his goods that afternoon, and the next morning at 5:30 a.m., he had a rehearsal for the *Today* show."

In New York, Jim and Jane moved into the same Beekman Place building where Burr Tillstrom lived, and Jerry found an apartment nearby on First Avenue.

Not all of the Muppet team, however, made the trip north—Bob Payne stayed behind.

"Jim said he was going to New York, and he didn't say anything about taking me . . . so they went off to New York, and I went into the art department [of WRC], and I asked if they had anything, and they said yes," Payne said. "And so I was working for the studio." But this would not be the last that Bob Payne saw of Jim and the Muppets.

The Muppets were live in the studio at *Today* each week with Dave Garroway's successor, Hugh Downs. (The *Today* representative assigned to coordinate the Muppets' appearances was a young news writer named Barbara Walters.) The segments were very similar to *Sam and Friends* episodes—self-contained bits

When the Muppets moved to New York, Jim announced the news via an advertisement in the *Washington–Baltimore AFTRA Directory, 1963*. This local publication was distributed to all major production centers throughout the country. Courtesy SAG-AFTRA Archives and Special Collections.

with a beginning, middle, and ending. And now that the Muppets were in New York, they were a full-fledged part of the *Today* family, with Jim even pressed into service on one occasion to model men's clothing alongside other members of the show's cast.

Esskay, which had enjoyed a boost in sales as the sponsor of *Sam and Friends,* was not ready to say a final goodbye to their longtime pitch-puppets despite having canceled their show. While Jim and his growing team were going national on *Today,* they continued to return to Washington, D.C., from time to time, to shoot commercials for the meat company. Joined by human spokesperson Pat McKenzie, Kermit, Harry, and other *Sam and Friends* cast members appeared in several stand-alone commercials for Esskay. The spots ended in 1963, but not before a new member of the Muppet troupe had a chance to sell Esskay meats—a character originally created to sell food for a different species.

In 1962, Purina Dog Chow had commissioned Jim to create a pair of characters for a Canadian commercial campaign. Jim designed Rowlf the Dog and his lesser-known sidekick Baskerville, and, to build the puppet, he turned to Don Sahlin, whom Jim and Jane first met at the Detroit Puppeteers of America festival in 1960. Sahlin was a fine craftsman whose precise puppet-building expertise was an ideal complement to Jim's creative vision.

Rowlf would find a spot starting in September of 1963 on ABC's *The Jimmy Dean Show,* a weekly variety hour hosted by the man who had a No. 1 hit with "Big Bad John." Jim Henson provided Rowlf's voice and performed his head and left hand, and manipulating Rowlf's right hand was the latest Henson hire, Frank Oz, who had by now graduated from high school. Oz arrived in New York just one month before the show's premiere. Over the course of *The Jimmy Dean Show*'s three-season run, Dean's "hound dog buddy" Rowlf would become the first nationally known Muppet celebrity. Washington, D.C., viewers were, no doubt, delighted to hear Jim's familiar voice as Rowlf as he bantered and sang with Jimmy Dean, who had been another popular D.C. television fixture in the 1950s.

Even two years after *Sam and Friends* ended its run, its characters were still popular in Washington, D.C., appearing in a print ad for Steuart Motor Co., a local Ford dealership. Under a photo of Kermit, Moldy Hay, Yorick, Harry, and Sam, the copy proclaimed that "Puppets do exactly what they're told. Some car buyers are that way, too." Steuart proudly stated that it sold "the finest Fords ever built—for knowing humans, not puppets."

This would have been a prime promotional opportunity for *Sam and Friends* if the show was still on the air—and if Jim Henson had

The Steuart Motors advertisement in the April 23, 1963, issue of *The Evening Star* emphatically says, CONGRATULATIONS FOR NOT BEING A PUPPET.

been consulted. Henson sent a very strongly worded letter to Steuart Motor Co. informing them that the characters were owned by him and "the use of the puppet characters is in direct violation of the law and you are herewith directed to cease and desist in the use thereof." Sam Brown, Media Director of Steuart's agency, Alvin Epstein Advertising, sent a letter of apology, explaining that the photo was supplied by WRC and that the agency did not intend to imply an endorsement. He assured Jim that the ad would not be repeated and said he had been with the agency for only a short time. "I am not wise in the way of doing things," he wrote. "I am a former announcer."

For the next few years, Jim Henson, Jerry Juhl, Don Sahlin, and Frank Oz were the main Muppet creative team, working on short films, commercials, TV appearances, industrial films.

They would sometimes take trips to D.C. for commercial shoots for Wilkins and other clients, and Del Ankers was occasionally brought up to New York to shoot some industrial films with the Muppets as well. For a time, Jim even continued to rent space at the Rodel studio in Georgetown to store the sets for his library of Wilkins-style commercials.

The 1960s were filled with variety show appearances for the Muppets—usually in a self-contained segment like the ones on *Sam and Friends* and the other WRC shows on which the Muppets appeared. But while the segments were similar to *Sam and Friends*, the characters were not. Kermit remained a member of the Muppet cast, but the rest of the *Sam and Friends* repertory company gradually went into retirement, replaced by new puppet characters designed by Jim and built by Don Sahlin. When Frank Oz received his draft notice in 1965, Jim brought on a new performer to the team, Jerry Nelson, who would go on to become a core member of the Muppet performers for decades. (Frank did not pass his Army physical and eventually returned to Muppets Inc.)

Coincidentally, Jerry Nelson had crossed paths with Jim Henson before while a student at American University in Washington.

"After I got out of the Army in 1956, I worked at WRC in Washington, D.C., in the basement of the Wardman Hotel, so I'd seen Jim," Nelson said in a 2012 interview with Henson biographer Brian Jay Jones. "I of course knew who he was, kind of, because he had advertisements on the television. . . . I was a [studio] page there, so I delivered mail and I would walk across the floor and see Jim and Jane getting ready to do *Sam and Friends*."

Over the course of twenty-five appearances on *The Ed Sullivan Show* and guest spots on other variety programs of the 1960s, Jim and his team gradually developed new sketches and characters to fill roles formerly occupied by the *Sam and Friends* company. But amid all the changes, Kermit remained a core member of the Muppet cast and thrived, appearing often throughout the 1960s before landing a new series gig.

Sesame Street (1969), produced by Children's Television Workshop (now known as Sesame Workshop), made Kermit a much bigger star and introduced a new cast of Muppets to the world. Not only did new Muppets Big Bird and Oscar join the human cast members in the street scenes, Kermit, Cookie Monster, Bert, Ernie, Grover, The Count, Prairie Dawn, and many others starred in their own sketches and songs interspersed throughout the hour. These self-contained segments were not unlike *Sam and Friends* episodes, and for the first five years of *Sesame Street*, many Muppet inserts were written by Jerry Juhl.

The new show's characters may have been different, but there was an essence that evoked their predecessors. Though he briefly appeared once, the voracious Yorick was effectively retired in favor of the equally insatiable Cookie Monster (performed by Frank Oz), and the frantic Professor Madcliffe was displaced by an equally frenetic (but not as scientific) Jim Henson character Guy Smiley.

As *Sesame Street* became incredibly popular with children, Jim turned to developing a show that would allow him to bring his Muppets to a wide audience of all ages, including that sophisticated adult crowd he first found in the WRC days.

He piloted the idea with a couple of prime-time specials on ABC, *The Muppets Valentine Show* (1974) and *The Muppet Show: Sex and Violence*. In 1975, to promote the latter, Jim brought the characters to *The Tonight Show Starring Johnny Carson,* where he had made his network TV debut nineteen years earlier (albeit with a different host and originating from a different coast). To commemorate his earlier appearance, Jim performed the same *Sam and Friends* segment he and Jane had done on Steve Allen's version of the show—"I've Grown Accustomed to Your Face," with Kermeena and Yorick—this time with Frank Oz as his performing partner.

The ABC specials proved the concept, but American broadcast networks were not convinced and declined to order *The Muppet Show* as a weekly show. Fortunately, English media impresario Lew Grade saw potential and ordered a syndicated series to be produced by Jim in London and distributed to a global audience.

With *The Muppet Show,* Jim achieved his goal of having a weekly half-hour variety show for the whole family, but in many ways, this long-form show was constructed using elements of the short-form *Sam and Friends*. In fact, Jim's earliest notes on a variety show date back to the *Sam and Friends* era. In 1960 or 1961, he sketched out characters and concepts for a show called *Zoocus*—a combination of "zoo" and "circus"—which was to be a half hour of variety television with a new cast of characters. *Zoocus* never got off the ground, but *The Muppet Show* did, and there is clearly a lot of *Sam and Friends'* DNA in that production—not the least of which was the participation of Jerry Juhl and Bob Payne.

Jerry served as head writer, and Bob as a puppet designer/builder, but Jane Henson was only sometimes in the studio. Throughout this time, Jane was primarily busy with a houseful of kids, as Lisa and Cheryl had been joined by Brian in 1963, John in 1965, and Heather in 1970.

The new show's connection to *Sam and Friends* was not confined to the production team.

Sam and Friends stalwart Kermit ("the Frog" officially a part of his name since the late 1960s) was front and center as host, but he was surrounded with a mostly brand-new cast of characters—and the Muppets' first network star, Rowlf the Dog. As with *Sesame Street*, the characters may have been new, but some of them filled similar roles to those of Jim's earlier creations. Frank Oz's Animal was like Yorick in some ways—a minimally verbal id with a single-minded hunger. Harry the Hipster was gone, but Jim's Dr. Teeth and Jerry Nelson's Floyd filled the void. Professor Madcliffe's scientific (albeit warped) mind emerged in a more laid-back way with Dr. Bunsen Honeydew (performed by Dave Goelz).

Just as Kermit, Harry, and Madcliffe discussed the backstage goings-on at WRC and their plans for the show, the format of *The Muppet Show* also gave us a look at what was happening both onstage and off. And, just in *Sam and Friends*, many sketches had somewhat disastrous conclusions (leading to some characters receiving concussions). It was, as Frank Oz put it in the foreword to this book, "controlled, affectionate anarchy."

The musical numbers of *The Muppet Show* were also reminiscent of those on *Sam and Friends*, and on some occasions, actual numbers from *Sam and Friends* were re-created for the half-hour show, including "Glow Worm" and "Tweedle Dee." The song "Inchworm" was performed twice on *The Muppet Show*—backstage by its originator Danny Kaye in Season 3 and initially by Charles Aznavour in a Season 1 performance that echoed the visual presentation of its WRC broadcast, right down to the silhouettes of children singing in the schoolhouse window.

Bits developed during Jim's 1960s variety show era (like "Mahna Mahna" and "Java") were also used on *The Muppet Show,* in most cases as initially conceived and presented. However, with a larger budget and cast now at his disposal, Jim could also present full-scale production numbers alongside his smaller, more intimate vintage pieces. Despite all the increased capabilities *The Muppet Show* provided, one segment in each episode continued to be very reminiscent of *Sam and Friends*.

In England and other areas outside of the United States where television programming generally had fewer commercials, *The Muppet Show* had to be two minutes longer than the version shown on U.S. television. These two minutes were filled with what became known as "U.K. spots," stand-alone songs or sketches that could be easily excised from the episodes without causing any continuity issues from their absence.

The U.K. spots had to be taped on a tight schedule with limited takes and without the appearance of guest stars. Throughout the run of *The Muppet Show*, these spots continued to resemble the *Sam and Friends* format, often shot with a single camera and sometimes featuring some of those charming imperfections that Jane Henson described. In the case of the song "Any Old Iron," a pupil falls off a background Muppet chorus member's eyeball as Fozzie begins to sing. With time constraints preventing a retake, the pupil-less performance went out over the air and remains in the show to this day.

The Muppet Show used a wide variety of preexisting songs—from Tin Pan Alley standards to contemporary hits—but unlike with *Sam and Friends*, this new show didn't have to rely on phonograph records. Each week, Jim and his fellow performers and guest stars would record new vocals for four or five songs, with Jack Parnell's band backing them up.

A *Muppet Show* musical number was usually about three minutes long—which was the approximate length of a *Sam and Friends* episode without the commercial—and some were even shorter. According to *Muppet Show* music consultant Larry Grossman, Jim thought any musical number longer than two minutes was indulgent.

The big difference between *The Muppet Show* and *Sam and Friends*, besides the running time, was the guest star. *Sam and Friends* had its own guest stars, but they were mostly unknowing participants whose performances were played from records. For *The Muppet Show,* Jim had the real thing—big stars traveling all the way to England for the express purpose of performing with the Muppets. As Kermit sang in the last *Sam and Friends* episode, "They come for to sing." It must have pleased Jim to welcome some of the same stars he lip-synced to in Washington to his big production in London.

As the Muppets moved on to feature films, the direct connection to *Sam and Friends* started to fade, but the old gang made an appearance on *The Muppets: A Celebration of 30 Years* in 1986. After watching an archival clip reel, Harry, seated at a banquet table, posed a logical question to the frog of honor. "How come you look so much better now than you did then?"

"That's one of the advantages of being a Muppet," replied Kermit, right before Yorick began to devour him for old time's sake. Kermit the Frog, now a superstar, continued to work, but "Kermit the First" (as the proto-Muppet was informally designated within the company) and the rest of the *Sam and Friends* gang were sent on the road in a series of *Art of the Muppets* touring museum exhibitions starting in 1979.

When The Jim Henson Company was sold to the German company E.M. TV for a short time in the early 2000s, the new owner acquired the rights to Jim's characters, but all historical puppets (those in nonperformable condition) remained the property of Jim's children, with the original Kermit residing in a Midtown New York City bank vault.

This is when discussions began about the eventual disposition of Jim's first group of Muppet characters. The Jim Henson Legacy, a nonprofit organization founded by Jane Henson, administered the family's two thousand-plus-item collection of historical puppets and worked to create new exhibitions in which to display them. Eventually, after a successful touring exhibition mounted by the Legacy and the Smithsonian Institution Traveling Exhibition Service, major portions of the Henson family collection were donated to the Museum of the Moving Image in Queens, New York, and the Center for Puppetry Arts in Atlanta, Georgia, where permanent exhibitions were established. The Henson children had worked with The Jim Henson Legacy to make the final decisions on where most of the puppets would eventually find permanent homes (with the Legacy's then-Executive Director Bonnie Erickson spearheading the process), but when it came to *Sam and Friends,* the Hensons deferred to their mother Jane's wishes as to where those characters should go.

Jane felt that Jim's first Kermit and the other *Sam and Friends* characters should go home to Washington, D.C. Before donating the puppets to the Smithsonian's National Museum of American History, however, Jane tested the waters by agreeing to include them in a short-term exhibit called *Muppets and Mechanisms* in 2006. Willard Scott, Jane Henson's colleague from WRC's *Afternoon* program, served as master of ceremonies for the opening event, and for the first time in almost fifty years, the original Kermit and the *Sam and Friends* cast appeared before a delighted public in Washington, D.C. The exhibition's success confirmed to Jane that Washington was where these characters belonged.

The Henson family made the generous gift of the *Sam and Friends* cast to the Smithsonian in 2010.

Jane Henson and fellow WRC alum Willard Scott at the opening ceremony of *Muppets and Mechanisms* in 2006. Photo by the author.

In 2010, Willard Scott and Jane Henson returned to the National Museum of American History for the deed-of-gift ceremony, as Jane officially signed the paperwork transferring ownership of the *Sam and Friends* puppets over to the Smithsonian Institution. They were now the property of the American people.

"People come and they go in television, and they mostly go," Willard Scott said at the ceremony as he surveyed his former fellow *Afternoon* cast members lined up on a table to his left. "But not the Muppets. They went on and got better and better and better and better."

Exhibited intermittently since then, the characters will be regularly featured in the museum's new permanent entertainment exhibition in 2022.

The cast of *Sam and Friends* in the vault at the National Museum of American History. Photo by the author

Kermit, Harry, and Sam as they looked in 2019. Photo by the author

In 2013, twenty more of Jim's characters were donated to the Smithsonian, joining Kermit the First and the *Sam and Friends* cast, as well as Oscar the Grouch, and a later version of Kermit that had previously been donated to the Smithsonian's permanent collection.

The Smithsonian's *Sam and Friends* collection includes Kermit, Harry, Sam, Yorick, Professor Madcliffe, Mushmellon, Chicken Liver, Icky Gunk, and even Jim's pre-*Sam and Friends* creation, Pierre the French Rat. Where is Omar? Well, he was found in storage a few years later and donated to the Center for Puppetry Arts. A second Yorick—remember those episodes in which we met Yorick's siblings and parents?—was found and included as part of the Museum of the Moving Image's Henson collection. So whether you visit New York, Atlanta, or Washington, you'll be able to see a little bit of *Sam and Friends*.

Omar at the Center for Puppetry Art's Worlds of Puppetry Jim Henson collection. Photo by the author

The *Sam and Friends* display at the Museum of the Moving Image in Queens, New York.

The city of Hyattsville, Maryland (adjacent to University Park, Maryland, where Jim had lived with his parents), commemorated Sam, Kermit, Harry, and the rest of the *Sam and Friends* cast in 2016 with the dedication of a bas-relief planter sculpted by Bill Culbertson. Located in David C. Driskell Community Park, the eight-sided structure is made to resemble vintage television screens, each displaying a vignette from *Sam and Friends*. Stone benches featuring Muppet-style eyes and quotes from Jim Henson surround the planter.

The Sam and Friends planter in Hyattsville, Maryland. Photo by the author

* * *

In 2011, Jim Henson was honored as a "Disney Legend," a designation bestowed upon individuals who made outstanding contributions to the Walt Disney Company, which purchased the Muppets in 2004. The ceremony featured a live duet by Kermit the Frog and Rowlf the Dog, and in a nod to Muppet history, Jim's son Brian Henson and puppeteer Leslie Carrara-Rudolph also re-created a performance of the *Sam and Friends* favorite "I've Grown Accustomed to Your Face," with a generic frog sitting in for Kermit.

Brian Henson first developed this re-creation of his father's original piece as part of *Stuffed and Unstrung,* a live improvised puppet show that eventually became known as *Puppet Up!* Re-creations of Jim's self-contained early puppet pieces have been a part of *Puppet Up!* performances ever since.

Just as part of the early Muppet heritage lives on in Brian's show, *Sam and Friends* remains an inspiration to puppeteers today; performances similar to Jim's WRC broadcasts continue on in live puppet slams and in countless YouTube videos. At the dawn of the YouTube era, Jane Henson made the connection between the short videos seen on the internet service and the short pieces Jim made on local television. She said she knew that if Jim were starting out today, he would be working on YouTube and not on television. What YouTube and TikTok are to today's generation of young creators, television was to Jim Henson in 1955—a magical portal to communicate and engage with an audience. He saw the medium of television as a representation of the future, perhaps even *his* future. And indeed, what began on the WRC-TV studio floor in a repurposed hotel auditorium took Jim Henson to the Television Academy Hall of Fame.

Of his growing entertainment empire, Walt Disney once said, "I only hope that we never lose sight of one thing, that it was all started by a mouse." Now that the Walt Disney Company is the custodian of the one continuing star of *Sam and Friends* and his current cast of Muppet co-stars, it seems appropriate to offer a similar admonition regarding Jim Henson's creations. Let us never lose sight of the fact that it was all started by a frog—at a time when he wasn't really a frog at all.

PART II

The Sam and Friends Episode Guide

Sam and Friends

Credits

Writers:	Jim Henson
	Jerry Juhl (1961)
Directors:	John Chapin
	Carl Degen
Performers:	Jim Henson
	Jane Nebel Henson
	Robert Payne (1958-1961)
	Jerry Juhl (1961)
Broadcast: stations	WRC-TV, Washington, D.C. channel 4
	WBAL-TV, Baltimore, channel 11 (1958-1961)
Origination:	
1955-1958	WRC Studios
	Sheraton-Park Hotel
	Washington, D.C.
1958-1961	WRC Studios
	4001 Nebraska Avenue NW
	Washington, D.C.

Sam and Friends Air Schedule History

Sam and Friends was frequently moved around the broadcast schedule and usually aired at the tail end of a block of programming that contained WRC's news, sports, and weather broadcasts.

While it's almost impossible to list a complete schedule of the show's time slots through the years, thanks to the research done by Jim's biographer, Brian Jay Jones, and by careful examination of *The Washington Post* and *The Evening Star* television listings, and WRC print advertising, we can trace a fairly accurate history of *Sam and Friends'* broadcast schedule.

May 9, 1955
Sam and Friends premieres on WRC, airing Monday through Friday at 11:25 p.m.

August 26, 1955
Following the evening's broadcast, *Sam and Friends* is removed from the WRC schedule.

August 30, 1955
After viewer outcry, *Sam and Friends* returns to the air at 11:25 p.m., but, sadly, not for long.

October 10, 1955

Sam and Friends is replaced at 11:25 p.m. by a syndicated, Listerine-sponsored, five-minute filmed show featuring Les Paul and Mary Ford. With their own show on indefinite hiatus, Jim Henson and Jane Nebel continue to work on the WRC program *Afternoon*.

May 14, 1956

The Muppets become part of *Footlight Theater* with Paul Arnold, airing Monday through Friday, 6 to 6:45 p.m.

September 10, 1956

WRC moves *Footlight Theater* to 5:30 p.m. and returns it to its original purpose of showing old movies. The Muppets and Paul Arnold are now seen on *Sam and Friends with Paul Arnold*, which airs immediately after *Footlight Theater* in a shorter time slot, Monday through Friday, 6:30 to 6:45 p.m.

December 31, 1956

Sam and Friends with Paul Arnold adds a second daily broadcast, retaking its late-night time slot from Les Paul and Mary Ford. The show now airs 6:30 to 6:45 p.m. and 11:25 to 11:30 p.m.

February 25, 1957

Sam and Friends (or as a print ad in *The Washington Post and Times–Herald* refers to it, *Paul Arnold with Sam and Friends*) continues two shows a night, Monday through Friday, but the early show is now ten minutes long and moves to 6:50 p.m.

September 9, 1957

NBC's *Huntley-Brinkley Report*, which began in 1956 at 7:45 p.m., is moved to 6:45 p.m. The early broadcast of *Sam and Friends* is discontinued (for the time being) to allow time for Bryson Rash's news and the WRC weather report. The 11:25 p.m. broadcast continues.

September 8, 1958
WRC advertising no longer mentions Paul Arnold. The show is listed as *Sam and Friends—The Muppets* and continues airing at 11:25 p.m.

November 24, 1958
Sam and Friends, now sponsored by Esskay, returns to 6:30 p.m. Monday through Friday and adds Baltimore's WBAL-TV to its network of two stations for the early evening broadcast. The show also continues to air at 11:25 p.m., but only on WRC. On the following night's broadcast, the cast officially welcomes Baltimore viewers to the *Sam and Friends* network (of two stations).

January 4, 1959
Sam and Friends is now only airing at 6:30 p.m., followed by Tippy Stringer's weather forecast, Jim Gibbons with sports, and then the network news with Huntley and Brinkley. The 11:25 p.m. slot is occupied by the news with Bryson Rash.

March 9, 1959
Sam and Friends begins broadcasting in color Monday through Friday at 6:30 p.m.

May 26, 1959
Sam and Friends ends its season. Jim and Jane get married two days later.

August 3, 1959
Sam and Friends begins a new season, still airing Monday through Friday at 6:30 p.m. A WRC ad in *The Washington Post and Times–Herald* proclaims, "They're Back."

May 27, 1960
Sam and Friends ends its season. Jim, Jane, and the new addition to their family, Lisa, spend part of the summer break in Detroit for their first Puppeteers of America festival.

September 12, 1960
Sam and Friends begins its new season with a move to 6:40 p.m., making it WRC's direct lead-in to NBC's *Huntley-Brinkley Report*.

June 13, 1961
Sam and Friends airs its last show of the season. Jim and Jane embark on a cross-country trip with Lisa to visit the Puppeteers of America festival in Asilomar, California.

September 18, 1961
The show returns for its last season, albeit a partial one. For its final weeks, the show moves back to where it started—Monday through Friday at 11:25 p.m.

December 15, 1961
Sam and Friends airs its final show.

In addition to their own show, the Muppets were a regular part of the cast of *Afternoon,* which aired Monday through Friday on WRC. *Afternoon* premiered on March 7, 1955, in the 2:15 to 3 p.m. time slot.

Afternoon added an additional fifteen minutes on July 4, 1955, adjusting its airtime to 2 p.m.

On October 10, 1955, the show moved to 1 p.m. for several weeks before moving back to 2 p.m. on October 31, 1955.

On November 28, 1955, Inga Rundvold became the host of the show, and *Afternoon* became *Afternoon with Inga*. The show remained at 2 p.m. but was trimmed to thirty minutes. The Muppets continued to make occasional appearances until the show ended in May 1956.

The Muppets also made regular appearances on *In Our Town*, a WRC entertainment/interview program, which aired weekdays at 1 p.m. starting on June 30, 1958. The show moved to 1:30 p.m. on March 2, 1959, and remained there until the show ended in September of 1959.

Sam and Friends

Music List and Partial Episode Guide

This episode guide was compiled by cross-referencing surviving scripts, transcription acetate discs, record lists, and reel-to-reel audio air checks made by Jim Henson. Information about the songs and authors was referenced from the American Society of Composers, Authors and Publishers (ASCAP) and BMI databases, as well as discogs.com and other music databases.

Some airdates are approximations, based on the order of the archival recordings.

Since few exact airdates are available for the early years of the show, songs used on the show before late 1958 are listed by the date that the acetate records used during the broadcast were made. It is safe to assume that the first use of the song occurred shortly after its acetate recording was created. These music transcription discs were used for Muppet appearances on *Afternoon* and *In Our Town,* as well as *Sam and Friends.*

From late 1958 onward, live broadcasts are listed by their airdates. Some recordings and scripts were undated, and we have estimated where they occurred in the run whenever possible.

Both Jim and Jane recalled that the first song officially used by the Muppets (on *Afternoon*) was "Tweedle Dee," performed by Georgia Gibbs and written by Winfield Scott. For the song, Jim constructed two bird puppets. Decades later, Jaye P. Morgan, a vocalist who was heard on *Sam and Friends,* would perform the song on *The Muppet Show.*

Records transcribed on January 2, 1955:

"Meet Me in St. Louis": Performed by The Del Monico Four, written by Andrew B. Sterling, Kerry Mills

The Del Monico Four recorded this version of "Meet Me in St. Louis," which was written to herald the 1904 St. Louis World's Fair and regained popularity when used in the 1944 Judy Garland MGM film of the same title. Jim enjoyed using barbershop quartet music in *Sam and Friends,* especially in the early days, and in 1957, Jim and Jane's frequent use of barbershop music was acknowledged with an award from the Society for the Preservation and Encouragement of Barber Shop Quartet Singing in America.

"Daisy Bell (A Bicycle Built for Two)": Performed by unknown barbershop quartet, written by Harry Dacre

The 1892 song—in which a man who "can't afford a carriage" but has a tandem bicycle tries to get a woman named Daisy Bell to marry him—was written not too long after the invention of the title mode of transportation. The rendition used on *Sam and Friends* was a barbershop arrangement by an unknown quartet.

"A Bird in a Gilded Cage": Performed by unknown barbershop quartet, written by Arthur J. Lamb, Harry Von Tilzer

Published in 1900 and a sheet music bestseller, the song is a tear-jerker of a ballad about a woman whose "beauty was sold for an old man's gold." This version is a four-part harmony arrangement performed by an unknown barbershop quartet.

"Etiquette Blues": Performed by Butch Stone, orchestra conducted by Van Alexander, written by Gayle Grubb

In 1948, Butch Stone, a vocalist and saxophone player who would later join the Les Brown orchestra, released this patter song (heavy on the Brooklyn accent) that lists some simple rules of etiquette, including, "Never cut spaghetti up in pieces / eat it like a chicken eating worms. / When you're eating cake be sure you eat the frosting first / watch out for bacteria and germs." The song was popularized two decades earlier by The Happiness Boys (see next entry).

"Where Did You Get That Name?": Performed by The Happiness Boys (Billy Jones and Ernest Hare), Dave Kaplan at the piano, written by Bob Miller, Lew Klein

A song about people getting their names from their occupations took on greater meaning when performed by The Happiness Boys, a team who demonstrated brand loyalty by adapting their name as their sponsorship changed. After their stint on behalf of Happiness Candy Stores, Jones and Hare were known as The Taystee Loafers when Taystee Bread (a company that would later use the Muppets' Wilkins-style commercials for their product) became their radio sponsor.

Records transcribed on May 5, 1955

"I'll Remember": Performed by Cliff Nazarro, written by Burton Lane, Ralph Freed

This straightforward love song from the 1939 film *I'll Remember* was turned into a comedy record by double-talk comedian Cliff Nazarro. The song begins with Nazarro remembering his true love, then in a spoken soliloquy, his memories of her become a series of gibberish double-talk statements.

"News of the World": Performed by Cliff Nazarro

Nazarro, who appeared in more than fifty feature films, recorded this spoken-word piece in 1942. This parody of a radio news report—complete with commercial messages—frequently lapses into Nazarro's trademark double-talk.

"What Did He Say? (The Mumble Song)": Performed by The Charioteers, written by Charles Grean, Cy Coben

This is the first of two different songs with similar titles used on *Sam and Friends,* both with the premise of a person who can't be understood. In this song, the central character mumbles as the singing quartet tries to figure out what he's saying. *Sam and Friends* used another recording of "What Did He Say" performed by the Deep River Boys. Co-author Charles Grean is probably best known for writing Phil Harris's hit "The Thing."

"Donkey Tango": Performed by Ray Bloch and His Orchestra with narration by Leon Janney, written by Rudolph Goehr, Robert Weil

Orchestra leader Ray Bloch is probably best known for leading the orchestra on *The Ed Sullivan Show* during its entire run from 1948 to 1971. The Muppets made twenty-five appearances on Ed Sullivan's show starting in 1966. "Donkey Tango" is an instrumental accompanied by actor Leon Janney's narration of the story of a donkey named Pablo who moved in rhythm to a tango.

"Salt": Performed by The Vagabonds, written by Jack Adrian (a.k.a. Adrian Greenberg) (see page 89)

Records transcribed on May 12, 1955

"George Washington, Abraham Lincoln, Ulysses S. Robert E. Lee": Performed by Phil Harris and His Orchestra, written by Clancy Hayes

When picked on by a mean man named Big-Foot Joe, the singer reminds Joe about his given name—a long moniker derived from America's past. (Though it may seem odd today that someone would have both Abraham Lincoln and Robert E. Lee in their name.) As the first-person story song concludes, Phil Harris tells us in his familiar style that he's not just relying on his long name for self-defense. "I've got a bullet-proof vest, a razor-proof collar, a big forty-four that's gonna make you holler."

"The Preacher and the Bear": Performed by Phil Harris and His Orchestra, written by Joe Arzonia

A quick-tempo patter story song sung by Phil Harris in his breathless, nonstop style, it tells the tale of a preacher who happened to encounter a grizzly bear. When cornered by the bear, the preacher turns to prayer in the refrain: "Lord if you can't help me, for goodness' sake, don't help that bear."

"Eating Goober Peas": Performed by Rusty Draper and Vocal Group, orchestra conducted by David Carroll, traditional, adapted, and arranged by David Carroll, George Stone

This song about peanuts is a traditional folk song dating back to the Civil War. The song was briefly sung in passing by Patton Oswalt in a 2013 episode of *Parks and Recreation*.

Records transcribed on May 19, 1955

"The Guy with the Voodoo!": Performed by the Fletcher Peck Trio, written by Stan Freeman, Fletcher Peck

The refrain of this song is familiar to Henson fans for its paraphrased use in the film *Labyrinth* (1986). The original quote: "You remind us of the guy / What guy? / The guy with the voodoo / Who do? / You do / I do what? / You remind us of the guy."

"Open the Door, Richard": Performed by The Charioteers, written by John Mason, Don Howell, Jack McVea, Dusty Fletcher

This record had its origin as an African American vaudeville routine. The lead performer and background vocalists are returning home after a night out at the club. They knock on the door of their house, trying to get Richard's attention to let them in—Richard left the club early with the key. It's been recorded many times since its introduction; a CD released in 2012 compiled twenty-four different recordings, including this one by The Charioteers.

Records transcribed on June 9, 1955

"A Four-Legged Friend": Performed by Bob Hope and Jimmy Wakely, written by Jack Brooks

This song was featured in Bob Hope's 1952 film, *Son of Paleface*, introduced by the movie's co-star, King of the Cowboys, Roy Rogers. Hope sang a reprise of the tune while impersonating the Rogers in order to ride Trigger, only to be thrown off by the "one-man-horse." Hope (with Jimmy Wakely) and Rogers each released their own recordings of the song the same year *Son of Paleface* played theaters. More than twenty-five years later, Hope would sing "Don't Fence Me In" on *The*

Muppet Show with a Muppet horse played by Jerry Nelson. "A Four-Legged Friend" was featured in Rogers's and Dale Evans's *Muppet Show* episode as a U.K. spot, though they did not perform it.

"Morris": Performed by Mel Blanc, accompanied by Franklyn Marks and His Brothers, written by Richard Adler, Jerry Ross

Mel Blanc, legendary voice performer, sang this tune about the unlikely name of Morris—found on a burly wrestler, a movie star, and a gorilla. "It used to be that every other fellow's name was Joe / but now you hear a new name everywhere you go." The song was written by the team who would go on to write *The Pajama Game* (1954) and *Damn Yankees* (1955).

"He's a Tramp" (from *Lady and the Tramp*): Performed by Peggy Lee with orchestra directed by Sonny Burke, written by Sonny Burke, Peggy Lee

The performer of this Disney classic has her own connection to Muppet history. The original name of Miss Piggy, as listed on the character's copyright certificate, is Miss Piggy Lee. The Lee was dropped out of fear of legal action.

"Empty Saddles": Performed by The Buffalo Bills, written by Billy Hill

Popularized by the cowboy group Sons of the Pioneers, the tune is a melancholy cowboy lament. The recording used on *Sam and Friends* was from The Buffalo Bills' record entitled *Barbershop's Best* (1955).

Records transcribed on June 23, 1955

"Woodman, Woodman, Spare That Tree": Performed by Phil Harris and His Orchestra, written by Irving Berlin, Vincent Bryan

Co-written by Irving Berlin, one of the most successful songwriters in history, this Phil Harris patter song tells the tale of a man defending a tree from destruction not for environmental reasons, but because it's his refuge—he can climb it, but his wife can't.

"You Go Your Way (And I'll Go Crazy)": Performed by Cliff Nazarro, written by Harry Revel, Mort Greene

Double-talk comic Cliff Nazarro brought his unique style to this recording, which begins as a standard ballad before descending into unintelligible nonsense.

"She Never Left the Table": Performed by Art Carney, orchestra under the direction of Sid Feller, written by Roy Alfred, Al Frisch

Art Carney released this record in 1955. In it, he sings of a romantic dinner date with a lady who was more interested in satisfying her hunger for food than for love. He recounts everything she ordered from the menu and laments that "she never left the table." Best known at the time as *The Honeymooners'* Ed Norton, Art Carney would go on to work with Jim Henson in *The Great Santa Claus Switch* (1970), *The Perry Como Winter Show* (1972), and *The Muppets Take Manhattan* (1984).

"The Day I Read a Book": Performed by Jimmy Durante, orchestra conducted by Roy Bargy, written by Jimmy Durante, Jack Barnett

The "Old Schnozzola," as Durante was called, had a long career from vaudeville to television with a stint at MGM in between, where he was teamed with Buster Keaton for a brief time. This comedy song (co-written by Durante, himself) pokes fun at his apparent lack of literacy. "Why, if you walk into my house, you'll see lots of books. /

Believe me, they're not there just for appearances. I press an awful lot of butterflies."

Records transcribed on June 30, 1955

"Tongue Twisters": Performed by Danny Kaye, written by Roger Edens

In addition to his credits as a songwriter, Roger Edens spent many years as an arranger and associate producer in the famous Arthur Freed unit at MGM. This record takes classic tongue twisters like "Peter Piper" and makes them swing, with a choral refrain interspersed between Danny Kaye's rapid, rhythmic tongue-twisting verses. Interestingly, the "Moses Supposes" tongue twister pops up in the song—it was Roger Edens who (along with lyricists Betty Comden and Adolph Green) wrote the song "Moses Supposes" for *Singin' in the Rain* (1952), which was released just one year after this Danny Kaye record.

"Oooh Looka There, Ain't She Pretty?": Performed by The Charioteers, orchestra under the direction of Mitchell Ayres, written by Carmen Lombardo, Clarence Todd

Co-composer Carmen Lombardo's brother Guy Lombardo was a bandleader well known for his annual New Year's Eve performances. Carmen's collaborator for this tune, Clarence Todd, was an African American composer and musician. This song was probably their biggest hit, with recordings by Bob Crosby, Benny Goodman, Bill Haley and His Comets, Frankie Avalon, and Guy Lombardo and his band, the Royal Canadians. The Charioteers' recording is a swinging party, with lots of "ooh-ah-oohs" ideal for Muppet lip-sync performances.

"Little Man You've Had a Busy Day": Performed by Patti and Jerry Lewis with orchestra conducted by Dick Stabile, written by Maurice Sigler, Al Hoffman, Mabel Wayne

Released as a single in 1953, the song begins with Jerry Lewis's wife, Patti, singing a straight version of this lullaby standard as she is putting her "little man" to bed. Jerry interrupts with a mile-a-minute recap of his busy schedule. Though his then-partner Dean Martin does not perform on the record, he is mentioned when Jerry sings about a submarine christening mishap: "The bottle I mean, / wound up breaking on Dean, / the sub made no motion, / but Dean's in the ocean."

"I'll Pay as I Go": Performed by Thurl Ravenscroft with the Jeff Alexander Quartet, written by Jeff Alexander, Marve Fisher

Thurl Ravenscroft, best known as the longtime voice of Tony the Tiger and the vocalist behind "You're a Mean One, Mr. Grinch" and many Disney theme park recordings, provides the lead vocal on this tune, which was on the flip side of "Dr. Geek" (see next song). This song is a jaunty march in which the singer refuses to pay for love on installments. "I'll pay as I go, owing nothing to no one. / I'll pay as I go, leaving no balance due. / I'll never again put my heart in a pawn shop. / I'll never again be indebted to you."

"Dr. Geek" (from Tanganyika): Performed by Thurl Ravenscroft with the Jeff Alexander Quartet, written by Jeff Alexander, Marve Fisher

In this song, which falls more strongly in the novelty category than "I'll Pay as I Go," Thurl describes Dr. Geek, the rich witch doctor psychiatrist: "He'll shrink your head and make your troubles small."

"Tennessee Hillbilly Ghost": Performed by Phil Harris, written by Beasley Smith, Marie Peterson

Phil Harris sings a ghost story cowboy song about a Tennessee hillbilly ghost who could play "the strangest mountain music you ever heard before."

Record transcribed on July 11, 1955

"I Went to Your Wedding": Performed by Spike Jones and His City Slickers, vocal refrain by Sir Frederick Gas, written by Jessie Mae Robinson

Jessie Mae Robinson, an African American songwriter, achieved success with "I Went to Your Wedding" as a hit for Patti Page in 1952. Spike Jones gave it a comedic spin soon after, releasing his version on the RCA label in early 1953. Vocalist Sir Frederick Gas (real name Earl Bennett) was a regular member of Spike Jones's band for several years. In Spike's arrangement, Sir Frederick sings, accompanied by a strumming guitar, only to break into laughter at the mention of the bride's face, struggling as he regains and loses his composure throughout the song. The record was banned in Boston on account of Earl Bennett's giggles.

Records transcribed on July 14, 1955

"The Natives Are Restless Tonight": Performed by Ray McKinley and His Orchestra, written by John Brooks, Alfie Fogel, Joe Darion

Band leader, singer, and drummer Ray McKinley released this swinging vocal in 1954. With lyrics like "the queen of the Congo is playing the bongo," it would be considered culturally insensitive today.

"My Gal Sal": Performed by The Buffalo Bills, written by Paul Dresser

"My Gal Sal" was written by popular songwriter Paul Dresser, whose best-known tune was "On the Banks of the Wabash, Far Away." Dresser's life was portrayed in a 1942 movie musical entitled *My Gal Sal,* its title inspired by this song, which lists the virtues of the singer's gal, Sal.

"The Corn Keeps A-Growin'": Performed by Dennis Day with Henri René and His Orchestra, written by Sammy Lerner, Ben Oakland

The verses of this lively song are a series of tongue-twisting anecdotes. One was about a brandy-loving, gin-hating man named Mulligan and a fellow named Milligan, who had the exact opposite tastes. "When someone switched their glasses, they drank each other's brew. / Now Milligan's a sober man and Mulligan's a stew." Each verse flows into the title refrain. Dennis Day spent many years as the tenor vocalist on *The Jack Benny Program* on both television and radio. Jim Henson shared the stage with Jack Benny on *The Tonight Show Starring Johnny Carson* in 1974 and had hoped to produce a Muppet Income Tax Day television special guest starring the famous comedian.

"The Thing": Performed by Phil Harris, written by Charles Grean

Phil Harris introduced his recording of "The Thing" in 1950, only weeks after recording it. A No. 1 hit on the Billboard chart, it's the story of the discovery of a mysterious object. The sound of three knocks is heard whenever the name of the object is attempted to be mentioned in the song.

**"What Happened to the Hair (On the Head of the Man I Love?)":
Performed by Pearl Bailey with orchestra directed by Don Redman, written by Steve Allen, Sammy Gallop**

The tune is a jazzy lament about the once glorious head of hair upon the head of a loved one: "He used to have a mess of fuzz / but now there's nothing where the fuzz once was." Show business legend Pearl Bailey, who performs the song, appeared as a guest star on the third season of *The Muppet Show*. Co-author Steve Allen gave Jim and Jane Henson their network television debut on *Tonight*.

Records transcribed on July 21, 1955

"Once in Love with Amy": Performed by Ray Bolger, written by Frank Loesser

Written for *Where's Charley* (1948), the musical version of the play *Charley's Aunt,* this Loesser tune would later be performed by Pops and Fozzie as a U.K. spot during Season 5 of *The Muppet Show*.

"Minnie the Mermaid": Performed by Phil Harris and His Orchestra, written by Bud DeSylva

Bud DeSylva's 1923 song "Minnie the Mermaid," as sung by Phil Harris, tells the story of a man and his mermaid dream girl: "She had the tail of a fish for a train / but just the same, she could sure entertain."

"Dufo (What a Crazy Guy)": Performed by Wally Cox, written by Wally Cox

Known to television viewers for his role on *Mister Peepers* (1952) and as the voice of Underdog, Wally Cox recorded this monologue—

which he had performed live for years—for RCA Records in 1953. In it, he recounts the various dangerous adventures of his old friend Dufo, punctuating the bizarre anecdotes with "what a crazy guy."

"It's a Sin to Tell a Lie": Performed by Somethin' Smith and the Redheads, written by Billy Mayhew

Originally introduced in 1936, "It's a Sin to Tell a Lie" is an incredibly sincere ballad. It would later be performed in 1964 by Rowlf and Jimmy Dean on *The Jimmy Dean Show*. The recording used on *Sam and Friends* was performed by Somethin' Smith and the Redheads, a 1950s vocal trio. This record was their biggest hit, making it to No. 7 on the Billboard Hot 100 chart.

Records transcribed on August 4, 1955

"Such a Night": Performed by Cab Calloway, Sy Oliver and Orchestra, written by Lincoln Chase

Cab Calloway's recording of "Such a Night," about an unforgettable moonlight kiss, was released in 1954. The popular song was also recorded by a variety of other artists, including The Drifters, Johnnie Ray, Dinah Washington, and Elvis Presley. Songwriter Lincoln Chase had what was probably his biggest and most enduring hit a decade later with Shirley Ellis's "The Name Game." Cab Calloway would later bring his unique vocals to *Sesame Street* in the 1980s.

"Down the Road Apiece": Performed by Ray McKinley and His Orchestra, written by Don Raye

A vocal jazz performance, "Down the Road Apiece" is a song about a little-bitty shack in the hills where you can get your kicks—that is, "if you want to hear some boogie."

"Wayfaring Stranger": Performed by Burl Ives, Traditional / "Woolie Boogie Bee": Performed by Burl Ives, written by Burl Ives

"Wayfaring Stranger" is an American folk song that dates to the mid-1800s. Burl Ives, today best remembered as the voice of Sam the Snowman in the classic *Rudolph the Red-Nosed Reindeer* TV special, used it as the title track on his 1944 album, as well as the title of his CBS radio program and his 1948 autobiography. The authorship of Ives's 1949 recording of "Woolie Boogie Bee" is credited to the singer, but the tune is based on the traditional folk song "I Wish I Was a Mole in the Ground," and both are based on an "I wish" premise that speculates how life would be different if the singer was a variety of different animals or objects.

"You Can't Do Wrong Doin' Right": Performed by Phil Harris and Jack Benny's Quartet with Walter Scharf and His Orchestra, written by Al Rinker, Floyd Huddleston

Phil Harris, a regular on Jack Benny's program for many years (several while doing double duty on his own radio show with wife Alice Faye), teamed up with fellow Benny regulars The Sportsmen Quartet (credited on the record as "Jack Benny's Quartet") for this recording. As the title indicates, the song implores the listeners to do the right thing: "Let old Satan know he's lost the fight / 'cause you can't do wrong doin' right."

Records transcribed on August 11, 1955

"Close the Door": Performed by Jim Lowe with Norman Leyden Orchestra, written by Fred Ebb, Paul Klein

Complete with a catchy refrain ("Close the door, they're coming in the window!") and sound effects, the lyrics to this novelty song were written by Fred Ebb, who went on to Broadway fame with John Kander. Several of the team's songs from *Cabaret* (1966) and *Chicago* (1975) would be performed on *The Muppet Show*.

"I Ain't Gonna Give Nobody None O' This Jelly Roll": Performed by Phil Harris and His Orchestra, written by Spencer Williams, Clarence Williams

Phil Harris recorded this song in 1949, almost thirty years after it was first recorded by Wilbur Sweatman's Original Jazz Band. It tells the story of Little Willy Green's inability to share the jelly roll his momma gave him: "Your lovin's awful sweet / but my jelly roll, it can't be beat." Over the years, versions have been released by Louis Armstrong, Sidney Bechet, Bobby Darin & Johnny Mercer, and Leon Redbone.

"The Sad Cowboy": Performed by The Sportsmen Quartet with orchestral accompaniment, written by Al Gannaway, Hoagy Carmichael, Walton Farrar

A plaintive, Western ballad, it was co-written by Hoagy Carmichael, whose long songwriting career began in the Stone Age (if we are to believe his guest appearance in a classic *Flintstones* episode). The Sportsmen Quartet was a regular fixture on *The Jack Benny Program* on both radio and television, and their harmonies can be heard on dozens of classic Warner Bros. cartoons.

"The Telephone No Ring": Performed by Nicola Paone, written by Nicola Paone

An example of dialect comedy that might now be considered culturally insensitive, Nicola Paone's 1949 tune is the story of an Italian person's trouble trying to make a telephone call. Paone, known as the Italian Bing Crosby, recorded more than 150 songs during his career and later ran a New York restaurant for several decades.

"Dig-Dig-Dig Dig for Your Dinner": Performed by Phil Harris with Walter Scharf and His Orchestra, written by Mack Gordon, Harry Warren

This spirited pseudo-gospel tune about the necessity of hard work and dues-paying was originally performed by Gene Kelly and Phil Silvers in the 1950 MGM film *Summer Stock*. This Phil Harris cover was released the same year.

"Possibilities": Performed by Phil Harris with orchestra conducted by Walter Scharf, written by Al Rinker, Floyd Huddleston

This is a typically up-tempo Phil Harris number proclaiming the virtue of seeing the potential in any given situation: "Ain't no miracle / too impossible / to anyone who sees / the possibilities." Christopher Columbus and Abraham Lincoln are offered as examples of those who saw the possibilities in their respective situations.

Records transcribed on August 18, 1955

"Sunday Driving": Performed by Jerry Lewis with Billy May and His Orchestra, written by Leon Pober

Supported by sound effects, Jerry Lewis delivers a fast-paced driving song in his high character voice. Billy May, whose orchestra accompanied the song, was a longtime collaborator of Stan Freberg and provided music for many of the Freberg records used on *Sam and Friends*.

"I'm a Little Busybody": Performed by Jerry Lewis with Billy May and His Orchestra, written by Leon Pober, Niccolò Paganini

The flip side of his 1950 Capitol single "Sunday Driving" is a breathless patter song (set to a Paganini theme) in which Jerry tells all about everyone he knows. Lyricist Leon Pober wrote Don Ho's theme song, "Tiny Bubbles."

"The Musicians": Performed by Dinah Shore, Betty Hutton, Tony Martin, Phil Harris, with Henri René and His Orchestra, written by Charles Grean, Tom Glazer

This high-powered quartet released this tune in 1952. Best known for its inclusion in two episodes of *The Dick Van Dyke Show,* the song was based on a German folksong. When *Sesame Street* augmented its original compositions with existing songs in its earliest episodes, this was one of the songs it used. Co-composer Tom Glazer would go on to write the songs for the film *A Face in the Crowd* (1957).

"I Cried for You": Performed by Jerry Colonna, written by Abe Lyman, Arthur Freed, Gus Arnheim

Mustachioed Jerry Colonna, who was best known as a comic foil for Bob Hope, starts this song as a serious ballad but is soon drowned out by a chorus of criers.

Records transcribed on August 19, 1955

"Ugly Chile (You're Some Pretty Doll)": Performed by Johnny Mercer with Paul Weston and His Orchestra, written by Clarence Williams

The song by Clarence Williams begins with a refrain about how the singer's parents once sang about his appearance ("You're so pretty, Oh! So pretty!") only to have his self-esteem shattered upon his first date with a girl who elaborates on how ugly he really is.

"It's a Quiet Town": Performed by Danny Kaye and The Andrews Sisters with Vic Schoen and His Orchestra, written by Bob Russell, Harold Spina

Danny Kaye and The Andrews Sisters sing about how quiet Crossbone County is, but based on this raucous song, it really isn't.

"Sheriff" Kermit sings "It's a Quiet Town" as Hank and Frank supply The Andrews Sisters' backup vocals.

Records transcribed on August 25, 1955

"Jack and the Beanstalk (Bebop's Fable)": Performed by Steve Allen, written by Steve Allen

Steve Allen, a musician and composer in addition to being a talk show host and comedian, released a record of four *Bebop's Fables* in 1953, with his hip takes on "Goldilocks and the Three Bears," "Cinderella," "Snow White and the Seven Dwarfs," and "Jack and the Beanstalk."

"Old, Old Vienna": Performed by Eddie Lawrence with orchestra directed by Nick Perito, written by Eddie Lawrence

Best known for "The Old Philosopher" and the many variations thereof, Eddie Lawrence's long career included Broadway, cartoon voices, television appearances, and motion pictures. In this tune, as Viennese music plays, Lawrence touts the praises of old, old Vienna.

"How Do'ye Do and Shake Hands": Performed by Betty Hutton, Dinah Shore, Phil Harris, Tony Martin, with Henri René and His Orchestra, written by Cy Coben and Oliver Wallace

Originally written for the Disney animated feature *Alice in Wonderland,* this 1951 recording was the flip side of the same starry quartet's version of "The Musicians." Another famous quartet consisting of Danny Kaye, Jimmy Durante, Jane Wyman, and Groucho Marx released a version of this song in the same year.

"There Is a Tavern in the Town": Performed by unknown barbershop quartet, written by William H. Hills

The song dates to the late 1800s as a college drinking song. Crooner Rudy Vallée had a hit with it in the 1930s under the title "The Drunkard Song." More recent generations would recognize the melody but would be more apt to sing it with very different lyrics: "Head, shoulders, knees, and toes." The version of the song used on *Sam and Friends* was recorded by an unidentified barbershop quartet with piano accompaniment and spoken word interludes.

"I've Got You Under My Skin": Performed by Stan Freberg with Les Baxter and His Orchestra and Chorus, written by Cole Porter (see pages 157–158 for a full summary)

Records transcribed on September 1, 1955

"I Can't Carry a Tune": Performed by Jerry Lewis, written by Arthur Quenzer, Franklin Marks

In this song released on Capitol Records in 1952, Jerry laments his lack of singing talent despite his hard work and musical lineage: "I'm a guy who likes to sing, something awful. / That's the way I sing, something awful."

"(I've Been So Wrong, For So Long—But) I'm So Right Tonight": Performed by Phil Harris and His Orchestra, written by By Dunham, Terry Shand

This tune is a typical up-tempo Phil Harris vocal about a man finally falling in love.

"The Bowery": Performed by unknown barbershop quartet, written by Charles H. Hoyt and Percy Gaunt

Originally introduced in the 1891 Broadway musical *A Trip to Chinatown*, "The Bowery" is a song about the wild things that happen on New York City's Bowery and how the narrator vows he'll "never go there anymore." This recording and the next two barbershop records transcribed on this day were recorded by the same unidentified barbershop quartet.

"The Bird on Nellie's Hat": Performed by unknown barbershop quartet, written by Alfred Solman, Arthur J. Lamb

The song, which dates to 1906, would later be used as a U.K. spot in the third season of *The Muppet Show*, with Miss Piggy as the Nellie of the song's title and Louise Gold providing the singing voice of the matronly female pig performing the tune.

"She May Have Seen Better Days": Performed by unknown barbershop quartet, written by James Thornton

The barbershop classic tells the sad story of a down-on-her-luck lady who is the target first of ridicule, then sympathy.

Records transcribed on September 14, 1955

"I Know an Old Lady": Performed by Phil Harris with Skip Martin and His Orchestra, written by Alan Mills, Rose Bonne

Phil Harris's recording is an adaptation of a classic cumulative children's verse in which an old woman swallows a fly and then swallows an animal to catch the fly, and so forth. In Season 2 of *The Muppet Show*, guest star Judy Collins performed the song while the actions were rendered beside her in shadow puppetry. A version of the song was also performed by José Feliciano on *Sesame Street*. Pete Seeger sang it on the 1974 album *Pete Seeger & Brother Kirk Visit Sesame Street*.

"Goofus" (theme for *Sam and Friends*): Performed by Joe "Fingers" Carr and His Ragtime Band, written by Wayne King, William Harold, Gus Kahn

This is an instrumental version of a song that has been recorded by a wide range of artists from Phil Harris to the Carpenters. Joe "Fingers" Carr was a pseudonym for record producer, musician, and songwriter Lou Busch, who had great success late in his career as the arranger and conductor for Allan Sherman's parody albums of the 1960s. The acetate recording's label indicates that the tune was a "theme for *Sam and Friends,*" so it was probably used more as intro and underscore music than for any specific performance.

Records transcribed on September 15, 1955

"Never Hit Your Grandma with a Shovel (Use an Ax Instead)": Performed by Spike Jones, written by Felix Hanemann

The 1942 track begins with the tight harmony singing all the reasons you should not hit your grandmother with a shovel and offers sweetly sung, wise advice: "Though it may prove a shock . . . respect her aged head / stay the shovel and instead / paste your dear old, sweet old grandma / with a rock."

"By the Light of the Silvery Moon": Performed by unknown barbershop quartet, written by Gus Edwards, Edward Madden

A popular song first published in 1909, it would later be performed briefly in the preshow of *MuppetVision 3D* at Walt Disney World and pop up in a Muppets web video and in one version of the live Magic Kingdom show *The Muppets Present . . . Great Moments in American History.*

"Don't Start Courtin' in a Hot Rod": Performed by Tennessee Ernie Ford and Molly Bee with Cliffie Stone's Orchestra, written by Ernest Ford

Molly Bee, who would be a frequent guest on *The Jimmy Dean Show* along with Rowlf, joined Tennessee Ernie Ford for this 1953 release. A commentary on 1950s car culture, it implores youth to start courtin' "in a buggy like your mom and dad" (mostly because the engine's noise would drown out the sounds of whispered sweet nothings).

"The Ugly Duckling": Performed by Danny Kaye, written by Frank Loesser

Composed by Frank Loesser for Danny Kaye's 1952 picture *Hans Christian Andersen*, the song is a musical retelling of Andersen's 1843 fairy tale "The Ugly Duckling."

"Inchworm": Performed by Danny Kaye, written by Frank Loesser

Written for the film *Hans Christian Andersen*, the song is the story of a businesslike inchworm sung against a countermelody of an addition table. The song would later be performed twice on *The Muppet Show*, once by Charles Aznavour and once by Danny Kaye himself. (For more on this segment, see pages 128–129.)

Records transcribed on September 22, 1955

"Murder He Says": Performed by Betty Hutton with Pete Rugolo and His Orchestra, written by Frank Loesser, Jimmy McHugh

Frank Loesser, who would go on to write the songs for *Guys and Dolls* (1950) and *How to Succeed in Business Without Really Trying* (1961), teamed with Jimmy McHugh (whose credits include *The Muppet Show* classic "I Won't Dance" and hundreds of other tunes) to create this lively 1942 love song, which predated the 1945 Fred MacMurray film of the same title. In this song, the vocalist's dilemma is her man's vocabulary—his repeated use of slang words like "murder," "solid," "dig," and "Jackson."

"Smoke! Smoke! Smoke! (That Cigarette)": Performed by Phil Harris, written by Merle Travis, Tex Williams

This song is a quick-tempo critique of cigarette culture. As it was written in 1947, however, it does not criticize the health risks but rather the aggravation caused when cigarette smokers have to drop what they're doing to grab a smoke.

"The Handout Song (There's a Handout on Panhandle Hill)": Performed by Danny Kaye with orchestra directed by Sy Oliver, written by Dick Sanford, Sammy Mysels

Danny Kaye implores those in need to come to Panhandle Hill for a distribution of all sorts of free items made possible by the generosity of a suddenly wealthy hobo named Vanderbilt Norgen McGill. "His partner, Jim Doyle / stubbed his toe and struck oil / on the sands of old Panhandle Hill."

"Sipping Cider Through a Straw": Performed by The Elm City Four, Traditional

Dating to the late 1800s, this folk song opens with the line, "The prettiest girl I ever saw / was sipping cider through a straw." This was the start of a romance in which the song's central character ends up with nineteen children. Jim Henson used a recording by The Elm City Four, a Midwestern barbershop quartet whose members included Philip Reep, Claude Reese, Darrel Woodyard, and Hubie Hendry.

Records transcribed on September 29, 1955

"A Couple of Swells": Performed by Fred Astaire and Judy Garland, written by Irving Berlin

Written by Irving Berlin for the 1948 picture *Easter Parade,* the song was performed by Fred Astaire and Judy Garland as vaudevillians costumed as hobos, singing about their high-toned behavior.

"Can't Stop Talking": Performed by Betty Hutton, written by Frank Loesser

In this song, Betty Hutton sings at breakneck speed about how she can't stop talking about the man she adores. The song, written by Frank Loesser, was featured in the 1950 Betty Hutton/Fred Astaire film *Let's Dance.*

"No Ring on Her Finger": Performed by unknown barbershop quartet, written by Frank Loesser, Manning Sherwin

The song was written for the 1937 film *Blossoms on Broadway* and tells the story of poor little Daisy McGee, who waits by the church every day for the hosiery salesman who promised he would return for her. (She goes on to have similar experiences with a cold cream salesman and a gas meter reader.) Although Frank Loesser later worked by himself, creating both music and lyrics, at this early point in his career, he joined forces with several collaborators. On this tune, he worked with Manning Sherwin, who is probably best known as the co-author of "A Nightingale Sang in Berkeley Square."

"The Man Who Broke the Bank at Monte Carlo": Performed by The Del Monico Four, written by Fred Gilbert

An 1891 composition very popular in British music hall performances, the song tells the story of a lucky man who finds his way to wealth at Monte Carlo. This barbershop arrangement was recorded by The Del Monico Four.

"She Is More to Be Pitied Than Censured": Performed by unknown barbershop quartet, written by William B. Gray

The story of a "a girl who had fallen to shame," the song dates to 1898. We are told not to scorn the woman and laugh at her downfall but to remember that a man "was the cause of it all."

"Wait 'till the Sun Shines, Nellie": Performed by unknown barbershop quartet, written by Harry Von Tilzer, Andrew B. Sterling

Recorded many times since its introduction in 1905, the song had become popular again in the *Sam and Friends* era after the release of a film by the same name in 1952.

Records transcribed on October 13, 1955

"Lazy River": Performed by Phil Harris and His Orchestra, written by Hoagy Carmichael, Sidney Arodin

Phil Harris's recording of "Lazy River" is one of dozens of versions Jim could have chosen from. Louis Prima, Louis Armstrong, The Mills Brothers, The Ames Brothers, and co-composer Hoagy Carmichael all released their own interpretations.

"Silas Lee": Performed by Phil Harris and His Orchestra, written by Johnny Lange, Hy Heath

Although Phil Harris hailed from Indiana, he had a flair for delivering songs about the American South. This one is about a fiddling square dance caller from Tennessee named Silas Lee who turns a high-class fancy affair into a down-home jamboree.

"The Doughnut Song": Performed by Burl Ives with orchestra under the direction of Norman Leyden, written by Bob Merrill

Bob Merrill, whose later credits with Jule Styne include *Mister Magoo's Christmas Carol* (1962) and Broadway's *Funny Girl* (1964), wrote this song in 1950. The jaunty melody and lyrics convey a positive philosophy to "watch the doughnut, not the hole."

Records transcribed on October 19, 1955

"The Yellow Rose of Texas": Performed by Stan Freberg with Billy May's Orchestra (Yankee Snare Drumming: Alvin Stoller), original song written by Don George

As Kermit tries to get through his stirring Texas anthem, two overzealous musicians (a drummer and a banjo player) get carried away with their accompaniment. This 1955 Stan Freberg record was used on one of the Muppets' earliest network appearances on *The Steve Allen Show*.

Records transcribed on November 8, 1955

"Sixteen Tons": Performed by Tennessee Ernie Ford with orchestra conducted by Jack Fascinato, written by Merle Travis

The song, written and originally released by Merle Travis in 1947, was then covered by Tennessee Ernie Ford, whose version was released only weeks before Jim Henson had this transcription record made for use on *Sam and Friends*. Orchestra leader Jack Fascinato served as musical director for *Kukla, Fran and Ollie* until Burr Tillstrom switched networks from NBC to ABC in 1954. Fascinato remained at NBC and began working on Ford's recording and television projects. Later in his career, Fascinato composed music for some animated *Sesame Street* films.

"Atchoo (The Sneezing Record)": Performed by Joey Faye, written by Sam Carlton, Dan Dougherty

Vaudeville, Broadway, film, and television performer Joey Faye was known for being one of show business's funniest sneezers and released this song to take advantage of his unique talents. In it, Faye sneezes throughout and explains how his nonstop sneezing has ruined his life.

"You Laughed When I Cried Over You (The Laughing Record)": Performed by Joey Faye and Ralph Young, written by Cy Coben, Charles Grean

On the flip side of "The Sneezing Record," Joey Faye starts laughing uncontrollably as Ralph Young sincerely sings.

"After the Ball": Performed by The Del Monico Four, written by Charles K. Harris

An 1891 melancholy waltz, it tells the story of a brokenhearted man who never married because he saw his sweetheart kissing another man at a ball, only to learn many years later that the man was the woman's brother. It was one of the top sheet music sellers in history.

"Bill Bailey, Won't You Please Come Home": Performed by The Del Monico Four, written by Hughie Cannon

A 1902 composition, it was very popular among early twentieth-century jazz bands and vocalists. This barbershop quartet version by The Del Monico Four begins with the rarely sung verse:

On one summer's day, the sun was shining fine.
The lady love of old Bill Bailey was hanging clothes on the line
In her backyard and weeping hard.
She married a B&O brakeman that took and throw'd her down.
Bellering like a prune-fed calf with a big gang hanging 'round;
And to that crowd she yelled out loud:
Won't you come home, Bill Bailey . . .

"The Fountain in the Park": Performed by The Del Monico Four, written by Ed Haley

An 1884 composition, the song is best known not by its title but by its first line: "While strolling through the park one day . . ." As the song continues, its narrator (or narrators, as in this barbershop arrangement by The Del Monico Four) is "taken by surprise by a pair of roguish eyes." Kermit would go on to perform the tune in a sketch with Heather Locklear on *Muppets Tonight* in 1997.

Records transcribed on November 10, 1955

"Just a Bum (Ma Pomme)": Performed by Maurice Chevalier with Henri René and His Orchestra, written by Charles Borel-Clerc

Maurice Chevalier was a popular performer in France and America from the 1920s and '30s (when he was famous enough to be a major gag in the Marx Brothers' *Monkey Business* as the shipboard celebrity the Marx stowaways must impersonate to disembark) to the 1960s, when his career resurged with an appearance in MGM's *Gigi*. Jim had three Chevalier songs put on acetate on the same day.

"Place Pigalle": Performed by Maurice Chevalier, orchestra directed by Jacques Helian, written by Alex Alstone, Maurice Chevalier

Inspired by a Paris public square of the same name, "Place Pigalle" was recorded by Chevalier in 1946.

"Valentine": Performed by Maurice Chevalier with Henri René and His Orchestra, written by Henri Christiné, Albert Willemetz

Chevalier performed "Valentine" in French in Paramount's first musical, 1929's *Innocents of Paris*. The recording used on *Sam and Friends* is an English version of the romantic tune about a man's first love, a beautiful girl named Valentine. When the narrator runs into her years later, he does not recognize the much older woman.

"Barnacle Bill the Sailor": Performed by Candy Candido, written by Carson Robison, Frank Luther

"Barnacle Bill the Sailor" is based on a traditional folk song. This recording was made by Candy Candido, who was known for his ability to speak in very high and very low registers, which he does to great effect here. After comedy team Bud Abbott and Lou Costello split up, Abbott briefly teamed with Candido to form Abbott and Candido, but the new team played just a handful of live engagements.

Record transcribed on November 14, 1955

"Mad Dogs and Englishmen": Performed by Danny Kaye, written by Noël Coward

Introduced by Beatrice Lillie in a 1931 Broadway revue entitled *The Third Little Show,* the song would later be performed by not-quite-mad dogs Rowlf and Baskerville on the second season of *The Muppet Show*.

Records transcribed on December 13, 1955

"The Old Chimney": Performed by The Wilder Brothers, written by George Weidler, Walter Weidler, Warner Weidler, John N. Wilson

Sam and Friends would always bring in the holiday season with special music selections. This is a Christmas tune about Santa coming down "the old chimney."

"Santy's Movin' On": Performed by Homer and Jethro, written by Hank Snow, Homer Haynes, Jethro Burns

Homer and Jethro's guitar and mandolin accompany the story of Santy as he makes a variety of unlikely moves: "Santy was a sad old man / when he backed into the electric fan . . . he's movin' on."

"Santa Brought Me Choo Choo Trains (But Daddy's Having Fun)": Performed by Spike Jones and His City Slickers, vocal by George Rock, written by Bob Sadoff, Paul S. Lasky

In this song, a lucky kid gets the trains he wanted for Christmas, only to have his daddy (voiced by Thurl Ravenscroft) monopolize them.

"Santa Claus Looks Like My Daddy": Performed by Danny Kaye, written by Russ Carlyle, Art Sutton

Danny Kaye released this holiday song on Decca Records in 1951. In his little boy voice, Kaye sings about the startling resemblance between Santa Claus and his own father—except for his beard . . . and his red nose—and now, Santa is kissing his mother. It suddenly dawns on the kid that Santa seems to look different in every department store.

"I Tant Wait Till Quithmuth": Performed by Mel Blanc, orchestra conducted by Buddy Cole, written by Lois Jean Ridgely, Don Ricardo

Mel Blanc's enthusiastic little boy character can't wait for Christmas to arrive and sings about the gifts he wants to give his family: "I donna buy my mommy a house an' new fur coat / I donna buy my daddy some money 'cause he's bwoke."

"Christmas Chopsticks": Performed by Mel Blanc, orchestra conducted by Buddy Cole, written by Fred Heider

On the flip side of "I Tant Wait Till Quithmuth," in his little boy voice, Mel Blanc sings to the tune of "Chopsticks," then breaks into spoken word to offer his Christmas list, sprinkled with animal imitations.

Records transcribed on December 23, 1955

"The Little Fiddle (Symphony for Unstrung Tongue)": Performed by Danny Kaye with orchestra and sound effects under the direction of Johnny Green, written by Sylvia Fine

In a song composed by his wife, Sylvia Fine, Danny Kaye leads a tongue-twisting guide to the orchestra.

"Lucky Pierre" (from *New Faces of 1952*): Performed by Robert Clary, Virginia De Luce, Rosemary O'Reilly, Patricia Hammerlee, Bill Mullikin, written by Ronny Graham

Robert Clary, who plays the title character in this song and is best known as Corporal LeBeau on *Hogan's Heroes,* made his first big splash in *The New Faces of 1952* revue. Songwriter Ronny Graham had a long career as an actor, comedian, and screenwriter. His writing credits include collaborating with Mel Brooks on *Spaceballs* (1987) and writing seven episodes of *M*A*S*H.*

"Cry Me a River": Performed by Julie London, orchestra conducted by Felix Slatkin, written by Arthur Hamilton

This classic torch song was a big hit for Julie London, who would go on to a long run as Nurse Dixie McCall on the 1970s hit *Emergency!* alongside her husband, musician and songwriter Bobby Troup. On *Sam and Friends,* the song was lip-synced by Kermeena (played by Kermit) and shot through a fish-filled aquarium.

"When You See a Pretty Girl": Performed by Jerry Colonna, written by Ross Bagdasarian

With his big eyes and handlebar mustache, Colonna was like a human Muppet. A comic foil to Bob Hope for many years, Colonna appeared in many of Hope's radio and television programs, as well as on Hope's USO tours. This brief comic song written by the man who would go on to create *Alvin and the Chipmunks* ponders all the changes of behavior that can happen "when you see a pretty girl."

"Sifting, Whimpering Sands": Performed by Homer and Jethro, written by V. C. Gilbert, Mary M. Hadler Gilbert

This is a parody of "Shifting, Whispering Sands," a song/poem in which a gold prospector tells the story of his adventure and a very close call in the valley of the Shifting, Whispering Sands. In Homer and Jethro's version, the valley isn't as treacherous. Homer and Jethro exchange a series of observations about their experience: "And stopping to rest, I heard a tinkling, whispering sound. / It was the Good Humor Man, so I ordered a double dip of tutti frutti." One of the straight recordings of the song featured the voice of *Sam and Friends* regular Ken Nordine and the music of Billy Vaughn and His Orchestra.

"They Laid Him in the Ground": Performed by Homer and Jethro, written by Patrick McAdory

This 1955 record is a sad and doleful series of comic-tragic anecdotes all leading to a person's demise.

"The King's New Clothes": Performed by Danny Kaye, written by Frank Loesser

Written by Frank Loesser for the Samuel Goldwyn picture *Hans Christian Andersen*, the song is a musical retelling of Andersen's "The Emperor's New Clothes."

Records transcribed on January 8, 1956

"This is a Wife? (What is a Wife?)": Performed by Homer and Jethro, written by Gene Piller, Ruth Roberts, William Katz

Homer and Jethro provide a spoken-word commentary consisting entirely of wife jokes (with a few mother-in-law jokes for good measure). "When a wife says that she's got an open mind, it just means one thing. She's got a hole in her head." All of this is backed by a soft organ accompaniment.

"A Little Beauty": Performed by Art Carney and Friend, written by Ross Bagdasarian, arranged and conducted by Milton Delugg

The 1955 song begins as a straight number with Carney crooning to his "little beauty." But his girl's giggling fits push Carney into an over-the-top comic aggravation. Ross Bagdasarian (a.k.a. David Seville) wrote the song, which was arranged and conducted by Milton Delugg, the longtime NBC music director who became well known on camera as the bandleader on *The Gong Show*.

"The Trouble with Harry": Performed by Alfi and Harry (David Seville), written by Floyd Huddleston, Herbert Eiseman, Mark McIntyre

Alfred Hitchcock's movie of the same title inspired this novelty record from David Seville (a.k.a. Ross Bagdasarian) before the Chipmunks came along.

"Old MacDonald Had a Farm": Performed by The Sportsmen Quartet*, Traditional

This children's song goes back to 1917 and has been interpreted on many recordings. This one, likely performed by The Sportsmen Quartet, is more grown-up in nature and includes lines about Old MacDonald's golf game and the farmer's proverbial daughter. "And when he saw those salesmen there, e-i-e-i-o . . . / a boom-boom here, and a bang-bang there / Here a boom, there a bang, everywhere a buckshot."

* While the quartet performing this song sounds like The Sportsmen, it could not be confirmed that this recording was indeed made by the well-known quartet.

Records transcribed on January 16, 1956

"Outfox the Fox" (from *The Court Jester*): Performed by Danny Kaye with Jud Conlon Singers and Orchestra, written by Sylvia Fine, Sammy Cahn

The Paramount film *The Court Jester* (1955) was a triumph for Danny Kaye, memorable for its "Vessel with the Pestle" routine and a score filled with new songs. In "Outfox the Fox," Danny Kaye warns that no one can outfox the brave hero, the Black Fox.

"Too Young": Performed by Spike Jones and His City Slickers, vocal refrain by Sara Berner, Paul Frees, and the Jud Conlon Choir, written by Sylvia Dee, Sidney Lippman

Nat King Cole had a No. 1 hit with this song in 1951. Twenty-one years later, fourteen-year-old Donny Osmond had his own hit record cover of the tune. In this Spike Jones version, voice legend Paul Frees croons in a French accent as Sara Berner (best known as switchboard operator Mabel Flapsaddle on *The Jack Benny Program*) interrupts, calling the Frenchman a variety of famous movie star names (Cary, Errol, Clark, Gregory, etc.). After the first verse, the routine is switched with Berner singing and Frees calling out the names of female movie stars. All of this happens over a lush choral backing provided by Jud Conlon's choir, until, in true Spike Jones fashion, the record ends with a train crash.

Record transcribed on February 27, 1956

"The Book Was So Much Better Than the Picture": Performed by Jerry Lewis with orchestra conducted by Dick Stabile, written by Mel Leven

Although Dean Martin was the featured singer in their act, while they were still working as a team, Jerry Lewis signed with Capitol Records as a solo recording artist. This track was recorded on January 10, 1952, and is a rant about how different a movie is from the book it was based on.

Records transcribed on March 12, 1956

"Listen to the Gooney Bird": Performed by Homer and Jethro, written by Jethro Burns, Homer Haynes

In this comedic take on "Listen to the Mockingbird," Homer and Jethro sing about the unusual title character and its unique qualities: "Though she is a scrappy bird, she's an unhappy bird. / 'Cause she weighs three pounds and lays a five-pound egg."

"Good Ol' Mountain Dew": Performed by Kenny Roberts, Traditional

This folk standard refers to moonshine and not the neon-colored manufactured soft drink. Written during Prohibition, the song originally ended with a trial. When alcoholic beverages once again became legal, the song was overhauled. Rowlf the Dog would perform the song with Jimmy Dean on *The Jimmy Dean Show* in 1966.

Record transcribed on April 19, 1956

"Interview with Shorty Petterstein": Performed by Henry Jacobs, Professor Leaf Woodrow, written by Henry Jacobs

From the album *Radio Programme No. 1 Audio Collage: Henry Jacobs' Music and Folklore* (1955), this track is an "interview" with a jazz musician who blows a French horn. Shorty Petterstein was played by Henry Jacobs, a broadcaster and ethnomusicologist who frequently explored music history in both factual and satirical recordings. The record was later adapted into an animated film by Ernest Pintoff, who later won an Academy Award for his short *The Critic*.

Recorded on June 25, 1956

SKETCH: "Louis Looselid: Private Eye": A rare surviving recording of an original sketch from the *Footlight Theater* era, this hard-boiled detective parody features Kermit as Louis Looselid, a private eye hired by Lady Farthingham to locate her missing husband, Lord Farthingham. The trail leads to the stately Farthingham home, where Looselid immediately suspects the butler, Jarvis. "As a private eye, I'm always suspicious of the butler." But in this case, the butler didn't do it—the lord is found safe in the house but looking a little worse for the wear. "Just look at you. You look as if you slept in a barn for two days," says Lady Farthingham. "I did," he replies. The case closed, Looselid returns to his office, where his next adventure is teased—a face-off against his fiendish nemesis Dr. Boriarity. (It is unknown if further Louis Looselid adventures were presented.) The story of Lord Farthingham's disappearance was told in two parts, airing on consecutive days. As this predated Jim Henson's performances of vocals, the voices on this recording were most likely provided by Paul Arnold.

Record transcribed on June 25, 1956

"Old MacDonald Had a Farm" (with The Three Haircuts introduction): Performed by The Sportsmen Quartet, Traditional

This recording of "Old MacDonald" (see page 268) is preceded by a brief introduction excerpted from the record "You Are So Rare To

Me" by The Three Haircuts, a parody vocal trio consisting of Sid Caesar, Carl Reiner, and Howard Morris, who made several appearances on Caesar's *Your Show of Shows.*

Records transcribed on July 30, 1956

"Standing on the Corner" (from *The Most Happy Fella*): Performed by Andy Griffith with Glenn Osser and vocal group, written by Frank Loesser

A vocal group begins to sing the chorus of Frank Loesser's catchy tune and is interrupted by Andy Griffith from time to time so he can insert a quick word of wisdom in commentary to the song's lyrics.

"Silly Signs Song": Performed by Art Carney with Jimmy Carroll and His Orchestra and Chorus, written by Ervin Drake, Jimmy Shirl

Art Carney released this Columbia record in 1956, a jaunty comic number recounting some of the silly signs the singer has seen.

"Oh Boy! (Ain't It Great to Be Crazy)": Performed by Art Carney with Jimmy Carroll and His Orchestra and Chorus, written by Don George

On this, the flip side of "Silly Signs Song," Art Carney and a chorus of kids sing about the virtues of being crazy.

"Alfred the Airsick Eagle": Performed by Ray Heatherton with eagle courtesy of the Bronx Zoo, orchestra conducted by Archie Bleyer, written by Don Gohman, Lowell Salaway

Ray Heatherton (father of singer Joey Heatherton, who would work with Jim Henson on *The Perry Como Winter Show* in 1972) and a chorus of kids sing the tale of Alfred the Airsick Eagle.

Records transcribed on August 6, 1956

"Steamboat Bill": Performed by unknown vocal group, written by Leighton Bros., Ren Shields

This 1910 song, performed on *Sam and Friends* by an unidentified vocal group reminiscent of The Mills Brothers, has been recorded many times over the years. The tune is familiar to Disney fans as it was whistled by Mickey Mouse in the first sound cartoon, *Steamboat Willie* (1928).

"The Band Played On": Performed by unknown barbershop quartet, written by Charles Ward, John Palmer

Though no visual record exists, one can easily imagine the visuals this 1895 song inspired: "Casey would waltz with a strawberry blonde / and the band played on. / He'd glide 'cross the floor with the girl he adored / and the band played on. / But his brain was so loaded it nearly exploded; / The poor girl would shake with alarm. / He'd ne'er leave the girl with the strawberry curls / And the band played on."

"Goodbye My Lover, Goodbye": Performed by unknown barbershop quartet, written by T. H. Allen

This traditional song dates to the 1880s. Additional and alternate verses have been added through the years, but the general story remains the same—it is a farewell song sung from a departing boat to a lover on the shore.

"You're Not the Only Pebble on the Beach": Performed by unknown barbershop quartet, written by Stanley Carter, Harry Braisted

Published in 1896, the song offers a philosophy of life: "She's not the only pebble on the beach. / That is the sort of lesson you must teach. / If you want to win her hand / let the maiden understand / that she's not the only pebble on the beach."

"Be My Guest": Performed by Buddy Hackett and Alan Dale with orchestra directed by Dick Jacobs, written by Wilson Stone, Ad Edwards

Though he went on to a successful career as a solo comic, in the mid-1950s, Buddy Hackett attempted to team with singer Alan Dale as a Martin-and-Lewis-style team. This track and the next one constitutes their entire discography, released on one 45 record.

"Pardners": Performed by Buddy Hackett and Alan Dale with orchestra directed by Dick Jacobs, written by Jimmy Van Heusen, Sammy Cahn

This is the flip side of the 1956 Hackett/Dale record. Since Alan and Buddy were trying to be like Martin and Lewis, someone thought they should record the title song to Dean and Jerry's comedy *Pardners* (1956).

Record transcribed on November 21, 1956

"I Just Goofed": Performed by Ernie Englund and His Orchestra, written by Ernie Englund

In this song, punctuated by trumpet hits, the narrator describes his misstep with his date. "Now, what I should have said was, 'Baby, you got a face just like a heifer'—that's a cow, you know. / But now, now, I guess it's a little bit too late to be clever."

Records transcribed on December 5, 1956

"Egghead": Performed by Jill Corey with Jimmy Carroll and His Orchestra, written by Al Hoffman, Dick Manning, Milt Story

This 1956 song is a sweetly sung critique of a man who's smart, but not when it comes to certain things: "Come kiss me, Egghead, and you will learn a lot about an awful lot / because there's an awful lot you don't know." The song's co-author, Milt Story, was a well-known cartoonist who extended the Egghead concept with a line of 3D plastic "Egghead" premiums that could be found inside Kellogg's breakfast cereals.

"While the Lights are Low": Performed by The King Sisters, written by Ray Stanley

The King Sisters, six sibling big band singers who gained popularity in the 1930s, later transitioned to television and included more family members to create The King Family. The song is a romantic one with lots of cuddling and pressing of lips "while the lights are low."

Record transcribed on December 31, 1956

"'Erbert": Performed by The Naturals, orchestra conducted by LeRoy Holmes, written by Sam Denoff, Eugene Klavan

A song about "the chap what stole her heart away," the American song's choral hook revolves around the cockney-voiced singers dropping the H in Herbert's name. Although the record credits composers "Andrew" and "Donald," ASCAP records indicate that the song was written by *Dick Van Dyke Show* writer Sam Denoff and radio personality/author Eugene Klavan.

Records transcribed on January 2, 1957

"Sam's Song (The Happy Tune)": Performed by Vicki Benet, written by Lew Quadling, Jack Elliott

This lively tune was later performed as a U.K. spot in the fourth season of *The Muppet Show,* sung as a backstage serenade to the Muppets' later character named Sam—Sam the Eagle.

"The Party's Over": Performed by Doris Day with Frank De Vol and His Orchestra, written by Jule Styne, Betty Comden, Adolph Green

The song was written for the 1956 Broadway hit *Bells are Ringing*. The version used on *Sam and Friends* was recorded as a pop cover by Doris Day the same year.

"Dancing Chandelier": Performed by Sylvia Syms, written by Bob Hilliard, Philip Springer

A bright and up-tempo number, the song is about a party in the apartment above—hence, the dancing chandelier. The singer awaits a call from her lover to invite her to the festivities. Performer Sylvia Syms was a New York-based nightclub singer and recording artist.

"The Ballad of Roger Boom": Performed by The Voices of Walter Schumann, soloist Kenneth Harp, written by Bob Hilliard

Laden with sound effects and a comic vocal performance, this seems more like a Spike Jones record than a presentation by The

Voices of Walter Schumann, a group better known for their serious lush vocal harmonies. The song is about a man with an aptitude for blowing things up, a tune that the Muppets would certainly know how to visualize. Interestingly, two versions of this song came out in 1956. The other recording, titled simply "Roger Boom," was also performed by an unlikely orchestra—that of champagne music maker Lawrence Welk, with vocals by Larry Hooper. (Even Welk wanted to capitalize on the novelty song craze of the 1950s.) Subsequent *Sam and Friends* performances of the song would feature the more well-known Welk/Hooper recording.

"The Ballad of Sir Lancelot": Performed by The Naturals, orchestra conducted by LeRoy Holmes, written by Alan Lomax

This is a version of the closing theme for the U.K.-produced *Adventures of Sir Lancelot*, a television series that ran on NBC from 1956 to 1957.

Records transcribed on January 18, 1957

"Calico Pie": Performed by Dorothy Olsen, written by Jack Segal, Marvin Fisher

Dorothy Olsen, known as "the Singing Schoolteacher," released several records—primarily for children—after winning $25,000 on *Name That Tune* in 1955. *Billboard* described her "Calico Pie" as a "charming, lilting novelty that will appeal to the kiddies."

"Green Door": Performed by Jim Lowe, written by Bob Davie, Marvin Moore

Fozzie Bear would later perform "Green Door," a song about a wild (but secret) midnight party, in a fourth-season *Muppet Show* opening number.

"What Did He Say? (The Mumble Song)": Performed by the Deep River Boys, written by Charles Grean, Cy Coben

This is another version of "What Did He Say? (The Mumble Song)" (see page 236) as performed by the Deep River Boys, an African American quartet whose career spanned from the 1930s to the 1980s. The Deep River Boys recorded the song in 1948, one year after The Charioteers. We have no way of knowing if Jim switched versions for a reason, but he did go back to using The Charioteers' record after this.

"Roger Boom": Performed by Larry Hooper and Lawrence Welk, written by Bob Hilliard (see pages 276–277)

Records transcribed on January 29, 1957

"Hold 'em Joe": Performed by Harry Belafonte with Hugo Winterhalter and his Orchestra, written by Harry Thomas

The song was written for the Broadway revue *John Murray Anderson's Almanac* (1953). The show was notable for the Broadway debut of Harry Belafonte, who would later appear on one of the most memorable episodes of *The Muppet Show*.

"I Dreamed": Performed by Betty Johnson with Lew Douglas and His Orchestra, written by Charles Grean, Marvin Moore

Betty Johnson's long career began as a member of The Johnson Family Singers, a North Carolina-based gospel group. "I Dreamed" was the biggest hit of her solo career, which has continued into the twenty-first century. The song was written by Charles Grean ("The Thing," "What Did He Say?" "The Musicians"), who happened to be married to Johnson for a brief time. The song is a lively tune in which the singer recalls a series of adventurous and romantic dreams.

"Mama from the Train (Throw Mama Down the Stairs Her Hat of Blue)": Performed by Homer and Jethro, written by Irving Gordon

Homer and Jethro took the song "Mama from the Train (A Kiss, a Kiss)" and gave it their own spin, changing the sentimental song about throwing a kiss to a beloved mother from a departing train into a song about literally throwing a mother-in-law from a train ... and down the stairs.

"Goodnight Ladies": Performed by The Sportsmen Quartet, written by Edwin Pearce Christy

The Sportsmen released this arrangement of the mid-1800s folk song in 1948 and performed it on radio and television. The song was once again popularized in 1957 when Meredith Willson incorporated it into his musical *The Music Man*.

Records transcribed on February 7, 1957

"The Maladjusted Jester": Performed by Danny Kaye, written by Sylvia Fine

Written for Danny Kaye's *The Court Jester* (1955) by his wife, Sylvia Fine, the song is the story of how a jester becomes a jester. After trying many occupations, a hapless person uncertain of his future decides to literally "make a fool of myself."

"Pum-Pa-Lum (The Bad Donkey)": Performed by Steve Lawrence with chorus and orchestra directed by Dick Jacobs, written by Al Wood

This song is about a naughty donkey in Kingston, Jamaica, performed by that unlikely performer of island music, Steve Lawrence.

"Old King Cole": Performer unknown, Traditional

Nursery rhymes like this one became an ongoing source of inspiration for Jim Henson. "Old King Cole" appeared in a *"Sesame Street News"* segment as well as an episode of *Mother Goose Stories*. This children's record (and the next track listed) are brightly sung choral arrangements by an unidentified group.

"Three Blind Mice": Performer unknown, Traditional

A children's nursery rhyme used for years as *The Three Stooges'* theme, "Three Blind Mice" showed up in an early *Sesame Street* Muppet insert.

Records transcribed on February 21, 1957

"M.T.A. (The Boston Subway Song)": Performed by Will Holt, written by Bess Hawes, Jacqueline Steiner

This song, protesting transit fare increases, tells the story of a man named Charlie, "the man who never returned," who is forever riding the Boston subway because he could not pay a five-cent exit charge. In 2006, the Massachusetts Bay Transit Authority named its contactless smart card the CharlieCard in honor of the song's central character.

"Round and Round": Performed by Perry Como with Mitchell Ayres and His Orchestra and The Ray Charles Singers, written by Lou Stallman, Joe Shapiro, arranged by Joe Reisman, Ray Charles

An up-tempo Perry Como vocal with choral backing, the song directs the listener to find a wheel and follow its path as it "leads you to the one you love." Once you get there, find a ring and put it on the "one you've found, found, found." Recording artist Perry Como would later welcome the Muppets to his television specials in 1965 and 1972. He joined Julie Andrews for *Julie on Sesame Street* in 1973.

"Stone Cold Dead in the Market (He Had It Coming)": Performed by Ella Fitzgerald, Louis Jordan and his Tympany Five, written by Wilmoth Houdini

The legendary Ella Fitzgerald and Louis Jordan sing of a domestic conflict born out of a woman's revenge on her abusive husband. The tragic outcome is wrapped in a bright tempo tune sung with West African accents.

Records transcribed on April 1, 1957

"The House": Performed by The Four Tophatters, orchestra conducted by Archie Bleyer, written by Sonny Curtis, Bob Schell, Fred Weismantel

The song tells the story of a crazy house "built from the upstairs down." (Co-writer Sonny Curtis would go on to write "I Fought the Law" and the theme to *The Mary Tyler Moore Show*.)

"The Cricket Song": Performed by Ray Bolger with orchestra and chorus directed by Sy Oliver, written by Bobby Gimby, Johnny Wayne

Ray Bolger sings about the sweet song of the cricket. The chirping cricket featured in the "duet" was named Davy Cricket, a reference to Disney's popular 1950s *Davy Crockett* television show. This tune was the flip side of "Once in Love with Amy," also recorded by Ray Bolger, who is best known for starring as the Scarecrow in *The Wizard of Oz* (1939).

"Dreamers' Bay": Performed by Patience and Prudence with the Mark McIntyre Orchestra, written by George McConnell, Harold Spina

Patience Ann McIntyre and Prudence Ann McIntyre were fourteen and eleven years old, respectively, when they first entered a recording studio. The children of orchestra leader Mark McIntyre, the sisters recorded sporadically between 1956 and 1965 before retiring from show business. "Dreamers' Bay" is a wistful tune that sounds like the result of combining "Moonlight Bay" and "On the Good Ship Lollipop."

"I'm Popeye the Sailor Man": Performed by Spike Jones and His City Slickers, vocals by Windy Cook, Mary Virginia, written by Sammy Lerner

Popeye's theme dates to the debut of his Max Fleischer animated cartoons in 1933, and in it, the sailor announces to the world that he is "strong to the finich 'cause I eats me spinach." Though the most famous version is performed by Popeye's longtime voice artist Jack Mercer, the recording Jim used was released by Spike Jones and His City Slickers in 1957 on Verve Records, with Windy Cook providing the Popeye vocal and Mary Virginia as Olive Oyl.

Live broadcast: April 8, 1957

GUEST STAR: Stan Freberg

No documentation survives, but Bernie Harrison of *The Evening Star* reported that "Stan Freberg, the old puppeteer, really flipped over WRC's Muppets, whom he had never seen prior to his Monday night visit. He was especially taken with Kermit and Harry and his only disappointment Monday was that time ran out before he could pay his proper respects." According to Freberg's recollection, the appearance involved him poking his head into frame and asking the Muppets for credit for using his records in their broadcasts only to receive a mallet hit to the head.

Live broadcast: May 27, 1957 (11:25 p.m.)

INTRO: Paul Arnold is with Sam as Paul discusses the "Festival of Magic," an episode of NBC's *Producers' Showcase* that aired earlier that evening. Paul is disappointed that the *Sam and Friends* gang didn't get the call to perform along with the world's greatest magicians. He is certain he could have gotten them booked in the festival if he sawed Sam in half. "Of course, that's been done so often," says Paul, as he gets an idea for a great new trick. Paul picks up an axe—and Sam disappears quickly. One of the magical stars of the "Festival of Magic," Milbourne Christopher, had appeared on *Sam and Friends* in March.

THEME/OPEN

MUPPET SONG: "The Maladjusted Jester": Performed by Danny Kaye, written by Sylvia Fine (see page 279)

OUTRO: Paul is still trying to come up with a magic trick. He suggests the bullet catch but can't get anyone to give it a try.

Records transcribed on July 24, 1957

"S-S-S'Wonderful (Hector the Nearsighted Rattlesnake)": Performed by The Kirby Stone Four, snake rattle played by Archie Bleyer, orchestra conducted by Archie Bleyer, written by George and Ira Gershwin

This record turns the Gershwins' standard "'S Wonderful," written for the 1927 musical *Funny Face,* into a novelty song, extending the "s" sound into a snake hiss delivered by Hector, a nearsighted rattlesnake.

"Ivy League": Performed by Tennessee Ernie Ford with orchestra conducted by Jack Fascinato, written by Tennessee Ernie Ford, Jack Fascinato

A commentary on the "Ivy League look" as defined by Brooks Brothers and other high-class clothiers, this song is about a man who purchases some new threads and feels transformed—like a real Ivy Leaguer.

"Gotta Get to Your House": Performed by David Seville, written by Skipper Adams

This is a simple and repetitive song in which the singer has a driving intention to "gotta get to your house" and starts to get flustered and confused as the song goes on.

"Dragnet Goes to Kindergarten": Performed by Ricky Vera, orchestra directed by George Cates, written by Walter Schumann, special dialogue by Steve Allen.

Jack Webb's hit crime drama was always ripe for parody. This one was created by Steve Allen and narrated by child actor Ricky Vera. Instead of Jack Webb as Joe Friday, this record gives us young Ricky Vera as Detective Saturday Morning, who is trying to track down his missing lollipop as his dry narration and interrogation efforts are accompanied by authentic *Dragnet* theme music and underscore.

Live broadcast: August 15, 1957

GUEST STAR: Bob Hope

On this date, Bob Hope came to WRC-TV, and although there is no script or audio recording to document it, a newspaper article mentions that he would be appearing on *Sam and Friends* on this date.

Live broadcast: August 19, 1957

COLD OPEN: Paul Arnold has loaned his watch to Sam, who has loaned it to Professor Madcliffe. Paul wonders if that has something to do with the fact that Professor Madcliffe has been asking around to borrow a watch spring.

THEME/OPEN

INTRO: Paul sends Sam to Professor Madcliffe for the watch.

PAUL ARNOLD SONG

MUPPET SONG: "I Just Goofed": Performed by Ernie Englund and His Orchestra, written by Ernie Englund

Mushmellon lip-syncs to the song (see pages 274-275).

SKETCH: Professor Madcliffe tells Paul that his watch wasn't very good—it fell apart as soon as he took the back off. Madcliffe agrees to repair the watch.

MUPPET SONG: "The Maladjusted Jester": Performed by Danny Kaye (Kermit), written by Sylvia Fine (see page 279)

Live broadcast: August 20, 1957

COLD OPEN: Paul Arnold misses his watch, and he's not happy with the replacement—an alarm clock strapped to his wrist.

THEME/OPEN

PAUL SPEAKS/SINGS/INTRO

MUPPET SONG: "Zip Zip": Performed by The Diamonds, written by Anthony Colombo, Barry Kaye, Harry Booros

In this song, the lead singer of the quartet describes his girl as his "Zip Zip" who makes him "flip flip." The 1957 record was performed by The Diamonds, a Canadian group formed in 1953.

SKETCH: Paul asks Professor Madcliffe how long it will take to repair his watch. The Professor is upset by the constant interruptions. "I wish you wouldn't bother me with your problems; I have problems of my own. Right now I have a watch to fix."

Records transcribed on August 28, 1957

"Person to Pearson": Performed by Stan Freberg and Daws Butler, music by George Bruns, written by Stan Freberg, Daws Butler

A parody of Edward R. Murrow's *Person to Person,* this 1954 Stan Freberg comedy track is an interview between Freberg's Edward N. Nonymous and Daws Butler's J. Pierrepoint Pearson, a man who sleeps behind the A&P store—because they kicked him out from sleeping behind the Piggly Wiggly. Daws Butler was a frequent Freberg collaborator but is probably best known as a Hanna-Barbera voice artist. The voice he uses on this track is similar to that of Elroy Jetson. The Muppets would lip-sync to another *Person to Person* parody when Spike Jones's "Poisen to Poisen" is released in 1959.

"The Drummer and the Cook": Performed by Harry Belafonte, written by Paul Campbell

In this folk song dating to the mid-1800s, Belafonte sings of a clandestine relationship between a drummer and a one-eyed cook.

"The Man on the Flying Trapeze": Performed by Spike Jones and His City Slickers, commentary by Doodles Weaver, written by Alfred Lee, George Leybourne, arranged by Spike Jones and Doodles Weaver

Written in 1867, the circus-themed song's refrain is still known today: "He'd fly through the air with the greatest of ease / That daring young man on the flying trapeze." The Spike Jones version's vocalist, Doodles Weaver, is tongue-tied throughout, turning the lyrics into an endless string of spoonerisms: "He floats by his hair with plates full of cheese . . ." The parody originated with comic actor Joe Twerp on the 1935 radio show *Komedie Kapers.* Doodles Weaver began performing his version in nightclubs in 1944 before recording it for RCA with Spike

Jones and His City Slickers in 1947 for release the following year. In the fourth season of *The Muppet Show,* Miss Piggy begins to sing the song with Kermit performing as the title character. She doesn't get a chance to finish because Kermit's act ends abruptly with a fall.

"It's Magic": Performed by Jonathan and Darlene Edwards (Paul Weston and Jo Stafford), written by Jule Styne, Sammy Cahn

The performing duo of Jonathan and Darlene Edwards was a purposely bad lounge-singing act that was created by the actually good musician Paul Weston and his talented wife, singer Jo Stafford. After entertaining friends at parties with the characters, they recorded several albums, keeping their identities secret for as long as they could. As Jonathan and Darlene Edwards, Weston played the songs in rhythmically unique ways while Stafford sang off-key. The song "It's Magic" was introduced in the 1948 film *Romance on the High Seas*. Appropriately, when illusionist Doug Henning appeared on *The Muppet Show,* "It's Magic" was performed by Miss Piggy while Kermit magically disappeared and reappeared all around her.

Record transcribed on January 11, 1958

"Old Man Atom": Performed by Sons of the Pioneers, written by Vern Partlow, Irving Bibo

The song is a rarity for the 1950s—a country-western song about modern technology. It is a cautionary tale about atomic energy that ends with, "So listen folks, here is my thesis: / Peace in the world or the world in pieces!"

Record transcribed on January 14, 1958

"The Green-Eyed Dragon": Performed by John Charles Thomas, written by Greatrex Newman, Wolseley Charles

Broadway and opera baritone John Charles Thomas released this song in the 1930s. It's a fast-paced fairy tale about a thirteen-tailed dragon who stands guard at a castle and feasts on such delights as little boys, puppy dogs, and big fat snails. While John Charles Thomas had a varied repertoire, he had a great animosity toward the new fad of rock 'n' roll music and spoke out against the subject in two appearances on Groucho Marx's *You Bet Your Life* in 1957.

Record transcribed on January 29, 1958

"Silhouettes": Performed by Andy Griffith, orchestra under direction of Billy May, written by Frank C. Slay, Jr., Bob Crewe, special material by Andy Griffith and Ainslie Pryor

The song at the center of this recording is "Silhouettes," the story of a romance as glimpsed from the outside of a house through a closed window shade. The original version was released by a group called The Rays, but in this version, an unnamed doo-wop group sings the song as the pre-Mayberry Andy Griffith periodically interrupts to analyze the action from his folksy point of view.

"How Do'ye Do and Shake Hands": Performed by Betty Hutton, Dinah Shore, Tony Martin, Phil Harris, with Henri René and His Orchestra, written by Cy Coben and Oliver Wallace (see page 252)

Records transcribed on April 15, 1958

"Income Tax": Performed by Bob Corley, written by Bob Corley

Sam and Friends celebrated income Tax Day with a performance to this 1956 spoken-word record. Comedian Bob Corley delivers an

Andy Griffith-style monologue, playing a moonshiner recounting the time he tried to get help with his income tax return.

"Perfidia": Performed by Count Von Blitzstein, written by Alberto Dominguez, Milton Leeds

In this 1958 novelty tune, a performer billed only as "Count Von Blitzstein" badly plays and sings the tune "Perfidia" in a restaurant as a desperate French waiter implores him to stop because the customers are leaving.

Record transcribed on June 10, 1958

"The Country's in the Very Best of Hands": Performed by *Li'l Abner* Original Broadway Cast (featuring Stubby Kaye), written by Johnny Mercer, Gene de Paul

Although this song lists a lot of bad behavior and aggravating political situations, the title refrain emphasizes a positive outlook. The Broadway production of *Li'l Abner* opened in 1956, and Jim had seen the Broadway production on a trip to New York.

The following records were transcribed and would have been performed after Jim Henson left for Europe on June 19, 1958:

Records transcribed on July 28, 1958

"She's a Lady": Performed by Betty Hutton and Perry Como with Mitchell Ayres and His Orchestra, written by Cy Coben

In this song, Betty Hutton insists she's a high-class lady, but her vocal performance and lyrics say otherwise. Conversely, Perry Como's side of the duet expresses his less-than-stellar behavior.

"Anything You Can Do (I Can Do Better)": Performed by *Annie Get Your Gun* Original Broadway Cast (featuring Ethel Merman and Ray Middleton), written by Irving Berlin

The Muppets lip-synced to Ethel Merman on *Sam and Friends,* but Merman showed up in person in the first season of *The Muppet Show,* performing a duet of her showstoppers with Kermit the Frog, who momentarily took offense when, in "You're the Top," Merman compared him to "Mickey Mouse."

"The Musicians": Performed by Dinah Shore, Betty Hutton, Tony Martin, Phil Harris, with Henri René and His Orchestra, written by Charles Grean, Tom Glazer (see page 250)

"John Henry": Performed by Harry Belafonte, accompanied by Millard Thomas, guitar, written by Paul Campbell

The legend of "steel-driving man" John Henry is said to be based on a real railroad worker who raced against a steam drill. The folk song about his story was sung by many artists. This Harry Belafonte version was recorded in 1954. Credited writer Paul Campbell was actually a collective pseudonym for the folk group The Weavers. One of the group's members, Pete Seeger, would later perform "John Henry" on *Sesame Street.*

"This Ole World": Performed by Stuart Hamblen, written by Stuart Hamblen

A more global take on the popular song "This Ole House," also written by country singer-songwriter Stuart Hamblen, the lyrics tell the story of the narrator, who is tired of the numerous changes that have beset "this ole world" and decides to leave it in a mighty rocket.

"Rock Island Line": Performed by Stan Freberg and His Sniffle Group, interruptions by Peter Leeds, written by Lonnie Donegan, special arrangement by Stan Freberg

Right down to parodying the name of Lonnie Donegan's group (Lonnie Donegan and His Skiffle Group), Stan Freberg targets Donegan's 1955 recording of the classic folk song, which begins with a rather extended spoken introduction. In Freberg's version, introduced the year after Donegan's record, the introduction goes on so long that it's interrupted by a record producer (Peter Leeds) asking him if he's actually going to sing the song or just read it.

"Yosemite Sam": Performed by Mel Blanc, music by Billy May, written by Alan Livingston, Billy May

Mel Blanc brought his popular Warner Bros. cartoon character to Capitol Records with this 1951 single extolling the virtues of Sam's shooting skills—particularly when ducks and rabbits are involved. Orchestra leader Billy May, a frequent Stan Freberg collaborator, teamed with Alan Livingston to write the song. Livingston, who created Bozo the Clown for the record label, went on to a long career as an executive for Capitol Records and NBC.

"Life Gits Tee-Jus, Don't It?": Performed by Peter Lind Hayes, written by Carson Robison

Entertainer Peter Lind Hayes delivers a casual monologue about the little things in life. The song would go on to be performed by the Muppets' own Gogolala Jubilee Jugband on a first-season episode of *The Muppet Show*.

The following records were transcribed after Jim returned home on August 2, 1958.

Record transcribed on August 8, 1958

"Elderly Man River": Performed by Stan Freberg, Daws Butler, written by Jerome Kern, Oscar Hammerstein II, Pete Barnum, Stan Freberg

In a segment from Stan Freberg's 1957 CBS network radio show, Freberg's performance of "Old Man River" is interrupted by a censor from the "Citizens' Radio Committee" whenever a questionable word is uttered. This forces Stan to improvise quick, inoffensive, and grammatically correct fixes throughout.

Records transcribed on August 13, 1958

"Jubilation T. Cornpone": Performed by *Li'l Abner* Original Broadway Cast (featuring Stubby Kaye), written by Johnny Mercer, Gene de Paul

A showstopper for *Guys and Dolls* veteran Stubby Kaye, the song tells the story of Dogpatch's Civil War hero, who in actuality did very little that was heroic.

The cast of the Broadway production of Li'l Abner, as photographed by Jim Henson.

"None But the Lonely Heart": Performed by Spike Jones and His City Slickers with Helen Grayco, violin solo by Dick Gardner, written by Peter Tchaikovsky, arranged by Eddie Brandt, Spike Jones

With background music by Tchaikovsky, this Spike Jones 1949 RCA Victor release begins as a "Soaperetta" in which vocalist Helen Grayco's Mary suggests she and her lover John (Jones) must part: "You have another wife, and I have another husband, and he has another wife, and she has another husband." The record then descends into typical Spike Jones horn music and man-made sound effects before allowing John's rebuttal, in which, despite all of the excess husbands and wives, he urges reconciliation. Mary refuses, as she's about to be married. Vocalist Helen Grayco was Spike Jones's wife.

Records transcribed on August 21, 1958

"Etiquette Blues": Performed by Butch Stone, orchestra conducted by Van Alexander, written by Gayle Grubb (see page 235)

"To Keep My Love Alive": Performed by Ella Fitzgerald, written by Richard Rodgers, Lorenz Hart

The song was written by Rodgers and Hart for a 1943 revival of *A Connecticut Yankee*. In it, the character Morgan le Fay sings about the various ways she eliminated her fifteen husbands, all in the interest of keeping her love alive.

Records transcribed on September 8, 1958

"Abominable Snowman": Performed by Stan Freberg, written by Stan Freberg

In this excerpt from Freberg's 1957 radio show, Stan interviews the Abominable Snowman (also voiced by Freberg), who discusses his taste in sneakers (size 23) and the finer points of terrorizing mountain climbers.

"Oh, Happy Day": Performed by *Li'l Abner* Original Broadway Cast, written by Johnny Mercer, Gene de Paul

From the musical *Li'l Abner,* the song is sung by a group of scientists who imagine the joy of a future that would be completely run by science.

Records transcribed on September 18, 1958

"The Peony Bush": Performed by Danny Kaye, written by Meredith Willson

Meredith Willson wrote "Peony Bush" in 1949, about eight years before his hit musical *The Music Man* opened on Broadway. The song hails the virtues of a peony bush in the singer's garden, which attracts the eye of the object of his affection. Danny Kaye, whose vocals on "Peony Bush" alternated from soft and gentle vocals to loud and boisterous interludes, was Willson's first choice to play Professor Harold Hill, but he declined the role.

"Dinah": Performed by Danny Kaye, written by Harry Akst, Sam M. Lewis, Joe Young

The song "Dinah," published in 1925, was recorded by many artists, including Ethel Waters (who introduced it), Louis Armstrong, Bing Crosby and The Mills Brothers, and Thelonious Monk. Danny Kaye's version is notable for the extended scat-singing interlude and his pronunciation of the title character (and all associated rhyming words) as "Dena," which, perhaps not coincidentally, is the name of his daughter.

"Ain't Nobody's Business But My Own": Performed by Tennessee Ernie Ford, Dorothy Gill, conducted by Jack Fascinato, written by Tennessee Ernie Ford, Irving Taylor

Tennessee Ernie Ford recorded two versions of this song, one with Dorothy Gill and another with Kay Starr. The song is a lively duet—essentially a sung argument between a couple. When each is reminded by the other of an infraction, the response is "It ain't nobody's business but my own."

"You Can't Hurt Me Now Cuz I'm Daid": Performed by Hank Fort, written by Hank Fort, C. Murray, B. Jacobson

Hank Fort, born Eleanor Louise Middleton Hankins, had a long career both as a performer and a songwriter with more than four hundred songs to her credit. In this one, the figuratively dead narrator explains that her man can't hurt her now—and if he proposes marriage, she'll come back to life; if not, she'll remain dead to him.

"There's a New Sound": Performed by Tony Burrello, written by Tony Burrello, Tom Murray (see page 74)

Recorded by Jim Henson on September 19, 1958

SKETCH: "Drain Dweller": Harry announces a public service feature of the program, introducing correspondent Kermit with his traveling microphone speaking from the kitchen of a fashionable Northwest Washington, D.C., restaurant and interviewing Orwell Filchmouth, a drain dweller who lives in the U-shaped part of the drainpipe under the kitchen sink. Filchmouth discusses the hazards of living in such a precarious location. The interview concludes with Orwell leaving a parting thought: "Next time you look down the drain and see someone looking back—just remember that a home isn't a home without a watchdog at night, a cricket on the hearth, and a drain dweller in the drain."

Records transcribed on September 23, 1958

"Sincere": Performed by *The Music Man* Original Broadway Cast (featuring The Buffalo Bills), written by Meredith Willson

The Buffalo Bills was an existing barbershop quartet in Buffalo, New York, when they were hired to play the singing school board in Meredith Willson's *The Music Man* on Broadway. Several of the quartet's records were used on *Sam and Friends*.

"The Sadder-But-Wiser Girl" Performed by *The Music Man* Original Broadway Cast (featuring Robert Preston), written by Meredith Willson

In this song from *The Music Man,* Professor Harold Hill explains his philosophy regarding women: "I spark, I fizz, for the lady who knows what time it is. / I cheer, I rave, for the virtue I'm too late to save." Robert Preston was best known as a dramatic film actor before playing Harold Hill.

Record transcribed on September 24, 1958

"Lullaby of Bird Dog" (long and short version): Performed by Homer and Jethro, song written by George Shearing

Homer and Jethro take on jazz as they shake up George Shearing's "Lullaby of Birdland," adding words to turn it into a song about trying to identify the breed of a bird dog. "Can it be that he's a basset hound / built too close to the ground? / Lullaby of bird dog / this can't be Lassie, I know. / This is Joe!"

Recorded by Jim Henson on September 26, 1958, re-edited for length, October 20, 1958

SKETCH: "Ghost Interview": Kermit conducts a live interview from Gabriel Park Memorial Cemetery with the ghost of Lord Randall Worthington. (See pages 173–183 for the full script.)

Recorded by Jim Henson on October 1, 1958, second take on October 2, 1958

SKETCH: "Madcliffe Interview": Kermit interviews Professor Madcliffe about his specialty—failure. (For more on this episode, see page 45.)

Moldy Hay performs "Pachalafaka"

Records transcribed on October 20, 1958

"Pachalafaka": Performed by Earl Brown, written by Irving Taylor

A song later used on *The Muppet Show*, "Pachalafaka" was introduced on composer Irving Taylor's album *Terribly Sophisticated Songs*, released the same year it made its *Sam and Friends* debut. According to the song, the word "pachalafaka" is a tender word of love and gives the singer a thrill unlike any other romantic phrase, but by the end of the tune, we find out that he really doesn't know the meaning of the word.

"G'wan Home, Your Mudder's Callin'": Performed by Jimmy Durante, written by Ralph Freed, Sammy Fain

This song, sung by Jimmy Durante from a tough kid's point of view, is the story of a kid being summoned home. "G'wan home, your mudder's callin' / your father got caught in the wash machine. / G'wan home, your mudder's bawlin' / she can't get the laundry out clean."

Records transcribed on November 8, 1958

"Salt": Performed by The Vagabonds, written by Jack Adrian (a.k.a. Adrian Greenberg) (see page 89)

"What Did He Say? (The Mumble Song)": Performed by The Charioteers, written by Charles Grean, Cy Coben (see page 236)

"I Love Me (I'm Wild About Myself)": Performed by Mel Blanc, written by Edwin J. Weber, Will Mahoney, Jack Hains

First released as a Capitol single in 1953, Mel Blanc's recording is an unrepentant celebration of self. It was earlier recorded in 1923 by vaudeville artist Billy Murray.

Records transcribed on September 3, (year unknown)

"Good Old 149": Performed by Danny Kaye, writer unknown

Danny Kaye attended New York's Public School 149 and celebrated his alma mater in 1953 by releasing his performance of the school's fight song on Decca. The school, located in Brooklyn, is now named after Kaye.

"Tschaikowsky (And Other Russians)": Performed by Danny Kaye, written by Ira Gershwin, Kurt Weill

Danny Kaye introduced this song in the Broadway musical *Lady in the Dark* in 1941. Delivered at breakneck speed, the song is simply a list of the names of Russian composers.

Undated transcriptions

"Sh-Boom": Performed by Stan Freberg with The Toads and orchestra conducted by Billy May, written by James Keyes, Claude Feaster, Carl Feaster, Floyd F. McRae, William Edwards

In this 1954 recording, Stan Freberg does his best to urge the vocal group to be as unintelligible as possible when singing the lyrics and blows a whistle when he can actually understand the words.

"Banana Boat (Day-O)": Performed by Stan Freberg, interruptions by Peter Leeds with Billy May's Music, written by Stan Freberg

Immediately following Stan Freberg's opening shout of "Day-O!," he is repeatedly restrained and shushed by a hip, laid-back, bongo-playing musician: "Wow, man. I'll have to ask you not to shout like that. It's, like, right in my ear, man." This goes on throughout the entire song. The Freberg single was released in 1957, the year after Harry Belafonte's version was a Top 10 hit. When Belafonte appeared on *The Muppet Show,* he also could not get through a performance of this, his trademark song, without several interruptions.

"My Future Just Passed": Performed by Don Cherry with Ray Conniff and His Orchestra, written by George Marion, Jr., Richard Whiting

In this tune, the singer sees a girl walk by and imagines her to be the girl of his dreams—his future. He doesn't muster up the courage to speak to her, but the song ends with him deciding to follow her home to see where she lives, thus, the invention of the stalker.

"Six Months Out of Every Year": Performed by *Damn Yankees* Original Broadway Cast (featuring Shannon Bolin), written by Richard Adler, Jerry Ross

In this song from *Damn Yankees,* Meg Boyd laments the six months out of every year that the baseball season keeps her husband's attention from her.

"Swan Lake": Performed by Andy Griffith, written by Andy Griffith

In this comic monologue, recorded live at an engagement in Nashville, Griffith describes the action of the ballet *Swan Lake* from his homespun, Southern perspective.

"Face the Funnies": Performed by Stan Freberg, Daws Butler, June Foray, Peter Leeds, written by Stan Freberg, Pete Barnum

An excerpt from Stan Freberg's CBS radio series, "Face the Funnies" is a parody of panel discussion programs but focusing on fictional characters and the probing questions surrounding them: "Does or does not Orphan Annie have more than one red dress?" Heard among the panelists are Peter Leeds and cartoon voice legends Daws Butler and June Foray.

"Sam, Don't Slam the Door!": Performed by Ray McKinley and His Orchestra, written by Sammy Marks, Gene Gifford

Bandleader Ray McKinley plays this swing number, a warning to Sam that if he slams the door, he "ain't gonna be 'round here anymore."

"I'm a Lonely Little Petunia (in an Onion Patch)": Performed by The Smith Bros. with Sid Bass and His Orchestra, written by Billy Faber, Johnny Kamano, Maurie Hartmann

This is a simple, lilting novelty tune about a lonely little petunia. Being in an onion patch, all it does is cry all day.

Yorick (the Lonely Petunia) in an onion patch.

"I Got the Shiniest Mouth in Town": Performed by Butch Stone with Les Brown and His Band of Renown, written by Stan Freberg

One of the few songs written by Stan Freberg and not recorded by him, the song is a boastful proclamation of the quality of the singer's smile—gold bridgework and all. Performer Butch Stone was a sax player and vocalist who started out with Van Alexander's orchestra and joined up with Les Brown in 1941.

"Rain No More": Performed by The Honey Dreamers, written by Bob Davis

Based on the traditional folk song, this 1957 recording was described in a music trade publication as a "refreshing and exciting new version of the familiar oldie." The calypso-flavored arrangement was performed by The Honey Dreamers, a vocal quintet (three men and two women) first formed in the mid-1940s. The group's Keith Textor would go on to work with Jim, writing music for several of his *Sesame Street* counting films, including "The King of Eight," and arranging the music for *The Muppets Valentine Show* (1974).

"Muskrat": Performed by Merle Travis, written by Harold Hensley, Merle Travis, Tex Ann

Country singing legend Merle Travis sings this children's song with successive verses about the muskrat, groundhog, rooster, jaybird, and tomcat.

"What'd He Say?": Performed by Joe Reisman and His Orchestra and Chorus, written by Lee Pockriss, Paul Vance

Not to be confused with "What Did He Say? (The Mumble Song)," also used on *Sam and Friends,* this song was a 1958 novelty record composed by the same team who would go on to create "Itsy Bitsy Teenie Weenie Yellow Polka Dot Bikini." This song has a similar premise as "What Did He Say? (The Mumble Song)"—there's this guy who can't be understood, but in this case, the person doesn't mumble—he lapses into chipmunk-like sped-up sound.

∗∗∗

Note: From this point on, Jim Henson preserved audio of the live *Sam and Friends* broadcasts, and those episodes summarized here are arranged by their airdate. Eventually, Jim only recorded the initial broadcasts of musical lip-sync performances and not their subsequent uses, so there are gaps in airdates. Also, when he began this process, Jim methodically spoke the air date on the tape before each episode as an audio slate, but this practice eventually ended, and on some tapes, Jim's written documentation was incomplete. In those cases where precise information does not exist, an airdate range has been estimated.

Unless otherwise noted, all episodes start with the *Sam and Friends* title card, theme music, and opening announce: "*Sam and Friends* . . . brought to you . . . by Esskay." Some episodes begin with a cold open before the title card, and those are specified. Most episodes end with a title card and a music/announce outro similar to the show's open. Some installments feature a comedic tag after the "*Sam and Friends* . . . brought to you . . . by Esskay" closing announcement, and those are noted.

Along with this listing of live broadcasts, a few additional records have been listed by the dates that their control-room acetates were created, as we do not have precise airdates for them (if they were used on the air at all).

November 24, 1958 *(on* **In Our Town***)*

RECORD: "Song of the Sewer": Performed by Art Carney, orchestra under the direction of Sid Feller, written by Art Carney, Matt Dubey, Harold Karr

With "Song of the Sewer," Art Carney capitalizes on the popularity of his Ed Norton character from *The Honeymooners*. Although Norton is not mentioned by name in the song, he does happen to share an occupation with the song's narrator, and Carney essentially sings in character, "Together we stand, with shovel in hand, to keep things rolling along."

November 24, 1958

RECORD: "The Yellow Rose of Texas": Performed by Stan Freberg with Billy May's Orchestra (Yankee Snare Drumming: Alvin Stoller), original song written by Don George (see page 260)

COMMERCIAL: Professor Madcliffe chastises Moldy Hay for waving to friends during the program. "I was noddin' to my little old mother. She's watching 'cause I told her all about us goin' on the air for Esskay and how poppin' proud we are to be on five nights a week for such a rep-a-rep-a-rep-u-table company." Madcliffe corrects him: "Moldy, the word it reputable, meaning to be held in high regard. To have a name one is justly proud of—a quality name like Esskay." Moldy asks, "Do you want a head bustin' on your hands? You think Ma don't know all about Esskay? Why, she's been tastin' the difference quality makes for over one hundred years." Madcliffe: "Moldy, your mother can't be that old." Moldy: "No, but Esskay is. How else you think they know so much about good meat?" Madcliffe: "But you said your mother . . . awww—" Moldy: "Man, you sure can mess up a good commercial. I guess I told him, huh, Ma?"

November 25, 1958

INTRO: The show begins with Omar welcoming Baltimore to the *Sam and Friends* network. "Let's see, how many stations does that make now?" he asks. "Two!" shouts Professor Madcliffe. Omar then introduces the song.

RECORD: "The Musicians": Performed by Dinah Shore, Betty Hutton, Tony Martin, Phil Harris, with Henri René and His Orchestra, written by Charles Grean, Tom Glazer, (see page 250)

COMMERCIAL: With Thanksgiving approaching, Esskay Turkeys are the featured product. Moldy Hay begins the spot with, "Thanksgiving is a-comin' and the old gray goose is fat." He is immediately corrected by Kermit for mentioning a goose and not their sponsor's poultry. "We don't mention that word around here seeing that our revered sponsor is none other than Esskay—purveyor of the most scrumptious tastebud-ticklin' turkey in the world today!" Viewers are reminded that Esskay quality turkeys are completely clean and oven ready, with the giblets packed separately. "You wouldn't want all those giblets rollin' 'round loose, would you?"

Note: Starting this week, *Sam and Friends* aired in Baltimore on WBAL at 6:30 p.m. as well as on WRC in Washington, D.C.

November 26, 1958

RECORD: "I Know an Old Lady": Performed by Phil Harris with Skip Martin and His Orchestra, written by Alan Mills, Rose Bonne (see page 254)

COMMERCIAL: Moldy Hay is upset—"I am seven shades of wild-eyed purple fury!"—because his cousin Doozey May has purchased a turkey that's not an Esskay. Kermit asks him if he told her the virtues of an Esskay quality bird, but Moldy is not speaking to her. Kermit tells him that his behavior is not helping the situation. "What did you do?" Kermit asks. "I hit her," Moldy Hay says.

TAG: Moldy has a final word. "Hey, Sam, I bet that old woman was like my cousin Doozey May that I was telling Kermit about. She'd eat just about anything, too."

November 27, 1958

RECORD: "Inchworm": Performed by Danny Kaye, written by Frank Loesser (see page 256)

COMMERCIAL: Omar is wearing a pilgrim hat. Harry asks, "Hey, daddio, how come the crazy lid? What's the big deal?" Omar explains that he has been selected to offer Thanksgiving greetings to the viewers. "Dear friends, on behalf of our sponsor, Esskay, their employees and dealers, our cast and myself, may I say, happy, happy Thanksgiving to you all. May your blessings this holiday season be as bountiful as our good wishes for you. Thank you."

November 28, 1958

RECORD: "Roger Boom": Performed by Larry Hooper and Lawrence Welk, written by Bob Hilliard (see page 276–277)

COMMERCIAL: Harry sets up the commercial with an elaborate musical fanfare, then Kermit delivers a "message of pure joy"—a pitch for Esskay Breakfast Links.

December 1, 1958

RECORD: "The Hunting Song": Performed by Tom Lehrer, written by Tom Lehrer

This tune about a hunter who shot his limit—"two game wardens, seven hunters, and a cow"—was written and performed by Tom Lehrer, a popular musical satirist and college professor. In the 1970s, Lehrer contributed songs to *The Electric Company*.

COMMERCIAL: Kermit begins the commercial but is interrupted by Professor Madcliffe, who calls it off because the delivery of the commercials is getting sloppy. (See pages 111–112 for full text of this commercial.)

RECORD: "Lullaby of Bird Dog": Performed by Homer and Jethro, song written by George Shearing (see page 297–298)

December 2, 1958

COMMERCIAL: Omar tries to make conversation: "Scrapple, anyone?" But Harry critiques his conversation starter. "Omar, dad, like, honk, you're for weirdsville." Harry explains that you start a *day* with scrapple—not a conversation. "Especially when it's Esskay Skrapple."

RECORD: "I've Grown Accustomed to Your Face": Performed by Rosemary Clooney, written by Frederick Loewe and Alan Jay Lerner

As Kermeena sings to a sweet face, she doesn't realize that the face is actually a disguised Yorick, who devours the face disguise and then goes after Kermeena.

December 3, 1958

COMMERCIAL: Kermit is trying to figure out a new, exciting way to tell people about Esskay quality. Harry tries to solve his problem with his new poem about Esskay: "Esskay! Quality quality quality quality—pure! Pure! Pure! Quality quality quality quality pure . . ." Kermit stops him. "Now, wait a minute, Harry. What kind of poem is that?" "It's beatnik poetry, man!" Kermit expands on Harry's Beat message with more details about Esskay.

RECORD: "Looking at Numbers": Performed by Ken Nordine and The Fred Katz Group, written by Ken Nordine, Fred Katz

As a bongo accompaniment plays, Ken Nordine looks at numbers one at a time, describing their appearance and incorporating metaphors and similes.

TAG: Jim Henson's voice riffs on the Ken Nordine piece by looking at the letters S . . . and K . . . "Together, the two letters mean much more than either by themself. They stand for the sponsor of our show. That's who *they* stand for."

December 4, 1958

COMMERCIAL: Omar delivers a poem, "Ode to an Esskay Sausage": "Oh, sun, awake the sleeping brood. / The roosters crowed. The cow has mooed. / 'Tis time for eggs and Esskay Sausage. / 'Tis time that begs for . . ." Omar's poem trails off with a mumble. "Just a minute, hold everything," Professor Madcliffe says. "Look here, Omar. I don't mind your coming on here and talking about Esskay. I don't mind your reading poems." But Madcliffe wants to know what the mumbled ending to his poem was supposed to be. "If you've got something to say, speak out." Omar has an explanation: "Did you ever try to find a word that rhymes with sausage?"

INTRO: The cast gathers for the song. A pitch pipe is blown for their opening note, and even though the *Sam and Friends* vocal group is off-pitch, they begin . . .

RECORD: "Down by the Old Mill Stream": Performed by Randy Van Horne Swing Choir, written by Tell Taylor

This barbershop quartet favorite was published in 1910 and was used quite frequently in media. The record used here was recorded by Randy Van Horne's vocal group, which, in addition to recording several albums, sang as studio singers on notable TV theme songs, including *The Flintstones* and *The Jetsons*.

December 5, 1958

RECORD: "Beep Beep": Performed by The Playmates, written by Carl Cicchetti, Donald Claps

This 1958 recording was a Top 10 hit for The Playmates, a vocal trio hailing from Connecticut. The song begins very slowly and gradually increases in tempo. The central subject of the song is a Cadillac that is tailed and eventually overtaken by a horn-honking Nash Rambler. The popularity of the song had an impact on sales of the Rambler, a car manufactured between 1950 and 1954 by Nash and again between 1958 and 1968 after Nash was consolidated into the new American Motors.

COMMERCIAL: After a non-Henson recorded Esskay jingle, Kermit tells viewers that if they feel "plum tuckered out" in the morning, they should ask the head chef of the house to fix up a pile of

Esskay Sausages for breakfast. Moldy Hay says the commercial reminds him of when he used to live back on the farm. "I used to take care of a bunch of cows my daddy had." This leads in to what may be the first Muppet use of the "herd of cows" routine (see pages 42–43 for the full exchange).

December 8, 1958

RECORD: "Banana Boat (Day-O)": Performed by Stan Freberg, interruptions by Peter Leeds with Billy May's Music, written by Stan Freberg (see pages 300–301)

COMMERCIAL: Same as November 26, 1958

TAG: At the conclusion of the commercial, Kermit realizes, "Egad we're late!" and a sped-up version of the "Sam and Friends" outro plays.

Records transcribed on December 9, 1958

"A Shine on Your Shoes": Performer unknown*, written by Arthur Schwartz, Howard Dietz

Though written for a 1932 musical revue called *Flying Colors*, it's best remembered as a Fred Astaire dance number in the MGM musical *The Band Wagon* (1953). An energetic number, the song praises the value of having a shine on your shoes, claiming it will lead to a "singable, happy feeling."

* The version used on *Sam and Friends* could have been the Fred Astaire performance from *The Band Wagon*, Jerry Lewis's 1956 recording, or a 1958 record by The Hi-Lo's with Frank Comstock and His Orchestra. (The version cannot be confirmed since the acetate could not be accessed.)

"Herman Horne on Hi-Fi": Performed by Stan Freberg, written by Stan Freberg, Pete Barnum

The high-fidelity craze was at its peak in the late 1950s, when Stan Freberg presented this "expert" segment on his CBS radio program. Freberg's Herman Horne explains the need for state-of-the-art audio equipment, despite seemingly more important priorities: "All women are troublemakers who would like to take the money their husbands need desperately for a new and better speaker and selfishly squander it on things like . . . shoes for the children, homogenized milk, or perhaps a second dress."

December 9, 1958

INTRO: Moldy Hay tells Sam he's been having deep philosophical thoughts lately. He asks Sam if he has thoughts like that. "Do you ever think about what you want to get out of life? For instance, do you want to be a genius? Or be famous? Or have a lot of girls? Now, you take Mushmellon over there . . . he knows what he wants out of life. He only wants one thing . . ."

RECORD: "Money": Performed by Mel Blanc, orchestra conducted by Billy May, written by Stan Freberg, Ruby Raskin

Mel Blanc released this recording of Stan Freberg and Ruby Raskin's song in 1954. It was a Henson favorite and would later be performed by the Muppets on *The Mike Douglas Show* and *The Tonight Show Starring Johnny Carson* in 1966 and presented as a Dr. Teeth solo number in a first-season episode of *The Muppet Show*. When the Muppets contributed Muppet moments to *Good Morning America* in 1992, the song was used in a sketch in which Fozzie Bear's taxes were audited.

COMMERCIAL: Same as November 28, 1958 (without Harry's musical fanfare)

December 10, 1958

INTRO: Omar presents a peony bush and tells viewers that this is one that Kermit loves with all his heart.

RECORD: "The Peony Bush": Performed by Danny Kaye, written by Meredith Willson (see page 295)

COMMERCIAL: "The *Sam and Friends* Mystery Theater" presents a terrifying commercial drama. "What Happened to Bacon for Breakfast?" is the mystery. According to Detective Omar, it was last seen on Sunday morning, but where has it been all week? "The real crime is that people are eating small, cold breakfasts for weekdays when they need energy-giving bacon for breakfast most," Professor Madcliffe says, going off script. As the commercial fades out, Madcliffe is still raving about the qualities of Esskay Bacon.

December 11, 1958

COMMERCIAL: Harry is "completely bugged" and "gonesville"—he can't get the Esskay quality message out of his head. Kermit calms him down. "Of course, the outstanding quality of Esskay products is in your mind." Harry: "I dig, man. But, ohh, here it comes again!"

RECORD: "Open the Door, Richard": Performed by The Charioteers, written by John Mason, Don Howell, Jack McVea, Dusty Fletcher (See page 238)

December 12, 1958

COLD OPEN: Harry asks the director for a little room, a little bit more, a little bit more . . . and then cues the opening: "I'd like you to know we have a swinging little show here what go by the name of *Sam and Friends* . . .

TITLE CARD/ANNOUNCE: After the initial musical fanfare, Harry cues each snippet of theme music individually and delivers the opening announcement in his own inimitable fashion. "We'd like you to know that the gig is being brought to you . . . go, man. (MUSIC) Crazy . . . by a little organization what is known to the more discriminating of our viewing populace as Esskay. . . . (MUSIC) And now, as they say in the language of the television, on with the gig."

RECORD: "Nuttin' for Christmas": Performed by Stan Freberg with Billy May's Music, written by Sid Tepper, Roy C. Bennett

This is a fairly straight Stan Freberg cover of a song about a kid who has earned his way to Santa's naughty list, that is, until the arrival down the chimney of a man with a bag over his shoulder. After the kid assists the burglar and receives his cut of the loot, the two sing the closing chorus.

COMMERCIAL: When Moldy Hay is homesick for farm breakfasts, Professor Madcliffe reminds him that there's a ton of Esskay Hickory Smoked Bacon waiting to be bought right there in the city. Moldy Hay tells him that most days "hustlin' city folk" don't take time for a real breakfast. "Positively criminal! People should take time every morning to enjoy breakfast with Esskay Hickory Smoked Bacon. Particularly weekdays when they need energy most.

It should be illegal not to enjoy it. I'll sue! Write my congressman! Someone get me a cheap lawyer!"

December 15, 1958

RECORD: "Maggie": Performed by Stan Freberg with Cliffie Stone's Music, written by Cliffie Stone, Stan Freberg

As a chorus sings behind him, Stan Freberg expresses his love for Maggie but is overtaken by a spell of hiccups. With the lead singer eventually unable to go on, the chorus finishes the song.

COMMERCIAL: Omar interviews Yorick, who has just eaten four Esskay Hams. While his responses to most of the questions are unintelligible, when Omar asks if he could taste the difference Q-wal-ity makes, Yorick can be heard giving a very definitive, albeit guttural, "Yes." (A few hiccups follow, playing off the Stan Freberg song, with one hiccup heard after "brought to you by Esskay.")

December 16, 1958

TITLE CARD/ANNOUNCE: The opening logo is interrupted by Omar saying, "Once again, *Sam and Friends* is brought to you by Esskay."

RECORD: "Old, Old Vienna": Performed by Eddie Lawrence with orchestra directed by Nick Perito, written by Eddie Lawrence (see page 252)

COMMERCIAL: Harry has a riddle: "What's bald, plump, and tender and makes your nose light up?" Moldy Hay says his father is bald and plump. "You're out, man," Harry says. "It's Esskay Oven Ready Turkey. They're so clean! They're bald as a billiard ball." After

Professor Madcliffe yells at Harry for describing the sponsor's product as bald and delivers a straight, impassioned pitch, Moldy pipes up: "Harry, I got the bald, plump, tender part, but that don't make my nose light up." Harry replies: "It will, boy, when you smell it roasting. It will. Makes me wish I had a nose."

December 17, 1958

RECORD: "The Night Before Christmas": Performed by Stan Freberg with Babette Bain and Billy May's Music, written by Stan Freberg, Jack Brooks

On this 1955 record, Stan Freberg recites the Clement Moore poem in his own unique way as his niece tries to keep him on track and remind him that Santa doesn't have any reindeer named Marilyn or Gina Lollobrigida.

COMMERCIAL: Professor Madcliffe promises to perform a magic trick—making an Esskay Oven Ready Turkey appear out of thin air—and as he does so, he reminds the audience to buy one for their families' Christmas feasts.

December 18, 1958

RECORD: "Wild Bill Hiccup": Performed by Spike Jones and His City Slickers (featuring George Rock, Freddy Morgan, Jack Golly), written by Eddie Brandt, Freddy Morgan, Spike Jones

This 1949 RCA record is a silly Western ballad in classic Spike Jones style, filled with sound effects and fast-paced vocal performances.

COMMERCIAL: Harry delivers a Beat-style commercial for Esskay's Oven Ready Turkeys: "They're gone on the gums, wet with the white meat, draggin' with the dark meat." Kermit translates: "Delicious. Lots of moist white meat. Rich, man-sized drumsticks." Harry continues: "Swingin-est, wildest, in-est, most-est, gone, gone, gone."

December 19 and December 22, 1958

INTRO: The program begins with a solemn announcement that tonight's show is one of a more mature and serious nature.

RECORD: "It's Magic": Performed by Jonathan and Darlene Edwards (Paul Weston and Jo Stafford), written by Jule Styne, Sammy Cahn (see page 288)

COMMERCIAL: Harry paints a portrait one hundred years in the making—a sandwich made of Esskay Fully Cooked Ham. Professor Madcliffe asks why he just painted a picture of a sandwich instead of delivering the commercial. Madcliffe talks about all the things Harry could have mentioned about Esskay. "You haven't said one word about Esskay quality." Harry explains that someone said one good picture is worth a million words. "And, man, was he right—especially when there's a blabbermouth like you around."

Note: On December 22, the show ends with Harry explaining that the show may seem repetitious. "Leave us say that on Friday, the technicians discovered to their great dismay that chewing gum is not a good conductor of electricity. We hope that we'll be back tomorrow for Esskay—audio and video." (Apparently, a technical problem on Friday, December 19, prevented either the audio or video from being transmitted, so the show was re-performed on Monday, December 22.)

December 23, 1958

COLD OPEN: Moldy Hay reminds viewers that the Muppets are guesting on Jack Paar later in the evening and invites them to tune in at 11:30.

TITLE CARD/ANNOUNCE

COMMERCIAL: Moldy begins a Shakespearian recitation: "Friends, Romans, and Countrymen, lend me your ears. I has [sic] come to bury Caesar and not to praise him." Professor Madcliffe interrupts. "Shakespeare is fine, but not on this show. What do you think you're doing?" Moldy explains that he was told to talk like a ham. "You were told, my hominy gritted friend, to talk *about* ham—an Esskay ham to be specific." Moldy then launches into the commercial. "If you've never tried an Esskay Fully Cooked Ham, then you've never tasted ham at all."

RECORD: "Let Me In": Performed by Red Ingle and The Natural Seven, written by Bob Merrill

In this song, the main character desperately wants to get into a closed room because he can hear laughter and music inside. Singer Red Ingle was a member of Spike Jones's City Slickers for several years before starting his own group, Red Ingle and The Natural Seven. A version of this segment with Jim Henson singing the live vocal was performed on *The Tonight Show Starring Johnny Carson* on December 31, 1965.

December 24, 1958

COMMERCIAL: Omar is quietly wrapping an Esskay Sausage as a Christmas gift when Kermit convinces him that it's not right to give a single sausage. "You're not thinking big enough. Maybe an

Esskay Fully Cooked Ham or an Esskay Oven Ready Turkey will do as a gift, but not *one* Esskay Sausage. Omar says that he happens to be fond of Esskay Sausage. "Who isn't?" Kermit says. "But it ain't socially proper to give one Esskay Sausage." Omar is convinced. He'll give a whole case of Esskay Sausage.

RECORD: "The Chipmunk Song": Performed by David Seville, written by Ross Bagdasarian (see page 81 for more on the creation of the Chipmunks)

After "The Chipmunk Song," the Muppets segue into a sped-up Chipmunk-style version of Danny Kaye's "Tschaikowsky (And Other Russians)"—and even the *Sam and Friends* outro is sped up.

December 25, 1958

TITLE CARD/ANNOUNCE: As "Jingle Bells" plays instead of the regular opening music, Omar announces that *Sam and Friends,* on this Yuletide Day, is brought to you by Esskay."

RECORD: "Carol of the Bells": Performed by The Randolph Singers, conducted by David Randolph, Traditional

COMMERCIAL: Moldy Hay cues the commercial jingle, but instead of an Esskay jingle, a choral excerpt from Stan Freberg's "Green Christmas" is played: "We wish you a Merry Christmas, we wish you a Merry Christmas, we wish you a Merry Christmas, now please buy our beer." Moldy Hay protests: "Aw, come on now, that's not our jingle!" He threatens to quit, but Madcliffe tells Moldy that everyone elected him to the job—he urges Moldy to make the planned speech. Moldy delivers a sincere Christmas greeting on behalf of Esskay. "Folks, this wonderful day is almost over, but we can't consider it perfect 'til we wish you all a very Merry, Merry

Christmas. All of us here, and all the people that make Esskay products, hope you've had a joyful day on this day of all days."

RECORD: "God Rest Ye Merry Gentlemen": Performed by The Randolph Singers, conducted by David Randolph, Traditional

December 26, 1958

COLD OPEN: Omar chastises Yorick for eating all the Esskay Sausage in the house—as well as the rest of the Christmas turkey (bones and all), the platter, the tablecloth, and all the dishes, but he went too far when he ate all the Christmas tree ornaments. "We had high hopes of using them again next year."

TITLE CARD/ANNOUNCE

RECORD: "Christmas Tree": Performed by The Voices of Walter Schumann, vocal by Bill Lee, written by Jay Daniel, Sid Robin

With its call-and-response style, this energetic tune from Walter Schumann's *The Voices of Christmas* album (1955) was inspired by the German sing-along song "Schnitzelbank." "Is this not a Christmas tree? / Yes, this is a Christmas tree!" The Voices of Walter Schumann was a twenty-person vocal ensemble formed by orchestra leader Schumann.

COMMERCIAL: Same as December 10, 1958

December 29, 1958

COMMERCIAL: Same as December 4, 1958

RECORD: "The Hat I Got for Christmas Is Too Beeg": Performed by Mel Blanc, written by David Gussin, Marv Fisher

Singing in a Mexican accent, Mel Blanc performs a joyous song about the holidays but is upset because the hat he received for Christmas is too large for him.

December 30, 1958

COLD OPEN: Ken Nordine's "Bubble Gum" recording begins (with Yorick acting it out onscreen), only to be interrupted by Omar: "Wait a minute, Yorick. We've got to start the show first."

TITLE CARD/ANNOUNCE: The *Sam and Friends* opening announce begins but is interrupted after "brought to you . . ." with the resumption of the Nordine track. Omar again interrupts: "No, no, no! Not yet, Yorick!' The opening is finally allowed to finish with "by Esskay." "All right, Yorick. If you're ready, now," Omar says.

RECORD: "Bubble Gum": Performed by Ken Nordine featuring The Fred Katz Group, written by Ken Nordine, Fred Katz

"Word jazz" creator Ken Nordine makes a confession that he has become a "bubble gum fancier." As he speaks, he chews and chews, all while a jazz combo plays behind him. He explains that he's getting pretty good at blowing bubbles, insisting that he blew one yesterday so big that he almost floated away.

COMMERCIAL: Same as December 12, 1958

December 31, 1958

COMMERCIAL: The commercial begins as the December 5, 1958, spot did, but the Esskay jingle was revoiced by Jim Henson. Kermit then goes into his sales pitch, but Moldy is not involved (and we don't get the "herd of cows" gag).

RECORD: "That Old Black Magic": Performed by Louis Prima and Keely Smith, written by Harold Arlen, Johnny Mercer (see page 142 for a full summary)

TAG: The ending drumbeats of "That Old Black Magic" are heard after the "by Esskay" outro.

January 2, 1959

COMMERCIAL: Omar begins to make a New Year's resolution, but when Yorick joins him, he chastises Yorick for not eating breakfast. "How many times do I have to tell you breakfast is one of the most important meals in the day? . . . Have you ever tasted Esskay Bacon and a couple of Esskay Eggs to start the day right?" Yorick grunts a response. "That's just what I thought," Omar says, and he then continues to sing the praises of an Esskay breakfast. Omar asks Yorick to sign a resolution that he will have an Esskay Bacon breakfast every morning. Yorick eats the pen instead.

RECORD: "M.T.A. (The Boston Subway Song)": Performed by Will Holt, written by Bess Hawes, Jacqueline Steiner (see page 280)

January 5, 1959

COMMERCIAL: Omar reads a poem:

> In the bright year just passed, we've been happy to say,
> One hundred years old, that's our sponsor, Esskay.
> And the people did cheer, and the band they did play,

And the world seemed to chorus "happy hundredth birthday."
But today, there are no bands, and no people to shout,
For the bell has just tolled their one hundredth year out.
Gone are the cheers, the big year is done,
And nobody cares when you're one hundred and one.

Professor Madcliffe energetically reminds everyone that Esskay still knows more than anyone about quality. Omar ends the spot by wishing the sponsor a happy one hundred and first birthday.

RECORD: "Abominable Snowman": Performed by Stan Freberg, written by Stan Freberg (see pages 294–295)

January 6, 1959

RECORD: "Proud New Father": Performed by Johnny Standley with Horace Heidt and His Musical Knights, written by John Standley

Comedian and musician Johnny Standley recorded this routine in which he tears apart the problematic "bit of literature, 'Rock-a-bye Baby.'" He questions the viability of a proud new father jumping out of bed at three in the morning to take his crying baby and its cradle outside to search for a tree from which to rock his child to sleep. "Have we nothing better to do than to place a poor, helpless infant high in a tree and wait for the wind to blow?"

COMMERCIAL: Same as December 2, 1958

January 7, 1959

RECORD: "Jubilation T. Cornpone": Performed by *Li'l Abner* Original Broadway Cast (featuring Stubby Kaye), written by Johnny Mercer, Gene de Paul (see page 293)

COMMERCIAL: Same as December 1, 1958

January 8, 1959

COLD OPEN: "Harry the Hipster": Performed by Ronny Graham, written by Ronny Graham

In this excerpt from his revue, *Take Five*, Ronny Graham's Harry calls the class to order and sings a bit of the Slim Gaillard song "Cement Mixer (Put-ti Put-ti)" before the recording is interrupted by . . .

TITLE CARD/ANNOUNCE: A sped-up version of the *Sam and Friends* opening title plays.

RECORD: "Cecilia": Performed by David Seville, written by Dave Dreyer, Herman Ruby

Originally written in 1926, this version was recorded by David Seville (Ross Bagdasarian) in 1957. In Seville's version, he can't quite remember his dance partner's name as he scrambles to express his fondness for her.

COMMERCIAL: Same as November 28, 1958

TAG: "Harry the Hipster": Ronny Graham's song concludes the episode with the end of his rambling spoken-word piano-accompanied routine. The "How do you get to Carnegie Hall? / Practice" joke is included before class is dismissed and the closing theme is played.

January 9, 1959

RECORD: "Myrtle": Performed by Joe Pryor with Loulie Jean Norman with orchestra conducted by Henry Mancini, written by Irving Taylor

From Irving Taylor's album *Terribly Sophisticated Songs,* Joe Pryor's vocal sings the praises of a woman named Myrtle as her voice echoes. "'Til the day I change your last name, the time will go slow as a turtle / but the first name to me, will always be Myrtle." The orchestra and vocals for the album were conducted by Henry Mancini.

COMMERCIAL: Moldy Hay begins to recite a poem appropriate for cold weather:

> Little Willie from the mirror licked the mercury right off,
> Thinking in his childish error it would cure the whooping cough.
> At his funeral, Willie's mother sadly said to Mrs. Brown,
> 'Twas a chilly day for Willie when the mercury went down.

Kermit then enters, searching for a new, exciting way to tell people about Esskay quality. Harry obliges with a repeat of his Beat poem from December 3, 1958.

Records transcribed on January 12, 1959

"Coplas": Performed by The Kingston Trio, Traditional, arranged by Dave Guard

The Kingston Trio recorded this Mexican folk song partially in Spanish with periodic English translations. In any language, the song is not exactly a serious one, involving green peppers, a mule, and cat in a sombrero and long pants.

"Little Brass Band": Performed by David Seville, written by Ross Bagdasarian

In this non-Chipmunk David Seville tune (whose melody is evocative of his song "Witch Doctor"), Seville sings about the little brass band that plays in his heart whenever he kisses his girl.

"Where is the Beast in You?" (from the musical *Goldilocks*): Performed by Elaine Stritch, written by Leroy Anderson, Joan Ford, Walter Kerr, Jean Kerr

While the title makes it sound like an adaptation of "Goldilocks and the Three Bears," the Broadway musical *Goldilocks* (1958) was a story set in the early days of film. The legendary Elaine Stritch sings this song in which she wonders about the lack of beastly behavior in her man.

"The Carnival Song": Performed by *Say, Darling* Original Broadway Cast (featuring David Wayne, Vivian Blaine, Steve Condos), written by Betty Comden, Adolph Green, Jule Styne

Say, Darling was a 1957 play about the writing of a musical and included songs from the show within the show. One of these songs, "The Carnival Song," is a patent medicine sales pitch for "Dr. Rizzuto's Royal Rejuvo-Regenerator."

January 12, 1959

RECORD: "Anything You Can Do (I Can Do Better)": Performed by *Annie Get Your Gun* Original Broadway Cast (featuring Ethel Merman and Ray Middleton), written by Irving Berlin (see page 291)

COMMERCIAL: A Henson-voiced announcer introduces "The *Sam and Friends* Storybook!" After a horn fanfare, Harry proceeds to deliver the swingin'est thing in orbit—the beatnik fairy tale "Chicken Little": "Now, this chicken digs Esskay the most. Like, she wants to join up. Well, the Esskay kingpin, he says, 'Like, honk, we only take chickens that are U.S. government certified grade A for perfect quality. Then, they gotta be inspected for wholesomeness. Ya' gotta be farm fresh . . . plump and luscious . . . so you can be cut up, ready to cook, and quick frozen to seal in your goodness.' The chicken flips. 'Oooh! If I could only slip into the blue and orange Esskay wrapper, I'd feel like a movie star.' The kingpin offers as how maybe some smart lady will fry her in Esskay's famous shortening, Essko. It's super creamed, pure white, and digestible as butter. Well, the chicken is go-o-o-one. She says, 'Oooh! I'll be the difference quality makes.'"

January 13, 1959

RECORD: "Elderly Man River": Performed by Stan Freberg, Daws Butler, written by Jerome Kern, Oscar Hammerstein II, Pete Barnum, Stan Freberg (see page 293)

COMMERCIAL: Same as December 10, 1958

January 14, 1959

RECORD: "Yon-u-ary": Performed by Danny Kaye, written by Sylvia Fine

This is a jaunty song set in Capetown with the calendar-based chorus sung in a dialect that reflects the way the word January is spelled in the title. The verse is sung in Danny Kaye's regular singing voice.

COMMERCIAL: Professor Madcliffe implores the cast to "beef up this show!" He says they need to tell people about beef that bears the Esskay brand. After the beef passes the government inspections, it still must meet Esskay's highest standard of perfection. Harry is touched. "I may weep. It's just like winning the Academy Award." Madcliffe agrees. "Esskay's quality control guarantees the finest performance whenever Esskay beef is served." Harry is on board. "Well, man, let's get with it. Like, I mean, let's do it. Let's beef up the show, man. Beef up the show! Now, let me hear those golden words." And, of course, those words are "taste the difference quality makes."

January 15, 1959

COLD OPEN: The show starts with an excerpt from Ronny Graham's "Harry the Hipster": "Before we commence the commencement . . . rise, turn east, and face Decca." (A comic beatnik's prayer to the mighty Decca record label.) Note: The cold open track is from the cast recording of the live revue, *Take Five* (1957). Though Graham's hipster shares a name with the Muppet, *Sam and Friends'* Harry predated Graham's character by several years.

TITLE CARD/ANNOUNCE

RECORD: "Git Up Off'n the Floor, Hannah! (A Bitter New Year's Eve)": Performed by Red Ingle and The Natural Seven, written by Foster Carling, Joe Washburne, Red Ingle

The flip side of the delightfully titled "Moe Zart's Turkey Trot," this is a 1948 story song in which farm girl Hannah refuses her mother's offer of a blanket to use during a sleigh ride with young Charles to the village New Year's party. When she sits motionless on the bitter cold ride, Charles decides to take her home, and as soon as she arrives, she collapses, frozen. Charles tenderly takes her hand and delivers the title directive: "Git up off'n the floor, Hannah, them hogs have got to be fed."

COMMERCIAL: Kermit tells the story of "Good King Mushmellon," the owner of the finest of all fresh frozen chickens, an Esskay Maryland Frying Chicken. "But, alas, good King Mushmellon was proud but sad. For he lacked the perfect shortening to fry his precious chicken to a golden brown. Then, up popped a minstrel and told him about Esskay's famous shortening, Essko—super creamed, pure white, digestible as butter. The perfect way to fry foods and bake goodies. King Mushmellon beamed with delight and said, 'You shall have the hand of my fairest daughter and we shall feast on Esskay Farm Fresh Frozen Chicken, fried to a royal gold in Essko!' So they lived happily ever after, tasting the difference that quality makes."

January 16, 1959

RECORD: "Pachalafaka": Performed by Earl Brown, written by Irving Taylor (see page 299)

COMMERCIAL: Kermit tells the audience about the pure goodness of Esskay Frying Chickens and is then interrupted by Professor Madcliffe, who tells him that he doesn't have enough "sell." "You gotta tell 'em that Esskay's Maryland Frying Chickens are U.S. government certified grade A for perfect quality and every one is inspected for wholesomeness." Kermit responds, "I was getting to that," to which Madcliffe says, "Be quicker about it, or you'll never have time to tell them the way to protect the flavor of something as delicious as Esskay Chicken is to use Esskay's famous shortening, Essko!" Kermit finishes with a straight pitch, imploring viewers to buy the product and, of course, "Taste the difference quality makes."

RECORD: "If'n": Performed by Jaye P. Morgan and Eddy Arnold, written by Matt Dubey, Harold Karr

Jaye P. Morgan, who would go on to appear on *The Muppet Show*, recorded this up-tempo duet in 1956 with country singer Eddy Arnold as a pop cover for a Broadway show tune. The song was written for the musical *Happy Hunting* (1956), which starred another *Muppet Show* guest, Ethel Merman.

January 19, 1959

RECORD: "C'est Si Bon": Performed by Stan Freberg with the George Bruns Quartet, written by Henri Betti, Andre Hornez, Jerry Seelen (see page 151 for a full summary)

COMMERCIAL: Moldy Hay tells Kermit he's very proud because his prize steer Jeremiah has been bought by Esskay. "He's going to bear the Esskay brand. He passed the most rigid government inspections and then he met all of Esskay's extra-high standards, so they accepted him. Oh, Kermit, I'm so busted proud, I don't know what to do." Kermit is very impressed. "There's not many that can come up to Esskay's high standards." Moldy replies, "Oh, I'm so happy. I think I'll write a commercial or something."

January 20, 1959

RECORD: "When the Crabgrass Blooms Again": Performed by Jimmy Joyce, written by Irving Taylor

Another track from Irving Taylor's *Terribly Sophisticated Songs*, "When the Crabgrass Blooms Again" is a satirical melancholy tune targeted at the midcentury suburban obsession with lawn care: "Ladybugs will meet their men / and though I know you'll be gone then / will you miss me and my lawn then / when the crabgrass blooms again." Vocalist Jimmy Joyce led an eponymous vocal ensemble on *The Smothers Brothers Comedy Hour* and *The Red Skelton Hour*. The Jimmy Joyce Singers also were in the cast of Nancy Sinatra's Las Vegas show in the late 1960s alongside the Muppets.

COMMERCIAL: Same as January 12, 1959

January 21, 1959

INTRO: The guys are watching *Rock 'n' Roll for Young 'n' Ole* on television. Moldy turns up the volume and we transition to . . .

RECORD: "Heartbreak Hotel": Performed by Stan Freberg, written by Tommy Durden, Elvis Presley, Mae Axton

This 1956 take on Elvis Presley's hit of the same year pokes fun at Presley's vocal and physical gymnastics as Freberg's voice becomes almost unrecognizable as he adds syllables to words, rips his jeans while gyrating, and eventually becomes so immersed in echo effects that they cover the entire melody.

COMMERCIAL: Same as December 12, 1958

January 22, 1959

COMMERCIAL: Braving the elements, Kermit conducts a door-to-door impartial survey—and the lady of the house (played by Harry) sings the praises of a familiar brand. "I dig Esskay the most . . . I swing for that finely grained, extra tender, extra flavorful beef that bears the Esskay brand. Sonny, it's gonesville!" Kermit responds, "Why, madam, I'm delighted to hear you say that. Now, is there any particular reason you chose that particular meat?" The lady says, "Sonny, Esskay is the outmost. Every piece of Esskay beef passes the most rigid government inspection, then meets Esskay's own extra-high standards before it gets that ever-lovin' Esskay brand. Sonny, this beef is in orbit." Kermit replies, "Madam, you've been certainly most helpful. May I ask you your name?" To which the lady says, "I'd have sagged if you hadn't. I'm Mrs. Esskay. Mrs. TastetheDifference-QualityMakes Q. Esskay. So long, Sonny!" Kermit signs off: "Well, commercially speaking, we've done our duty for the day. Now I'm getting in, because, baby, it's cold outside. Song cue!" Kermit can't help but continue with the inevitable, "You're welcome," grimacing at his own gag.

RECORD: "Baby It's Cold Outside": Performed by Homer and Jethro with June Carter, written by Frank Loesser

Originally written by Frank Loesser to perform with his wife, Lynn Garland, at parties, the song was later used in the 1949 Esther Williams picture *Neptune's Daughter* and won an Academy Award for best song. This version gives a folksy, homespun approach to the song, with June Carter (Johnny Cash's future wife) joining Homer and Jethro and turning the duet into a trio. The duet was later performed by Miss Piggy and Rudolf Nureyev on *The Muppet Show*. In recent years, Miss Piggy joined Vince Gill and Michael Bublé on subsequent performances of the song.

January 23, 1959

INTRO: Kermit introduces Yorick, who has put together the day's episode, and while we don't understand Yorick's grumbles, Kermit can understand that Yorick will present a musical number . . .

RECORD: "Fish": Performed by Leona Anderson, written by Tony Burrello, Tom Murray

Leona Anderson began her career in silent films, and considering her later music career, it's not surprising that she didn't make an immediate transition to talkies. Her shrill musical recordings were popularized on *The Ernie Kovacs Show* and included on a CD compilation of songs featured on Kovacs's shows.

COMMERCIAL: Same as December 11, 1958

January 26, 1959

INTRO: The record of "That Old Black Magic" is stuck. Harry hits it to get the music going.

RECORD: "That Old Black Magic": Performed by Louis Prima and Keely Smith, written by Harold Arlen, Johnny Mercer (see page 142 for a full summary)

COMMERCIAL: A variation of the commercial from December 1, 1958, but this time, instead of Kermit, Omar begins the spot. He is interrupted by Professor Madcliffe, who calls off the commercial because the delivery is getting sloppy. He mentions the special qualities of the product during his pep talk. "Try it, Omar. And give it some gumption!" Omar responds, "I can't. Our time is up."

January 27, 1959

COLD OPEN: Harry tells the viewers that the subject for the evening is controversial and advises that those who "can't take it, had better leave the room."

TITLE CARD/ANNOUNCE

INTRO: Harry introduces the subject for the night's show—marriage. "As I stand here looking into the sea of faces before me, and I can see some of these faces need looking into, I see some of you out there are bachelors. Those are men who never make the same mistake once." Harry then recites some facts from the research staff: "Fifty percent of all married people are women . . . who wrote this, anyway?" He then presents a group of vocalists to espouse their experience on the subject.

RECORD: "I Got a Wife": Performed by The Mark IV, written by Edward Mascari, Erwin Wenzlaff

This song is a fast polka recounting a stereotypical wife's complaints. The music is interrupted with a sped-up recording of the wife herself.

COMMERCIAL: Same as January 16, 1959

END TITLE/ANNOUNCE

TAG: After the closing announce, a brief excerpt from "I Got a Wife" is played.

January 28, 1959

RECORD: "The Quest for Bridey Hammerschlaugen": Performed by Stan Freberg with June Foray and Billy May's Music, written by Stan Freberg

In this 1956 Capitol single, Stan places a woman named Goldie Smith (June Foray) into a trance and ends up interviewing a young girl named Bridey Hammerschlaugen, a Roman citizen making her living in 200 A.D. as an usherette in the Colosseum. The track pokes fun at *The Search for Bridey Murphy*, a book (and record) by amateur hypnotist Morey Bernstein, who claimed that he was able to contact a deceased woman named Bridey Murphy through the hypnosis of Colorado housewife Virginia Tighe. A film adaptation was rushed into production and reached theaters the same year the book was published.

COMMERCIAL: Same as January 19, 1959

January 29, 1959

INTRO: Harry introduces a guest speaker, who will re-create his days of misguided youth.

RECORD: "Dufo (What a Crazy Guy)": Performed by Wally Cox, written by Wally Cox (see pages 245–246)

COMMERCIAL: Same as January 15, 1959

January 30, 1959

COLD OPEN: The opening music is played backward, and Harry tells the musicians that he knows it's Friday and it's been a long week but he asks them to try it again from the top.

TITLE CARD/ANNOUNCE (Played normally)

RECORD: "Somebody Else, Not Me": Performed by Phil Harris, written by Ballard MacDonald, James F. Hanley

Phil Harris mostly talks through this story song about a couple of difficult situations (escaped Bengal tigers, an eyewitness to murder) and says how these tough spots are an opportunity for great heroism, for "somebody else, not me."

COMMERCIAL: Same as January 22, 1959

February 2, 1959

RECORD: "Rock Island Line": Performed by Stan Freberg and His Sniffle Group, interruptions by Peter Leeds, written by Lonnie Donegan, special arrangement by Stan Freberg (see page 292)

COMMERCIAL: Variation on November 26, 1958, but not specifically about turkey

February 3, 1959

COMMERCIAL: Same as December 4, 1958

RECORD: "Rock Around Stephen Foster": Performed by Stan Freberg with Billy May's Orchestra, written by Stan Freberg, Stephen Foster

What begins as a lilting rendition of Stephen Foster's "I Dream of Jeannie" transforms into a full rock 'n' roll Foster medley, complete with a Bill Haley-inspired counting sequence, all under the direction of Freberg's shouted instructions.

February 4, 1959

COLD OPEN: Harry: "To the youth of America, we present . . ."

TITLE CARD/ANNOUNCE

INTRO: Harry begins, "To those who like rock 'n' roll music, Sam will say a small something considered square by all but the sideburns set."

RECORD: "All American Boy": Performed by Bobby Bare, written by Bobby Bare

A sort of an "instructional" country ballad on how to become a rock 'n' roll star, this song was written and recorded by Bobby Bare right before he entered the service. The song ends with Uncle Sam interrupting the all-American boy's career, just as he had with Elvis Presley in 1958.

COMMERCIAL: Same as January 12, 1959

February 5, 1959

RECORD: "The Great Pretender": Performed by Stan Freberg with The Toads and Billy May's Music, written by Buck Ram

The Platters had released "The Great Pretender" in 1955. In Freberg's version, released the next year, the piano player balks at playing the repetitive chords of the song. Freberg's lead singer keeps the musician on track whenever he tries to play something else. "You play that 'cling-cling-cling' jazz or you won't get paid tonight." But the pianist can't be contained, leading to an homage to Freberg's own "The Yellow Rose of Texas" as the singer complains, "He ruined the ending—one of the lovely parts in the whole (DRUM FILL) piece!"

COMMERCIAL: The spot is the first commercial for Esskay's "Load O' Loot" contest. Jim Henson (in what sounds like his normal speaking voice) offers a list of prizes (a 1959 Chevy Impala, a fourteen-foot motorboat, a mink stole, a freezer with $500 worth of Esskay meat, etc.) and the rules for the contest. All you have to do is think of the one word that describes the taste and quality of Esskay's new Hickory Smoked Sliced Bacon.

TAG: A car crash and a Stan Freberg "Wow."

February 6, 1959

RECORD: "Hunger Is From": Performed by Ken Nordine with The Fred Katz Group, written by Ken Nordine, Fred Katz (see page 157 for a full summary)

COMMERCIAL: A spot for Esskay's new and improved Hickory Smoked Sliced Bacon is read by Jim in his normal speaking voice and ends with a mention of the "Load O' Loot" contest.

TAG: A few closing notes of "Hunger Is From"

February 9, 1959

RECORD: "Person to Pearson": Performed by Stan Freberg and Daws Butler, music by George Bruns, written by Stan Freberg, Daws Butler (see page 287)

COMMERCIAL: Another spot in Jim Henson's normal voice: "Just one word and you can win this whole truckload of prizes in Esskay's 'Load O' Loot' contest."

February 10, 1959

RECORD: "G'wan Home, Your Mudder's Callin'": Performed by Jimmy Durante, written by Ralph Freed, Sammy Fain (see page 299)

COMMERCIAL: Professor Madcliffe and Harry deliver a spot for the "Load O' Loot" contest. From context, it is apparent that Harry is laden with glitzy accessories. Madcliffe says Harry looks like something out of a glassworks explosion. Harry explains that he represents the Esskay "Load O' Loot contest." "Don't I look rich? Rich beyond your wildest dreams?" Madcliffe responds: "Tell me, Diamond Lil, why aren't you wearing some of those glorious prizes?" Harry says, "Well, you couldn't exactly expect me to wear a new 1959 Chevrolet Impala sedan, could you, sonny? And I'm certainly not vamping around the likes of you in a $1,000 Lutetia mink stole or a $1,000 diamond ring . . . or any of the dozens of other fantabulous prizes! See, sonny?" Madcliffe is not impressed. "I wish they were giving away a diamond-studded revolver, honey. 'Cause I'd sure let you have it." The commercial concludes with instructions on finding the contest entry on Esskay packaging.

February 11, 1959

COLD OPEN: Harry informs the audience that the chicken in the following song is, in fact, an Esskay Chicken.

TITLE CARD/ANNOUNCE

RECORD: "Please Pass the Biscuits": Performed by Gene Sullivan, written by Gene Sullivan

A 1957 country song that doesn't have a lot of singing, this record is essentially an extended monologue with musical backing as Gene Sullivan tries to get someone at the huge dinner table to pass him as biscuit.

COMMERCIAL: Same as February 6, 1959

February 12, 1959

INTRO: Moldy Hay greets the viewers of the modern metropolis and presents a look down below at the subway.

RECORD: "Ambrose (Part Five)": Performed by Linda Laurie, written by Linda Gertz, Lou Sprung, Wes McWain

The inaccurately titled "Ambrose (Part Five)"—there were not four previous installments—is the spoken story of a girl walking and talking her way through a dark subway tunnel with her boyfriend, Ambrose. Ambrose's only line in the record is a deep-voiced, "Just keep walking." Performer Linda Laurie, who provided both voices on the record, is the stage name of co-writer Linda Gertz, who created the song while attending high school in Brooklyn. She later recorded a follow-up, which was called not "Ambrose (Part Six)" but "Forever Ambrose."

COMMERCIAL: "Vroom! Vroom!" Moldy Hay is pretending to drive his new 1959 Chevrolet Impala sedan—practicing for when he wins it in the "Load O' Loot" contest. He then tells the audience how to enter.

February 13, 1959

RECORD: "What Did He Say? (The Mumble Song)": Performed by The Charioteers, written by Charles Grean, Cy Coben (see page 236)

COMMERCIAL: Same as February 9, 1959

TAG: Harry reminds viewers that it's Friday the 13th, "and we got by the show without a hitch." As soon as he says it, a series of big crash sounds begins and continues over the closing music and announce.

February 16, 1959

RECORD: "The Old Philosopher": Performed by Eddie Lawrence, written by Eddie Lawrence

Comedian and actor Eddie Lawrence first introduced "The Old Philosopher" in 1956, and the record became an unexpected hit. As a soft arrangement of "Beautiful Dreamer" plays in the background, Lawrence speaks directly to the listener, asking a series of sad, pitiful, and increasingly depressing questions: "You say your wife went out for a corned beef sandwich last weekend, and the corned beef sandwich came back but she didn't?" Just when the questions get as sad as they could get, Lawrence asks, "Is that what's troubling you, friend?" At that point, the boisterous "National Emblem March" kicks in, and Lawrence becomes an energetic voice of inspiration, commanding the listener to "never give up, never give up . . . [TWO DRUMBEATS] . . . that ship!" The whole thing repeats, but the Old Philosopher struggles to take his own advice and the record ends abruptly and tragically. Lawrence repeated the format of "The Old Philosopher" with subsequent recordings, including "The New Philosopher," "The Merry Old Philosopher," "The Philosopher Strikes Back," and "The Old Philosopher and the Single Girl."

COMMERCIAL: Same as February 6, 1959

February 17, 1959

COMMERCIAL: Yorick makes the discovery that the cast of Sam and Friends may not be eligible to enter the Esskay "Load O' Loot" contest. (See pages 113–114 for full summary.)

RECORD: "Barnacle Bill the Sailor": Performed by Candy Candido, written by Carson Robison, Frank Luther (see page 263)

February 18, 1959

RECORD: "Good Ol' Mountain Dew": Performed by Kenny Roberts, Traditional (see page 270)

COMMERCIAL: Same as February 6, 1959

February 19, 1959

RECORD: "Sh-Boom": Performed by Stan Freberg with The Toads and orchestra conducted by Billy May, written by James Keyes, Claude Feaster, Carl Feaster, Floyd F. McRae, William Edwards (see page 300)

COMMERCIAL: Same as February 10, 1959

February 20, 1959

RECORD: "The Guy with the Voodoo!": Performed by the Fletcher Peck Trio, written by Stan Freeman, Fletcher Peck (see page 238)

COMMERCIAL: Same as February 9, 1959

SEGUE: Omar tells Kermit that they have time for only a short song. He asks Kermit to sing his school song.

RECORD: "Good Old 149": Performed by Danny Kaye, writer unknown (see page 300)

February 23, 1959

RECORD: "That's My Boy": Performed by Stan Freberg with orchestra and chorus conducted by Les Baxter, written by Stan Freberg

On this early Freberg record released in 1951, a father proudly sings about the son who brings him joy and all the adorable things his little guy does—like playing with poison darts and an axe, carrying a knife, setting the mailman on fire, and throwing acid on the rug. Freberg sings, "I'm mighty thankful for what I've got / but I'm sure glad he's such a lousy shot."

COMMERCIAL: Same as February 10, 1959

February 24, 1959

RECORD: "You Need Feet": Performed by Bernard Bresslaw, written by Roy Irwin, adapted by Sid Colin

English actor Bernard Bresslaw released this record in 1958. The song, a comic twist on Max Bygraves's "You Need Hands" released that same year, is a celebration and clarification of why feet are necessary. The primary need that the song's narrator has for feet is to "run away from you."

COMMERCIAL: Same as February 12, 1959

February 25, 1959

COMMERCIAL: Omar is being punished—he must recite "new and improved Esskay Hickory Smoked Sliced Bacon" over and over because on a recent commercial, he made the mistake of saying only "Esskay Bacon" and not the "new and improved." The commercial ends with a plug for the "Load O' Loot" contest. Omar then mentions the product once more. "I think I've earned my pay in this commercial."

INTRO: A soft-spoken classical music announcer (in Jim's voice) introduces Kermit with a performance of "Dizzy Fingers."

RECORD: "Dizzy Fingers": Performed by Jonathan Edwards (Paul Weston), written by Edward Elzear "Zez" Confrey

Composer Zez Confrey was known for creating eccentric novelty piano solos, including 1921's "Kitten on the Keys." This recording of Confrey's quick-tempo song "Dizzy Fingers" was made by Paul Weston, playing in character as bad lounge musician Jonathan Edwards.

February 26, 1959

RECORD: "Salt": Performed by The Vagabonds, written by Jack Adrian (a.k.a. Adrian Greenberg) (see page 89)

COMMERCIAL: Same as February 17, 1959

February 27, 1959

RECORD: "Love Poems: Togetherness": Performed by Andy Griffith and Billy May's Chamber Group, written by Andy Griffith, Billy May, poetry by the Beautiful Barbara Edwards

As chamber music plays, Andy Griffith recites poetry, juxtaposing the flowery poetic figures of speech with his homespun manner and Southern drawl. On the 45, the poetry is credited to the "Beautiful Barbara Edwards," which happens to be the maiden name of Griffith's wife at the time.

COMMERCIAL: Same as February 9, 1959

RECORD: "It's Never Too Late to Fall in Love": Performed by *The Boy Friend* Original Broadway Cast (featuring) Geoffrey Hibbert and Dilys Lay, written by Sandy Wilson

This song is from the musical *The Boy Friend* (1954), which had a long run in London's West End and is notable for being the Broadway debut of Julie Andrews, who would go on to work with Jim Henson on several occasions, including as a guest star on *The Muppet Show*. The 1971 film adaptation of *The Boy Friend* starred another future *Muppet Show* guest, Twiggy.

March 2, 1959

RECORD: "The Sad Cowboy": Performed by The Sportsmen Quartet with orchestral accompaniment, written by Al Gannaway, Hoagy Carmichael, Walton Farrar (see page 248)

COMMERCIAL: Professor Madcliffe is in carnival barker mode as he invites viewers to step right up and enter the "Load O' Loot" contest with one word to best describe Esskay's new and improved Hickory Smoked Sliced Bacon. As he lists some of the prizes, he is repeatedly interrupted by a little boy (Harry) reciting the words he wants to use. "Esskay-rumptious . . . Esskay-rutiatingly wonderful . . . Esskay-stiest . . ."

March 3, 1959

RECORD: "Alvin's Harmonica": Performed by David Seville and the Chipmunks, written by Ross Bagdasarian

This Top 10 hit was the second Chipmunks record, following the 1958 No. 1 Christmas tune, "The Chipmunk Song." The Chipmunks' voices were created by Ross Bagdasarian by recording his voice on a tape recorder running at half speed, then playing the tape back at full speed. In this song, despite David Seville's protests, Alvin insists on playing his harmonica rather than the planned number. (For more on David Seville, see page 81.)

COMMERCIAL: Same as February 12, 1959

TAG: After the closing announce, harmonica music is heard as Harry tells Alvin to stop: "All right, Alvin. Do like the man says. Cut it out."

March 4, 1959

COLD OPEN: Omar describes the color television camera: "Tonight, friends, as an educational feature of our show, we'd like to explain the TV color camera. Here on the front of the camera, you'll see the lens turret. On top, you'll see the radiator. Behind the lens turret, here, we have a shortwave radio, a vacuum cleaner, an image orthicon tube, the sacroiliac, the clavicle, the polarity regulator, the horizontal cue, the cerebellum, the femur, and in the middle, the drive shaft." Omar explains that they've just bought a new multimillion-dollar color camera (with whitewall tires) for the show, and he starts it up, only to hear a loud motor sound effect. "Oh no, it's stuck in reverse!" After a loud crash, Omar makes a request: "Would you mind asking the director to order a couple more of those?"

TITLE CARD/ANNOUNCE

RECORD: "Eloise": Performed by Kay Thompson, orchestra conducted by Archie Bleyer, written by Kay Thompson, Robert Wells

Thompson provides the spoken vocals for Eloise and Nanny as a male chorus sings about the precocious six-year-old girl who lives on the top floor at New York's Plaza Hotel. Though today best known as the author of the *Eloise* books, Kay Thompson was an acclaimed vocal arranger at MGM and a popular nightclub performer.

COMMERCIAL: Same as February 10, 1959

March 5, 1959

RECORD: "Lay Somethin' on the Bar (Besides Your Elbows)": Performed by Jerry Lewis with orchestra conducted by Dick Stabile, written by Billy Austin, Sheldon Smith

Jerry Lewis released this solo Capitol record in 1951 while still teamed with Dean Martin. In this novelty song, the bartender narrator appeals to customers to pay their tabs and "lay somethin' on the bar besides your elbows."

COMMERCIAL: Professor Madcliffe tells the cast that they received a letter from the sponsor. Harry responds, "Letters, we have letters, we've got—man, this show is getting more like Perry Como every night." Madcliffe says that everyone's been talking so much about the "Load O' Loot" contest prizes that they haven't sufficiently mentioned Esskay's new and improved Hickory Smoked Sliced Bacon. Harry concludes the spot with another mention of the product and the contest. "You'll find instructions on how to win the 'Load O' Loot' in every package of this bacon. Please buy some today. Our life here is going to be miserable until you do."

March 6, 1959

RECORD: "Serutan Yob (A Song for Backward Boys and Girls Under 40)": Performed by Red Ingle and The Unnatural Seven, vocal by Karen Tedder and Enrohtwah, written by eden ahbez

Red Ingle's record is a hillbilly take on "Nature Boy," a song popularized by Nat King Cole. The song is the story of a "strange, enchanted boy" who wandered the world spreading a philosophy of love. Songwriter eden ahbez, a free-spirited forefather of the hippie movement (thus the lowercase spelling of his name), was said to have based the title character on himself.

COMMERCIAL: Same as February 25, 1959

TAG: After the closing title card and announce, the characters are hard at work against a backdrop of construction noises. Harry points out that on the previous night's show, one of the placards fell down, and since they're going to be in color next Monday, he's having the cast "put the stage and sets all shipshape." He calls out some instructions to Moldy Hay, who is adjusting the lights, and Omar, who is painting. A bucket falls on Harry's head. "Omar! Did you turn out the lights?"

March 9, 1959 (first color broadcast)

RECORD: "The Chick": Performed by Lee and Paul, written by Lee Pockriss, Paul Vance

The song is about the hatching of three chicks from eggs left by the Easter Bunny. One of the chicks is not content to be an Easter chick but instead wants to play bass guitar in a rock 'n' roll band. This disgruntled chick occasionally interjects spoken complaints throughout the song ("Man, like, I don't dig feathers") and sings his rock 'n' roll chorus. Songwriter Lee Pockriss went on to have a long career, including composing many songs for *Sesame Street*. His and Paul Vance's biggest hit, however, was 1960's "Itsy Bitsy Teenie Weenie Yellow Polka Dot Bikini," which Miss Piggy recorded in 1993 for the *Muppet Beach Party* CD.

COMMERCIAL: Same as February 17, 1959

March 10, 1959

RECORD: "The Ugly Duckling": Performed by Danny Kaye, written by Frank Loesser (see page 256)

COMMERCIAL: Same as March 2, 1959

March 11, 1959

RECORD: "The Good Old Days": Performed by Eddie Lawrence, written by Eddie Lawrence

Eddie Lawrence, best known for "The Old Philosopher," spends this entire recording complaining about rock 'n' roll and angrily, yet fondly, reminiscing about the good old days.

COMMERCIAL: Same as March 5, 1959

March 12, 1959 (first on-camera mention of the show being in color)

COLD OPEN: Following the crow of a rooster, Harry announces, "The following gig is being laid on you in indefatigable color." Omar asks what happened to the NBC peacock. "For your edification, cat, the only birds on this show will be Esskay chickens."

TITLE CARD/ANNOUNCE

RECORD: "Dinah": Performed by Danny Kaye, written by Harry Akst, Sam M. Lewis, Joe Young (see page 295–296)

COMMERCIAL: Same as February 12, 1959

March 13, 1959

RECORD: "The Kids on the Corner": Performed by Phil Foster, written by Phil Foster, containing "That Old Gang of Mine," written by Ray Henderson, Billy Rose, Mort Dixon

This 1954 song kicks off with a vocal of "That Old Gang of Mine." After the first line, the instrumental backing continues as Phil Foster launches into a spoken soliloquy in which he wonders what happened to his old friends from the corner—Beans, Knuckles, Four-Eyes, and Bushel-Head. Brooklyn stand-up comedian Phil

Foster is probably best remembered as Frank DeFazio, Laverne's father on *Laverne & Shirley*.

COMMERCIAL: Same as February 10, 1959

March 16, 1959

COLD OPEN: Harry announces, "The following gig is being brought to you in living— Er, the following gig is being brought to you in color. . . . Yorick, I thought I told you to leave that bird alone." (We can only imagine what Yorick was doing to NBC's peacock logo.)

TITLE CARD/ANNOUNCE

RECORD: "I've Got You Under My Skin": Performed by Louis Prima and Keely Smith, written by Cole Porter

Introduced in the 1936 movie *Born to Dance,* this Oscar-nominated Cole Porter tune has been recorded many times, and three different versions were used on *Sam and Friends*. This version is a Louis Prima/Keely Smith duet with a driving percussion rhythm and horn section punctuation.

COMMERCIAL: Same as February 25, 1959

March 17, 1959

RECORD: "Tango": Performed by Mike Nichols and Elaine May, written by Mike Nichols and Elaine May, containing background music, "Jalousie," performed by Marty Rubinstein, written by Jacob Gade

Mike Nichols and Elaine May, who would each go on to impressive filmmaking careers, had a successful run as an improvisational comedy team in the late 1950s and early '60s. One of their records, *Improvisations to Music* (1958), contained this track, a dialogue taking place during a tango in which most of the discussion is about the new postal zone system. Jim Henson would go on to collaborate with Elaine May when she worked on a script revision for *Labyrinth*.

COMMERCIAL: Same as February 17, 1959

TAG: The closing announce is interrupted by the final piano arpeggio and "olé" of the Nichols and May record.

March 18, 1959

RECORD: "Outer Space": Performed by Ken Nordine, written by Ken Nordine

From his *Son of Word Jazz* album (1957), this Ken Nordine track recounts an attempt to communicate with outer space. The odd sounds of the alien questions are interpreted and answered by Nordine. "Yes, we have many, many women here on Earth. They're beautiful, actually. They're different from men, and we revere them. In fact, women are extremely important to us."

COMMERCIAL: Same as December 23, 1958, but Kermit and Harry are playing the roles originally played by Moldy Hay and Professor Madcliffe in the original spot.

March 19, 1959

RECORD: "Leather-Winged Bat": Performed by Burl Ives, Traditional

Burl Ives first recorded his version of the English folk song on his album *The Wayfaring Stranger* in 1944. He rerecorded it for his

1958 album, *Capt. Burl Ives' Ark*. Judy Collins would later perform the song on *The Muppet Show*.

COMMERCIAL: Same as December 15, 1958

RECORD: "On Top of Old Smokey": Performed by Burl Ives, Traditional

This American folk song was popularized by The Weavers in a 1951 recording and Burl Ives released the version used on *Sam and Friends* shortly thereafter. Tom Glazer turned the tune into a popular children's record of the 1960s with an edible update: "On Top of Spaghetti." Grover sang his own version of the original song on the 1975 *Sesame Street* album, *Bert & Ernie Sing-Along*.

Kermeena discovers "The Thing" in a great big wooden box floating in the bay. Photo by Jim Henson

March 20, 1959

RECORD: "The Thing": Performed by Alice Pearce, written by Charles Grean

This recording is from *Monster Rally,* a 1959 concept novelty album featuring both covers and original funny songs in the horror theme and wrapped inside a sleeve illustrated by Jack Davis (who would later illustrate early *Sesame Street* calendars and merchandise). Jim used several *Monster Rally* tracks on *Sam and Friends.* Alice Pearce, best known as Mrs. Kravitz on *Bewitched,* provides the vocal on this reworking of the hit Phil Harris record.

COMMERCIAL: Same as December 19, 1958

TAG: Omar has purchased "The Thing" from a little girl—and sells it to Harry. He opens it and is eaten (presumably by Yorick).

POST LOGO TAG: After the closing announce, we hear the little girl from the record laughing.

March 23, 1959

RECORD: "I Love Me (I'm Wild About Myself)": Performed by Mel Blanc, written by Edwin J. Weber, Will Mahoney, Jack Hains (see pages 299–300)

An unidentified character performs the song at a piano.

COMMERCIAL: Moldy Hay explains that they're not quite ready for the commercial. He shows a picture of an Esskay Fully Cooked Ham (in its golden foil), but he says they had asked the Esskay people to prepare one with all the trimmings so the audience could see what it would look like for their Easter dinner. They had sent Omar to the Esskay plant to pick it up, but Moldy learns Omar has returned without the ham. "Technical difficulties, ladies and gentlemen," Moldy says. "Due to conditions beyond our control, the commercial you were about to see at this time has been canceled—Omar ate it."

TAG: The pianist prepares to play again. "And now for my next number..." Instead, a new song, "I Love Me" starts to repeat. "Hey, that's the same thing you just did," Omar says. The pianist doesn't mind. "I not only like me, I like my music. I wrote it," he says, continuing to scat-sing and play until the show ends.

March 24, 1959

RECORD: "I Went to Your Wedding": Performed by Spike Jones and His City Slickers, vocal refrain by Sir Frederick Gas, written by Jessie Mae Robinson (see page 243)

COMMERCIAL: Professor Madcliffe calls for the Muppets to "fall in" to hear a new directive from the Esskay people. Madcliffe explains that too many people are buying new and improved Esskay Hickory Smoked Sliced Bacon to enter to "Load O' Loot" contest. But it's now Easter time and, "Ham is what we gotta sell now!" The cast is encouraged to tell people to buy Esskay Fully Cooked Hams—and Harry does so, but he can't resist adding a pitch for bacon.

March 25, 1959

RECORD: "The Invisible Man": Performed by Alice Pearce, written by Joel Herron, Fred Hertz

In this original song from the *Monster Rally* album, Alice Pearce's character explains that although no one has been able to see her romance, she's been going steady with the Invisible Man.

COMMERCIAL: After reading a book (*Do-it-Yourself Hypnosis: Self Taught in Ten Easy Lessons or Five Hard Ones*), Omar has accidentally hypnotized himself into thinking he's an Esskay Fully Cooked Ham. "I am an Esskay Fully Cooked Ham. So thoroughly cooked, you can serve me just as I come from the gold foil wrapper."

Omar continues the commercial under hypnosis. At the end, Harry observes, "We have lost a friend, but we gained a ham."

March 26, 1959

RECORD: "Going on a Hike": Performed by Tom D'Andrea and Hal March, with harmonica accompaniment by Jerry Hilliard, written by George Cates, Tom D'Andrea, Hal March

Actors Tom D'Andrea and Hal March teamed in a short-lived 1955 NBC service comedy called *The Soldiers,* based on characters they developed on variety show appearances. On this record, soldiers Tom and Hal complain about taking a hike.

COMMERCIAL: Same as March 23, 1959

The *Sam and Friends* presentation of "On the Good Ship Lollipop." Photo by Jim Henson

March 27, 1959

RECORD: "On the Good Ship Lollipop": Performed by Shirley Temple, written by Richard Whiting, Sidney Clare

First sung by Shirley Temple in the 1934 film *Bright Eyes,* the song became identified with the child star and landed on the American Film Institute list of the one hundred most popular songs in movies.

COMMERCIAL: Same as March 24, 1959

RECORD: "I'm Five": Performed by Danny Kaye, written by Milton Schafer

"I'm Five" was introduced on Danny Kaye's 1958 album, *Mommy, Gimme a Drinka Water*. Kermit's nephew, Robin, sang the song on a second-season episode of *The Muppet Show,* but only after Kermit nixed his original choice, "They Call the Wind Maria." The track was also included on *The Muppet Show 2* album.

March 30, 1959

RECORD: "Mama from the Train (Throw Mama Down the Stairs Her Hat of Blue)": Performed by Homer and Jethro, written by Irving Gordon (see page 279)

COMMERCIAL: Same as March 2, 1959

RECORD: "I've Got You Under My Skin": Performed by Stan Freberg with Les Baxter and His Orchestra and Chorus, written by Cole Porter (see pages 157–158 for a full summary)

March 31, 1959

RECORD: "Life Gits Tee-Jus, Don't It?": Performed by Peter Lind Hayes, written by Carson Robinson (see page 292)

COMMERCIAL: Same as February 5, 1959

April 1, 1959

INTRO: Omar has difficulty saying hello and asks how to greet the audience.

RECORD: "How Do'ye Do and Shake Hands": Performed by Betty Hutton, Dinah Shore, Tony Martin, Phil Harris, with Henri René and His Orchestra, written by Cy Coben and Oliver Wallace (see page 252)

COMMERCIAL: Same as February 6, 1959

April 2, 1959

RECORD: "The Book Was So Much Better Than the Picture": Performed by Jerry Lewis with orchestra conducted by Dick Stabile, written by Mel Leven (see pages 269–270)

COMMERCIAL: Same as February 12, 1959

TAG: Kermit ends with a mention of Academy Awards season, "so we thought we'd get our nomination in." He rattles off a list of award categories for *Sam and Friends* to enter: "Best Actor, Best Actress, Best Directed Show, Best Photography, Best Sound, Best Art Direction . . ." Kermit continues reading categories as the show fades out.

April 3, 1959

RECORD: "Monster Rally": Performed by Hans Conried and Alice Pearce, written by Joel Herron, Fred Hertz

The title track from the *Monster Rally* album, this song announces the title event and lists all the famous monsters who will be in attendance. The voices are provided by Alice Pearce and Hans Conried, who is probably best remembered for his cartoon voices. Conried provided the voice of Captain Hook in Walt Disney's *Peter Pan* (1953) and Snidely Whiplash in Jay Ward's *Dudley Do-Right*. Fans of classic TV may remember Conried from his many on-camera appearances, including a recurring role as Uncle Tonoose on Danny Thomas's *Make Room for Daddy*.

COMMERCIAL: Same as February 9, 1959

TAG: Harry and Sam are lost in unfamiliar territory. "You know, if you were the kind of cat who gets scared, this place here might scare ya," Harry says. "But we're not the kinda cats who get scared, are we? You bet your life we're not." When they hear one cackling laugh, Harry suggests they make a quick exit as one more line from "Monster Rally" is repeated: "You'll be lucky to get out alive!"

April 6, 1959

COLD OPEN: After a rooster crows, Harry announces: "The following gig is being brought to you in living color, and for those cats without color sets, it's being brought to you in dull black and white and motley shades of gray."

TITLE CARD/ANNOUNCE

RECORD: "My Baby": Performed by Ken Nordine and The Fred Katz Group, written by Fred Katz

In this track from his *Word Jazz* album, Ken Nordine gives a laid-back monologue about "his baby" as Fred Katz's jazz plays beneath.

As the record begins, through jazz slang we are led to believe think the baby referred to is Nordine's date, but the piece culminates with a performance from his baby—a real baby.

COMMERCIAL: Same as February 17, 1959

April 7, 1959

RECORD: "I Just Goofed": Performed by Ernie Englund and His Orchestra, written by Ernie Englund (see pages 274–275)

COMMERCIAL: Same as February 9, 1959

RECORD: "The Maladjusted Jester": Performed by Danny Kaye, written by Sylvia Fine (see page 279)

April 8, 1959

RECORD: "The Man on the Flying Trapeze": Performed by Spike Jones and His City Slickers, commentary by Doodles Weaver, written by Alfred Lee, George Leybourne, arranged by Spike Jones and Doodles Weaver (see pages 287–288)

COMMERCIAL: Same as March 5, 1959

April 9, 1959

RECORD: "Don't Sing Along (On Top of Old Smokey)": Performed by Homer and Jethro, Traditional, special lyrics by Homer and Jethro

Homer and Jethro take on the sing-along craze in this 1959 record "On Top of Old Smokey." Homer feeds lines to the sing-along singers in every musical pause, but not the correct ones. "On top of old Smokey / all covered with trees / I stood in the water / from up to my ankles."

COMMERCIAL: Same as February 25, 1959

April 10, 1959

RECORD: "Face the Funnies": Performed by Stan Freberg, Daws Butler, June Foray, Peter Leeds, written by Stan Freberg, Pete Barnum (see page 302)

COMMERCIAL: Same as February 9, 1959

April 13, 1959

TITLE CARD/ANNOUNCE: "Rhapsody from Hunger(y)": Performed by Spike Jones and His City Slickers, vocal refrain by Freddy Morgan and Helen Grayco, written by Franz Liszt, arrangement by Spike Jones

Instead of the regular theme, Omar delivers the *Sam and Friends* opening announce over the instrumental introduction ("Hungarian Rhapsody") of Spike Jones's "Rhapsody from Hunger(y)." After a romantic couple makes a couple of toasts, they break their glasses when clinking, and the record abruptly changes to . . .

RECORD: "Never Trust a Woman": Performed by Phil Harris and His Orchestra, written by Jenny Lou Carson

Phil Harris released "Never Trust a Woman" in 1948. Interestingly, the fairly sexist song was, in fact, written by a woman. Prolific songwriter Jenny Lou Carson was the first woman to write a song to hit No. 1 on the country music chart (1945's "You Two-Timed Me One Time Too Often").

COMMERCIAL: Same as March 2, 1959

April 14, 1959

RECORD: "Lida Rose and Will I Ever Tell You": Performed by *The Music Man* Original Broadway Cast (featuring The Buffalo Bills and Barbara Cook), written by Meredith Willson

From Meredith Willson's 1957 Broadway hit, *The Music Man*, the song begins with the school board barbershop quartet singing "Lida Rose." The song becomes a counterpoint as Marian the Librarian sings "Will I Ever Tell You." This presentation pauses for a commercial just before the counterpoint begins.

COMMERCIAL: Same as February 6, 1959

RECORD: The song resumes with Marian singing her "Will I Ever Tell You" counterpoint as the quartet's "Lida Rose" continues.

April 15, 1959

RECORD: "Income Tax": Performed by Bob Corley, written by Bob Corley (see pages 289–290)

COMMERCIAL: Same as February 10, 1959

April 16, 1959

INTRO: Harry introduces a learned speaker lecturing on high fidelity.

RECORD: "Herman Horne on Hi-Fi": Performed by Stan Freberg, written by Stan Freberg, Pete Barnum (see page 312)

COMMERCIAL: Same as February 9, 1959

TAG: Sound effects from Stan Freberg's record

April 17, 1959

COLD OPEN: Harry says they asked the Bolshoi Ballet to perform a number written especially for *Sam and Friends*, but the dance company refused. So instead, they are presenting chapter two in the love life of Ambrose.

TITLE CARD/ANNOUNCE

RECORD: "Forever Ambrose": Performed by Linda Laurie, written by Sidney Jacobson, Linda Laurie, Lou Stallman

Linda Laurie followed up on the success of "Ambrose (Part Five)" with "Forever Ambrose," but this time, Ambrose gets more dialogue as the couple looks back on their past. "Bright Eyes" (as Ambrose calls her), however, is far more romantic than Ambrose. Linda Laurie would go on to write the theme song to the Sid and Marty Krofft series *Land of the Lost*.

COMMERCIAL: Same as February 12, 1959

April 20, 1959

INTRO: Omar explains that he asked Yorick to dig up hi-fi sounds to share on the show. At twenty-three feet down, this is what he discovered:

RECORD: "There's a New Sound": Performed by Tony Burrello, written by Tony Burrello, Tom Murray (see page 74)

COMMERCIAL: Same as February 25, 1959

April 21, 1959

RECORD: "The Lone Psychiatrist": Performed by Stan Freberg with Daws Butler and June Foray, orchestra conducted by Billy May, written by Stan Freberg, Daws Butler, Larkin, Calvelli

In 1955, Stan Freberg combined the popularity of television's *The Lone Ranger* with the science of modern psychiatry, creating a masked man roaming the West offering psychoanalysis.

COMMERCIAL: Unknown

April 22, 1959

RECORD: "A Brooklyn Baseball Fan": Performed by Phil Foster, chorus and orchestra directed by Dick Jacobs, written by Phil Foster, contains "Take Me Out to the Ball Game," written by Albert Von Tilzer, Jack Norworth

Credited on the record as "Brooklyn's Ambassador to the U.S.A.," Phil Foster delivered this spoken-word tribute to the enthusiastic fans of the Brooklyn Dodgers in 1954. The team abandoned

Brooklyn for sunny Los Angeles in 1957. (Phil Foster would eventually do the same, co-starring on *Laverne & Shirley* in the 1970s.)

COMMERCIAL: Same as February 17, 1959

April 23, 1959

RECORD: "Mostly Ghostly": Performed by Hans Conried and Alice Pearce, written by Joel Herron, Fred Hertz

This track from the *Monster Rally* novelty album is a tribute to a girl who is, indeed, mostly ghostly and, according to the song, is "clearly the most different girl I've ever seen. / Truly ghoulie . . . every day with her is Halloween."

COMMERCIAL: Same as March 5, 1959

SKETCH: Omar introduces a new feature, "The Poet's Corner." As lush organ music plays, they recite. Moldy Hay: "Thirty days hath Octember, / Juniary and no wonder. / All the rest have peanut butter, / except grandmother, and she has a Volkswagen. Thank you." Harry: "Roses are red, violets are blue, I can row a boat . . . canoe?" Kermit: "Roses are red. Violets are blue. What colors are yours?" Professor Madcliffe: "A funny old bird is a pelican. / His beak can hold more than his belly can. / He can hold in his beak, / enough food for a week . . . well, I don't know how." Omar invites viewers to send in their poems and gives the address for WRC-TV. Jim would later perform a variation on the "Thirty Days" poem on *The Muppets on Puppets* (1968) and *The Dick Cavett Show* (1971).

April 24, 1959

RECORD: "Nowhere": Performed by Red Ingle and The Natural Seven, written by Edward Heyman, John Green, arranged by Country Washburne, Foster Carling

Red Ingle's "Nowhere" is a brisk two-step celebrating the place (or lack thereof) called nowhere. Within the song is a substantial homage to Phil Harris's "That's What I Like About the South": "Did I tell you 'bout the place called Didma Duty? / It ain't no city, but it's a beauty. / And that's where I met my sweet patootie. / I did my duty!"

COMMERCIAL: Same as February 6, 1959

April 27, 1959

RECORD: "Silhouettes": Performed by Andy Griffith, orchestra under direction of Billy May, written by Frank C. Slay, Jr., Bob Crewe, special material by Andy Griffith and Ainslie Pryor (see page 289)

COMMERCIAL: Same as March 2, 1959

April 28, 1959

RECORD: "Hey, Boy! Hey, Girl!": Performed by Louis Prima and Keely Smith, Sam Butera and The Witnesses, written by Jimmie Thomas, Oscar McLollie

This swinging duet was the title song for the 1959 film that starred Louis Prima and Keely Smith.

COMMERCIAL: Same as February 9, 1959

April 29, 1959

RECORD: "The Pocketbook Song": Performed by Leroy Van Dyke, written by Landrew Smith, Percy Terry, Lee Hazlewood

This rockabilly song essentially lists the contents of a woman's purse: "She had corn pads, matches, and some kind of token / tickets for a show way up in Shamokin." Co-writer Lee Hazlewood is probably best known for writing the Nancy Sinatra hit "These Boots Are Made for Walkin.'"

SEGMENT: "The Poet's Corner": Moldy Hay recites "Perseverance" (actually a comedic take on Edgar Guest's "It Couldn't Be Done"): "They told him that it couldn't be done. / With a smile he went right to it. / He tackled the thing that couldn't be done . . . and couldn't do it." Harry: "It is better to have loved a short guy, than never to have loved a'tall." Professor Madcliffe: "I knew a girl named Passion. / I asked her for a date. / I took her out to dinner, / and, gosh, how Passion ate." Omar closes with a request to viewers to send in poems.

COMMERCIAL: Same as February 10, 1959

April 30, 1959

RECORD: "Do I Worry?": Performed by The Ink Spots, written by Stanley Cowan, Bobby Worth

By the time this gentle ballad was used on *Sam and Friends,* The Ink Spots had been disbanded for several years.

COMMERCIAL: Same as February 25, 1959

May 1, 1959

RECORD: "It's a Quiet Town": Performed by Danny Kaye and The Andrews Sisters with Vic Schoen and His Orchestra, written by Bob Russell, Harold Spina (see page 251)

COMMERCIAL: Same as February 6, 1959

SEGMENT: "The Poet's Corner": Professor Madcliffe: "I often pause and wonder at fate's peculiar ways, / for nearly all our famous men are born on holidays." Moldy Hay: "Down the street the funeral goes, and wails and sobs diminish. / He died from drinking shellac they say, he had a lovely finish. Thank you." Harry: "I bought a wooden whistle, but it wouldn't whistle, so I bought a steel whistle, but steel it wouldn't whistle, so bought a lead whistle, steel, it wouldn't lead me whistle. So I bought a tin whistle. And now, I tin whistle." Omar closes by mentioning the poetic tidbits were contributed by the audience.

May 4, 1959

RECORD: "The King's New Clothes": Performed by Danny Kaye, written by Frank Loesser (see page 267)

COMMERCIAL: A three-bedroom home, a 1959 Studebaker Lark, and an all-new kitchen and laundry room are among the prizes in a "Name This Steer" contest sponsored by the Visking Company, makers of the sausage casings used in manufacturing Esskay Franks. Viewers are instructed to look for the contest sticker on Esskay Franks for entry information.

May 5, 1959

RECORD: "She's a Lady": Performed by Betty Hutton and Perry Como with Mitchell Ayres and His Orchestra, written by Cy Coben (see page 290)

COMMERCIAL: Harry presents a wild invention—the "dreamicator," which will show what anybody is dreaming about in wonderful Technicolor. The machine shows that Moldy Hay is dreaming about the three-bedroom house offered in the Visking contest. Professor Madcliffe is dreaming about finding a name for the steer—the challenge presented in the contest as the best name wins. Yorick is dreaming about the package of Esskay Franks that contains the entry form (all he ever dreams of is food).

May 6, 1959

TITLE CARD/ANNOUNCE: The announce is made over the harmonica solo of the episode's featured song instead of the regular theme, and this opening title segues directly into the lip-sync performance.

RECORD: "I Found My Mamma": Performed by Rosemary Clooney with Eddy Manson on the harmonica and orchestra under the direction of Percy Faith

In this novelty song from 1950, Rosemary Clooney swings a version of "Mary Had a Little Lamb"—and the lamb's responses are harmonica sounds.

COMMERCIAL: Professor Madcliffe asks the audience to "excuse the commercial tonight"—they're featuring Esskay Franks this month, and Omar has never done a commercial for franks. "So the Professor here is going to teach me how to do it tonight," Omar says. Madcliffe tells Omar to show the people how much he's learned. Omar begins the commercial, holding up a single frankfurter, only to have Madcliffe tell him he has the product turned the wrong way. "Everyone knows the front end of the frank should be to the left and back end to the right." To Omar, both ends look the same. Madcliffe concurs but asks Omar to keep the right end of the frank pointed to his right side and the left end of the frank pointed to his left side. Omar concludes: "I guess Esskay must have hickory smoked the right and left sides right off of this one. Folks, even if they don't have a front and back, left side or right, they sure taste good."

SEGUE: Harry announces that in honor of the Esskay Franks commercial, they have a bit of happy hot dog music—and to sing it, they have the happy hot dog harmonizers . . .

RECORD: "Hot Dog Polka": Performed by Len Dresslar, written by Harry Coon, Paul Severson

This lively song includes the refrain "There ain't no bones in a hot dog." Performer Len Dresslar worked often in the advertising industry, and his most recognizable performance was as the voice of the Jolly Green Giant.

May 7, 1959

RECORD: "A Four-Legged Friend": Performed by Bob Hope and Jimmy Wakely, written by Jack Brooks (see pages 238–239)

COMMERCIAL: Kermit asks Yorick to hold up a package of Esskay Franks while Kermit does the commercial for the Visking contest to name the steer. He lists the prizes and then asks Yorick to show the contest entry sticker, which is the only thing remaining from the package after Yorick got to it. "Yikes, Yorick," Kermit says, "you almost ate the commercial."

TAG: Harry thanks the Academy of Television Arts & Sciences for the local Emmy Award received the previous night. On behalf of the whole group, Harry thanks Esskay, the ad agency VanSant Dugdale, director John Chapin, "and the three empty-headed puppeteers Bob Payne, Jane Nebel, and Jim—" Harry is muffled (apparently by a human hand) before he can get out the rest of Jim's name.

May 8, 1959

RECORD: "The Five Pennies Saints (When the Saints Go Marching In)": Performed by Danny Kaye and Louis Armstrong, Traditional, adapted by Sylvia Fine

Danny Kaye played bandleader Red Nichols in the 1959 film *The Five Pennies* and recorded this song with co-star Louis Armstrong (who played himself) for the film's soundtrack.

COMMERCIAL: Same as May 4, 1959

May 11, 1959

RECORD: "None But the Lonely Heart": Performed by Spike Jones and His City Slickers with Helen Grayco, violin solo by Dick Gardner, written by Peter Tchaikovsky, arranged by Eddie Brandt, Spike Jones (see page 294)

In this presentation, the song is paused halfway through for a commercial.

COMMERCIAL: Same as May 4, 1959

RECORD: "None But the Lonely Heart" concludes.

TAG: "The Poet's Corner": Moldy Hay: "Some farmers say a cow gives milk autumn, winter, spring, and summer, / but I say a cow doesn't give milk, you've got to take it from her. Thank you." Harry: "I only drink my nerves to calm / my steadiness improve, / last night I got so steady, / I couldn't even move." Professor Madcliffe: "A divinity student named Tweedle / refused to accept his degree. / He didn't object to the Tweedle, / but he hated the Tweedle-D.D." Omar thanks the viewers for the poems featured on "The Poet's Corner."

May 12, 1959

INTRO: Professor Madcliffe tells Sam they're ready to try the dreamicator machine to interpret Sam's thoughts. He tells Sam to think of something. The music to "That Old Black Magic" starts, but the Professor tells him to think of something serious like philosophy, nuclear fission, or the Pythagorean theorem. After an explosive sound effect, the music begins.

RECORD: "Ain't A-Hankerin'": Performed by Bob Hope and Rosemary Clooney, orchestra conducted by Gus Levene, written by Budd Burtson, Arthur Altman

This song is from the Western comedy *Alias Jesse James* (1959), but the recording used here is a pop cover. While Bob Hope reprises his performance, Rosemary Clooney's half of the duet in the film was performed by Rhonda Fleming.

COMMERCIAL: Same as May 5, 1959

May 13, 1959

COMMERCIAL: Same as May 6, 1959

RECORD: "Interview with Shorty Petterstein": Performed by Henry Jacobs, Professor Leaf Woodrow, written by Henry Jacobs (see pages 270–271)

May 14, 1959

RECORD: "Yosemite Sam": Performed by Mel Blanc, music by Billy May, written by Alan Livingston, Billy May (see page 292)

COMMERCIAL: Same as May 7, 1959

May 15, 1959

RECORD: "Dance of the Hours": Performed by Spike Jones and His City Slickers, commentator Doodles Weaver, written by Amilcare Ponchielli, arranged by Doodles Weaver and Spike Jones

The 1949 RCA recording begins with an instrumental fanfare and quickly transitions to a racetrack call by Doodles Weaver with Ponchielli's "Dance of the Hours" serving as background music.

COMMERCIAL: Same as May 4, 1959

SKETCH: "The Poet's Corner": Moldy Hay: "I once had a classmate named Guesser, / whose knowledge grew lesser and lesser. / It at last grew so small, / he knew nothing at all, / and now he's a college professor." Professor Madcliffe: "Old Mother Kangaroo / has a bag for her kids, too, / but when they grow old, they scram and never come back, / leaving the old lady holding the sack." Omar delivers a poem that is apparently an old Navy saying: "When in trouble or in doubt, / run in circles, scream, and shout." Harry: "Mary had a little lamb, / its fleece was white as snow, / why fleas is white instead of black / is what I'd like to know." Omar closes with, "You've been listening to 'Poet's Corner,' which is designed for the literary enhancement of our youth."

May 18, 1959

RECORD: "The Matador": Performed by Sammy Shore with orchestral accompaniment, written by Sammy Shore

Stand-up comedian Sammy Shore, who sang this novelty song about the greatest bullfighter, went on to co-found the Comedy Store comedy club in Los Angeles. In the "Miss Piggy's Hollywood" segment of *The Jim Henson Hour*, Fozzie Bear auditions at the club.

COMMERCIAL: Same as May 4, 1959

May 19, 1959

INTRO: Omar is trying to contact outer space with the dreamicator machine. He soon makes contact with someone (or something) speaking in gibberish. This launches into the classic "You Don't Say" gag: "You don't say . . . you don't say . . . you don't say." / "Who was it?" / "He didn't say."

RECORD: "Flying Saucer": Performed by Hans Conried, written by Joel Herron, Fred Hertz

Another track from the *Monster Rally* album, this song is in the form of an announcement with Hans Conried singing a request for the owner of the flying saucer to move it to another location or receive a parking ticket.

COMMERCIAL: Same as May 5, 1959

May 20, 1959

RECORD: "Dante's Inferno": Performed by The Mark IV, written by Edward Mascari, Erwin Wenzlaff

This is an up-tempo, harmonic tune welcoming deserving folks to Dante's Inferno. "You pushed your way into the bus, / you didn't want to wait. / You only had two blocks to walk, / but you were rather late. / The driver took your transfer, / but your thumb was on the date. / Welcome to Dante's Inferno."

COMMERCIAL: Same as May 6, 1959

SKETCH: "The Poet's Corner" is performed over a lush arrangement of "When You Wish Upon a Star." Omar recites: "A stable attendant named Morse, / whose manner was ever so coarse, / neglected to feed / a disgruntled steed, / and was kicked in the head by the horse." Moldy Hay: "A certain young miss from Nantucket, / while milking a cow in a bucket, / gave a terrible wail / when swished with a tail, / her problem is learning to duck it. Thank you." Professor Madcliffe: "A fella with the moniker Fink / once owned a profitable ice-skating rink. / But he looked like a fool / for freezing the pool / when the skaters began to sink." Harry closes by saying that "The Poet's Corner" is dedicated to "the cultural and intellectual downfall of our nation's literature."

May 21, 1959

INTRO: Omar tries to open the show, but Professor Madcliffe interrupts him. "Oh no! Yorick just ate my typewriter!" Harry announces that his hi-fi set and all of his Guy Lombardo records have also been eaten. "Lucky I have my Lawrence Welk records hidden away . . . I think." But a closer look reveals that Yorick also got to Harry's Lawrence Welk records—labels and all. "That boy's gone over the hill for good," Harry says. The music begins.

RECORD: "I Need a Vacation": Performed by Jim Backus, written by Mort Garson, Bob Hilliard

Actor Jim Backus, best remembered as *Gilligan's Island*'s Thurston Howell III and the voice of Mister Magoo, recorded this track in 1958. The song is a breakneck rhythm of instrumental and background vocals with Backus periodically (and anxiously) interjecting his desire for a vacation.

COMMERCIAL: Same as May 7, 1959

May 22, 1959

RECORD: "St. George and the Dragonet": Performed by Stan Freberg, Daws Butler, June Foray, Hy Averback (announcer) with Walter Schumann and orchestra, written by Stan Freberg, Daws Butler, Walter Schumann

This 1953 No. 1 hit was Stan Freberg's parody of Jack Webb's *Dragnet,* placed in medieval times with Freberg's St. George as the no-nonsense knight in pursuit of the facts (and the dragon). The recognizable voices of Daws Butler and June Foray play the other roles, and Hy Averback, best known as a television director, is the announcer. Walter Schumann (composer of the original *Dragnet* theme) and his orchestra provide the music.

COMMERCIAL: Same as May 4, 1959

May 25, 1959

RECORD: "Inchworm": Performed by Danny Kaye, written by Frank Loesser (see page 256)

COMMERCIAL: Same as May 4, 1959

May 26, 1959

INTRO: Harry begins the show by telling the audience of "loyal, faithful followers" that the show will be taking a few weeks off. "Professor Madcliffe here is teaching Sam a course in higher mathematics (numbers over ten), Yorick has a part-time job at a garbage disposal company, and I'm going to Florida to get a suntan." He asks viewers to keep buying Esskay products all summer.

RECORD: "Goodnight Ladies": Performed by The Sportsmen Quartet, written by Edwin Pearce Christy (see page 279)

The quartet starts to sing "Goodnight Ladies," then Harry cuts in to add a good night to men, boys, girls, dogs, goldfish, and all other viewers "whatever you are." The quartet continues, then wraps up with a syncopated ending.

Sam and Friends takes a break for Jim and Jane's May 28, 1959, wedding and their brief honeymoon in Rehoboth Beach, Delaware, with a longer trip around New England to follow.

Note: As the new *Sam and Friends* season begins, Esskay's sponsorship remains on summer hiatus, so the episodes begin and end with a temporary Esskay-less title card and do not include commercials until the company resumes its sponsorship on August 24, 1959.

Sam and his friends make their way back to Washington after a few weeks off.

August 3, 1959

INTRO: Harry is ready for the first show back, but he says Sam and some of the others haven't returned to Washington yet and Professor Madcliffe isn't happy about it. Harry hears a car approach, carrying Sam and the others. Harry asks Sam what he's going to say to Professor Madcliffe.

RECORD: "How Do'ye Do and Shake Hands": Performed by Betty Hutton, Dinah Shore, Tony Martin, Phil Harris, with Henri René and His Orchestra, written by Cy Coben and Oliver Wallace (see page 252)

TAG: Madcliffe tries to tell the audience about what he has planned for upcoming shows. Kermit interrupts, wanting to talk about his plans for the show. As they bicker, Harry enters and says, "Preview of things to come on *Sam and Friends,* namely mayhem."

August 4, 1959

INTRO: Omar is doing a crossword when Professor Madcliffe interrupts—he has seen a snake. After Madcliffe leaves, Omar announces that a new character, Icky Gunk, has joined the "staff" and will be performing with Kermit and Harry in the next number.

RECORD: "S-S-S'Wonderful (Hector the Nearsighted Rattlesnake)": Performed by The Kirby Stone Four, snake rattle played by Archie Bleyer, orchestra conducted by Archie Bleyer, written by George and Ira Gershwin (see page 284)

August 5, 1959

INTRO: Harry begins speaking French and Kermit translates, although it soon becomes clear that Harry just knows a few random words and phrases. Kermit's "translations" explain that the theme of the day's show is "French." The musical number for the evening is a recently released song from a currently running Broadway show. The title of the song (and the Broadway show) is "La Plume de Ma Tante," which Kermit translates as, "The tail of the ostrich is teasing my mother."

RECORD: "La Plume de Ma Tante": Performed by Hugo and Luigi, their orchestra and children's chorus, written by Al Hoffman, Dick Manning

As a children's chorus sings in French, then translates the phrase into English—"The pen of my aunt is on the bureau of my uncle"—a deep voice provides occasional backup vocals, punctuating both

French and English lyrics. The credited performers on this track (and its producers), cousins Hugo (Peretti) and Luigi (Creatore) were also composers.

TAG: Professor Madcliffe wants to know who wrote Harry's French script from the top of the show. Harry says he wrote it himself. "You did?" "Oui!" Harry says. "We? You and who else?" Madcliffe asks. After some further confusion, Harry is asked why he is speaking with a French accent. He says he got a job at Bonelli's pizza restaurant. When told that Bonelli's is Italian, Harry quickly changes accents. (Lou Bonelli was the WRC record librarian.)

August 6, 1959

RECORD: "The Peony Bush": Performed by Danny Kaye, written by Meredith Willson (see page 295)

SKETCH: Icky Gunk confides in Omar that he is planning to take over the weather show. Omar asks if Frank Forrester (WRC's then-new meteorologist) knows about this. Icky says this is the first hurdle. Icky asks if Frank remembers the previous weather person. Before Omar can utter Tippy Stringer's full name, Icky shushes him. "No names." Icky then asks if Omar thinks the new weather person is pretty like the last weather girl. "Well, no," Omar says. "Does he model fashions every night?" Icky asks. "No, but . . ." Before Omar can get another word out, Icky apparently dons a dress and introduces himself as the next weather girl. "Behold! A ravishing beauty!"

August 7, 1959

SKETCH: "Drain Dwellers": This is a revised and rerecorded version of the episode originally created on September 19, 1958. Once again, Kermit interviews drain dweller Orwell Filchmouth, whose voice Jim created by inhaling while speaking. The discussion becomes philosophical when Kermit asks about the difficulties of living in the drain when liquids are poured down the sink. "Yes, Kerm, we learn that there are times when we have to hold on to what we've got and watch everything else pass us by."

August 10, 1959

RECORD: "Sunshine Girl": Performed by *New Girl in Town* Original Broadway Cast, music and lyrics by Bob Merrill

From the 1957 Broadway musical *New Girl in Town* (based on the play *Anna Christie*), the song's refrain cheerfully tells us that the "sunshine girl has raindrops in her eyes."

SKETCH: Harry announces that this season, they're bringing back the cultural part of the show: "The Poet's Corner." Omar: "I remember, I remember, ere my childhood flitted by, / it was cold then in December, it was warmer in July. / In the winter there were freezings, in the summer there were thaws, / but the weather isn't now at all like it used to was." Kermit: "There was an old man from Nantucket, / who kept all his cash in a bucket, / but his daughter named Nan / ran away with a man, / and as for the bucket, Nan took it." Harry: "'Twas in a restaurant they met, / Romeo and Juliet, / he had no cash to pay the debt, / so Romey owed what Julie et. Get it?" Moldy Hay: "They walked in the lane together, / the sky was covered with stars. / They reached the gate in silence, / he lifted down the bars. / She neither smiled nor thanked him / because she knew not how, / for he was just a farmer's daughter / and she a Jersey cow." Harry next delivered Marc Antony Henderson's "Hiawatha" parody, "The Song of Milkanwatha": "He killed the noble Mudjokivis, / of the skin he made him mittens. / Made 'em with the fur side inside, / made 'em with the skin side outside. / He to get the warm side inside, / put the inside skin side outside. / He to get the cold side outside, / put the warm side fur side inside. / That's why he put the fur side inside, / why he put the skin side outside, / why he turned them inside outside . . . so Romey owed what Julie et . . . Get it?" Omar invites viewers to submit their poems. Harry: "So Romey owed what Julie et." Omar: "Oh, shut up, Harry."

August 11, 1959

RECORD: "Beat Love at First Sight": Performed by Al Collins, written by Sol Schlinger

Al Collins (known as Jazzbo) was a disc jockey and musician who released this recording in 1959, just a few months before it was initially used on *Sam and Friends*. It's a love song for the Beat generation: "At first, I dug you to be a square. / You had a job and that's a sin. / But you were no slob and you quit your job. / Now you're Beater than you've ever been."

SKETCH: Professor Madcliffe explains that after watching the show for several days, he believes the missing element is humor—and he has designed a laugh meter (which Moldy Hay assembled for him) to measure the intensity of the laughter of the studio audience in a part of the show called "The Jokebook Nook." Harry: "Did you hear about the auto mechanic who crawled out from under the car, and he told the owner there was a short circuit in the ignition? She said, 'Well, don't just stand there, man . . . lengthen it.'" A titter of canned laughter is heard. Kermit: "Did you know you can't starve in the Sahara Desert because of the sand-which-is-there?" Another titter is heard. Kermit offers another: "You know, Eve wasn't afraid of catching the measles because she had Adam." Another titter. Omar: "Sir Lancelot was selling his coat of armor, so King Arthur said, 'How much are you charging?' and Lancelot said, 'Four cents an ounce. That's First Class mail.'" Another titter. Moldy Hay delivers a simple, "Good evening, friends" and receives a big laugh—he continues: "A feller asked me how long cows should be milked, and I told him, 'Just about the same as short cows.'" He gets a big laugh from the machine. Madcliffe: "Why does the stork stand on one foot? Because if he lifted the other foot, he'd fall down." He gets no response. "Moldy," he says, "this laugh meter isn't working." Moldy says it worked for him, and he tries another joke: "Open the screen door when you shout, Mother. You'll strain your voice!" He gets a big laugh. "See?" Madcliffe is not happy. "This program is fixed!" Moldy Hay invites viewers to send jokes to *Sam and Friends*.

August 12, 1959

RECORD: "Banana Boat (Day-O)": Performed by Stan Freberg, interruptions by Peter Leeds with Billy May's Music, written by Stan Freberg (see pages 300–301)

TAG: A radio announcer sent by NBC comes to investigate the faulty laugh meter used on the previous day's show and plugs the next day's show—a version of "The Three Little Pigs," which he is presenting to expand the dramatic content of the show. This new character is initially named Theodore but will eventually become known as Chicken Liver. Jim may have been planning to do several fairy-tale sketches on *Sam and Friends,* as he listed a few other stories on the reverse of his handwritten script, including "Jack and the Beanstalk," "Cinderella," "Rumpelstiltskin," and "Goldilocks." Fairy tales would become a rich source of content for Jim over the years, ranging from the full-length *Tales from Muppetland* specials to Kermit's regular "*Sesame Street* News Flash" segments.

Theodore (a.k.a. Chicken Liver) joins the cast as an NBC radio announcer before settling in as one of the gang.

August 13, 1959

SKETCH: Theodore, the radio announcer from the previous show, narrates "The Three Little Pigs," as Harry, Kermit, and Icky Gunk play the eponymous roles. The story is delayed when Kermit says he is not happy with the character name Dinky, which the announcer pronounces as "Stinky." Once Kermit's character is renamed George, the story continues with Yorick playing the part of the wolf. (Yorick's insatiable appetite does not bode well for the pigs in this version of the story.) Icky's house of straw (soda straws) is quickly demolished after a few huffs and puffs, and Yorick quickly devours Icky's pig character. Harry's pig has built his house from an old gasoline can, and Yorick "huffed and he puffed and he lit a match and blew his house up." After the explosion, Yorick devours Harry's pig character. Kermit's pig's house is indeed made of bricks—in fact, it's Harry's garage (Harry's pig rises from the dead when he hears about it). Unable to blow the house down, Yorick goes around back, climbs onto the roof, jumps down the chimney, and lands in a pot of boiling water. "Here's a bar of soap, you old wolf, now come clean," Kermit's George pig says. The narrator explains that, "The wolf apologized for eating the two little pigs, so George pig let him out of the boiling pot, and he ate George pig, and thus ending our story because we are now out of pigs."

August 14, 1959

RECORD: "The Thing": Performed by Alice Pearce, written by Charles Grean (see pages 353–354)

SKETCH: We are told that the faulty laugh meter from the previous "Jokebook Nook" segment has been repaired. Theodore introduces another "Jokebook Nook" segment, promising it will be honest and spontaneous. This time, everyone except Professor Madcliffe receives enthusiastic responses to their jokes. Moldy Hay even gets big laughs with the same joke he told earlier in the week. Madcliffe insists the machine is fixed, the show is crooked, and the entire studio audience has been bribed. "I can't stand a poor loser," Theodore says to one big final laugh and thunderous applause.

August 17, 1959

INTRO: Harry cautions Sam about loaning his car to Beatrice—she's a sweet girl but a lousy driver. After we hear a crash, then we go into the song. (While Harry mentions the name Beatrice, it's likely Jim meant to say Bernice. We never hear the name Beatrice again.)

RECORD: "Never Trust a Woman": Performed by Phil Harris and His Orchestra, written by Jenny Lou Carson (see pages 361–362)

SKETCH: "The Poet's Corner" segment begins with Kermit and Theodore reciting "Father William" in tandem. Though they attribute the poem to Lewis Carroll, the poem they deliver is actually an anonymous parody of Carroll's "You Are Old, Father William." This version of "Father William," as well as several other "The Poet's Corner" offerings, was published in a 1920 compilation entitled The Book of Humorous Verse by *Carolyn Wells*. The show concludes with a limerick from Professor Madcliffe: "There was an old man of St. Bees, / who was stung in the arm by a wasp. / When asked, 'Does it hurt?' / He replied, 'No, it doesn't. / I'm so glad that it wasn't a hornet.'" Madcliffe acknowledges his poor poetry. "That last one may have been bad, but remember—it could have been verse!"

August 18, 1959

SKETCH: Harry says that since Theodore joined them, he's been trying to do a dramatic show. "Stand back, cause here it comes," Harry says.

RECORD: "Mysterioso": Performed by Mike Nichols and Elaine May with Marty Rubinstein at the piano, written by Mike Nichols, Elaine May, Marty Rubinstein

From Nichols and May's album *Improvisations to Music,* the track is a dialogue between two espionage agents who meet on a train in mysterious circumstances.

August 19, 1959

INTRO: Icky Gunk tells us he has programmed the evening's show. He tells us it's called "Music with a Message."

RECORD: "The Hunting Song": Performed by Tom Lehrer, written by Tom Lehrer (see page 308)

RECORD: "To Keep My Love Alive": Performed by Ella Fitzgerald, written by Richard Rodgers, Lorenz Hart (see page 294)

While the recording of Ella Fitzgerald was the same one used in August of 1958, in this performance, the pitch was changed so Ella sounds a little like the Chipmunks (who had made their recording debut the prior Christmas season).

TAG: Harry reminds the viewers that the music was selected by "sneaky, snakey" Icky Gunk, and the others had nothing to do with it. "For those of you who think our program is going to the dogs—er, snakes—we want you to know Esskay will be back with us on Monday." Kermit closes with a plug for the next day's Western drama "Powderburn."

August 20, 1959

SKETCH: "Punsmoke (Powderburn)": A parody of *Gunsmoke*. (See pages 144–145 for a full summary.)

August 21, 1959

RECORD: "You Need Feet": Performed by Bernard Bresslaw, written by Roy Irwin, adapted by Sid Colin (see pages 343–344)

SKETCH: "The Jokebook Nook": Since Moldy Hay rigged the laugh meter, Professor Madcliffe has changed the concept of "The Jokebook Nook" segment from telling jokes to making funny faces. Kermit and Harry's faces get mild responses. Madcliffe's face elicits a few coughs but no laughs. A simple "hi there" from Moldy gets a big reaction. We then learn that the audience is made up of 163 members of Moldy's family.

Note: Esskay sponsorship resumes with the next episode, but from this point on, Jim's recordings do not usually include the Esskay commercial.

August 24, 1959

RECORD: "M.T.A. (The Boston Subway Song)": Performed by Will Holt, written by Bess Hawes, Jacqueline Steiner (see page 280)

August 25, 1959

RECORD: "When the Crabgrass Blooms Again": Performed by Jimmy Joyce, written by Irving Taylor (see page 331)

August 26, 1959

SKETCH: "The Poet's Corner" features the cast delivering a few poems, including a brief verse submitted by Lt. and Mrs. Richard Wells of Alexandria: "Mary had a little lamb, / its feet were black as soot, / and everywhere that Mary went, / its sooty foot he put." After that, they recite "Jabberwocky" by Lewis Carroll. The Muppets would go on to perform the poem on the Brooke Shields episode of *The Muppet Show*.

August 27, 1959

INTRO: Everyone has been lost in the wilderness with no food supply . . . for nearly thirty-seven minutes. (We later learn that the impenetrable forest they're lost in is D.C.'s Rock Creek Park.) Harry packed only perishables, and all the ice cream and popsicles have melted. Kermit chides that he should have packed some staples.

"Yeah, our staple gun is completely empty," Moldy Hay says. Professor Madcliffe arrives to bolster their spirits by leading a sing-along.

RECORD: "The Battle of Kookamonga": Performed by Homer and Jethro, written by J. J. Reynolds, Jimmie Driftwood

A parody of "The Battle of New Orleans," the song is the story of a scout troop from Camp Kookamonga on a trip to study nature (and the nearby Girl Scout troop).

August 28, 1959

RECORD: "Song of Reproduction": Performed by Flanders and Swann, written by Michael Flanders, Donald Swann

British comedy team Flanders and Swann were known for their comedy songs from the mid-1950s to the mid-1960s. The reproduction referred to in this record is high-fidelity reproduction.

TAG: Kermit says there's no question about the high fidelity of this program—WRC-TV has the sound of quality.... "What does quality sound like, anyway?" Harry asks. "Sort of like this," Kermit says as he cues a sound effect of bubbles, *boing*s, and a machine winding down.

August 31, 1959

RECORD: "Elderly Man River": Performed by Stan Freberg, Daws Butler, written by Jerome Kern, Oscar Hammerstein II, Pete Barnum, Stan Freberg (see page 293)

September 1, 1959

SKETCH: Kermit is trying to fix the laugh meter before "The Jokebook Nook" segment begins so the machine doesn't just laugh at Moldy Hay's jokes. When "The Jokebook Nook" finally starts and Moldy's joke gets little response, he undoes Kermit's repair and gets his big laugh. Kermit redoes his repair and gets a big laugh on his "sand-which-is-there" joke. Professor Madcliffe's joke, "It's raining cats and dogs outside—I just stepped in a poodle," gets a reaction from the machine, but just the sound of barking dogs. "How'd you do those dogs barking, Kermit? That's a pretty good trick," Moldy asks. "I guess I just know how to *lead* a dog's *laugh*." Moldy is impressed. "Lead a dog's laugh—that's a pretty good joke," Moldy says. "Button number three," Kermit says. "Right," Moldy says as he activates the show's final laugh on the machine.

Jim's doodle of Professor Madcliffe and the laugh meter on a list of fairy-tale ideas.

September 2, 1959

RECORD: "Open the Door, Richard": Performed by The Charioteers, written by John Mason, Don Howell, Jack McVea, Dusty Fletcher (see page 238)

September 3, 1959

RECORD: "(All of a Sudden) My Heart Sings": Performed by Spike Jones, vocals by Paul Frees and Loulie Jean Norman, written by Harold Rome, Jamblan, Henri Herpin

For his album *Spike Jones in Hi-Fi: A Spooktacular in Screaming Sound,* Spike Jones takes the song popularized by Paul Anka and other pop artists and turns it into a romantic duet between Count Dracula (Paul Frees) and Vampira (Loulie Jean Norman). Jim Henson made note of another recording of this song (by Edie Adams) on his song lists, but there is no confirmation the Adams version was used on-air.

September 4, 1959

RECORD: "Wun'erful, Wun'erful!": Performed by Stan Freberg with Billy May's Music, featuring Peggy Taylor, Daws Butler, Chuck Schrouder, and The Lemon Sisters, accordion medley by Billy Liebert, written by Stan Freberg with excerpts from songs by Frank Loesser, Bob Calame, Lawrence Welk ("Bubbles in the Wine"), Richard A. Whiting, Leo Robin ("Louise"), Leo Robin, Ralph Rainger ("Please")

Champagne music maven Lawrence Welk was incredibly popular in the 1950s, appearing on his own weekly television series. Stan Freberg parodied Welk's broadcast with this 1957 recording that pokes fun at various elements of the show—including generously thanking viewers for their cards and letters. Fans of *Svengoolie* may recognize Freberg's "thank you for all those cards and letters" jingle from Sven's weekly letters segment.

September 7, 1959

SKETCH/INTRO: Icky Gunk is looking through a telescope as Kermit enters. "Hey, Icky, what're you doin'?" Icky quickly gets defensive. "Nothing. I haven't moved a thing. I never touched it." Kermit doesn't care. "It's not my telescope.... It's probably one of Professor Madcliffe's things." Icky tells Kermit that it's neat to look through. "You can see planets and stars." Kermit is intrigued. "You can see stars by looking through it?" Icky invites him to try it, and Kermit looks through the telescope. "Hmmm. I don't see any." Professor Madcliffe enters. "What are you doing?" he says, as he gives Kermit a whack. That did it. Kermit is now seeing stars (just not through the telescope). Madcliffe is upset that Kermit and Icky are fouling up his telescope. "We only wanted to look at the stars," Kermit says. Madcliffe explains that his telescope is not for looking at stars, it's for looking at planets—specifically Mars. Kermit concedes that he knows very little about "astronism." Professor Madcliffe corrects him. "It's not astronism, it's astronomy and I, I'll have you know, am an astromoner!" Icky looks skyward and wonders what people are like up there. "Just wait till we get rocket travel between the planets," Kermit says. "Yeah—just imagine the popular music we'll have then," Icky says. The script does not indicate what song this bit introduces, and there is no recording of the episode, but the song "What Do You Hear from the Red Planet Mars?" from the Hans Conried/Alice Pearce *Monster Rally* album was on Jim's song lists, and its running time matches the timing written on the script page. The song is a sci-fi take on an old-fashioned Tin Pan Alley tune.

September 8, 1959

INTRO: Icky Gunk prepares to perform his song as Professor Madcliffe enters. "Icky, I hope you won't mind if I work on my rocket during your number—it's going to be ready for its first flight tomorrow." Madcliffe promises to keep the noise down, but he suggests Icky sing loudly—not a difficult request as Icky will be lip-syncing to a Jerry Lewis record. But Madcliffe still manages to distract as he and Harry search for his missing hammer as Icky sings. "Pliers we got—screwdrivers and monkey wrenches we got, but do we got a hammer? No, we do not. So I have to do all my construction hammering with a hunk of two-by-four. It's disgraceful—that's what it is, disgraceful."

RECORD: "I Keep Her Picture Hanging Upside Down": Performed by Jerry Lewis with orchestra conducted by Dick Stabile, written by Arthur Quenzer, Earl Hatch

In this song, Jerry Lewis is a heartbroken man who hangs his girl's picture upside down "'Cause I can't stand the sight of her face."

TAG: The Professor invites viewers to "watch me fly my rocket ship tomorrow on this show."

September 9, 1959

SKETCH: "Rocket Ship": Professor Madcliffe presents his rocket ship, built with his own two hands. He calls it "The Silver Swallow." The Professor asks Kermit and Harry to go aboard for the trip to Mars. Kermit objects. "Look, Captain Vidio [sic], I think we'll sort of sit this one out." Harry adds, "I get space sick real easy." Madcliffe doesn't want to take no for an answer. "Don't you feel the call of adventure? Haven't you read the space comic books? Haven't you read your obligations in your NBC contract?" Kermit and Harry relent and take their positions as co-pilot and navigator, but Kermit starts the launch countdown at 6,347 because he's not in a hurry to leave. When the ship finally launches, it goes backward. Harry admits he was always a lousy navigator.

September 11, 1959

SKETCH: "The Poet's Corner": Professor Madcliffe introduces "that part of the show that deals with what Wordsworth spoke of as 'emotion recollected in tranquility' or what Edgar Allan Poe called 'the rhythmical creation of beauty' or what Samuel Taylor—" Madcliffe is interrupted by Omar. "What Professor Madcliffe is trying to do is introduce 'The Poet's Corner.'" Kermit begins with "The sultan got mad at his harem / and invented a scheme for to scare 'em. / He caught him a mouse, / which he loosed in the house. / The confusion is called a harem-scarem." Harry follows with another limerick: "There was a young girl of West Ham, / who hastily jumped on a tram. / When she had embarked, / the conductor remarked: / 'Your fare'—'Well they do say I am.'" Moldy is up next: "There was an old fellow named Green, / who grew so abnormally lean, / and flat and compressed, / that his back touched his chest, / and sideways he couldn't be seen." The Professor then introduces "The Rhythm of the Ancient Mariner" by Samuel Taylor "Colerumph." The others tell him that he's not "in the spirit of things," and he has to do a limerick. He doesn't know any, so Omar says he'll hold a cue card with a limerick for him. After the Professor unsuccessfully tries to read a backward cue card, Omar turns the card around and Madcliffe recites: "A major with a wonderful force, / called out in Rock Creek Park for a horse. / All the flowers looked 'round, / but no horse could be found, / so he just rhododendron, of course." The Professor doesn't get it.

September 21, 1959

RECORD: "Proud New Father": Performed by Johnny Standley with Horace Heidt and His Musical Knights, written by John Standley (see page 323)

September 22, 1959

INTRO: Moldy Hay starts the show. "Tonight, friends, we're gonna have a little pickin' and singin'—a little country tune. "With very little tune," Professor Madcliffe interrupts.

RECORD: "Don't Sing Along (On Top of Old Smokey)": Performed by Homer and Jethro, special lyrics by Homer and Jethro, Traditional (see pages 360–361)

September 23, 1959

INTRO: Harry introduces the evening's "musical monstrosity." Icky Gunk takes exception to that description since he's singing the song. Kermit explains that Icky won't really be singing—Kermit will play a record and Icky will pretend he's singing "like we usually do." Harry is upset to learn that the whole show is a "fake." Kermit invites Harry into the control room to play the record.

RECORD: "Lo, Hear the Gentle Lark": Performed by Edie Adams, orchestra under the direction of Henry Mancini, written by Henry Bishop

Edie Adams, who was appearing at this time in husband Ernie Kovacs's television programs, recorded this nineteenth-century tune for her 1959 album, *Music to Listen to Records By: Edie Adams Sings?* As Icky lip-syncs to the track, Kermit and Harry adjust the speed of the record in the control room so Edie's voice is altered throughout the song.

September 24, 1959

INTRO: Harry introduces Sam with a song to make up for the "long-hair music" (a term once used to describe classical music) played on the previous show. Harry describes the selection as "sideburn music."

RECORD: "All American Boy": Performed by Bobby Bare, written by Bobby Bare (see page 337)

September 25, 1959

RECORD: "Wild Bill Hiccup": Performed by Spike Jones and His City Slickers (featuring George Rock, Freddy Morgan, Jack Golly), written by Eddie Brandt, Freddy Morgan, Spike Jones (see page 316)

September 28, 1959

SKETCH: Kermit discovers a seed for a "marination" flower—a cross between a marigold and a carnation. He waters it, and when he goes to get Harry to show him the seedling, Yorick discovers the flower—and eats it. This happens several times. "This could go on all day," Kermit says. Eventually, Kermit sneakily stakes out and catches Yorick, who promises not to eat any more flowers but instead devours the whole bag of seeds. He soon has marinations growing out of him.

September 29, 1959

RECORD: "Somebody Else, Not Me": Performed by Phil Harris, written by Ballard MacDonald, James F. Hanley (see page 336)

September 30, 1959

RECORD: "The Trouble with Harry": Performed by Alfi and Harry (David Seville), written by Floyd Huddleston, Herbert Eiseman, Mark McIntyre (see page 268)

SKETCH: Kermit has been sent up in an airplane for a 6:30 p.m. spot check on the hurricane. (Hurricane Gracie had recently hit the Southeast, and its downgraded remnants were producing rain in the Maryland/D.C. area.) "I should be within sight of the eye of the hurricane very soon, yes, I think I see it up ahead there . . . you should be able to see it on your home receivers at any second." The eye of the hurricane is then revealed to be the eye logo of rival network CBS. "I think I got the eye of the wrong hurricane."

Although Kermit was working at NBC, he found another network's logo in the eye of the hurricane.

October 1, 1959

RECORD: "She's a Lady": Performed by Betty Hutton and Perry Como with Mitchell Ayres and His Orchestra, written by Cy Coben (see page 290)

October 2, 1959

RECORD: "The Cricket Song": Performed by Ray Bolger, with orchestra and chorus directed by Sy Oliver, written by Bobby Gimby, Johnny Wayne (see pages 281–282)

October 5, 1959 & October 6, 1959

Sam and Friends pre-empted for World Series broadcasts.

October 7, 1959 (first Baltimore broadcast of the season)

INTRO: Professor Madcliffe gathers the cast to start the show. Yorick's grunts tell Madcliffe that Yorick is disappointed that his team didn't win the World Series, but Yorick bet on neither the Dodgers nor the White Sox. Madcliffe asks who Yorick did bet on, and Yorick gives an unintelligible reply, which Madcliffe nevertheless understands. "Yorick, the umpire doesn't play in the game," Madcliffe says. We can actually make out Yorick's reply: "Now he tells me." Madcliffe implores the cast to do a good job and do the show right because it's their first show this season in Baltimore.

RECORD: "I've Got You Under My Skin": Performed by Stan Freberg with Les Baxter and His Orchestra and Chorus, written by Cole Porter (see pages 157–158 for a full summary)

The song ends abruptly and the characters freeze. Kermit asks them to move . . . they oblige by falling down, an action accompanied by a big crashing sound. Kermit excuses himself to do the commercial. "I guess we fixed him" says Harry. "Yeah, but who's gonna fix us?" Icky Gunk, one of the vocalists, asks.

October 8, 1959

RECORD: "A Gnu": Performed by Flanders and Swann, written by Michael Flanders, Donald Swann

This 1957 Flanders and Swann animal wordplay song would later be performed on a fifth-season episode of *The Muppet Show*.

October 9, 1959

RECORD: "Pachalafaka": Performed by Earl Brown, written by Irving Taylor (see page 299)

SKETCH: "The Poet's Corner": Omar introduces the segment and cues the music, but rather than the organ music, a horn fanfare is heard. Finally, the correct music is cued. Kermit begins: "A man and his lady love, Min, / skated out where the ice was quite thin. / Had a quarrel, no doubt. / For I hear they fell out. / What a blessing they didn't fall in." Yorick then shares a poem—even though no one can understand him. Harry hails it as one of the best poems they ever had on "The Poet's Corner."

October 12, 1959

RECORD: "C'est Si Bon": Performed by Stan Freberg with the George Bruns Quartet, written by Henri Betti, Andre Hornez, Jerry Seelen (see page 151 for a full summary)

October 13, 1959

SKETCH: "The Big Introduction": Kermit asks Bernice to tell Sam that they're ready to do the show. Bernice is puzzled. She asks Kermit which one Sam is. Kermit decides to introduce the characters and has rigged the laugh meter into an applause meter in order to have some kind of audience reaction when each character enters. Kermit introduces each member of the cast, and each receives applause—except Professor Madcliffe, whose appearance receives only some scattered coughs from the machine, and Kermit, who receives no reaction at all. With only three puppeteers, it was quite a challenge to perform all fourteen characters in three minutes. Jim carefully planned who would do what on the back of the episode's script.

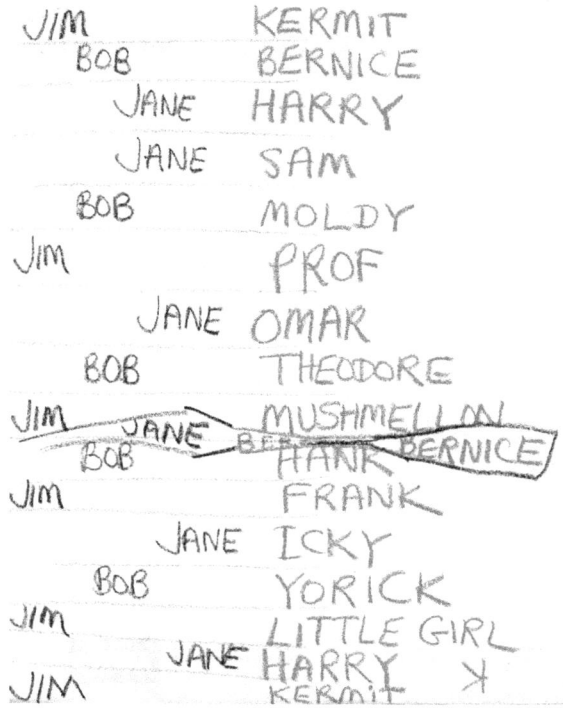

Jim's character/performer list for "The Big Introduction."

October 14, 1959

RECORD: "(All of a Sudden) My Heart Sings": Performed by Spike Jones, vocals by Paul Frees and Loulie Jean Norman, written by Harold Rome, Jamblan, Henri Herpin, (see page 391)

October 15, 1959

RECORD: "Standing on the Corner" (from *The Most Happy Fella*): Performed by Andy Griffith with Glenn Osser and vocal group, written by Frank Loesser (see page 272)

October 16, 1959

COLD OPEN: Kermit is taking a door-to-door survey and Bernice answers. Kermit asks what her favorite TV show is, and she responds *Sam and Friends*. Kermit asks why and who her favorite character is. She says she likes the opening and closing music best. She says she doesn't watch the rest of the show.

TITLE CARD/ANNOUNCE

RECORD: "The Musicians": Performed by Dinah Shore, Betty Hutton, Tony Martin, Phil Harris, with Henri René and His Orchestra, written by Charles Grean, Tom Glazer (see page 250)

October 19, 1959

INTRO: Kermit is fishing. Harry asks how many he's caught. "Well, if I catch the one I'm fishing for, and two more, I'll have three."

RECORD: "Cry Me a River": Performed by Julie London, orchestra conducted by Felix Slatkin, written by Arthur Hamilton (see page 266)

October 20, 1959

RECORD: "Dufo (What a Crazy Guy)": Performed by Wally Cox, written by Wally Cox (see page 245–246)

October 21, 1959

SKETCH: "*Sam and Friends* News Report": Professor Madcliffe begins, "From the four corners of the globe . . ." Harry points out that the globe is round—it doesn't have four corners. "Have you seen our globe?" Madcliffe says as he introduces the "*Sam and Friends* News Report." (See pages 184–187 for the full script.)

October 22, 1959

RECORD: "The Good Old Days": Performed by Eddie Lawrence, written by Eddie Lawrence (see page 349–350)

October 23, 1959

RECORD: "This is Your Death / Two Heads Are Better Than One": Performed by Spike Jones, Paul Frees, George Rock, written by Eddie Brandt, Spike Jones

Recorded for 1959's *Spike Jones in Hi-Fi: A Spooktacular in Screaming Sound,* this track is a parody of the Ralph Edwards TV show *This is Your Life*, with monster-making mad scientist Doctor Von Steiner as the guest of honor. When a two-headed monster is introduced, he (they?) performs a musical interlude.

October 26, 1959

INTRO: Professor Madcliffe introduces an unrehearsed performance of "Autumn in New York."

RECORD: "Autumn in New York": Performed by Jonathan and Darlene Edwards (Paul Weston and Jo Stafford), written by Vernon Duke

The intentionally mediocre lounge-singing act Jonathan and Darlene Edwards play and sing an off-tempo and out-of-tune version of Vernon Duke's jazz standard.

October 27, 1959

RECORD: "What Did He Say? (The Mumble Song)": Performed by The Charioteers, written by Charles Grean, Cy Coben (see page 236)

October 28, 1959

RECORD: "The Invisible Man": Performed by Alice Pearce, written by Joel Herron, Fred Hertz (see page 355)

October 29, 1959

RECORD: "Poisen to Poisen": Performed by Paul Frees, Spike Jones, written by Spike Jones, Eddie Brandt (see pages 145–146 for a full summary)

October 30, 1959

RECORD: "Tammy": Performed by Spike Jones, Paul Frees, Loulie Jean Norman, George Rock, written by Jay Livingston, Ray Evans

Presented by *Sam and Friends* as the culmination of several Halloween-themed episodes, this monstrous version of the Debbie Reynolds hit "Tammy" is sung as "Clammy," The track comes the horror-themed album *Spike Jones in Hi-Fi: A Spooktacular in Screaming Sound*, with Loulie Jean Norman and Paul Frees singing in character as Vampira and Dracula, respectively.

November 2, 1959

RECORD: "Abe Snake for President": Performed by Stan Freberg with orchestra conducted by Billy May, written by Stan Freberg, Ruby Raskin

This rousing 1952 campaign song is for Freberg's Abe Snake, a circus acrobat whose platform is filled with promises to legalize gambling and bring back vaudeville.

November 3, 1959

SKETCH: A representative from the Committee for Honest Programming (played by Icky Gunk) enters and tells Harry he's been sent to make sure the program doesn't try to pull the wool over the eyes of the public. Harry assures him that they're honest. "Honesty is merely the fear of being caught," says the Honest Programming rep. He says he will stick around to watch and asks Harry to proceed—and he almost immediately catches Professor Madcliffe in an exaggeration regarding the "thousands" of letters requesting "The Jokebook Nook." Madcliffe admits that there were not thousands of letters—only one from his mother . . . and she didn't really request the segment . . . Madcliffe requested that she request it. Kermit begins "The Jokebook Nook": "A feller went in a bookstore, and the clerk handed him a book and said, 'This book'll do half your work for you,' so the feller said, 'Good, I'll take two.'" Harry has one: "There was these two cats walkin' down the street. One cat says, 'I'm getting hungry, let's go eat up the street.' The other cat says, 'No, man, I don't like the taste of asphalt.'" When these two jokes get a big laugh from the laugh machine and the Professor's joke ("I've decided to quit the TV business; I'm gonna start a bakery if I can raise the dough") doesn't, the Professor is convinced the whole thing is a fake. The Honest Programming rep concurs, but Harry encourages him to try it himself. The programming rep repeats the Professor's joke, which, this time, gets a big laugh. The rep concludes that the show is legit.

November 4, 1959

RECORD: "Salt": Performed by The Vagabonds, written by Jack Adrian (a.k.a. Adrian Greenberg) (see page 89)

November 5, 1959

RECORD: "Barnacle Bill the Sailor": Performed by Candy Candido, written by Carson Robison, Frank Luther (see page 263)

November 6, 1959

RECORD: "Sincere": Performed by *The Music Man* Original Broadway Cast (featuring The Buffalo Bills), written by Meredith Willson (see page 297)

RECORD: "My Baby Just Cares for Me": Performed by The Buffalo Bills with banjo, written by Gus Kahn, Walter Donaldson

Introduced by Eddie Cantor in the film *Whoopee!* (1930), "My Baby Just Cares for Me" was recorded by The Buffalo Bills for their 1959 album, *Barber Shop!*

November 9, 1959

RECORD: "I've Grown Accustomed to Your Face": Performed by Rosemary Clooney, written by Frederick Loewe and Alan Jay Lerner (see page 308)

November 10, 1959

RECORD: "The Yellow Rose of Texas": Performed by Stan Freberg with Billy May's Orchestra (Yankee Snare Drumming: Alvin Stoller), original song written by Don George (see page 260)

November 11, 1959

SKETCH: Professor Madcliffe announces the invention of Fisby the Robot—a robot that can do mathematics without mistakes. But Fisby's demonstration of simple math problems soon gets out of hand. Fisby shocks Kermit, Professor Madcliffe, and Harry, sending them to the floor so he can run off with a television camera: "WHEN YOU LOOK AT ME, SUGAR PLUM WITH YOUR IMAGE ORTHOCON [sic] TUBE GLOWING . . . BEEP, BEEP. BEEP, BEEP." The camera returns the affection and invites Fisby to go somewhere where they can be alone.

November 12, 1959

RECORD: "Lay Somethin' on the Bar (Besides Your Elbows)": Performed by Chuck Murphy, written by Billy Austin, Sheldon Smith

Previously performed on *Sam and Friends* with a Jerry Lewis record (March 5, 1959, see page 347), this version of the song was recorded in 1951, the same year as Lewis's single.

November 13, 1959

RECORD: "Face the Funnies": Performed by Stan Freberg, Daws Butler, June Foray, Peter Leeds, written by Stan Freberg, Pete Barnum (see page 302)

November 16, 1959

RECORD: "The Five Pennies Saints (When the Saints Go Marching In)": Performed by Danny Kaye and Louis Armstrong, Traditional, adapted by Sylvia Fine (see page 371)

November 17, 1959

SKETCH: "The Poet's Corner": Bernice begins with: "A canner exceedingly canny, / one morning remarked to his granny, / a canner can can, / anything that he can. / But a canner can't can a can, can he?" Next up is Moldy Hay: "A doctor fell into a well and broke his collar bone. / The doctor should attend the sick and leave the well alone." Harry contributes a poem by Oliver Wendell Holmes: "The Reverend Henry Ward Beecher / called a hen a most elegant creature. / The hen, pleased with that, / laid an egg in his hat. / And thus did the hen reward Beecher." Professor Madcliffe chides Harry with a whimsical (and unattributable) bit of verse: "Harry, a pun is the lowest form of wit. / It does not tax the brain a bit. / One merely takes a word that's plain / and picks out one that sounds the same. / Perhaps some letter may be changed / or others slightly disarranged. / This to the meaning gives a twist / which much delights the humorist. / A sample now may help to show / the way a good pun ought to go. / It isn't the cough that carries you off. / It's the coffin they carry you off in." Bernice remarks: "That reminds me, Professor, I never go cycling with my boyfriend." Professor: "No? Why not?" Bernice: "I prefer to cyclone." The Professor introduces Yorick with a song . . .

RECORD: "Whence That Wince": Performed by Mike Stewart, Fia Karin, written by Walt Kelly, Norman Monath

From Walt Kelly's *Songs of the Pogo* album, the short but sweet track is a nimble bit of word gymnastics.

November 18, 1959

INTRO: With Professor Madcliffe translating into English, Harry welcomes the audience in French and announces that the theme of the show is French. Hank and Frank are there to sing a French folk song.

RECORD: "Sur La Route": Performed by Theodore Bikel and Cynthia Gooding, Traditional, adapted by Theodore Bikel, Cynthia Gooding

Though best known as an actor, in 1956, Theodore Bikel released an international folk music album with Cynthia Gooding entitled *Young Man and a Maid: Love Songs of Many Lands*. "Sur La Route" ("On the Road") is a French song about a road worker's encounter with a beautiful lady.

November 19, 1959

RECORD: "Singin' in the Rain": Performed by Edie Adams, orchestra conducted by Henry Mancini, written by Arthur Freed, Nacio Herb Brown (recording sped up for the broadcast) (see page 158 for a full summary)

RECORD: "Robin, He Married": Performed by Burl Ives, arranged by Burl Ives, Traditional

Burl Ives performs this fast folk song about a man named Robin, his wife from the West, and a wheel of cheese that got away from them.

November 20, 1959

RECORD: "Rock Island Line": Performed by Stan Freberg and His Sniffle Group, interruptions by Peter Leeds, written by Lonnie Donegan, special arrangement by Stan Freberg (see page 292)

November 23, 1959

RECORD: "Old, Old Vienna": Performed by Eddie Lawrence with orchestra directed by Nick Perito, written by Eddie Lawrence (see page 252)

November 24, 1959

RECORD: "Good Ol' Mountain Dew": Performed by Kenny Roberts, Traditional (see page 270)

November 25, 1959

INTRO: After the opening title, Hank and Frank are reciting the addition table—each uttering one number at a time. When Harry enters, they are startled and quickly exit. According to Harry, the twins speaking on *Sam and Friends* is a rare occurrence and he encourages them to return. "I don't believe this. How come you're talking?" Harry asks. Hank and Frank explain that they have been practicing. Harry asks why they split up the words between them. Alternating words as they respond, Hank and Frank explain that they are bashful, and by speaking in this manner, neither of them has to do all the talking. Harry asks them to introduce the folk song.

RECORD: "Eggs and Marrowbone": Performed by Richard Dyer-Bennet, Traditional

Englishman Richard Dyer-Bennet was a self-described minstrel who recorded many folk songs during his career. This one, "Eggs and Marrowbone," is about a wife's attempt to kill her husband.

November 26, 1959

RECORD: "Inchworm": Performed by Danny Kaye, written by Frank Loesser (see page 256)

November 27, 1959

RECORD: "The Hazy Yon": Performed by Mike Stewart, written by Walt Kelly and Norman Monath

From Walt Kelly's *Songs of the Pogo*, "The Hazy Yon" is a lilting ballad with a choral backing. Co-composer Norman Monath also contributed music to the films *Blackboard Jungle* (1955) and *Valley of the Dolls* (1967).

RECORD: "Lines Upon a Tranquil Brow": Performed by Walt Kelly, written by Walt Kelly, Norman Monath

Cartoonist Walt Kelly provides the vocal for this track from *Songs of the Pogo*, a poetic, meandering, yet comedically crass tune: "Have you ever cried out while counting the snow, / or watching the tomtit warble 'Hello': / 'BREAK OUT THE CIGARS! This life is for squirrels! / We're off to the drugstore to whistle at girls'?"

November 30, 1959

RECORD: "The Sad Cowboy": Performed by The Sportsmen Quartet with orchestral accompaniment, written by Al Gannaway, Hoagy Carmichael, Walton Farrar (see page 248)

December 1, 1959

RECORD: "Real Gone Galoot": Performed by Yogi Yorgesson, written by Harry Stewart

Songwriter and comedian Harry Stewart sings this song in character as Yogi Yorgesson, a man with an exaggerated Swedish accent.

OUTRO: Professor Madcliffe gives a brief outro and wonders about the whereabouts of the guy who promised him payola to play the record. Icky Gunk arrives, upset that the record was used. "I promised you the payola if you *wouldn't* play the record on this show . . . now it'll never be a hit."

December 2, 1959

SKETCH: "The Poet's Corner": As organ music plays, Moldy Hay begins with a poem about fleas: "Great fleas have lesser fleas, and these have less to bite 'em. / *These* fleas have lesser fleas and, so, ad infinitum." (This is a tweaked excerpt from Augustus De Morgan's 1872 poem "Siphonaptera.") After Hank and Frank deliver a tandem poem, Harry introduces the song.

RECORD: "Don't Sugar Me": Performed by Fia Karin, written by Walt Kelly, Norman Monath

"Don't Sugar Me," a torch song from Walt Kelly's *Songs of the Pogo* album, was later performed as a two-minute U.K. spot during the first season of *The Muppet Show*.

December 3, 1959

INTRO: Harry introduces the folk song of the week.

RECORD: "Viva Jujuy": Performed by Theodore Bikel and Geula Gill, Traditional

"Viva Jujuy" is an Argentinian folk song from the album *Theodore Bikel and Geula Gill Sing Folk Songs from Just About Everywhere* (1959).

December 4, 1959

SKETCH: Moldy is rehearsing a joke for "The Jokebook Nook"—even though it's not happening until Monday. He says he gets the strangest reaction when he tells this joke: "Every dog has his day, and those with broken tails have their weekends." He is met with a cacophony of dog barks.

RECORD: "Very Square Dance": Performed by Steve Allen, chorus and orchestra directed by Dick Jacobs, written by Steve Allen

The talk show host and prolific songwriter calls a "very" square dance, inserting new, hip words into traditional square dance rhythms: "Davy Crocket dreamed and planned, / and he plays trombone with Basie's band. / . . . At 45 it may sound great, / but spin this record at 78."

December 7, 1959

SKETCH: "The Jokebook Nook": Professor Madcliffe has installed a sense of humor into Fisby the Robot so he can tell jokes on "The Jokebook Nook." Madcliffe says, "Just think, Kermit, we'll have the very first artificially created jokes." When the segment begins, Omar recites his dog joke from the previous episode, with the same reaction from the dogs. Harry presents a joke for the horses in the audience: "One day when Kermit was a little boy, he said to his mother, 'Mother, I've just seen a man who makes horses.' And Kermit's mother said, 'Are you sure?' and Kermit said, 'Yes, mother, he had a horse nearly finished when I saw him. He was just nailing on his feet.'" The sound of galloping hooves indicates a big response from the horses in the audience. Kermit offers a brief joke: "I went to see a spiritualist last night." "Was he good?" Harry asks. "No, just medium." Ghostly laughter is heard in response. The Professor introduces Fisby with a joke for the machines in the audience. Fisby emits a series of beeps and sound effects. The laugh meter's response is off the chart.

December 8, 1959

RECORD: "It's Never Too Late to Fall in Love": Performed by *The Boy Friend* Original Broadway Cast (featuring) Geoffrey Hibbert and Dilys Lay, written by Sandy Wilson (see page 345)

RECORD: "The Voice Coach": Performed by Bob and Ray, background music directed by Dick Jacobs, written by Bob Elliot, Ray Goulding

Released as a single, this sketch features Ray Goulding interviewing monotone voice coach Chesley L. Beamish (Bob Elliott). Employed to assist actors on television, Beamish explains the various thrilling experiences that influence his direction of performances, but his bone-dry Jack Webb-esque delivery belies his ability.

December 9, 1959

SKETCH: "The Poet's Corner": Omar introduces "The Poet's Corner," but Harry tells him they're not ready. Moldy Hay has the only copy of the poem and he fell asleep while rehearsing it. They try to wake him up to recite.

RECORD: "Love Poems: To the Lovely Juanita Beasley": Performed by Andy Griffith, chimes by Billy May, written by Andy Griffith, Billy May

As lush accompaniment plays, Andy Griffith recites love poems.

December 10, 1959

RECORD: "The Man on the Flying Trapeze": Performed by Spike Jones and His City Slickers, commentary by Doodles Weaver, written by Alfred Lee, George Leybourne, arranged by Spike Jones and Doodles Weaver (see pages 287–288)

December 11, 1959

RECORD: "Never Hit Your Grandma with a Shovel (Use an Ax Instead)": Performed by Spike Jones, written by Felix Hanemann (see page 255)

December 14, 1959

RECORD: "Etiquette Blues": Performed by Butch Stone, orchestra conducted by Van Alexander, written by Gayle Grubb (see page 235)

December 15, 1959

RECORD: "The Chipmunk Song": Performed by David Seville, written by Ross Bagdasarian (see page 81 for more on the creation of the Chipmunks)

After "The Chipmunk Song," they segue into a sped-up Chipmunk-style version of Danny Kaye's "Tschaikowsky (And Other Russians)."

December 16, 1959

INTRO: Harry talks about the Christmas season. "This is the time of year that people think about things like peace and goodwill toward men . . . and people stop thinking about materialistic things . . . like money."

RECORD: "Five Pound Box of Money": Performed by Pearl Bailey, written by Jack Barker, Pearl Bailey

Pearl Bailey co-wrote this song and released her recording in 1959 Appropriate for a *Sam and Friends* holiday season presentation, the song is Pearlie Mae's request to Santa for a five-pound box of money.

December 17, 1959

INTRO: Kermit thinks about Christmastime in his childhood days. "You were once a little boy?" Harry asks. "Well, I was more like a little Kermit." Kermit recalls the one year he didn't think he was going to get anything for Christmas.

RECORD: "Nuttin' for Christmas": Performed by Stan Freberg with Billy May's Music, written by Sid Tepper, Roy C. Bennett (see page 314)

December 18, 1959

INTRO: Harry introduces their Christmas show, mentioning the decorations and that Icky Gunk is in the rafters to sprinkle snow during the song.

RECORD: "Santy's Movin' On": Performed by Homer and Jethro, written by Hank Snow, Homer Haynes, Jethro Burns (see page 264)

OUTRO: Harry complains about the song selection—and the lack of snow. He asks for more, and Icky obliges, dumping everything he has left onto Harry. Bernice then enters and notices Harry is standing under the mistletoe. Harry quickly orders the decorations be taken down. "Gotta get ready for Washington's birthday . . . and Easter, you know . . . come on, you guys, get busy dyeing them Easter eggs." In this episode, Jane Henson provides the voice of Bernice (usually voiced by Bob Payne).

December 21, 1959

RECORD: "Numba One Day of Christmas (The Twelve Days of Christmas)": Performed by Ed Kenney with Luther Henderson and His Orchestra, written by Eaton Magoon, Jr., Ed Kenney, Gordon N. Phelps

This is a Hawaiian version of "The Twelve Days of Christmas," as recorded on the 1959 album *Season's Greetings: A Christmas Festival of Stars!*

December 22, 1959

INTRO: Harry is skeptical they can get through the next song without messing up.

RECORD: "Christmas Tree": Performed by The Voices of Walter Schumann, vocal by Bill Lee, written by Jay Daniel, Sid Robin (see page 320)

December 23, 1959

RECORD: "Jingle Bells" (in Japanese): Performer unknown, Traditional

This version of the 1857 holiday standard is a lush arrangement for an orchestra and vocal group, but it happens to be sung entirely in Japanese, with Omar leading the lip-sync performance.

INTERRUPTION: Professor Madcliffe interrupts: "Hold it! Hold it, you guys. Sheesh! I asked the group for something original, but this is ridiculous." Kermit invites Omar to join the group for an American-style Christmas song.

RECORD: "We Wish You a Merry Christmas": Performed by The Weavers, Traditional

This classic Christmas carol would later be performed on several Henson projects, including *A Muppet Family Christmas*.

December 24, 1959

RECORD: "The Night Before Christmas": Performed by Stan Freberg with Babette Bain and Billy May's Music, written by Stan Freberg, Jack Brooks (see page 316)

December 28, 1959

INTRO: Harry greets the audience and hopes everyone had a Merry Christmas. He mentions the gifts they received. "Pancho Kermit got a new hat."

RECORD: "The Hat I Got for Christmas Is Too Beeg": Performed by Mel Blanc, written by David Gussin, Marv Fisher (see pages 320–321)

December 29, 1959

INTRO: Harry is playing chess with Kermeena. Harry says that she doesn't seem to have her mind on the game. "You said you wanted to ask me something when we finish the game," Harry asks as the music begins. "Can you ask it now?"

RECORD: "What Are You Doing New Year's Eve?": Performed by Margaret Whiting, written by Frank Loesser

Presented here two days before New Year's Eve, the singer in this Frank Loesser song asks someone about their holiday plans. In the *Sam and Friends* performance, Kermeena lip-syncs to the Margaret Whiting track as Harry responds to the vocals throughout in his own voice. When asked what he's doing New Year's Eve, Harry explains (during a long instrumental break) that Yorick is giving a party in the kitchen—a costume party where everyone is supposed to come dressed as their favorite recipe—but Harry says he's not going to that one. He also mentions a party that the Esskay people are giving. "At midnight, they throw luncheon meat and bacon out the window instead of confetti. Last year, I was wearing my red stripes up and down and Mr. Schluderberg threw me out the window thinking I was a charred strip of bacon. I fell in the middle of a group of bon-fire girls singing Christmas carols because their calendar was a week late." When asked the musical question, "What are you doing New Year's Eve?" one final time, Harry replies, "I told you! I told you! I'm busy! Sheesh."

December 30, 1959

RECORD: "That's My Boy": Performed by Stan Freberg with orchestra and chorus conducted by Les Baxter, written by Stan Freberg (see page 343)

December 31, 1959

INTRO: Harry introduces a special song for New Year's Eve.

RECORD: "Git Up Off'n the Floor, Hannah! (A Bitter New Year's Eve)": Performed by Red Ingle and The Natural Seven, written by Foster Carling, Joe Washburne, Red Ingle (see page 329)

January 4, 1960

RECORD: "Pass the Football": Performed by *Wonderful Town* Original Broadway Cast (featuring Jordan Bentley), written by Leonard Bernstein, Betty Comden, Adolph Green

Based on the play *My Sister Eileen,* the 1953 Broadway musical *Wonderful Town* is about two sisters seeking success in New York City. In the show, this song is performed by Wreck (Jordan Bentley), a pro football player, as he explains his path to success, which relied solely on his ability to pass the football. In 1956, Jim Henson designed the program and poster for the University of Maryland's production of the show.

January 5, 1960

COLD OPEN: Kermit's watch has stopped, and he asks what time it is. Professor Madcliffe exclaims that it's 1960! "It's time to reevaluate our values, temper our temperances, integrate our integrity, marinate our merits, and turpentine our turpitude." Kermit then asks Mushmellon what time it is. Mushmellon nonverbally indicates his response. Kermit concurs. "I thought so. It's time to do the *Sam and Friends* show!"

TITLE CARD/ANNOUNCE

RECORD: "Gone": Performed by Homer and Jethro, written by Smokey Rogers

This melancholy tune, a parody of Ferlin Husky's record of the same title, reflects on all that has happened since the singer's love has gone. "Our baby boy is hard to beat. / He's grown another foot, my sweet. / He looks so strange with three feet."

January 6, 1960

INTRO: Harry introduces Icky Gunk with a song from Gilbert and Sullivan's *The Sorcerer.*

RECORD: "My Name Is John Wellington Wells": Performed by Danny Kaye, written by W. S. Gilbert, Arthur Sullivan

Danny Kaye recorded a collection of Gilbert and Sullivan music for Decca records in 1949. In this patter song, sorcerer John Wellington Wells introduces himself: "My name is John Wellington Wells. / I'm a dealer in magic and spells. / In blessings and curses, / and ever-filled purses, / in prophecies, witches, and knells."

SEGUE: Harry suggests using Gilbert and Sullivan tunes to convey messages. "For instance, what would it be like if the chemistry professor at Harvard started teaching chemistry like Gilbert and Sullivan?"

RECORD: "The Elements": Performed by Tom Lehrer, written by Tom Lehrer

Musical satirist and mathematics professor Tom Lehrer set the periodic table of the elements to Gilbert and Sullivan's "I Am the Very Model of a Modern Major-General" in 1959.

January 7, 1960

INTRO: Harry mentions that they've received mail from all over the area about the folk songs they've been doing each week. "But in spite of all those responses, we're still gonna do another folk song." He introduces Kermit's performance.

RECORD: "Big Rock Candy Mountain": Performed by Burl Ives, Traditional, arranged by Elie Siegmeister

Burl Ives first recorded this folk classic in the mid-1940s and included it on several of his subsequent albums. It imagines a sort of hobo paradise with lemonade springs and hens that lay soft-boiled eggs.

January 8, 1960

SKETCH: Professor Madcliffe introduces a new feature, "Words of Wisdom." Kermit, inside a very famous crystal ball (thrown away by that very famous WRC weather forecaster Frank Forrester), offers such words of wisdom as: "A bird in the hand gathers no moss," "You can lead a horse to water, but you can't make him sink," and "People who love in glass houses shouldn't." Omar pulls Kermit out, and as they try to find a new spirit of the crystal ball, they ask Harry to do something to kill time.

RECORD: "Harry the Hipster": Performed by Ronny Graham, written by Ronny Graham

Used previously as brief cold openings on *Sam and Friends*, this is a longer excerpt from Comedian Ronny Graham's New York cabaret revue cast recording *Take Five*. In this segment, Graham's Harry, as performed onscreen by the Muppet with the same name, noodles on the piano while talking about some of the cats he's met—including a real cat. The bit concludes with a quick chorus of the Slim Gaillard song "Cement Mixer (Put-ti Put-ti)."

TAG: Moldy Hay has replaced Kermit as the spirit of the crystal ball, but he's not much better than Kermit. "Opportunity knocks once and the neighbors the rest of the time." "A bird in the hand is bad table manners." "If thine enemy wrong thee, buy each of his children a drum."

January 11, 1960

SKETCH: Omar has three pennies to add to his piggy bank, but somebody took the bank. It's clear from the jingling sound Mushmellon makes when he walks that he ate the bank. "There's only one thing to do," Omar says. He has Mushmellon hold his head up so Omar can deposit his three pennies. Then into . . .

RECORD: "Money": Performed by Mel Blanc, orchestra conducted by Billy May, written by Stan Freberg, Ruby Raskin (see pages 312–313)

January 12, 1960

RECORD: "Hunger Is From": Performed by Ken Nordine with The Fred Katz Group, written by Ken Nordine, Fred Katz (see page 157 for a full summary)

January 13, 1960

RECORD: "The Old Payola Roll Blues (Like the Beginning)": Performed by Stan Freberg, featuring Jesse White, music by Billy May with The Toads, written by Stan Freberg

In this 1959 record, Obscurity Records producer Barney Schlock (Jesse White) is trying to put together a hit rock 'n' roll record but is missing a teenage idol. Fortunately, a kid fitting the bill (Clyde Ankle, played by Freberg) just happens to be walking by the studio. When the music producer learns the guy can't sing, he immediately invites him in to record a song—all the kid has to do is sing "high school" over and over and throw in an occasional "oooh oooh." The title is a play on the classic song "The Old Piano Roll Blues," payola referring to the illegal practice of record companies secretly paying radio stations and disc jockeys to play records. The whole story of Clyde Ankle is enacted and sung over two sides of a 45, totaling about nine minutes and ending with a swinging big band finale. Even one side would be too long for the *Sam and Friends* time slot, so the show presented an edited version of part one, subtitled, in keeping with the slang of the day, "Like the Beginning."

January 14, 1960

RECORD: "The Ugly Duckling": Performed by Danny Kaye, written by Frank Loesser (see page 256)

January 15, 1960

RECORD: "Yankee Doodle": Performed by the Chipmunks with David Seville, Traditional

The Chipmunks record begins to play, with Alvin causing trouble as usual. After a chorus, when David Seville invites listeners to sing along,

Harry reluctantly complies: "Yankee Doodle went to Laurel riding on a racehorse, / stuck a billfold in his hat and called it payola." Kermit then takes over: "Yankee Doodle break it up, / Yankee Doodle dandruff, / mind your manners and your mother, / and when in school play hookey."

OUTRO: Harry consults the crystal ball for political forecasts. The spirit (Kermit) predicts Tippecanoe and Tyler Too (a reference to the 1840 campaign slogan of William Henry Harrison and John Tyler) by a landslide. He also predicts Lincoln will be assassinated by someone standing in John Wilkins's telephone booth.

January 18, 1960

RECORD: "Many Harry Returns": Performed by Fia Karin, written by Walt Kelly, Norman Monath

This sweet and whimsical birthday tune from *Songs of the Pogo* is a clever bit of Walt Kelly wordplay.

RECORD: "I'm Five": Performed by Danny Kaye, written by Milton Schafer (see page 357)

January 19, 1960

RECORD: "Tango": Performed by Mike Nichols and Elaine May, written by Mike Nichols and Elaine May, containing background music, "Jalousie," performed by Marty Rubinstein, written by Jacob Gade (see pages 351–352)

January 20, 1960

INTRO: Moldy Hay and Harry prepare to introduce "the big bit"—the boss's record. They introduce Jim Henson's own record.

RECORD: "The Countryside": Performed by Jim Henson, written by Jim Henson

In this fast tune (the flip side of "Tick-Tock Sick") laden with sound effects, Jim is a farm boy singing about his path from the farm to the city and back to the countryside.

OUTRO: Harry acknowledges that we just heard their boss, Jim Henson, with his new record. He asks if Jim liked the way they did the record. While we can't hear Jim's response, we hear the rustling of paper money repeatedly as Harry continues his shameless plug for "The Countryside." Kermit finally interrupts. "Friends, I hate to break up this friendly exchange of pleasantries, but the management respectfully suggests we do the commercial for Esskay."

January 21, 1960

COLD OPEN: Harry tells Yorick that they're going to be on Dave Garroway's *Today* show tomorrow morning. Yorick isn't going to watch. "Why not?" Harry asks. "I've seen your show," Yorick grunts.

TITLE CARD/ANNOUNCE: This is a variation on the regular opening, with Moldy Hay announcing the show's title, Harry delivering "brought to you," and Professor Madcliffe concluding with an emphatic "*by* Esskay!" This version would be used sporadically.

RECORD: "Do I Worry?": Performed by The Ink Spots, written by Stanley Cowan, Bobby Worth (see page 367)

January 22, 1960

SKETCH: Harry talks about being on the *Today* show and how it's made them more conscious of politics. They decide to consult the crystal ball to get a look at the future. The spirit (Kermit) briefly considers a future as a rock 'n' roll singer when he notices the echo his voice has when he's inside the ball, but after vocalizing with some Elvis Presley lyrics, the spirit enters his trance to see the future. Harry asks the spirit who's going to be the next president. "Herman R. Puddlestorf," Kermit says. "He's going to be the next President of the United States?" "No," Kermit replies. "He's going to be the next president of Puddlestorf Incorporated. They make crystal balls." Harry implores the spirit for another prediction. Kermit offers a weather report forecasting snew. "What's snew?" Harry asks. "I don't know—what's snew with you?" replies Kermit the spirit. This may be the first Muppet occurrence of a joke that was later used several times, including in the reindeer sketch on *Perry Como's Kraft Music Hall* and *The Ed Sullivan Show* and Dizzy Gillespie's episode of *The Muppet Show*.

January 25, 1960

RECORD: "Sweet Violets": Performed by Dinah Shore, written by Charles Grean, Cy Coben

This is a whimsical story song written with a "censored" or subverted rhyme, in which an anticipated rhyming word is not actually mentioned in the verse; instead an unexpected word is substituted or the word is moved to begin the next line: "There once was a farmer who took a young miss / in back of the barn where he gave her a / . . . lecture on horses and chickens and eggs / and told her that she had such beautiful / . . . manners." The subverted rhymes are strung continuously throughout the song.

January 26, 1960

INTRO: The sound of an orchestra tuning up is heard as Jim Henson's classical music announcer voice welcomes us to Consternation Hall in the nation's capital, "where our orchestra is warming up for our distinguished guest, the teenage idol Shaking Sam." The announcer narrates as Shaking Sam checks his microphone for the right amount of echo, checks his guitar to see if it's in tune, checks his shoulder to make sure it's shaking to the beat, and checks his check to make sure he's been paid enough money. With the checklist completed, Sam begins his performance.

RECORD: "Heartbreak Hotel": Performed by Stan Freberg, written by Tommy Durden, Elvis Presley, Mae Axton (see page 331)

January 27, 1960

COLD OPEN: The show starts with an excerpt from "Harry the Hipster," performed by Ronny Graham, written by Ronny Graham (see page 328).

TITLE CARD/ANNOUNCE

RECORD: "Cocktails for Two": Performed by Jonathan and Darlene Edwards (Paul Weston and Jo Stafford), written by Sam Coslow, Arthur Johnston

Purposely bad lounge act Jonathan and Darlene Edwards perform their version of the 1934 tune, which was introduced in the film *Murder at the Vanities*.

January 28, 1960

RECORD: "Yon-u-ary": Performed by Danny Kaye, written by Sylvia Fine (see page 328)

January 29, 1960

SKETCH: "The Poet's Corner": Harry explains that for the past few weeks, they've neglected "The Poet's Corner" and plan to make up for that with an entire program of poems and limericks. Moldy Hay: "I once had a cow named Zephyr, / she seemed such an amiable heifer. / But when I drew near, / she kicked my left ear, / and now I'm considerably deafer." Harry: "'My supper's cold!' he swore with vim. / And then she made it hot for him." Kermit: "An elephant lay in his bunk, / in slumber his chest rose and sunk. / He snored and he snored, / till the jungle folk roared, / so his wife tied a knot in his trunk." Professor Madcliffe: "There was a young lady of Crete, / who was so exceedingly neat, / when she got out of bed, / she stood on her head, / to make sure of not soiling her feet." Harry: "A mouse in her room woke Miss Dowd. / She was frightened, it must be allowed. / Soon a happy thought hit her, / to scare off the critter, / she sat up in her bed and meowed." Moldy: "It was a cold and windy night, a man stood in the street. / His aged eyes were full of tears, his shoes were full of feet." Kermit breaks for the commercial (which apparently takes place backstage at a rehearsal of *Romeo and Juliet*).

COMMERCIAL

TAG: They return for more poems. Professor: "Mary had a little lamb, / a little pork, a little jam, / a little egg, a little toast, some pickles, and a great big roast, / an ice cream soda topped off with fizz, / and Boy! How sick our Mary is." Harry: "There was an old man from Peru, / who dreamt he was eating his shoe. / He awoke in the night, / in a terrible fright, / and found it was perfectly true." Moldy: "As I was sitting in my chair, / I knew the bottom wasn't there, / nor legs, nor back, but I just sat, / ignoring little things like that." Moldy falls down as Harry wraps up the show: "That concludes 'The Poet's Corner.' If you'd like to see more of 'The Poet's Corner,' well, uh . . . don't hold your breath, 'cause we're out of poems." Harry wasn't entirely accurate, as Jim's script, written in pencil on the back of an AFTRA member report, contained a crossed-out limerick that was to have been delivered by Kermit. "A cheerful old bear at the zoo, / could always find something to do. / When it bored him, you know, / to walk to and fro, / he reversed it and walked fro and to."

February 1, 1960

INTRO: Kermit has found two fellas who sing like Homer and Jethro and has promised them a job, but Harry is hesitant to hire them. Kermit persuades Harry to give them a listen.

RECORD: "Oh That's Terrible": Performed by Homer and Jethro, written by Cy Coben

From their 1959 album *Life Can Be Miserable,* Homer and Jethro recount some unfortunate stories, always punctuating with the line, "Oh, that's terrible!" During the record's instrumental break, Harry and Kermit join in and add their own verses to the song. Harry: "You two fellows sing very bad. You'll never work on *Sam and Friends.*" Kermit: "Oh, that's terrible! I just paid them their salary and deducted it from your weekly fee." Harry: "Oh, that's terrible!"

OUTRO: Harry reluctantly agrees to hire the duo. "Kermit, you promised them a job, didn't you? But you didn't say what—so they'll start off waxing the floors, then washing the NBC mobile unit, painting the transmitter tower . . ." Homer and Jethro's sung response: "Oh, that's terrible!"

February 2, 1960

RECORD: "Night Heat": Performed by Ronny Graham and Gerry Matthews, written by Dee Caruso, Don Adams, Bill Levine

"Night Heat," from the revue *Take Five,* is a parody of an intense one-on-one television interview, with Ronny Graham as a disgraced former executive under scrutiny by a relentless television journalist armed with facts and surprise allegations. Among the writers of the segment were Don Adams, who would go on to play Control Agent 86 on *Get Smart,* and Dee Caruso, who later wrote for *The Monkees* and *Get Smart.* The third member of the writing team, Bill Levine, was a contributor to *Mad* magazine.

February 3, 1960

RECORD: "The Green-Eyed Dragon": Performed by John Charles Thomas, written by Greatrex Newman, Wolseley Charles (see pages 288–289)

February 4, 1960

SKETCH: Following up on his marination flower from the previous year, Kermit has developed a cross between a geranium and a chrysanthemum—a geranthemum. But each time he puts a seed into his electronic growth activator and sits back to watch it grow, some unseen thing or creature eats the seed (as we hear a high-pitched sound effect). But Yorick is asleep, so it's not him causing the trouble. Unable to solve the problem, Kermit considers taking up stamp collecting as a hobby.

February 5, 1960

INTRO: Icky Gunk sells lemonade. He has two bowls—all you can drink out of one bowl costs two cents. The other bowl is all you can drink for five cents. Kermit gladly pays for a drink from the two-cent bowl. "You know, you're not gonna make money selling lemonade that cheap," Kermit says. Icky explains that the special price is just for that bowl. "What's special about this bowl?" Kermit asks. "Well, my cat fell into this bowl a little while ago, and I thought I oughta sell it before word got around."

RECORD: "Looking at Numbers": Performed by Ken Nordine and The Fred Katz Group, written by Ken Nordine, Fred Katz (see page 309)

February 8, 1960

RECORD: "Let Me In": Performed by Red Ingle, written by Bob Merrill (see page 318)

February 9, 1960

SKETCH: Kermit makes faces into the TV camera as he tries to see the viewers at home. "I'm looking for viewers, but everything just looks dark in there." Kermit calls out a hello and receives a reply from the television camera, in a low, slowed-down voice. "I wonder if your cameraman knows you can talk," Kermit says. "Hey, Ed . . . I'm talking to your television camera." Ed the cameraman is startled, and we hear him quickly exit the studio. Kermit asks the camera what his name is. "My friends call me Camera Number Two." The camera invites Kermit into his parlor. Kermit says he has to do the commercial, but the camera sucks him up anyway.

February 10, 1960

INTRO: Kermit and Harry discuss the lack of music in the previous day's show. Kermit wants to present a melodious and lovely song. Harry suggests "Elvis Pelvis singing the Valentine Rock and Easter Egg Roll Cha-Cha-Cha." "No, no, something old-fashioned," Kermit says. "Mozart's Second Piano Boogie Woogie played by Screamin' Fats Monopoly?" They finally decide on "Maggie."

RECORD: "Maggie": Performed by Stan Freberg with Cliffie Stone's Music, written by Cliffie Stone, Stan Freberg (see page 315)

February 11, 1960

RECORD: "That Old Black Magic": Performed by Louis Prima and Keely Smith, written by Harold Arlen, Johnny Mercer (see page 142 for a full summary)

TAG: The ending drumbeats of "That Old Black Magic" are heard after the "By Esskay" outro.

February 12, 1960

INTRO: Kermit and Professor Madcliffe are lost while driving—probably because they're using a map of Ohio to navigate the D.C. area. "Let's get out of this neighborhood," Kermit says. "Over there are some fierce-looking dogs that might live here."

RECORD: "Home Sweet Home" (from *Lady and the Tramp*): Performed by The Pound Hounds (The Mellomen), written by Henry Bishop, John Howard Payne

Thurl Ravenscroft's quartet, The Mellomen, went to the dogs to provide the howling voices of the pound hounds in Walt Disney's *Lady and the Tramp* (1955). The recording of their rendition of "Home Sweet Home" from the film's soundtrack is used here.

February 15, 1960

RECORD: "Baby It's Cold Outside": Performed by Homer and Jethro with June Carter, written by Frank Loesser (see page 332)

February 16, 1960

INTRO: Harry and Professor Madcliffe are walking from Washington to Baltimore. "The sign here says 'Morrow'—I wonder how far away *it* is?" Madcliffe asks. They decide to ask a wanderer for directions.

RECORD: "To Morrow": Performed by Bob Gibson, written by Lew Sully, adapted and arranged by Bob Gibson

This silly and rambling song plays on the confusion between a place called Morrow and the word "tomorrow": "If you had gone to Morrow yesterday now don't you see / You could have gone to Morrow and returned today at three / For the train today to Morrow, if the schedule is right / Today it goes to Morrow and returns tomorrow night." The song dates to 1898, but the version used here was recorded and adapted by Bob Gibson. The Muppet Country Trio, consisting of puppets resembling Jim Henson, Frank Oz, and Jerry Nelson, would later perform the song on the first season of *The Muppet Show*.

February 17, 1960

INTRO: Harry gets the gang ready to sing, assigning parts for their barbershop quartet performance. "Sam, you'll sing baritone, 'cause you're the best baritone singer. Yorick, you're the ugliest, so you'll sing bass. I'll sing the lead—cause I'm the handsomest, and you'll [to Professor Madcliffe] sing tenor." "Why?" Madcliffe asks. "'Cause you've got the tinniest voice." Jim's handwritten script opens with Harry asking his fellow barbershop singers if their mustaches were in place, but the line was deleted. The script also indicates that the introduction was originally slated to be used for the song "Happy Days Are Here Again" but was switched to "Bye Bye Blackbird."

RECORD: "Bye Bye Blackbird": Performed by The Buffalo Bills, written by Mort Dixon, Ray Henderson

"Bye Bye Blackbird" would later be performed by Lou Rawls and The Electric Mayhem on *The Muppet Show,* though not in a barbershop arrangement.

February 18, 1960

INTRO: Kermit and Harry receive a chest from Jim Henson (whose novelty record "Tick-Tock Sick"/"The Countryside" was recently released on the Signature label). Harry says they've already done one side of "his silly record" and wonders what Henson wants now. Kermit reads a note: "*Dear* Sam and Friends, *please do the other side of my silly record.*" Harry resists. "We've done enough for him, so let's forget the whole thing." Kermit continues to read the note: "*I put a reminder in the chest, so I hope you won't forget the whole thing.*" Kermit and Harry open to reveal that the chest is filled with money. "Payola! That's what it is," an outraged Harry exclaims, referring to the illegal practice of paying bribes to disc jockeys in exchange for airplay. "He's trying to buy us off!" Kermit isn't outraged or insulted by the gesture. "Yeah, how about that. Let's do his record."

RECORD: "Tick-Tock Sick": Performed by Jim Henson, written by Jim Henson

Jim provides a soft and steady vocal rhapsodizing on various kinds of clocks and the ticks and tocks associated with them, accompanying a clock-like syncopated soundtrack. Jim frequently explored the concept of time and just five years later would receive an Academy Award nomination for his short film *Time Piece*.

February 19, 1960

RECORD: "Your Feet's Too Big": Performed by Fats Waller, written by Ada Benson, Fred Fisher

This jazz classic is all about the unusual size of a person's lower extremities: "From your ankle up, I'll say you sure are sweet. / From there down, there's just too much feet." The song would later be performed by a duo of monsters on *The Muppet Show*.

February 22, 1960

SKETCH: "Washington's Birthday": Moldy Hay and Harry want to celebrate George Washington's 228th birthday with a candle-laden cake, though Moldy admits that there isn't any cake under all the candles. "By the time I got 228 candles on it, there isn't any room left for any cake." When Harry ponders what George Washington would say, Moldy suggests Harry ask him by communicating to the first President with help from the spirit of the crystal ball (Kermit inside a glass globe). Spirit Kermit goes into a trance and places a long-distance call, then a longer-distance call, and eventually reaches Washington and wishes him a happy birthday. "Oh, thanks, Kermit. You know, it used to be people would play 'Yankee Doodle' on my birthday; now they sell television sets for thirty-five cents." Kermit asks Washington if he has any advice for the present generation. "In my day, I threw a silver dollar across the Potomac. Nowadays, they don't do that anymore. You know why?" Kermit responds immediately, "Yeah. A dollar doesn't go as far now as it used to." Kermit is suddenly disconnected from the call. "George? George? He hung up on me. He does that whenever I tell his punchline. But, gee whiz, he tells the oldest jokes."

February 23, 1960

INTRO: Harry warns Sam not to run away from the nice girl who's been pursuing him.

RECORD: "One Hundred Easy Ways": Performed by *Wonderful Town* Original Broadway Cast (featuring Rosalind Russell), written by Leonard Bernstein, Betty Comden, Adolph Green

In this song from *Wonderful Town,* Rosalind Russell's Ruth explains the many ways to lose a man.

February 24, 1960

RECORD: "Herman Horne on Hi-Fi": Performed by Stan Freberg, written by Stan Freberg, Pete Barnum (see page 312)

February 25, 1960

RECORD: "Harmony": Performed by Steve Lawrence and Eydie Gormé, written by Johnny Burke, James Van Heusen

From the 1947 Paramount Picture *Variety Girl* and originally performed by Bing Crosby and Bob Hope, this is a pop cover by the husband-wife duo Steve and Eydie. Another version, recorded by Johnny Mercer and Nat King Cole, also appeared on Jim's song lists, but its use on-air cannot be confirmed.

February 26, 1960

RECORD: "Money Is King": Performed by Bob Gibson, written by Bob Gibson

The philosophical calypso song is about the importance of money, or to be more specific, the importance of *not* having money.

RECORD: "I Come for to Sing": Performed by Bob Gibson, written by Bob Gibson, Chick Jung, William Wright (see page 206)

February 29, 1960

INTRO: Mushmellon is hopping up and down. Harry tries to get him to stop, but Kermit explains that Mushmellon must keep jumping all day. "February 29 is the extra day that's stuck in for leap year." "So?" Harry asks. "He's leaping!" Kermit says.

RECORD: "A Four-Legged Friend": Performed by Bob Hope and Jimmy Wakely, written by Jack Brooks (see pages 238–239)

March 1, 1960

RECORD: "Stereo Demonstration": Performed by Tony Randall, written by Tony Randall

Future *Muppet Show* guest Tony Randall recorded this lecture on stereophonic equipment in an English accent for his 1960 self-titled album. Randall is probably best known for his Emmy-winning portrayal of Felix Unger on TV's *The Odd Couple*.

March 2, 1960

RECORD: "My Baby": Performed by Ken Nordine and The Fred Katz Group, written by Fred Katz (see pages 359–360)

OUTRO: Harry teases that they're going to be on Dave Garroway's *Today* show the next morning, performing "Looking at Numbers," "Inchworm," and "A Visit to the Spirit of the Crystal Ball."

March 3, 1960

RECORD: "Rock Around Stephen Foster": Performed by Stan Freberg with Billy May's Orchestra, written by Stan Freberg, Stephen Foster (see pages 336–337)

March 4, 1960

SKETCH: Omar announces that they'll be conducting a public opinion telephone poll. Kermit misunderstood and had constructed a telephone pole. Omar tells Kermit to put the pole away and assigns him to pick random numbers from the phone book. While Kermit does so, Omar dials some random digits on his own. He reaches a lady and asks what her favorite television show is. She says, "*Sam and Friends*." "It is? Would you tell us why?" Omar asks. "Because it's so clever and so full of good, wholesome family entertainment," she says, "and because they play such good music on the show, and because my son works on the show." Kermit tells Omar, "Say hello to Mom for me, will you?" Omar asks, "How did I ever get your mother's telephone number?" Kermit replies, "I could ask the same question of you, sir." Omar continues to struggle with his poll as Kermit's first random phone number selection is a literal Random number—a toll call to Random, Maryland. Omar tries to explain that he didn't want to call a place *called* Random; "I just want a number haphazardly chosen." Kermit obliges with the number for a Mr. Haphazardly Q. Chosen.

March 7, 1960

SKETCH: Kermit is looking for Icky Gunk. Harry tells him that Icky just went down a hole—because he's a spelunker. "Well! He ought to be ashamed of himself!" Kermit says. Harry explains that a spelunker is someone who explores caves. "Listen—I think I hear a strange sound," Harry says. "Sounds to me like a new sound."

RECORD: "There's a New Sound": Performed by Tony Burrello, written by Tony Burrello, Tom Murray (see page 74)

March 8, 1960

RECORD: "With Plenty of Money and You": Performed by The Buffalo Bills, written by Al Dubin, Harry Warren

The barbershop quartet from *The Music Man* sings this tune, popularized in the film *Gold Diggers of 1937*, that declares how "life would be sunny" with plenty of money . . . and you.

RECORD: "The Squirrel": Performed by Bob Gibson, written by Bob Gibson

This children's song about the activities of a series of animals was recorded by Bob Gibson, who was heard on several *Sam and Friends* installments.

March 9, 1960

RECORD: "The Matador": Performed by Sammy Shore with orchestral accompaniment, written by Sammy Shore (see page 374)

March 10, 1960

RECORD: "It's a Quiet Town": Performed by Danny Kaye and The Andrews Sisters with Vic Schoen and His Orchestra, written by Bob Russell, Harold Spina (see page 251)

March 11, 1960

RECORD: "Abominable Snowman": Performed by Stan Freberg, written by Stan Freberg (see pages 294–295)

March 14, 1960

INTRO: "The Poet's Corner": Harry greets the audience, cues the organ music, and segues into . . .

RECORD: "Charles the Poet": Performed by Bob and Ray, written by Bob Elliott, Ray Goulding

In this track from the album *Bob and Ray on a Platter,* the team presents serious poetry. But Charles the Poet (Ray Goulding) continues to interrupt the solemn mood with silliness and laughter: "I took your hand in mine, our love to begin, / that guilty feeling, that of innocent sin, / add just a dash of gin."

March 15, 1960

RECORD: "Horse Named Bill": Performed by Bob Gibson, Traditional (see pages 154–155 for a full summary)

March 16, 1960 (date estimated)

INTRO: Harry begins by informing the audience that the group has been rehearsing all afternoon because their song is very complicated. "Luckily, we on this show, being a rather talented lot, possess the necessary musical background, the time-second splitting, uh split-second timing, and the synchronated syncopution, uh—the synthesized patronation—the chromated elocution—anyway, you name it and we've got it." Kermit takes offense at Harry telling the audience that he has elocution. "I've never had a sick day in my life," Kermit says. Harry stands corrected and then assigns the parts with Kermit on vocals, Bernice whistling, Yorick snorting, and Harry tooting his own horn. "Because, of course, it's a well-known fact that he who tooteth not his own horn getteth not his own horn tooted—or something like that—anyway, here's the number."

RECORD: Unknown. (While the script for the introduction exists, there is no recording of the show and no indication on the script as to which record it was intended to accompany.)

March 17, 1960

INTRO: "Tonight, friends, we take you from the soggy Eastern snows to a saga of the Old West," says Kermit as he offers a brief introduction. "You will notice we have eliminated the showing of real guns on the show due to the uneasiness shown concerning the depicting of violence and such relative matters on television."

RECORD: "Wyatt Earp Makes Me Burp": Performed by Spike Jones, vocals by Mousie Garner, Sir Frederick Gas, Sons of the Sons of the Pioneers, written by Spike Jones, Freddy Morgan

This is a Western story song delivered in typical Spike Jones style. Augmenting the record, Kermit can be heard periodically interrupting with his own lines and substituting spoken "bang-bang"s and "blam-blam"s for the burp sounds promised in the record's title. In this version of "Wyatt Earp Makes Me Burp," there isn't any burping at all. Although not credited on the record, Thurl Ravenscroft's voice is clearly identifiable as the song's narrator.

TAG: Harry "kills" Kermit at the end of the song. "Oh! You got me! Ow! I'm dying! You killed me dead," Kermit says. "Yeah, I didn't know how else I could have killed you," Harry says. Kermit decides not to die and instead does the commercial.

March 18, 1960

RECORD: "Oh, Don't Go Near Them Lion's Cage Tonight" (a.k.a. "Don't Go in the Lion's Cage Tonight"): Performed by Oscar Brand, written by E. Ray Goetz, John Gilroy

This version of the classic English music hall song was recorded by Oscar Brand. In it, a lady who works with lions every night is warned not to go near the lion's cage on one fateful night. Julie Andrews used a version as the title track of her 1962 album.

March 21, 1960

INTRO: Omar welcomes the audience of music lovers. "I have here a trombone, and because spring is here, I have decided to play my trombone for you." In view of the season, which brings with it blooming flowers and buzzing bees, Omar has decided to play "Flight of the Bumblebee."

RECORD: "The Sneezin' Bee": Performed by Spike Jones, written by Nikolai Rimsky-Korsakov, arranged by Spike Jones

"Flight of the Bumblebee" dates to 1900, written by Rimsky-Korsakov for an opera called *The Tale of the Tsar Saltan*. Spike Jones's "The Sneezin' Bee," from his album *Dinner Music for People Who Aren't Very Hungry* (1957), consists of a virtuoso Tommy Pederson trombone performance of "Flight of the Bumblebee" and an equally impressive Frank Leithner sneezing performance.

RECORD: "Ramona": Performed by Spike Jones, written by Mabel Wayne, L. Wolfe Gilbert

This track begins with a spoken introduction by Spike Jones, explaining that high fidelity can open up a new level of enjoyment to listeners by isolating a single instrument and bringing it up in the audio mix. Jones says that he likes drums, so when the song begins, the drum solo is overwhelming and drowns out the faint melody.

March 22, 1960

INTRO: Professor Madcliffe introduces "Folk Song Night," presenting Icky Gunk and his guitar to sing "that ballad of love and strife in old Mexico."

RECORD: "El Paso, Numero Dos": Performed by Homer and Jethro, written by Marty Robbins

Marty Robbins's Western ballad "El Paso" was released in 1959 and has become a classic tale of tragic romance. Homer and Jethro's version keeps the melody, but the lyrics have been thoroughly parodied, paying proper homage to the composer: "I asked a cab driver, 'Where's Rosa's Cantina? / I'd like to find it 'cause I can't stay long.'

/ He said, 'Why don't you go ask Marty Robbins? / 'Cause he's the hombre who made up this song.'"

March 23, 1960

RECORD: "The Pig & the Inebriate": Performed by Bob Gibson, Traditional

The short folk song is the story of a drunken man who ends up in the gutter, where a pig ends up beside him. When a passing lady says, "You can tell a man that boozes by the company he chooses," the pig slowly walks away.

RECORD: "True Love": Performed by The Buffalo Bills, written by Cole Porter

The famous barbershop quartet performs this Cole Porter tune that was composed for the 1956 MGM musical *High Society*. "True Love" would later be performed by Miss Piggy and Link Hogthrob in a third-season installment of *The Muppet Show*.

March 24, 1960

RECORD: "The Quest for Bridey Hammerschlaugen": Performed by Stan Freberg with June Foray and Billy May's Music, written by Stan Freberg (see page 335)

March 25, 1960

RECORD: "Flattery" (from *Whoop-Up*): Performed by Steve Lawrence and Eydie Gormé, written by Norman Gimbel, Moose Charlap

From the short-lived Broadway musical *Whoop-Up* (1958), this Steve Lawrence and Eydie Gormé pop cover duet was released in 1960. In the song, Steve and Eydie take turns tossing flattering verses at each other, while both insisting that "flattery will get you nowhere"—until they change their tune at the song's conclusion, agreeing that "flattery will get you somewhere."

March 28, 1960

SKETCH: Harry talks about the spring, a fitting time for a poem concerning birds and flowers and soft summer breezes and stuff. He introduces guest poet Moldy Hay, who delivers his poem entitled "Birds and Flowers and Soft Summer Breezes and Stuff." It is a whimsically silly poem that professes love for all the items mentioned in the title. It ends with, "I love the jabberknowled dinwitty in the park, / the chiggerbugger promecium in the dark, / the featherheaded flutterwoof that seldom turns blue, / the purpletiggered worflefeister that looks like snew." Harry interrupts to ask, "What's snew?" "Oh, I don't know. What's snew with you," Moldy replies. "Oooo! I knew it . . . I just knew it was comin'," Harry says in response to the second known *Sam and Friends* use of a gag that would become a Muppet standard. (Any Muppet joke worth using once is worth using many times.) As Moldy continues his recitation about calm and relaxing elements of nature, he falls asleep, not finishing his poem.

March 29, 1960

RECORD: "You're Just in Love": Performed by Mary Martin and Larry Hagman, written by Irving Berlin

Originally performed by Ethel Merman in *Call Me Madam* (1953), this version is sung by Mary Martin and her son, Larry Hagman.

The Muppets would go on to perform the song on Al Hirt's *Fanfare* and *The Jimmy Dean Show*. A snippet of the song was included in a medley when Merman appeared on *The Muppet Show* in Season 1, and the song was reprised the next season as a duet between Cleo Laine and The Swedish Chef.

March 30, 1960

INTRO: Harry introduces a recitation by Sam, which Harry will accompany on the piano.

RECORD: "There Once Was a Poor Young Girl": Performed by Oscar Brand, written by Charley Case

This spoken piece is a melodramatic parody—a story of a young girl who left her country home to seek employment in the big city because her father was hurt and the wolf was at the door. By the end of the story, not only does her father recover, but she inherits a fortune from a wealthy aunt.

SEGUE: Harry introduces their encore, "The Fountain in the Park."

RECORD: "The Fountain in the Park": Performed by Oscar Brand, written by Ed Haley

A barbershop quartet recording of the song was previously used on *Sam and Friends*. The version used on this episode was recorded by vocalist and music historian Oscar Brand.

March 31, 1960

INTRO: Bernice asks Harry what little boys are made of . . . Harry asks her to ask Kermit. This episode marks the second (known) time that Jane Henson voiced Bernice.

RECORD: "What Are Folks Made Of?": Performed by Bob Gibson, written by Bob Gibson

This folk song explores the stereotypical ingredients that go into making little boys and little girls (as well as old men and old women).

April 1, 1960

RECORD: "The Great Pretender": Performed by Stan Freberg with The Toads and Billy May's Music, written by Buck Ram (see pages 337–338)

April 4, 1960

RECORD: "They Laid Him in the Ground": Performed by Homer and Jethro, written by Patrick McAdory

This 1955 record is a sad and doleful series of comic-tragic anecdotes all leading to a person's demise. In the middle of the *Sam and Friends* performance of the song, Professor Madcliffe interrupts to say, "This number is a drag" and asks if the end of the song is near.

April 5, 1960

INTRO: Bernice is chewing gum. Omar asks her to blow a bubble. She can't. "You should see Yorick, he can really blow bubbles," Omar says.

RECORD: "Bubble Gum": Performed by Ken Nordine featuring The Fred Katz Group, written by Ken Nordine, Fred Katz (see page 321)

April 6, 1960

RECORD: "Herman Horne on Hi-Fi": Performed by Stan Freberg, written by Stan Freberg, Pete Barnum (see page 312)

April 7, 1960

INTRO: Omar has assembled the vocal group he calls "The Muppets 4": Frank, Kermit, Harry, and himself.

RECORD: "As Time Goes By": Performed by The Buffalo Bills, written by Herman Hupfeld

Best known from the classic film *Casablanca* (1942), the song was actually written ten years before its use in the movie.

April 8, 1960

SKETCH: Harry interviews Professor Von Madcliffe at Cape Cadaver about the weather satellite up above and the TV camera contained therein. The Professor explains how the satellite works—he can monitor the satellite's camera on his High Frequency Vidiotic Image Orthopedic Tube. Upon examination of the TV image from the satellite, Madcliffe locates a shooting star (with a sped-up voice) who wants to be a TV star. Madcliffe is then surprised to see Kermit transmitting from the satellite, but Kermit explains that he's the cameraman. "You can't use a television camera without a union cameraman," says Kermit, showing off his NABET (National Association of Broadcast Employees and Technicians) membership card. The Professor asks Kermit to turn his camera to take a shot of the Earth—he does so, revealing the Earth to be flat. "I always thought Christopher Columbus was a dunderhead," Kermit says. Madcliffe wraps up the show: "It all goes to show that modern science is taking another step—" Kermit interrupts, "Backwards."

April 11, 1960

RECORD: "G'wan Home, Your Mudder's Callin'": Performed by Jimmy Durante, written by Ralph Freed, Sammy Fain (see page 299)

April 12, 1960

RECORD: "Six Months Out of Every Year": Performed by *Damn Yankees* Original Broadway Cast (featuring Shannon Bolin), written by Richard Adler, Jerry Ross (see page 301)

OUTRO: Omar is trying to play ball with the rest of the gang, but he's having one problem—he can't catch the ball. "I'm bound to catch one sooner or later. After all, I've been here since nine o'clock this morning."

April 13, 1960

RECORD: "Income Tax": Performed by Bob Corley, written by Bob Corley (see pages 289–290)

April 14, 1960

RECORD: "Going on a Hike": Performed by Tom D'Andrea and Hal March, with harmonica accompaniment by Jerry Hilliard, written by George Cates, Tom D'Andrea, Hal March (see page 356)

April 15, 1960

RECORD: "The Chick": Performed by Lee and Paul, written by Lee Pockriss, Paul Vance (see page 349)

In this performance, Jim Henson replaced the rock 'n' roll chick's spoken remarks with Harry voicing similar disgruntled musings.

April 18, 1960

INTRO: Harry asks the President to throw out the first pitch, which hits Harry. (On this date, the Washington Senators began their season with a game at home against the Boston Red Sox. It would be their last season before relocating to Minnesota and becoming the Twins.)

RECORD: "A Brooklyn Baseball Fan": Performed by Phil Foster, chorus and orchestra directed by Dick Jacobs, written by Phil Foster, contains "Take Me Out to the Ball Game," written by Albert Von Tilzer, Jack Norworth (see pages 364–365)

April 19, 1960

INTRO: Harry introduces Yorick with a guitar solo and hands him his guitar, which Yorick proceeds to eat.

RECORD: "Muskrat": Performed by Merle Travis, written by Harold Hensley, Merle Travis, Tex Ann (see page 303)

April 20, 1960

RECORD: "Chinese Rock and Egg Roll": Performed by Buddy Hackett, written by Buddy Hackett

Comedian Buddy Hackett introduced his "Chinese Waiter" routine in 1953. Despite its offensive nature, it was a big hit (the times were different), and he gave it a rock 'n' roll twist for the 1956 record used in this segment. By 1960, the year this show aired, Hackett had already wisely retired the routine. He would enjoy a long career in stand-up comedy, film, and television, including a vocal performance on an episode of *Dinosaurs*.

April 21, 1960

RECORD: "Gotta Get to Your House": Performed by David Seville, written by Skipper Adams

Jim had used this song before (see page 284), but this time, apparently inspired by David Seville (Ross Bagdasarian)'s success with 1958's "The Chipmunk Song," Jim gave it the Chipmunk treatment by speeding up the recording for *Sam and Friends*.

SKETCH: "The Poet's Corner": The post-song edition of "The Poet's Corner" is also sped up, creating Chipmunk-like voices for the characters as they deliver limericks. The audio speed returns to normal just in time for the commercial.

April 22, 1960

INTRO: Harry provides an introduction as the music begins: "From somewhere way above and far out in never-ever land, today's number echoes down to us from the vaporous vacuums of perpetuosity. The languid love call of an infatuated enamored amorata—for, as Virgil says, 'amantes amentes,' which translated says, 'lovers are lunatics.'"

RECORD: "Myrtle": Performed by Joe Pryor with Loulie Jean Norman with orchestra conducted by Henry Mancini, written by Irving Taylor (see page 325)

April 25, 1960

RECORD: "The Old Philosopher": Performed by Eddie Lawrence, written by Eddie Lawrence (see pages 341–342)

April 26, 1960

RECORD: "Sortileges" (background instrumental): Performed by Roger Roger et son Orchestre, written by Roger Roger

SKETCH: "Omar Makes a Puppet": As the exotic instrumental music plays, Omar constructs a puppet. There are no further details on the sketch, but at the end, the voice of Icky Gunk is heard, so it is possible Omar's puppet came to life.

April 27, 1960

RECORD: "Nowhere": Performed by Red Ingle and The Natural Seven, written by Edward Heyman, John Green, arranged by Country Washburne, Foster Carling (see page 366)

April 28, 1960

INTRO: Pointing out that television is a complex and technical field, Professor Madcliffe calls over the show's cameraman to sum up his years of experience at NBC. We then hear an audio snippet from WRC cameraman Dodd Boyd (who, we assume, is played on camera by one of the Muppets): "After running a camera for fourteen years, I've said this all along . . . the guy who runs the camera, he ought to run the camera." Harry is in agreement. "Sure, Dodd. And you can quote him!"

RECORD: "Dinah": Performed by Danny Kaye, written by Harry Akst, Sam M. Lewis, Joe Young (see pages 295–296)

April 29, 1960

INTRO: Omar provides an introduction: "We now take you to the lobby of a New York hotel and a little girl who lives there who goes by the name of..."

RECORD: "Eloise": Performed by Kay Thompson, orchestra conducted by Archie Bleyer, written by Kay Thompson, Robert Wells (see page 347)

Kermit, in his Kermeena wig, plays the role of Eloise.

TAG: After the song, Harry calls for Eloise... Kermit says he'll send her in, but he returns moments later wearing a wig (as he did while playing Eloise in the song). "What happened to Kermit?" Harry asks. "I'll call him," Kermit says in a falsetto voice as he exits. "No, wait a minute, I wanted to talk to both of 'em," Harry says, explaining that he wanted to see if there was a family resemblance. When he notices that they don't appear on camera at the same time, Harry comes to a logical conclusion: "It doesn't look like they get along very well with each other."

May 2, 1960

SKETCH: In the first installment of a weeklong running storyline, Kermit is enjoying a spring day when his contentment is interrupted by the arrival of a chigger bug (Jim Henson's sped-up voice). The bug bites Kermit, who retaliates by spraying the area with bug spray. When the bug appears to succumb to the pesticide, Kermit feels remorse—until he is bitten again. "You double-crossed me! You were playing possum! I'll have no mercy next time," says Kermit, who then asks Yorick to watch the chigger while Kermit goes to get more insecticide. Yorick eats the bug. Kermit returns and is dismayed by Yorick's behavior. "Yorick! You didn't! How could you? He was my closest enemy." Kermit looks in Yorick's mouth—we hear the chigger still alive and biting Yorick from the inside.

May 3, 1960

INTRO: Harry is headed to meet Kermit in the woods. When Harry remarks that at this time of year, there aren't any mosquitoes or gnats or chiggers, he is, in fact, bitten by the chigger who was introduced the previous day. "Gee, that itches. I wonder if Kermit will know what to do for chigger bites."

RECORD: "Bonnie Wee Lassie": Performed by Burl Ives, Traditional

This traditional Scottish folk song is the story of a girl named Nell and her beau, Johnny. One little kiss between them turns into big problems.

TAG: Kermit tells Harry that there's only one thing to do for chigger bites: scratch.

May 4, 1960

INTRO: Harry is hoping they can get through the show without the chigger bothering them. Before he can introduce Kermeena's song, the bug returns and bites Kermeena, who then whispers to Harry that she wishes to dedicate her song to the chigger.

RECORD: "I've Got You Under My Skin": Performed by Peggy Lee, written by Cole Porter

Yet another version of the Cole Porter standard, this time by Peggy Lee. The song was later used on a Season 1 episode of *The Muppet Show*.

May 5, 1960

SKETCH: The show begins with the chigger still aggravating the cast. "Did you all see that chigger that just went by?" Harry says. "That chigger has been making life difficult for us ever since he showed up around here on Monday—" Before Harry can finish his sentence, the bug returns and bites him. "That did it! I'm gonna fix him but good!" says Harry, who runs offscreen and quickly returns with a hammer. Professor Madcliffe, who was also just bitten, joins Harry onscreen and together they give chase to the chigger. Harry takes aim and swings the hammer at the chigger, but it instead ends up in Madcliffe's mouth. Harry proposes they work out a plan to catch the bug. Harry suggests that Madcliffe be a decoy and as the chigger goes for the bait, Harry will sneak up and squirt him with insecticide. The bug returns but evades harm. Madcliffe suggests they give up and do the commercial.

May 6, 1960

RECORD: "Life Gits Tee-Jus, Don't It?": Performed by Peter Lind Hayes, written by Carson Robison (see page 292)

May 9, 1960

INTRO: Harry begins by saying, "The following number is dedicated to Jane Henson, to six-pound, ten-ounce Lisa Marie, and her proud new fatherrrrrr—" The audio slows down to a stop before Harry can mention Jim by name.

RECORD: "Proud New Father": Performed by Johnny Standley with Horace Heidt and His Musical Knights, written by John Standley (see page 323)

May 10, 1960

RECORD: "I Went to Your Wedding": Performed by Spike Jones and His City Slickers, vocal refrain by Sir Frederick Gas, written by Jessie Mae Robinson (see page 243)

May 11, 1960

INTRO: Professor Madcliffe asks Harry when he's going to get his broken glasses fixed. Harry promises to do so before the commercial.

RECORD: "Anything You Can Do (I Can Do Better)": Performed by *Annie Get Your Gun* Original Broadway Cast (featuring Ethel Merman and Ray Middleton), written by Irving Berlin (see page 291)

May 12, 1960

INTRO: Harry asks, "How do you like these glasses, Professor?" Professor Madcliffe responds, "They're terrible. How can you play pool with those?" "Pool?" Harry asks. "Sure. I just bought a pool table!"

RECORD: "Ya Got Trouble": Performed by Stan Freberg, The Jud Conlon Singers with Billy May's Orchestra, written by Meredith Willson

In 1958, Stan Freberg delivered a straight, nonparody version of this talk song from Meredith Willson's *The Music Man*, which had opened on Broadway the previous year. In later years, Freberg regretted not having the opportunity to play the role onstage.

May 13, 1960

INTRO: Professor Madcliffe begins by asking Harry if he's gotten a decent pair of glasses yet. Harry shows off his new spectacles, but the Professor says they're horrible. Madcliffe quickly changes the subject to announce that it's Friday the 13th—the birthday of Jubilation T. Cornpone.

RECORD: "Jubilation T. Cornpone": Performed by *Li'l Abner* Original Broadway Cast (featuring Stubby Kaye), written by Johnny Mercer, Gene de Paul (see page 293)

May 16, 1960

RECORD: "The King's New Clothes": Performed by Danny Kaye, written by Frank Loesser (see page 267)

May 17, 1960

INTRO: Professor Madcliffe asks Harry when he's going to get a pair of glasses that will look good on him. He asks Harry to take off the ones he's wearing now . . . he's never seen Harry without glasses. When Harry removes them, he is unrecognizable. (There is no indication in the script of what the specific gag was—if Harry actually appeared without glasses or if a different puppet stood in for him.) Madcliffe quickly changes the subject. "And speaking of explosions, has Yorick ever told you about his cousin Roger Boom?"

RECORD: "Roger Boom": Performed by Larry Hooper and Lawrence Welk, written by Bob Hilliard (see pages 276–277)

May 18, 1960

RECORD: "The Professor": Performed by Eddie Lawrence, written by Eddie Lawrence

From his 1958 album, *The Kingdom of Eddie Lawrence,* the comedian best known as "The Old Philosopher" becomes a professor to deliver a science lecture entitled "The Universe as a Whole in Three Parts." The German-sounding professor is periodically interrupted by an oompah band.

May 19, 1960

INTRO: As an instrumental of "Let Me Call You Sweetheart" plays, Harry recites a poem:

> Roses are red and violets are blue,
> And here's a bouquet that I offer to you,
> With chrysaniums orange and geranthemums pink,
> When I look at these flowers, I always think
> Of the perfumes that come from these lovely blooms,

Wind drifts sweetly through the hallways and rooms
Of my house where the smell of the blossoms is joined
With the odor from the kitchen of the cooking has been boined.
So when I think of this perfume, of this beautiful rose,
I wish most of all, that I had a nose.

Harry asks Kermit if he wants to smell Harry's flowers. Kermit does so and segues into . . .

RECORD: "Atchoo (The Sneezing Record)": Performed by Joey Faye, written by Sam Carlton, Dan Dougherty (see page 261)

May 20, 1960

RECORD: "Sh-Boom": Performed by Stan Freberg with The Toads and orchestra conducted by Billy May, written by James Keyes, Claude Feaster, Carl Feaster, Floyd F. McRae, William Edwards (see page 300)

May 23, 1960

RECORD: "The Kids on the Corner": Performed by Phil Foster, written by Phil Foster, containing "That Old Gang of Mine," written by Ray Henderson, Billy Rose, Mort Dixon (see pages 350–351)

May 24, 1960

RECORD: "Cecilia": Performed by David Seville, written by Dave Dreyer, Herman Ruby (see page 324)

May 25, 1960

RECORD: "Yaller Rose of Texas You-All": Performed by Homer and Jethro, written by Homer Haynes, Jethro Burns

This 1955 Homer and Jethro record has little in common with the Stan Freberg version of the classic folk song previously used on *Sam and Friends:* "There's a yaller rose of Texas, the cutest on this Earth. / Her right eye looks at Dallas, her left one at Fort Worth."

May 26, 1960

INTRO: Kermit announces "*Sam and Friends* present a golden adventure Muppet-acular" over the opening fanfare of the Spike Jones recording (below). After Kermit finishes, the record's actual announcer takes over.

RECORD: "I Search for Golden Adventure (In My Seven Leaky Boots)": Performed by Spike Jones, Joyce Jameson, Lynn Johnson, written by Carl E. Brandt, Eddie Brandt, Les Ecklund

From the Spike Jones album *Omnibust* (1960), the track is a fully scored production, the story of an African expedition to the lost city of Exoticus.

May 27, 1960

RECORD: "Goodnight Ladies": Performed by The Sportsmen Quartet, written by Edwin Pearce Christy (see page 279)

TAG/CREDITS: Kermit and Harry sign off for the season until the fall—they thank the ad agency and Esskay and ask the viewers to continue to buy Esskay products during the summer. Kermit concludes: "We wanted to end up by giving credit to a few of the people who've made this whole mess possible." The credits run, accompanied by circus music ("Alfred in the Circus" from *Musically Mad* (1959), performed by Bernie Green with the Stereo Mad-Men, written by Bernard Green).

NEW SEASON BEGINS

September 12, 1960

SKETCH: "Olympic Report Part 1": As "The National Broadcasting Company Management Orchestra" plays "The Stars and Stripes Forever," Kermit leads his fellow *Sam and Friends* cast members as they make their triumphant return from the Olympics in Rome. We learn that the Muppets competed in the "incidental sports—sports that might not have gotten some of the publicity, but important, nonetheless." Kermit first introduces the gold medalist in the marathon skip rope event, Sam, who, after skipping rope 173,461 times, is still skipping, but now without the rope. Kermit next introduces Icky Gunk, the hide-and-seek champion, but Icky does not show up. It seems that Icky took $10,000 from the ticket office before he started hiding and he still hasn't been found. The Tiddlywinks and mumblety-peg winners are next—Hank and Frank, who are confused about who exactly won what. Kermit next presents the gold medalist in freestyle pie-eating, Yorick, who devoured 472 pies in thirteen and a half minutes. Omar, a fellow member of the pie-eating team, protests Yorick's win by pointing out that Yorick ate the pie pans; he then hits Yorick with a pie. "You shouldn't have hit Yorick with that pie," Kermit says. "You wouldn't want to be called a bad sport." Omar replies, "Are you calling me a bad sport?" Kermit starts to say no, but he, too, is hit with a pie. With a mouth full of pie, Kermit tells viewers that the Olympic report will continue the next day

September 13, 1960

SKETCH: "Olympic Report Part 2": The second part of the Olympic report begins as Kermit continues to introduce the *Sam and Friends* Olympians to the cheering crowd. Mushmellon is introduced as the squash champion—who literally squashed the competition. Jazz musician Harry won the freestyle "Skoo-bee-doo." Kermit asks Harry to describe the event. "Like, the Skoo-bee-doo is incipiently a musical bit. You get yourself a swinging orchestracographer, a fifteen-man polyphonic allegrettomobile, and while they're ba-bumming in the background, you Skoo-bee-doo in the foreground." Harry then gives a quick demonstration to music: "Ba doo ba doo skoo bee dooo . . . ba dee ba deee skee booo deee . . . boo biddle-de-ba skittle-de-bee skoo-dle-de-boo skottle-e-bottle-de deddy-de-deh honk deddy-de-deh hoo deddy-doody-de-skoodyde de bop mop. Skoo boop be da *pow bam bang* bang blangety bang boom bad um beem!" Kermit admits that their team didn't have winners in some of the other incidental events such as the hopscotch match, the ten-meter peanut push, or the blind man's bluff. When prompted by Harry, Kermit wraps up the report by acknowledging his own win in the one hundred-meter leapfrog race. "Because I have a great many friends who are frogs, I got the gold medal."

September 14, 1960

INTRO: "Henrietta" says she's getting married. "I can't stop to talk about it now, darlings, I must run. So much to do . . ."

RECORD: "(We're All Invited to) Henrietta's Wedding": Performed by Marais and Miranda, written by Albert Diggenhof, Josef Marais

Marais and Miranda were a married singing duo who recorded folk and world music in the 1950s and 1960s. "Henrietta's Wedding," a song about a woman who is having a wedding but doesn't know who her husband is to be, would later be performed as a two-minute U.K. spot on *The Muppet Show*.

September 15, 1960

SKETCH: "The Coming Season": Kermit discusses what will be coming up on the show in the year to come, promising music, poetry, politics, and corny humor. The sketch contains "you don't say" drop-ins from the Spike Jones record "Chloe," with vocal by Red Ingle. (See pages 188–190 for the full script.)

September 19, 1960

INTRO: Moldy Hay introduces "Folk Song Day" with a song from Kermit, who starts to play the guitar intro but stops because he doesn't have a bucket. Moldy brings him one. Kermit starts to play again, but he stops again, this time because the bucket doesn't have a hole in it. Moldy is happy to oblige, taking the bucket offscreen. We hear a gunshot, and Moldy returns. "Here you are." Kermit sings . . .

RECORD: "There's a Hole in the Bucket": Performed by Bob Gibson, Traditional

This song, the story of a progressive (and eventually cyclical) problem whose solution presents a further problem, would later be performed by Jim Henson as an Anything Muppet on *Sesame Street*.

September 20, 1960

SKETCH: "Khrushchev Questionnaire Bit": Kermit has been asked by NBC News to go into the street to interview people about their reactions to Khrushchev's arrival in New York and his upcoming appearance at the United Nations. "I really enjoy being a newsman," Kermit says (foreshadowing his future career as a reporter for "*Sesame Street* News"). "Just think of the opportunities ahead. Huntley, Brinkley, and Kermit." Kermit finds a lady at home who agrees to be interviewed as soon as she's finished washing her hair. Kermit waits but is soon drenched with the rinse water the lady tosses out her window—and then is hit by her hair, which she dropped while wringing it out. Kermit finally finds someone—or, actually, "sometwo"—to interview, as Hank and Frank answer their door and speak their minds at the same time. Yorick is the last to be interviewed about Khrushchev, his guttural grunts mostly unintelligible until he tells the persistent correspondent to "go jump in a lake."

September 22, 1960

SKETCH: "The Poet's Corner": Omar opens with: "And now we here on *Sam and Friends* / to the height of culture we ascend, / to bring to you in rhythm and rhyme, / in lyrical verse and pantomime, / and haters of poetry will now dissent, / as we, 'The Poet's Corner,' present." Moldy recites: "She wore her stockings inside out all through the summer heat. / She said it cooled her off to turn the hose upon her feet." Then Kermit delivers: "There was a young lady of Niger, / who smiled as she rode on the tiger. / When they returned from the ride, / the lady was inside, / and the smile on the face of the tiger." After Hank and Frank wrestle with the Peter Piper tongue twister, Moldy Hay introduces Yorick to perform "Lines Upon a Tranquil Brow."

RECORD: "Lines Upon a Tranquil Brow" (from *Songs of the Pogo*): Performed by Walt Kelly, written by Walt Kelly, Norman Monath (see page 410)

September 27, 1960

SKETCH: "Sam for President: Part 1": Sam is chosen as a candidate for President by the Republicratic Party, and Kermit tries to prepare him for politics. "Remember, *all* candidates are good men, and we're not doubting their motives. We're *all* trying to accomplish the same good things for the nation . . . it's just our *methods* that are different. You see, we're using brand-new, tried-and-proven, good methods that won't cost the people any money . . . while the other candidates are using selfish, one-sided, inferior, sneaky, egotistical, decadent, pitifully inexcusable, and *wrong* methods that will bankrupt the country in a couple of days." Kermit drills the usually silent Sam with his all-purpose prerecorded campaign speech: "Friends, I say when the world situation is so hopelessly confused, you need a president who fits the situation." Kermit suggests Sam implement Moldy Hay's plan to get rid of the farm surplus by declaring a six-month-long holiday to be celebrated by one long picnic so the country can polish off the farm surplus. Moldy learns there's no pickle surplus, so the picnic plan won't work. "Another hopeless situation," Kermit says. "A pickle-less picnic certainly sounds pretty hopeless to me, too," Moldy adds. Sam concludes the show with his prerecorded speech.

September 28, 1960

SKETCH: "Sam for President: Part 2": Kermit and Harry continue to prepare Sam for his presidential campaign with a cheer and consider adopting a campaign song. (See pages 191–195 for the full script.)

September 29, 1960

INTRO: "Sam for President: Part 3": The group is talking about Sam being important now—he may run for President. They ask him how he became a success.

RECORD: "I Like People (The Friendly Song)": Performed by Jimmy Durante, Mitch Miller and Orchestra, written by Margaret Wise Brown, Marshall Barer, Ruth Patterson

Jimmy Durante sings this upbeat song about a man who used to hate everyone but now likes everyone he sees.

October 3, 1960

SKETCH: "Three Yoricks: Part 1": The opening is cut short as the theme music slows to a stop. Kermit asks what happened, and Harry explains that someone stole the record from the control room. Did Yorick eat the record? Harry and Kermit don't think so—he should be full for the day because he's already eaten Kermit's fountain pen, three tennis balls, a can of floor wax, two chrysanthemum bushes, a bowl of wax fruit, Harry's raincoat, car keys, two milk bottles, and the hall rug. When Yorick seems to be eating three times as much as he usually eats—including a station wagon—it becomes clear that he has visitors in town: his equally voracious mother and father. (Mom confesses to eating the station wagon.)

October 4, 1960

SKETCH: "Three Yoricks: Part 2": Kermit talks to Yorick about his mom and dad visiting and tells him not to be embarrassed because his parents ate so much. Kermit and Yorick are joined by another purple skull. "Yorick, is this your mother or your father?" In his guttural grunt vocals, Yorick says, "Neither." The new arrival is Yorick's brother. Kermit then learns Yorick is from Yoricktown, New Yorick. Kermit asks if there are any other siblings, and they are joined onscreen by another brother. "Gee, you all look so good together, you ought to do a three brothers act." Yorick grunts an affirmative. "You have an act?" Kermit asks. "Well, would you do it for us?"

RECORD: "Triplets" (from *The Band Wagon*): Performed by Fred Astaire, Nanette Fabray, Jack Buchanan, written by Howard Dietz, Arthur Schwartz

The song, a comic trio number from the MGM movie *The Band Wagon* (1953), was slowed so the vocals were similar to the low grunts uttered by Yorick.

October 7, 1960

SKETCH: "The Great Debate": Construction is underway as the Kennedy-Nixon debate will broadcast live later that evening from right down the hall in Studio A. Stagehands move equipment from the *Sam and Friends* studio as Kermit tries to carry on. (See pages 195–205 for the full script.)

October 10, 1960

INTRO: As applause subsides, Kermit thanks the unseen audience. "Thank you. Thank you. And now, I'd like to play for my next number, I'd like to play . . . baseball." Phil Foster's voice from his "Brooklyn Baseball Fan" record is cut in. "Pitch 'im, Carl! I'm wit' ya! I'm wit' ya, Carl baby! I'm wit' ya," Kermit continues. "Thank you, Sam. No, really, for my next number, I'll have the help of those two wonderful and gifted performers, Homer Wonderful and Jethro Gifted . . ."

RECORD: "Please Help Me, I'm Falling": Performed by Homer and Jethro, written by Don Robertson, Hal Blair

A parody of the Hank Locklin record about a man falling in love, this version is a little less romantic: "Please help me, I'm falling . . . for somebody new. / Anything I wind up with . . . will be better than you."

October 11, 1960

INTRO: Kermit introduces Harry as "that great Frenchman—that singer of French cafe songs, Monsieur Le Harry."

RECORD: "La Ploop de Ma Tante": Performed by Leonard Elliott and Irma Jurist, written by Leonard Elliott and Irma Jurist

From the 1959 album *Fuzzy Peach Pie and Other Lunacies,* Leonard Elliott and Irma Jurist perform a piano-accompanied bit of French silliness.

October 13, 1960

INTRO: Harry asks Kermit if he would like some chowder that Mrs. Murphy sent over. Kermit tries it and keels over. Harry asks Moldy Hay to dish some out to the audience as he takes over the piano-playing from Kermit.

RECORD: "Mrs. Murphy's Chowder": Performed by Oscar Brand, Traditional

From his album *Give 'Im the Hook! Songs That Killed Vaudeville*, Oscar Brand sings about the contents of Mrs. Murphy's chowder: "Silk hats, doormats, bed slats, Democrats, / cow bells, doorbells, beckon you to dine. / Meatballs, fish balls, mothballs, cannonballs. / Come on in, the chowder's fine!"

Professor Madcliffe presents his findings on high fidelity. Photo by Jim Henson

October 17, 1960

INTRO: Professor Madcliffe's topic for the day (and the show's theme for the week) is high fidelity. "On today's show, I plan to demonstrate to you my own personal very expensive ultra orthocoustic stereoscopic wide range polyphonetic AM-FM-ICBM multi-lateral vertical depth dimensional scareophonic gramophone and Victrola." When Madcliffe asks for assistance in explaining the fundamentals, a bit of Spike Jones's "How High the Fidelity" is played. In it, an expert (he must be an expert, he has a thick German accent) from the International Expert of Sound Technology offers his insights: "The secret is to make sure your transducer is looser than the juicer. Und once you got that straight, the tweeter will be sweeter than the heater." When Madcliffe asks for his speaker to be turned on, Kermit misunderstands and directs someone to give a speech. This transitions directly to . . .

RECORD: "Party Political Speech": Performed by Peter Sellers, written by Peter Sellers

This spoken-word track is Peter Sellers's take on a typical English politician's speech. Peter Sellers would go on to appear on *The Muppet Show* during its second season.

October 21, 1960

INTRO: Wrapping up a week dedicated to high fidelity, Professor Madcliffe has lowered a microphone into the ground to listen to the noise that worms make. Kermit sums up the week (some of which has been lost): "Monday, we did a bit about high fidelity. Tuesday, we had a lecture on high fidelity. Wednesday, you sang a song about high fidelity. Thursday, we had a stereo demonstration. And today, you're lowering your high-fidelity microphone down that hole." "So?" Madcliffe asks. Kermit replies: "Don't you think you're running this thing into the ground?"

RECORD: "There's a New Sound": Performed by Tony Burrello, written by Tony Burrello, Tom Murray (see page 74)

October 26, 1960 (date estimated)

RECORD: "The Frozen Logger": Performed by The Weavers, written by James Stevens

The Weavers performed this American folk song about a waitress's romance with a frozen logger.

October 27, 1960

INTRO: Moldy Hay sets up the scene—a girl sits beneath a tree and meditates on a lovely autumn day. A strolling guitar picker happens by; Moldy ponders if she may sing at him with her thoughts.

RECORD: "I Wonder When I Shall Be Married": Performed by Marais and Miranda, Traditional

The folk song is told from the point of view of a maiden and her hopes for a husband: "I wonder when I shall be married, / oh be married, oh be married. / I wonder when I shall be married, / for my beauty's beginning to fade."

October 28, 1960

RECORD: "I Only Have Eyes for You": Performed by Spike Jones, vocals by Paul Frees and Loulie Jean Norman, written by Harry Warren, Al Dubin

From *Spike Jones in Hi-Fi: A Spooktacular in Screaming Sound,* this rendition of the Warren and Dubin standard is a romantic duet between Count Dracula (Paul Frees) and Vampira (Loulie Jean Norman): "Are the bats out tonight? Let's forget them while we have a bite. For I only have eyes for you."

October 31, 1960 (date estimated)

INTRO: Kermit introduces a song to be performed by Icky Gunk and himself: "Good Peanuts." Kermit asks if Icky's guitar is in tune. A couple of plucks on the instrument confirm that it is. Kermit asks, "Do you have your choruses memorized?" Icky nods. "Even the last chorus?" Icky nods. "All right. We'll try to get through it, then."

RECORD: "Good Peanuts": Performed by Oscar Brand, Traditional

Oscar Brand sings this folk song, a catchy tune in praise of the generosity of spirit: "The man who owns them good peanuts and giveth his neighbor none, / he shall have none of my good peanuts when his good peanuts is gone." The verse is repeated with a variety of unusual and increasingly hard-to-sing items. A version of this song, called "Peanuts," was recorded on the *Sesame Street* album *Bert & Ernie Sing-Along*.

November 1, 1960

SKETCH: "The Hammer: Part 1": Hammering a loose nail on the set makes Kermit ponder the usefulness of the hammer, and he considers presenting a show about the tool's history. In mere moments, that show is a reality, with Kermit as its host. "The hammer—faithful servant to mankind, symbol of carpentry skill, and driver of nails. Where would man be without it?" Kermit asks. Harry says, "I don't know. Can you give me a *glue*?" Kermit responds to the pun with a swing of his hammer. "Ha! Missed me!" Kermit introduces tool historian Professor Madcliffe to deliver the history of the hammer, and he explains that it began with a starving inventor named Thomas A. Hammerschlaugen, cousin of Bridey Hammerschlaugen (as mentioned in a Stan Freberg song). "He was working away trying to figure out how to drive a nail into a piece of wood. You see, at that time, nobody knew how to use nails, therefore the nail manufacturers were starving. One day, Hammerschlaugen took off his shoe and was whacking a nail with the heel of it, when his bare foot stumbled across a peculiar-shaped stone. He picked up the stone and hit the nail with it." Madcliffe goes on to explain that the process worked very well, and soon everyone was using a stone Hammerschlaugen to hit nails with. The tool evolved, and eventually a handle was added and it was made of iron, then steel. "The name Hammerschlaugen was considered too long. People got tired of saying, 'Hand me the Hammerschlaugen,' and therefore it was shortened. So now, this very useful tool is known as . . . the Schlaugen." Moldy Hay introduces the commercial "for Esskay American Canned Ham-er, or something like that."

November 2, 1960

SKETCH: "The Hammer: Part 2": Kermit is again hammering the loose nail on the set (he never got to finish in the previous episode). Moldy Hay enters to share a poem he has written about the hammer. "In lives of labor and love of glamour, / there is no more important tool than the hammer. / For no tool there ever was such a clamor, / than the yammer and stammer for what? The hammer. / The tool for which I am most enamored, / the tool which leaves me most unhampered. / When a nail I try to slammer and blamer, / what do I use? My handy hammer. From every state, Maryland to Alabama, / ever'where, they use a hamma'. / They even say the Dalai Lama, / in his tool kit has a hama. / Thus we salute you, noble tool. / Who'll be taught in tool school? You'll." After Moldy's poem, Kermit returns to work hammering when he is interrupted by Harry. The two engage in a hammering contest to see who can hammer faster. When Kermit wins, Harry calls him a cheater, and the action devolves into a hammer battle with the two characters taking swings at each other.

November 3, 1960 (date estimated)

RECORD: "Down the Drain": Performed by Ken Nordine and The Fred Katz Group, written by Ken Nordine, Fred Katz

Ken Nordine shares his secret—that he has a "think it yourself kit" that he can use to let his mind go. He talks about taking hot baths and sit-down showers to relax. As the accompanying jazz music speeds up, he talks about sliding down the drain and ending up in the Caribbean.

November 4, 1960 (date estimated)

RECORD: "The Westerners (Two Face West)": Performed by Bob and Ray, written by Bob Elliott, Ray Goulding (see page 159 for a full summary)

November 8, 1960

SKETCH: "*Sam and Friends* Election Returns Report": Presented on the evening of the 1960 presidential election, *Sam and Friends* commentators are on hand with the returns. Kermit gives an update on regional returns, then Harry is tasked to check the turnout at polls, but he says that the poles are all locked up "in the pole vault"—which was tacked over with "pole tacks." The team goes to their ICBM Think-o-Vac computer to calculate the big winner, and after they put a nickel in the slot, kick it twice, and hit it, they receive a candy bar and the results, but the victors are neither Nixon and Lodge nor Kennedy and Johnson. The computer predicts that the winners of the election are Huntley and Brinkley, whose broadcast regularly followed *Sam and Friends* and who would later anchor that night's election coverage on NBC. (NBC's cutting-edge 1960 election coverage used the RCA 501 computer and not the Muppets' Think-o-Vac.) When Jim made the ICBM computer gag, little did he know he would be making industrial films for the actual IBM corporation beginning in 1965.

November 9, 1960 (date estimated)

RECORD: "Meet the Johnson Boys": Performed by The Weavers, Traditional

The Weavers' Ronnie Gilbert takes the lead on this rendition of a folk song about the Johnson boys, who, as the song says, "are too scared to pop the question."

November 10, 1960 (date estimated)

RECORD: "Ah-1, Ah-2, Ah-Sunset Strip": Performed by Spike Jones, written by Carl E. Brandt, Eddie Brandt, Les Ecklund

In 1960, Spike Jones took aim at the trend of music-driven private eye TV shows, especially *77 Sunset Strip*, with this jazz-punctuated recording. The swinging private eye on this record is looking for a new soundtrack that no one will want to steal and heads out to see Lawrence Staccato, who sounds a lot like Lawrence Welk. While listening to the square champagne music, a tenor turns up dead—the eighth one this week.

November 14, 1960

SKETCH: The show has been turned over to Moldy Hay, who will recite a poem. He wants to do something about what people are thinking about . . . like the Electoral College . . . or Cuba. He has trouble rhyming, even when Kermit and Harry are offering rhymes. He falls asleep and awakens with a poem: "Mary had a little lamb, a little ice cream, strawberry jam . . . / a little peanut brittle dipped in mustard, cotton candy dipped in custard, / chocolate-covered radishes, plum and apple pie, / candy-coated sandwiches, licorice on rye. / All this Mary ate one morning, / and feeling poorly she gave this warning: / I'd feel much better if I used my head / and had some delicious Esskay sausage instead." He adds: "How's that for a lead in to the commercial?"

November 15, 1960

SKETCH: Moldy Hay wonders why Kermit told him to get his clock fixed. Even though it's missing its hands, Moldy doesn't think there's anything wrong with it until he listens carefully to its *tick-tick-tick-tick* sound. "The trouble is obvious . . . it's missing one of its ticks. Let's see . . . it couldn't have gone far. . . ." While Moldy considers the problem, Harry enters, complaining about a mosquito bite. Moldy thinks Harry's bite is connected to his clock problem. "Ticks bite people, don't they? Maybe that's what bit Harry." Kermit finds the whole thing ridiculous. "Don't be silly—clocks don't have real ticks in them." But the missing tick shows up and is chased back into the clock by Kermit and Moldy. Moldy is satisfied with the way the clock sounds now, but Kermit points out that "even if the clock *is* ticking right, you still can't tell time with it. It doesn't have any hands." "Oh, that doesn't bother me," Moldy says. "I don't need to know the time exactly." Kermit tries to convince Moldy that his handless clock is useless, but Moldy seems to be able to tell time without the hands. If he leans his head in close enough, he can hear the tick telling him the time.

November 23, 1960

SKETCH: "Plymouth Rock": In celebration of Thanksgiving, *Sam and Friends* presents a reenactment of the Pilgrims' arrival with Harry as Miles Standoffish and Kermit as Captain John Smith. They meet a Native American who wants to sell them Manhattan Island for twenty-two bucks. "Why do you want to sell Manhattan, Chief?" Kermit (as Captain Smith) asks. "You been there? . . . Big, ugly buildings all over. Traffic jams. Taxi try to run you over. People all time run this way, that way. Never get anywhere." Miles Standoffish holds off on the deal. He can't conduct business. According to the calendar, it's a holiday—Thanksgiving.

November 28, 1960

SKETCH: "Tex": Kermit plays a vengeful cowboy who's been riding for three straight days without stopping—because he doesn't know how to get down. "Revenge is his motive, violence is his method, Tex is his name," intones the narrator. "Actually, I'm from Louisiana, but I didn't want to be called Louise," Kermit, as Tex, says. Meanwhile, back at the ranch, Harry is a villain threatening to foreclose on Violet Rose (Bernice)'s ranch if she won't marry him. "What would my husband say?" Her calls for help are heard by Tex, who happens to be that husband. Tex rides to the rescue and right through the front door, and then, when he doesn't duck below the kitchen doorway, he finally finds a way off his horse—and into unconsciousness. "You can't outsmart an hombre like that who uses his head," Harry, the villain, says. "I guess when he comes to, I'd better not be around, 'cause us bad guys always get shot at the end of these stories." Tex comes to and offers Harry a job on the ranch if he'll turn good. "Hot dog!" Harry says. "And I'll give you a date with my sister," Violet Rose says. "Hot dog!" Harry says. "And speaking of hot dogs," Violet Rose says, "I think it's time we did a commercial for some...." Harry chimes in with the last word(s): "Hot dogs!"

November 29, 1960

RECORD: "The Thing": Performed by Alice Pearce, written by Charles Grean (see pages 353–354)

TAG: It seems that Professor Madcliffe has purchased the title object from the little girl who sang about it in the previous song. Without knowing what it is or what it does, Madcliffe, in turn, sells it to Harry. "I wonder what's in here," Harry says before being pulled inside of the mysterious thing. "It's dark in here ... hey, let go of me ... help! Help!"

December 7, 1960

SKETCH: "Bird Watching": Professor Madcliffe, Kermit, and Harry are on a bird-watching expedition. Bird puns fly fast and furiously until a large bird mistakes Harry for a worm and Kermit for a frog and carries them off. Madcliffe decides to quit bird-watching and take up skin-diving instead. (Apparently, the bird knew something about Kermit's lineage that Kermit didn't yet.)

December 8, 1960

INTRO: The story picks up from the previous episode with Kermit and Harry in the gooney bird's nest, where the bird had brought them for dinner. "Boy, that was a good meal, gooney bird," Kermit says. "You know, yesterday, when you yanked us down there for dinner, I thought you were gonna eat *us*!" "Me, too, thanks for that delicious meal," Harry says, adding under his breath, "Sunflower seeds and breadcrumbs, uhh." Kermit is amused that the gooney bird has his own pet crow. "He's got a crow!"

RECORD: "I've Gotta Crow": Performed by *Peter Pan* Original Broadway Cast (featuring Mary Martin and Kathy Nolan), written by Mark Charlap, Carolyn Leigh

From the musical *Peter Pan* (1954), this song is sung by Peter (Mary Martin) after his shadow is reattached.

SEGUE: Kermit suggests that when a gooney bird has something to say, you should listen.

RECORD: "Listen to the Gooney Bird": Performed by Homer and Jethro, written by Jethro Burns, Homer Haynes (see page 270)

December 9, 1960

RECORD: "Miss Cone": Performed by Ken Nordine and The Fred Katz Group, written by Ken Nordine, Fred Katz

The Muppets get a night off (until the commercial, of course) as *Sam and Friends* presents Jim Henson's animated adaptation of Ken Nordine's "Miss Cone." (See pages 146–148 for a full summary.)

December 12, 1960

RECORD: A Christmas medley featuring "I've Got My Love to Keep Me Warm," written by Irving Berlin; "Let it Snow! Let it Snow! Let it Snow!" written by Sammy Cahn, Jule Styne; "Winter Wonderland," written by Felix Bernard, Dick Smith; "June in January," written by Leo Robin, Ralph Rainger; performed by Dean Martin with orchestra conducted by Gus Levene and Jo Stafford with Paul Weston and His Music from Hollywood, The Norman Luboff Choir, and The Starlighters

The audio for this broadcast began as a Henson-assembled medley of several holiday songs stitched together from Dean Martin's 1959 album *A Winter Romance*. But when Jim noticed that Jo Stafford's 1956 album *Ski Trails* with Paul Weston and The Norman Luboff Choir contained many of the same songs that were on Martin's album, he replaced Martin's choruses in the songs with Stafford's performances, creating a unique mash-up.

December 13, 1960

RECORD/INTRO: "Cocktails for Two": Performed by Spike Jones and His City Slickers with vocalist Carl Grayson, written by Arthur Johnston, Sam Coslow

Filled with sound effects and human-created noises, Spike Jones's treatment of this standard was his biggest hit, reaching No. 4 on the charts. Harry abruptly stops the Spike Jones silliness to present some serious, beautiful music.

RECORD: "As Time Goes By": Performed by The Buffalo Bills, written by Herman Hupfeld

The Buffalo Bills sing their tight four-part harmony version of "As Time Goes By," but the track is repeatedly interrupted by the glottal vocal sounds from the prior Spike Jones record.

TAG: Upset and ashamed, Harry says goodbye, punctuated by more Spike Jones noises.

December 14, 1960

RECORD: "Say 'Skada Wada Do'": Performed by Lou Carter, orchestra under the direction of Frank De Vol, written by Lou Carter

Former Jimmy Dorsey Band piano player and arranger Lou Carter released the album *How Deep Is Which Ocean* in 1960. His "Say 'Skada Wada Do'" is a novelty song that suggests a handy musical phrase to use when you don't have an answer to a question.

December 15, 1960

RECORD: "The Last Time I Saw Paris": Performed by Jonathan and Darlene Edwards (Paul Weston and Jo Stafford), written by Oscar Hammerstein II, Jerome Kern

This song was performed in the 1941 film *Lady Be Good* and won the Oscar for best original song. The recording used here is by the purposely mediocre team of Jonathan and Darlene Edwards.

December 16, 1960

SKETCH: "Omar's Puppet": Omar has been Christmas shopping and has purchased a present for his nephew. "It's a little doll-type thing. You put it on your hand, see? And it's called a puppet, you know, like they have on television." Omar wonders if perhaps he can be a puppeteer. He takes the bird puppet out of the package and gives it a try. He names the puppet Billy and makes him repeat Omar's statements: "Omar is wonderful," Omar says. "Omar is wonderful," Billy repeats. "And I am his slave," Omar says. "And I am his slave," Billy repeats. "For I am just a stupid puppet," Omar says. "You sure are!" Billy says. Omar puts Billy back in his box, vowing that he will never be a puppeteer.

December 19, 1960

SONG: "Jingle Bells": Performed by the *Sam and Friends* cast, Traditional

Kermit, Harry, and Moldy Hay perform this holiday classic to the accompaniment of a kazoo, toy piano, and variety of bells, whistles, and horns.

December 26, 1960

SKETCH: "The Poet's Corner": Omar welcomes the audience to a special Christmas edition of "The Poet's Corner." Harry begins with: "The bottle of perfume that Willy sent, / was highly displeasing to Millicent. / Her thanks were so cold, / they quarreled I'm told, / through that silly scent Willy sent Millicent." When Bernice corners Harry under the mistletoe, Harry quickly takes it down since it's after Christmas. Bernice counters with, "'Tis done beneath the mistletoe, / 'tis done beneath the rose. / But the proper place to kiss, you know, / is just beneath the nose." The episode concludes with a poem sent in by viewer Stuart Cowles of Towson, Maryland. A variation of "A Visit from St. Nicholas," Cowles's version features Robin Hood Santa robbing a house of its presents. "With a wink of his eye, he said, 'Man don't be greedy, / I'm heisting this stuff to give to the needy.'"

December 28, 1960

SKETCH: "Honk-Wattle-Piddle-Poo": Kermit tries to strum his banjo, but his song is interrupted when he learns that he's not allowed to play the instrument because he's not in the musicians' union. He instead forms a combo of music makers from the cast, giving Harry and Yorick nonsense phrases to repeat like "Honk-wattle-piddle-poo." While Jim had always provided multiple voices for *Sam and Friends*, in this episode, three of his characters were heard at the same time through the magic of audiotape. Harry sings the background beat, Yorick bum-bums the bass line, and Kermit sings an improvised melody with his nonsense words which somehow evolves into "The Stars and Stripes Forever." Kermit eventually segues to actual words with "Mary Had a Little Lamb" before the trio speeds up for their grand "Piddle-paddle-ponk" finale. Jim's script indicated the sections where Kermit would sing along to pre-recorded excerpts of his other characters.

January 6, 1961

SKETCH: "Huntley and Brinkley": Using snippets of real audio from Huntley and Brinkley, Kermit conducts an interview with the distinguished newsmen. (See page 143 for a full summary.)

January 13, 1961

INTRO: After some audio problems during the opening title (which Harry blames on Friday the 13th), Kermit dons his wig for a musical performance. Harry offers to fill in if the technical issues continue during the song.

RECORD: "How Deep Is the Ocean?": Performed by Miss Toni Fisher, written by Irving Berlin

No recording exists to accompany the script, but nightclub singer Toni Fisher's recording of this Irving Berlin standard seems to fit the routine, which calls for the song to be interrupted or stopped throughout, with Harry jumping in with his comic variations on lines when the record stops.

OUTRO: Harry wraps up, remarking that the performance wasn't bad "considering today's Friday the 13th and all."

January 24, 1961

SKETCH: "Open Ing": This is a parody of David Susskind's *Open End*, a sophisticated talk show of the era, notable because it initially did not have a set time limit for its nightly broadcast—it originated from New York City at 11 p.m. and stayed on the air until the host and guests ran out of things to say. Jim provides the voice for host David Suspenders as well as the other panelists: society leader Miss Elsa Marie Vincent Claire Van Go-Go; Austrian authority on medieval and modern chivalry Count Kermit Krabbleburgerholtzer (or was that Burgerholtzerkrabble? Even Kermit becomes confused about his name); and Professor Thaddeus Euphatic, author of *How to Be Polite*. The subject is etiquette, but the conversation quickly descends into arguments and disarray, with everyone speaking at once. Jim's audio track for this segment is very reminiscent of a Stan Freberg record. Significant production time was spent to allow all of Jim's characters to talk over one another.

January 30, 1961

INTRO: Swami Harry reads Bernice's tea leaves and sees a motorized musical fruit stand in her future. Bernice finds this prediction absurd, but after leaving the swami, she indeed encounters a motorized musical fruit stand and asks the proprietors, "Tell me sirs, do you have any bananas?"

RECORD: "Yes! We Have No Bananas": Performed by The Alley Singers (Phil Stern and Al Brennan, a.k.a. Freddy Morgan and Mousie Garner), written by Frank Silver, Irving Cohn

"Yes! We Have No Bananas" was first published in 1923 and has been recorded many times over the years. The recording used here is from the album *The Alley Singers: Side by Side* (1958), credited to two singers named Phil Stern and Al Brennan. But Phil and Al are actually Freddy Morgan and Mousie Garner from Spike Jones's band. In April of 1961, the Muppets would perform this recording as a remote cut-in to NBC's *Today* (but without the introductory Swami Harry segment). The tune was used twice on *The Muppet Show,* once in English and once in whatever language The Swedish Chef speaks.

February 9, 1961

INTRO: Harry mentions some of the popular musical genres of the modern world—rock 'n' roll and rhythm and blues—"but none of this stuff," he says, "compares to the great music of the past. Tonight, we have a hunk of this great past music, along with two great past musicians, and I think they just passed out. No, no, they didn't. Here they are now, and here they are to sing . . ."

RECORD: "Side by Side": Performed by The Alley Singers (Phil Stern and Al Brennan, a.k.a. Freddy Morgan and Mousie Garner), written by Harry Woods

This 1927 song would later be performed by Rowlf and Jimmy Dean on *The Jimmy Dean Show* and used on *The Muppet Show* as a duet between Fozzie Bear and guest Bruce Forsyth.

COMMERCIAL: Kermit introduces a great explorer, Sir Harry Pillory, "the man who has made more important discoveries than any other Englishman. Right, Sir Pillory?" He replies, "I wouldn't know. I'm from New Zealand." Kermit presses on, asking Pillory about his greatest discovery. Professor Madcliffe, as Sir Pillory, recounts an adventurous story of being driven deeper and deeper, not into the jungle, but into the food market. "They forced me forward, towards the meat counter. It was there that I found them—those incredible all-meat Esskay Franks." Sir Pillory continues to expound on the taste and quality of Esskay Franks. "Your greatest discovery, then?" Kermit asks. "Undoubtedly! With Esskay Franks you can taste the difference quality makes."

TAG: Harry plugs the next day's parody of *The Untouchables*.

February 10, 1961

SKETCH: "The Unmentionables": A parody of *The Untouchables*, a TV drama about federal agent Eliot Ness's fight against crime in 1930s Chicago, this is another full Freberg-like production with Jim providing the character voices and borrowing the real show's theme song. In the Muppet version, the chief of the squad is Eliot Mess. Every time Mess gets close to finding the bad guy, Bootleg Bernie Chemeeny, a blast of machine-gun fire silences the informer. Unlike Robert Stack's actual show, *The Unmentionables'* Eliot Mess does not come out on top. "You know the good guys can't always win," Bootleg Bernie (Harry) says after he blasts Mess.

February 13, 1961

RECORD: "The Reluctant Cannibal": Performed by Flanders and Swann, written by Michael Flanders, Donald Swann

This song, from the 1957 album *At the Drop of a Hat*, is about a cannibal who simply won't eat people and is berated by his fellow cannibals.

February 14, 1961

INTRO: Moldy mentions Valentine's Day and coaches Cupid, who keeps missing his target.

RECORD: "Love Poems: Togetherness": Performed by Andy Griffith and Billy May's Chamber Group, written by Andy Griffith, Billy May, poetry by the Beautiful Barbara Edwards (see page 345)

February 15, 1961 (date estimated)

RECORD: "Are You Lonesome Tonight?": Performed by Homer and Jethro, written by Lou Handman, Roy Turk

This tune dates to 1926, but it became a big hit in 1960 with Elvis Presley's recording. Homer and Jethro's version is not quite as sentimental and romantic: "You took me for a boat ride. I had to swim back. / Darlin,' I thought I'd never get out of that sack."

February 20, 1961

INTRO: Kermit is waiting on the corner for the Washington's Birthday parade. A small parade of two people goes by—they're saving the big one for Wednesday. (At the time, Washington's Birthday was still celebrated on February 22, his actual birthday.)

RECORD: "Hey, Look Me Over!": Performed by Mel Tormé and Margaret Whiting, written by Cy Coleman, Carolyn Leigh

From the 1960 Broadway musical *Wildcat*, the song was originally sung onstage by Lucille Ball. The version used here is a pop cover by Mel Tormé and Margaret Whiting. The Muppets would later perform the song on a 1973 ecology-themed TV special, *Keep U.S. Beautiful*.

February 21, 1961

COLD OPEN: "There's something fishy about the following show," an announcer says.

TITLE CARD/ANNOUNCE: A slight change is made to the regular opening: "*Salmon Friends* . . . is brought to you by . . . Esskay."

SKETCH: "Salmon Friends": As the announcer warned, there is indeed something fishy about this episode—piscatorial puns fly furiously as Professor Madcliffe takes Kermit and Harry on a field trip to a wharf to learn about fishing. "What's the porpoise of that?" Harry asks. "I'll ignore that," Madcliffe says. When the Professor asks if his students know about fish, Kermit offers a reply. "Yeah, every night I tuna in my favorite TV show, *Salmon Friends*—you know Salmon."

Only a script fragment survives for this episode, so we don't know for certain that it was intended to lead in to a record, but Frankie Laine's "Let's Go Fishin'" appeared on Jim's song lists and would have fit with the material.

February 22, 1961

RECORD: "Leetla Giorgio Washeenton (Little George Washington)": Performed by Alexander Scourby, written by Thomas Augustine Daly

Thomas Augustine Daly was a humorist and poet known for the incorporation of ethnic accents into his work. This piece is an Italian-flavored recitation about the young life of the father of our country (cherry tree and all). The track comes from a 1957 spoken-word humor album, *The Fun Makers*. Narrator Alexander Scourby was a film and stage actor who pioneered the field of audio books (originally created for the vision impaired), most notably as the first person to narrate the Bible, which he first recorded in 1953.

February 24, 1961 (date estimated)

INTRO: Bernice tells Kermit that since a lot of people watching don't have color TV sets (and because the show is in black and white in Baltimore), a lot of viewers don't know what color Kermit is. He explains that he is kind of a blue-green. He used to be just green, but now he's bluer than he used to be—emotionally speaking, that is. Bernice is off to meet her boyfriend but first asks what Theodore is doing behind them. "He's waiting for his song cue." "A song cue?" Bernice asks. "Song cue very much," says Kermit, leading into the song.

RECORD: "If You Felt Like I Did When We Said Goodbye": Performed by The Alley Singers (Phil Stern and Al Brennan, a.k.a. Freddy Morgan and Mousie Garner), written by Freddy Morgan

This is an original song written by one member of the duo. In it, Phil (Freddy Morgan) and Al (Mousie Garner) harmonize as a small combo plays accompaniment: "I'll always remember when I held your hand and you whispered, dear, I love you. / If you felt like I did when we said goodbye, then you'd know why I'm so blue."

March 2, 1961

SKETCH: "Mushmellon and Friends (Mushmellon Day)": Mushmellon is honored with National Mushmellon Day, receiving testimonials from the other characters (see pages 50–51).

March 6, 1961 (date estimated)

INTRO: Kermit mentions the beautiful spring day and the following song.

RECORD: "I Love Paris": Performed by Jonathan and Darlene Edwards (Paul Weston and Jo Stafford), written by Cole Porter

The fictional team of Jonathan and Darlene Edwards sing another Paris song; this oft-recorded Cole Porter standard was introduced in the 1953 Broadway musical *Can-Can*.

March 7, 1961

SKETCH: Kermit and Harry demonstrate how love songs are written, using cut-ins from The Buffalo Bills' barbershop recording of the 1916 song "If You Were the Only Girl in the World," written by Clifford Grey and Nat D. Ayer. Kermit theorizes that songwriters merely listen to a conversation between a boy and a girl in love and put it to music. Harry agrees to play the girl in the demonstration, and Kermit plays the boy, starting the dialogue with: "As I was saying, I wish you'd stop pestering me for a date—why, I wouldn't go out with you if you were the only girl in the world," says Kermit, then cueing the music to continue with ". . . if you were the only girl in the world . . ." This continues as Harry and Kermit take turns leading into lines from the song but straying from the sentimental and romantic tone. When The Buffalo Bills sing, "I would say such wonderful things to you . . .," Harry finishes the phrase ". . . like shut up or drop dead." Kermit finally concedes that this may not be how songwriters actually come up with songs.

March 8, 1961

SKETCH: "National Yorick Day": Kermit dedicates the show to Yorick and introduces the festivities of National Yorick Day. Special guests include his eighty-one-year-old mother, his sixteen-year-old sister, his father, twin cousins Horace and Morrace, his Uncle Borick (inventor of boric acid), and his Aunt Alice. Alice was a Shakespearean actress whose husband was, coincidentally, also named Yorick. Alice left her husband to join a traveling company of *Hamlet*. One night, onstage, one of the actors who happened to be a friend of her husband, said, "Alice, poor Yorick, I knew him well." Alice replied, "You didn't know him as well as I did or you'd have left him, too." The whole family bears a striking (almost identical) resemblance to Yorick—except for Big Yorick, who looks like the others but is huge. Although this differs from information shared in other episodes, we learn that Yorick was born in Yorick (York), Pennsylvania, and grew up in New Yorick (York) City. He attended P.S. 149 (which happens to be a school Danny Kaye popularized in a song played on *Sam and Friends*). Kermit introduces Yorick's former school principal, Thaddeus P. Madcliffe, who remembers the guest of honor for his voracious appetite. "He started off in the first grade by chewing the end off his pencil. By the second grade, he was eating the whole pencil, also any art gum erasers he could get. Third grade, he started on fountain pens, then he would drink the ink out of the ink bottle and then eat the bottle." We learn that Yorick is a book lover and has devoured such classics as *The Adventures of Tom Sawyer* and *Treasure Island*. Encyclopedia Britannica, *War and Peace,* and Webster's Unabridged Dictionary were harder for Yorick to digest, but he ate those, too, as well as a typewriter. And on his Graduation Day, Yorick ate the school. He still received his diploma, which (along with everyone else's) was locked in the office safe that he devoured with everything else on school property.

March 15, 1961

SKETCH: "Drums Bit": After a fast percussion opening announce (in place of the regular show open), Kermit explains to Harry that he's practicing his drumming. "I've been taking drumming lessons . . . from the very best, from Sammy Skin, NBC staff drummer. I'm learning to sing and accompany myself on the extra drum." "The what?" Harry asks. "The spare drum," Kermit says. "That's *snare* drum," Harry explains. Kermit demonstrates his drumming while singing a parody medley of Broadway show tunes. Harry is not impressed. "That sounds terrible. Do you know you'll never be a drummer drumming like that?" Kermit replies, "I don't think so. Hum a little bit of the melody." Harry takes over and says he took lessons from Chico Hamilton. He instructs Kermit that you have to visualize the beat. "Now, as I drum, watch and see if you can't practically see the beat." As Harry plays (with the help of Chico Hamilton), the beat is indeed seen—via Jim Henson's cut-out animation.

RECORD: "Drums West": Performed by The Chico Hamilton Quintet, written by Chico Hamilton.

Set to Chico Hamilton's 1959 record, the visual for this segment is a short film Jim Henson created by painstakingly moving tiny pieces of paper under his animation stand. The entire sequence, including

Kermit and Harry's introduction, was reprised on the *Today* show on April 10, 1961. Chico Hamilton later directly collaborated with Jim, creating music for other animated projects.

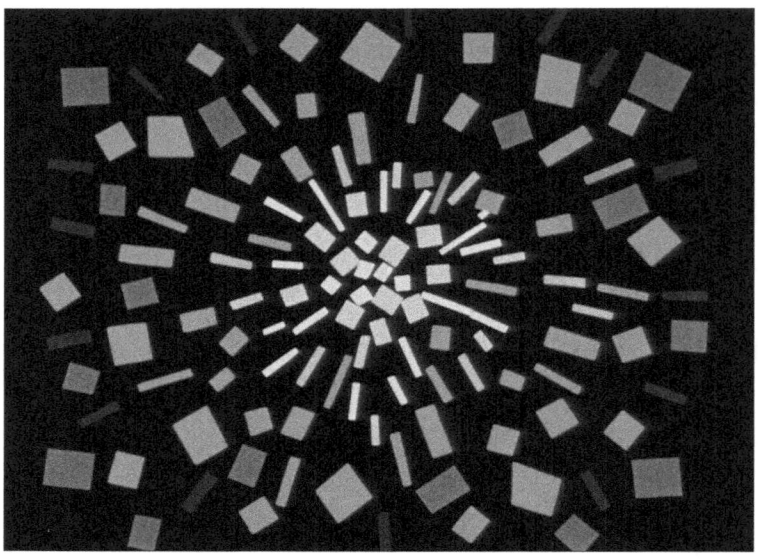

A frame of paper cut-out animation from "Drums West."

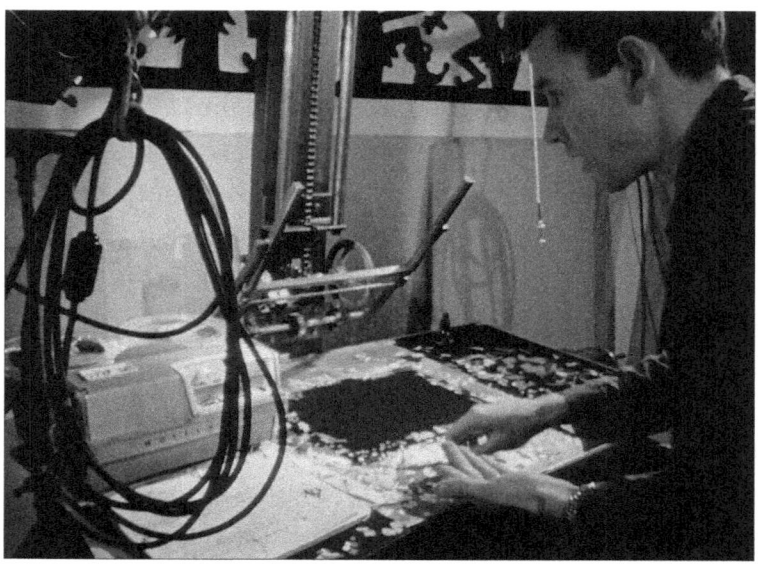

Jim at work on "Drums West"—a frame from the live-action tag seen at the end of the film.

March 17, 1961

SKETCH: "St. Patrick's Day": Kermit introduces Harry to play something special for St. Patrick's Day. Harry then launches into the record, and he can also be heard scatting and singing along as the music plays.

RECORD: "The Trouble with Harry": Performed by Alfi and Harry (David Seville), written by Floyd Huddleston, Herbert Eiseman, Mark McIntyre (see page 268)

March 20, 1961 (date estimated)

RECORD: "Mobile": Performed by The Confederates barbershop quartet, written by Robert Wells, David Holt

The Buffalo Bills were the most frequently used barbershop quartet on *Sam and Friends,* but this jaunty tribute to the city of Mobile, Alabama, is by a lesser-known quartet called The Confederates. Jim probably found the track because it was on an album called *Barbershop Battle,* which pitted the Southern music of The Confederates against the Northern songs of The Buffalo Bills.

March 22, 1961 (date estimated)

INTRO: Kermit stares at a triangle, trying to figure out his geometry homework. "Plane geometry?" Icky Gunk asks. "There's nothing plain about this geometry," Kermit says.

RECORD: "A Dollar Down": Performed by The Limeliters, written by Cisco Houston

The folk trio The Limeliters sings about a friend who bought an automobile (and lots of other things) for a dollar down and a dollar a week. Everything goes well . . . until it doesn't.

March 29, 1961

SKETCH: "The Poet's Corner": Kermit introduces "The Poet's Corner" and cues Harry to start playing the organ. Since Kermit wants the music to come in and out, Harry has mounted the organ on wheels so he can pedal it in and out. He demonstrates how he can pedal it all around the studio, but Harry crashes into the control room and a TV camera. When "The Poet's Corner" finally begins, Kermit starts with a poem about the stork. "The stork is a bird with a great big bill. / He brings us the babies whenever he will. / Then comes the doctor and when he's through, / you'll find that he has a big bill, too." After Kermit recites his non-rhyming St. Bees limerick (see page 386), Harry refuses to play music. "You didn't do a poem. That didn't rhyme." Kermit explains that it was blank verse and insists Harry play his music. Harry slaps the organ, making some banging noises and dull thuds. "That was blank music to go with your blank verse." Harry offers to close the show by reciting a poem and playing music at the same time. As he pedals and plays, he says, "Don't worry if your job is small and your rewards are few, / remember that the mighty oak was once a nut like you." As he finishes, Harry crashes into the camera, knocking it out of commission. "It's time to do the commercial, anyhow."

March 31, 1961

SKETCH: "Easter Bunny Bit": While exploring the woods, Kermit spots the one and only Easter Bunny—although the bunny was under the impression that he was the Wester Bunny. "I have no sense of direction at all, that's why I'm lost." The bunny has no idea where he is, but with Kermit's help, he gets back on track toward his destination: Baltimore. "That's where I'm supposed to deliver my Wester eggs." Kermit corrects him: "*Easter* eggs." Kermit concludes with a "Happy Easter" greeting to the audience.

April 1, 1961 (date estimated)

RECORD: "I Love Your Pizza": Performed by Homer and Jethro, written by Cy Coben

Home and Jethro get off to a rough beginning, but after a laughing false start, they sing their Italian food-flavored take on the tune "Oh Shenandoah." "Oh Mama Mia, I love your pizza . . . sprinkled on . . . with lots of sausage . . . lots of mushrooms . . . and anchovies . . . across the mozzarella."

April 5, 1961 (date estimated)

RECORD: "The Bear Chase": Performed by The Limeliters, written by Doc Bagby

"The Bear Chase" begins with an announcement to campers of the day's activity—a bear chase. This leads into a very fast account of the chase with some spoken interjections from reluctant participants: "I cannot understand why all of the guests are required to go out chasing a sweaty, old bear."

April 10, 1961 (date estimated)

RECORD: "Goodness Gracious Me": Performed by Peter Sellers and Sophia Loren, written by David Lee, Herbert Kretzmer

Peter Sellers and Sophia Loren co-starred in the 1960 film *The Millionairess,* in which Loren's socialite character sets her sights on an Indian physician played by Sellers. Although the movie was not a musical, this song was recorded by the duo, essentially in character, to promote the film. The song's co-writer Herbert Kretzmer would go on to write the lyrics for the musical *Les Misérables.*

April 12, 1961

RECORD: "Ma Says, Pa Says": Performed by Marais and Miranda, written by Josef Marais

This record is from Marais and Miranda's album *South African Folk Songs.* It's a song about a couple who are about to go dancing but are reminded by the girl's parents that they must keep on dancing always. The couple knows why: "For if we keep on dancing, we won't start romancing." Subsequent verses remind the couple to keep doing other things.

April 14, 1961

SKETCH: Omar recites an excerpt from "The Walrus and the Carpenter" from Lewis Carroll's *Through the Looking-Glass,* but before doing so, he informs the audience that he "is skipping a couple of verses because we don't have time to do the whole thing."

April 17, 1961

INTRO: Kermit presents a musical farm-and-country news report.

RECORD: "Lazy Jim Day's News": Performed by Lazy Jim Day, written by James Day

Jim Day, a hillbilly comedian, was a well-known radio personality on the Grand Ole Opry and other rural radio outlets until his death in 1959. One of his regular routines was a homespun presentation of news events set to music.

April 18, 1961 (date estimated)

RECORD: "Glow Worm" (guitar instrumental): Performed by Chet Atkins, written by Johnny Mercer, Paul Lincke (see page 153 for a full summary)

April 19, 1961 (date estimated)

INTRO: Harry asks Kermit if they can start yet. Kermit tells him they can't because the song is too short. "We have to kill this time to make the show the right length." After waiting a few moments, Kermit announces, "Now we can start."

RECORD: "Frogg": Performed by The Brothers Four, Traditional, new words and new music arranged by Bob Flick, Dick Foley, Mike Kirkland, John Paine

This record takes the centuries-old folk song "Frog Went a-Courtin'" and updates it, sending the title courting frog to the midnight show at the Coconut Grove, where he meets hat check girl Molly Mouse. The origin of this folk song dates all the way to the mid-1500s. Considering the central character, it's only logical that the Muppets would use it in the post-*Sam and Friends* era after Kermit officially evolved into being a frog. Kermit performed it in *The Muppets Valentine Show* in 1974, and Roy Rogers sang a brief snippet on *The Muppet Show*.

April 20, 1961 (date estimated)

RECORD: "Who's on First?": Performed by Abbott and Costello, dialogue created by Bud Abbott and Lou Costello, with contributing dialogue by John Grant

Bud Abbott and Lou Costello popularized and polished this routine in burlesque, then in radio, film, and television. In it, Abbott tries to brief Costello on the lineup of his baseball team and their unlikely nicknames.

April 24, 1961

INTRO: Harry mentions that they just returned from New York, where they did a bit on the *Today* show that morning. "They were very nice to us up there," Kermit says. "We were wonderful," Harry adds. Kermit cautions Harry not to brag, then introduces the day's song—an old English ballad with new words.

RECORD: "Variation on an Old English Theme": Performed by The Brothers Four, written by Harvey Geller, based on traditional theme

The S&H Green Stamps company was at the height of its popularity in the 1960s. To engender customer loyalty, retailers would give Green Stamps to their customers with their purchases. The customers would, in turn, redeem their stamps for catalog merchandise. Harvey Geller created a ballad about the Green Stamps phenomenon using the old English theme "Greensleeves."

OUTRO: After the song, Harry asks about the original words of the tune. The answer comes from another record; Pete Seeger of The Weavers explains that there are about forty verses to "Greensleeves" and each one is "dumber than the last."

April 25, 1961

SKETCH: Kermit and Harry discuss Elvis Presley. Kermit finds it interesting that "a guy like that—you know, a truck driver—could start singing, playing the guitar, and make millions of dollars." He calls Elvis a "phenonemum." "A what?" Harry asks. Kermit tries again. "Phemomenum." Harry corrects him. "You mean a phonemonin." "Phinuminum." Kermit and Harry struggle with the word, trying "phenoleum," "phenimonee," and "filodendrum" before deciding on the much simpler word: oddity. But as special as Elvis is, Harry insists that "just about anybody could sing as well as he can—with a guitar and an echo chamber. Why, even Sam would sound just as good, I betcha." Although only this section of script survives and there is no recording, it's a safe bet that this bit was paired with Stan Freberg's "Heartbreak Hotel," a comic cover of the No. 1 Elvis hit in which Freberg's lead vocalist asks for more and more echo throughout his performance.

April 1961 (exact date unknown)

SKETCH: "Visual Thinking": Kermit takes a course in visual thinking and demonstrates to Harry how he can make his thoughts appear above him. (See pages 148–149 for a full summary.)

Spring 1961 (exact date unknown)

INTRO: Moldy Hay professes his love for Bernice. To woo her, he asks a soothsayer for the formula for love.

RECORD: "Formula for Love": Performed by Nina & Frederik with Louis Armstrong, written by Kjeld Bonfils, Frederik van Pallandt, Nina van Pallandt

The husband and wife singing duo Nina & Frederik were popular in the 1950s and 1960s and recorded this performance with Louis Armstrong as the title song for their 1959 feature film. "Formula for Love" offers a straightforward recipe: "If you want the chick that you dig, / you've got to prove that you can love big. / And then she'll need a gentle shove / that's the formula for love."

Spring 1961 (exact date unknown)

RECORD: "Who Takes Care of the Caretaker's Daughter" (from *Lady, Be Good!*): Performed by Bobby Darin and Johnny Mercer, written by Chick Endor

In this song from the 1924 Broadway musical *Lady, Be Good!*, a clever person ponders the very difficult title question and a series of others.

Spring 1961 (exact date unknown)

RECORD: "Bullwinkle's Corner (Tom, Tom the Piper's Son and Peter Piper)": Performed by Bill Scott, Paul Frees, Walter Tetley, written by Paul Parnes, music arranged and conducted by Dennis Farnum

In this track from the 1961 album *Rocky & His Friends,* Bullwinkle tries to recite poems while being interrupted. Jay Ward's groundbreaking animated series of the same name premiered on November 19, 1959. This *Sam and Friends* episode may have been the first time Bullwinkle spoke through a puppet, but it wasn't the last. In September of 1961, when the show moved from ABC to NBC and was renamed *The Bullwinkle Show,* a puppet of Bullwinkle was used to introduce the cartoons.

May 4, 1961

SKETCH: Kermit and Harry are guests at a party. "The food is so good," Kermit says. "Yeah," Harry says. "Mouthwatering. Delicious. That's cause they're serving Esskay meats." Kermit reminds Harry that the commercial doesn't come until later in the show. While Kermit and Harry are enjoying the party, they don't know who is throwing it. "How did you happen to come to this, Harry?" "You invited me. Who invited you?" "I thought you did," Kermit says. "Speaking of party crashers," Harry says. "Do you hear someone knocking on the door?" Kermit tells Harry not to let him in. "Probably a party crasher." There is no recording of this episode, so we don't know for certain what record this script went with, but either The Charioteers' "Open the Door, Richard" or Red Ingle's "Let Me In" would fit.

TAG: This script makes no indication of which character is speaking, but viewers are informed that, "We're all gonna be watching our man in space tomorrow morning," referring to Astronaut Alan Shepard's historic Mercury space flight the next day. "Just imagine—out of this world, just like Esskay."

May 8, 1961

SKETCH: "Space Launch": Professor Madcliffe is about to launch a spaceship. "We'll be world famous," Kermit says, "just like Alan Shepard." Harry interrupts, wanting to read a poem he has written in honor of Shepard. "Hail to thee, our astronaut, / I bet you went higher than Castro thought. / And even Khrushchev opened his eyes / when we announced that we would televise. / Russia may be ahead as far as outer space, / but we have won the television coverage race." Madcliffe instructs Kermit to start the countdown before checking in with the launchpad to learn that their pilot isn't in place. Bernice is set to be the first "astronaut-ess" in outer space, but she is still making alterations to her space suit. She arrives in time . . . to see the ship launch without her.

May 17, 1961

SKETCH: "The First Annual TV Whammy Awards": *Sam and Friends* relinquishes its time slot to the presentation of the First Annual TV Whammy Awards presentation. Professor Madcliffe is introduced as the President of the Academy of Television Arts and Crafts. "We in the television medium feel the best reward for a job well done is money, but we also feel it's nice to have recognition from a group of your peers. And that's why we have selected as judges for the TV Whammy Awards George Peer, Martha Peer, and Clyde Peer." Astonishingly, Icky Gunk repeatedly wins in each category—beating out such nominees as Richard Nixon, John F. Kennedy, Jack Paar, and Ed Sullivan—but only because he also happens to be the official representative from the ballot-tabulating accounting firm of Cost and Waterhole (a nod to longtime award show tabulators, the accounting firm then known as Price Waterhouse).

May 19, 1961

SKETCH: "The Poet's Corner": The cast delivers another installment of "The Poet's Corner." First Omar delivers a poem about the yak. He regales viewers with the yak's positive traits before ending with, "Then tell your papa where the yak can be got, / and if he is awfully rich, he will buy you the creature—or else he will not, / I cannot be positive which." Moldy Hay and Harry each deliver a quick limerick before Hank and Frank finish with the same excerpt from "The Song of Milkanwatha" that was recited by Harry on August 10, 1959. The script is a brief one, but there is no recording to indicate which song was used in the episode.

May 25, 1961

SKETCH: Icky Gunk begins with, "And, uh, speaking of explosives, because after all, the Fourth of July isn't very far off . . ." Kermit interrupts. "Wait a minute, who's speaking of explosives? And the Fourth of July is over a month away." Icky insists on proceeding, telling Kermit that it is indeed very close, when you compare it to Halloween. Kermit says, "Halloween is a good day for you, Icky. Why don't you disappear until Halloween?" There is no recording to indicate if a song was paired with this script, but Icky calls for "Roger" to come out—likely a reference to Roger Boom, the title character of Lawrence Welk's song about an explosives expert. In the script, Kermit reacts with, "What are you doing with that firecracker? Don't you know you shouldn't play with fireworks? They're illegal." The bit ends with Kermit receiving a mouthful of firecracker, followed by an offscreen explosion and, most likely, Icky Gunk's lip-sync performance of "Roger Boom."

June 6, 1961

INTRO: Harry has arrived at a hotel that Kermit has recommended. "He said his niece lives here . . . and likes it very much . . . awfully cute little girl—Eloise." The frantic room clerk knows Eloise all too well and is trying to catch the mischievous child. The calls for "Eloise! Eloise!" lead into the record, which is no doubt performed by Kermeena as Eloise.

RECORD: "Eloise": Performed by Kay Thompson, orchestra conducted by Archie Bleyer, written by Kay Thompson, Robert Wells (see page 347)

June 7, 1961

INTRO: Harry makes an introduction: "Ladies and gentlemen, we take you now to the stage of a small, intimate, contemporary jazz-type club where a small, intimate, forty-five-piece jazz orchestra is warming up to accompany our contemporary jazz singer—leave us now join him as we hear him say . . ."

RECORD: "Hole in My Soul": Performed by Sascha Burland, orchestra conducted by Pat Williams, written by Sascha Burland

Released in 1961, this record is a rhythmic explanation and demonstration of soul as delivered by Sascha Burland, the musician responsible for the album *Huckleberry Hound for President*, which was used during Sam's election campaign. With Don Elliott, Burland conceived The Nutty Squirrels, jazz music's answer to Alvin and the Chipmunks.

June 8, 1961

INTRO: Harry addresses his opening remarks to music lovers: "We on the *Sam and Friends* staff like to do our best to stay up to date, modern, contemporary, and hip. . . . Today in our effort to remain hip, contemporary, modern, and up to date, we would like to introduce a new singer who strikes me as being very modern, up to date, hip, and contemporary." Harry introduces a fellow who has the newest thing in music: "The Gorilla Walk."

RECORD: "The Gorilla Walk": Performed by Sascha Burland, orchestra conducted by Pat Williams, written by Sascha Burland

Released with "Hole in My Soul," "The Gorilla Walk" is a dance record in which vocalist Sascha Burland directs listeners to return to primitive instincts: "Stick your elbows out, point your feet in, and stomp around!"

June 12, 1961

INTRO: Kermit begins with an announcement that the evening's show is not live. After Harry asks if the show is dead, Kermit explains, "Tonight, we're on videotape and therefore we're not in color in Washington, and of course we're never in color in Baltimore because the show is telecast there in black and white, but tonight we're especially black and white, even to the people with color sets in Washington or Baltimore, where we always are on in black and white that is . . . and to you people with black and white sets, we're . . . uh . . . just as black and white as usual . . . or perhaps more so." Kermit introduces the song after mentioning that they're getting ready to take a vacation after the next evening's show.

RECORD: "Goodnight Ladies": Performed by The Sportsmen Quartet, written by Edwin Pearce Christy (see page 279)

June 13, 1961

SKETCH: "Closing Credits 1961": Kermit and Harry explain that it's the last show of the season and that the Muppet crew is heading to the Puppeteers of America festival on the West Coast. Kermit thanks Esskay and the folks at their advertising agency, VanSant Dugdale. "And to all you good people in our audience, we'd like to say please continue to buy all those delicious Esskay Quality Meats products all summer." Harry reminds viewers to enter the Esskay Quality Meats contest. "And now, as is our custom," Kermit says, "we'd like to end the year by giving credit to all those people who have worked on the show and made it all possible. I imagine you'll be surprised to see how many people it takes to produce a little five-minute show like this. Let's have the credits, fellas." As the credits roll, the classic circus tune "Entrance of the Gladiators" is played.

NEW SEASON BEGINS

September 20, 1961

RECORD: "Dufo (What a Crazy Guy)": Performed by Wally Cox, written by Wally Cox (see pages 245–246)

September 21, 1961

INTRO: Professor Madcliffe greets the audience of music lovers. "Tonight's show is musical—unlike that rather sick monologue of last night about Dufo." On that, Kermit enters to lip sync Wally Cox's recurring line in the record presented the previous day: "What a crazy guy." "Anyhow, tonight, we're doing two songs of Americana," Madcliffe says and introduces Moldy Hay with the first tune. Kermit once again reacts with Wally Cox's "what a crazy guy."

RECORD: "You and I and George": Performed by Red Kelly and Stan Kenton's Band, arranged by Stan Kenton

A very brief song of an odd romance with an abrupt ending, this was a favorite piece of material of Jim Henson's. On Stan Kenton's album, *Kenton Live at the Las Vegas Tropicana*, Kenton is listed as the song's arranger, but there is no composer credited. Some experts attribute the tune to its vocalist (and Kenton band bass player) Red Kelly, but no one has officially accepted responsibility for the song's authorship. In addition to its use on *The Muppet Show*, Jim included it on Rowlf's album *Ol' Brown Ears Is Back*, and Rowlf sang it on several television guest appearances.

SEGUE: Madcliffe returns to introduce Sam with a song dedicated to fans of Elvis Presley. Kermit again chimes in with Wally Cox's "what a crazy guy."

RECORD: "You Are My Love": Performed by Dave Gardner, written by Biff Jones, Chuck Meyer

A comedic country song in which the narrator sings the praises of his true love, the tune is performed by Dave Gardner, who was professionally known as "Brother Dave Gardner," a drummer who found fame when he added comedy vocals to his act.

September 28, 1961

SKETCH: "Drill Team Soldiers": In one of the few *Sam and Friends* episodes that does not feature the regular cast, a blustery drill sergeant barks double-talk orders as soldiers try to follow. The soldiers finally get rid of their sergeant by proving that sometimes they can hit a target. This was one of the bits Jim and Jerry Juhl would perform in Hamburg, Germany, for the live USDA show (see pages 166–170).

Jim Henson and Jerry Juhl at work on the complex drill team soldiers' mechanism.

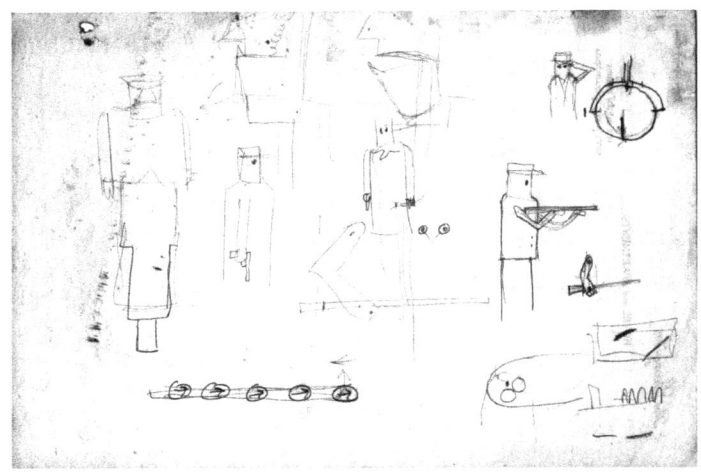

Jim's sketch for the design of the soldiers.

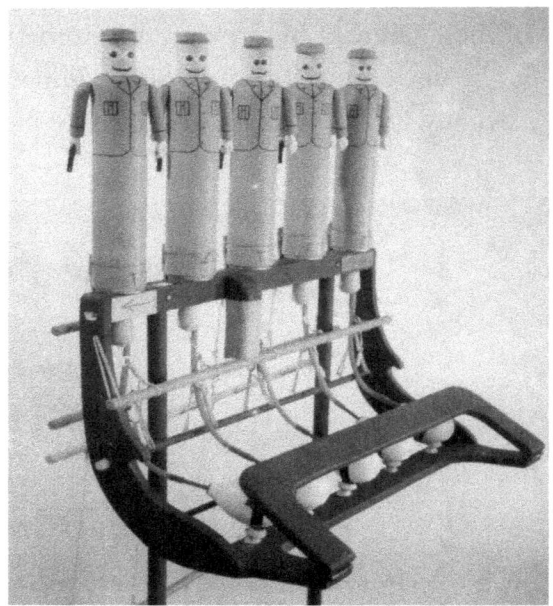

A close-up look at the drill team rig.

September 29, 1961

SKETCH: "Weather Warehouse": Harry presents "Wholesale Harry's Weather Warehouse," a new concept in weather shows on television. Unlike forecasters like WRC's Frank Forrester, who had just completed his forecast five minutes earlier, Harry isn't predicting the weather, he's selling it. (See page 150 for a full summary.)

October 4, 1961

INTRO: Chicken Liver delivers a serious introduction (written by Jerry Juhl) to an American song that has been reinterpreted by an English artist. "Since it has now undergone revision by a contemporary British artist of high repute, we feel that it now stands not only as a living historical document of our heritage, but as a mirror reflecting the current customs and mores of our society."

RECORD: "Does Your Chewing Gum Lose Its Flavor on the Bedpost Overnight?": Performed by Lonnie Donegan and His Skiffle Group, written by Billy Rose, Ernest Breuer, Marty Bloom

Originally written in 1924, the song became popular decades later as a hit by Lonnie Donegan and His Skiffle Group. Then, decades after its use on *Sam and Friends*, it was used on *The Muppet Show*.

October 6, 1961

COLD OPEN: Kermit shoots a hole in a bucket and then explains that there is a connection between this curious open and the show that will follow.

TITLE CARD/ANNOUNCE

RECORD: "There's a Hole in the Bucket": Performed by Art and Paul (Art Podell and Paul Potash), Traditional

Jim had previously used the Bob Gibson rendition of this folk classic on September 19, 1960 (see pages 463-464), but this version was recorded by folk duo Art Podell and Paul Potash for their album *Songs of Earth and Sky* (1960).

October 9, 1961 (date estimated)

COLD OPEN: The opening of "Person to Pearson": Stan Freberg's Edward N. Nonymous introduces himself and teases the upcoming interview.

TITLE CARD/ANNOUNCE

RECORD: "Person to Pearson": Performed by Stan Freberg and Daws Butler, music by George Bruns, written by Stan Freberg, Daws Butler (see page 287)

October 13, 1961

SKETCH: "Cool Jazz": Several gloved human hands dance to jazzy music—"Flying Home": Performed by Herbie Mann, Sam Most, written by Lionel Hampton, Benny Goodman—until another hand turns on a radio that plays "The Stars and Stripes Forever," written by John Philip Sousa. This leads to a heated conflict that is eventually resolved in a traditional Muppet manner—an explosion. This sketch would be later performed in Germany at the USDA show and on *The Mike Douglas Show*.

October 16, 1961 (date estimated)

COLD OPEN: An excerpt from "Sing Along": Performed by Mitch Miller and the Gang, written by Robert Allen

TITLE CARD/ANNOUNCE

SKETCH: "Sing Along": After the opening title/announce, Harry asks what the "thing" before the show was all about. Kermit explains the finer points of the sing-along and brings in his collection of sing-along records. At first, Harry is embarrassed that his vast musical knowledge has a blind spot, but when Kermit plays "The Old Grey Mare," Harry begs Kermit to stop the music. "You're trying to ruin me, man! If the wrong people knew I listened to that stuff, I'd be finished. They'd break my Charlie Parker records. They'd take away my Brubeck badge and revoke my scat license." Kermit urges him to give it a try—reminding Harry that he has some square records in his collection, too. When Kermit threatens to inform the Charlie Parker fan club, Harry gives in and they both sing along to "The Old Grey Mare," but Harry can't resist improvising and scatting and can't stick to the melody. The sing-along is interrupted by a phone call. Kermit takes the call and passes on a message from Mitch Miller, who would prefer that Harry *not* sing along. Mitch Miller, whose record was used in this installment, was a music producer and the host of a popular television program, *Sing Along with Mitch*, in which he led his "gang" in a sing-along with the home audience, who could view the lyrics superimposed on the screen. Bob McGrath—Bob of *Sesame Street*—was a member of Mitch Miller's gang from 1959 to 1964.

October 23, 1961

INTRO: "The Poet's Corner": Professor Madcliffe attempts to introduce a guest poet when he is interrupted by Kermit. "By the shores of Gitche Gumee . . ." Madcliffe tries to continue his introduction. Kermit begins another recitation. "Roses are red. / Violets are blue. / Here is Kermit with a poem for you." Madcliffe tells Kermit that "our guest poet is *not* you."

RECORD: Unknown, but this introduction could have been paired with one of several Andy Griffith comic poetry readings or other spoken-word records in the *Sam and Friends* repertoire.

Fall 1961 (exact date unknown)

SKETCH: In this bit written by Jerry Juhl, Kermit greets the armchair explorers in the audience and introduces them to Sir Icky Hickory (Icky Gunk paying homage to Mount Everest climber Sir Edmund Hillary), one of the "few men to find the lost country of Pachalafaka." Kermit interviews Sir Icky about his adventures, but when he asks the explorer to share visuals of his expedition with the audience, we learn that Sir Icky's photos were lost when his boat capsized, some of his film footage went up in a forest fire, and the rest was misplaced during a stampede, eaten by snakes, and devoured by a man-eating plant. The only surviving film captured a Pachalafakan native singing his traditional folksong.

RECORD: "Pachalafaka": Performed by Earl Brown, written by Irving Taylor (see page 299)

November 9, 1961

SKETCH: "The Robot (Machine H14)": A mechanical Muppet robot explains that machines are not understood by people and are superior to man in every way. "More accurate, more dependable, more powerful, better looking, and we have replaceable parts." His diatribe on the superiority and infallibility of the machine ends with his self-destruction. (Note: The concept of man versus machine is one that Jim would explore throughout his career—from IBM and AT&T industrial films to variety show appearances and segments on *The Muppet Show*.)

From Jim Henson's home movies: Jerry and Jim (obscured) help the Muppet robot self-destruct at the USDA Food Fair in Hamburg, Germany.

November 13, 1961

SKETCH: "Chef Omar": Omar prepares an incendiary salad. (See pages 151–152 for a full summary.)

RECORD: "Waltz of the Bubbles" (background instrumental): Performed by David Rose and His Orchestra, written by David Rose

November 17, 1961

INTRO: Theodore is standing at a fruit stand when Harry enters and asks for different fruits—none of which Theodore has. When Harry starts to leave, a sign pops up that reads TRY BANANAS. Harry then asks, "Got any bananas?"

RECORD: "Yes! We Have No Bananas": Performed by The Alley Singers (Phil Stern and Al Brennan, a.k.a. Freddy Morgan and Mousie Garner), written by Frank Silver, Irving Cohn (see page 484)

December 6, 1961

SKETCH: "The Dancing Donnellys": In a script written by Jerry Juhl, vaudeville team Mildred (voiced by Juhl) and Kermit sing, tap dance, and tell jokes to "Tea for Two." The gags range from awful to silly: "Who was that lady I saw you with last night?" Mildred asks. "That was no lady, that was you. We were looking at a mirror." They tap some more. "Mildred, did you put the cat out?" Kermit asks. "Put him out? I didn't even know he was on fire." They segue to a series of knock-knock jokes, finishing with, "Knock, knock / Who's there? / Edsel / Edsel who? / Edsel folks!" This kind of delightfully bad joke would frequently show up on *The Muppet Show* fifteen years later. Jerry once recalled a time when he noticed Jim staring intently at a *Muppet Show* script, carefully examining a particularly bad gag. He asked Jim if perhaps the joke was too bad to use in the show. "No," Jim replied. "It's an awful joke, but it's worthy of us."

December 12, 1961

SKETCH: "Scrooge Bit": In this spoken-word piece, we hear the story of Ebenezer Scrooge. But this version of Scrooge loved Christmas—because he was a toymaker. The narrator goes on to talk about Scrooge's high-tech line of toys, including his "Kiddie-Sell Hydrogen Bomb Kit" and its slogan: "Be the first one in your neighborhood to be the last one in your neighborhood." One night, Toymaker Scrooge is visited by the Ghost of Christmas Past, who shows him a child happily playing with a simple rubber ball. Scrooge immediately retools his factory to make only rubber balls instead of modern dolls, robots, and popular toys of the day. Three days later, Scrooge is bankrupt and dressed as Santa, collecting charity donations on the street corner. "There was a great difference in the old man, for now, he hated Christmas." The origin of this piece of material could not be traced, although the voice on the recording sounds like Jerry Juhl, so this could be an original script by Jerry.

December 15, 1961 (final show, see pages 206-207 for full summary)

INTRO: The characters discuss the culmination of the week's countdown to the final show.

COMMERCIAL: Harry is playing the piano as he and Kermit perform a rhythmic tribute to their sponsor. The commercial's script notes that the piece was written to be delivered to a track found on the album *Music Minus One, Volume 1*. Kermit and Harry alternate their verses:

KERMIT: Now, Pure Pork Sausages you will find
             Are made fresh daily—four different kinds:
             Dixie Made, Farm Fresh, Breakfast Links,
             And Country Style.

HARRY: Yeah yeah yeah yeah, but don't forget
            Esskay Pork 'n' Bacon Sausage—it's the best yet.

After going on to mention Esskay Franks, Skrapple, and Luncheon Meats, they wrap up with a familiar slogan: "Buy Esskay Meats, make no mistakes, and taste the difference quality makes."

SEGUE: Harry introduces Kermit to "sing" the final song.

RECORD: "I Come for to Sing": Performed by Bob Gibson, written by Bob Gibson, Chick Jung, William Wright

TAG: When Harry finds out it's the last show, he blows up the scenery and costumes.

The dates of the following episodes could not be determined:

SKETCH: "Average American Male": In this installment, summarized from a surviving script, the announcer introduces the average American male. The camera first focuses on a human hand outstretched against black. The hand points off-camera and the camera pans to Kermit. The announcer describes him: "Complexion: green; eyes: bulgy. He holds a good job and works hard at it." The hand holds up an Esskay package and Kermit pantomimes a commercial. As the announcer continues, Kermit reacts to each word in his description, and human hands count them on their fingers. "He is brave, courageous, strong, healthy, humble, kind, forgiving, loves his mother, and watches Jack Paar. This is the average American male. Only one thing can spoil his composure." A hand slaps a red heart on Kermit's chest. "And that one thing completely destroys him." Kermit tramples the hands and begins to sing. There is no recording of this episode, and the specific song is not indicated in the script. After the song, Kermit falls, and the hands enter, pick him up, and carry him off.

SKETCH: "Beat the Press": In a parody of *Meet the Press* (which originated from the same studio as *Sam and Friends*), a panel of columnists (Irma Firstleft and Kermit Secondturn) and moderator Stephen R. Moderator interview the President of the National Brotherhood of Swindlers, Hoods, and Confidence Men (otherwise known as the gangsters' union), James Forthright, and his Vice President, John Smith. A simple question about how long Forthright has served as union president garners this response: "I have nothing to hide, and if you want to know how I feel about a subject, just ask me openly, and I'll answer it openly in my own language as soon as my legal department can write it." Forthright is never quite forthright with that question but doesn't seem to mind being asked if he's an honest man. "This is a gangsters' union. We've got qualifications you have to meet . . . you can't have an honest man president of a bunch of crooks."

SKETCH: "The Curtain": Kermit is admiring a beautiful red curtain (many years before he would stand in front of one during each episode of *The Muppet Show*). He asks Sam to help work the curtain and sets up a simple cue: "How about when I say 'open' you open the curtain, and when I say 'close,' you close it, okay?" They rehearse a few times, and even when Kermit tries to catch him off guard, Sam's curtain pulling is on point. Kermit is impressed. "He's really on his toes." Sam closes the curtain in front of Kermit. "I said *toes,* I didn't say *close.*" Kermit asks Sam to reopen the curtain so he can get on with the show. Sam complies. "Now to get on with the show," Kermit says. "People often ask me if this green that I wear is my skin or my shirt. In other words, they want to know if I'm wearing clothes." Sam again closes the curtain, believing he heard the cue. This sort of thing continues until the end of the episode, with Sam opening and closing the curtain several times as Kermit tries to keep things on track.

1961 ESSKAY COMMERCIALS

While Jim Henson eventually stopped including commercials on his audio recordings of *Sam and Friends* episodes, he did save the scripts for the final batch of Esskay commercials that aired as part of the show. Summarized here are the commercials written in October of 1961 and used on the show during its final weeks on the air. Since films of a couple of these spots still exist separately from *Sam and Friends* episodes, it's possible that these commercials may have aired on their own after the end of the series, but that could not be confirmed.

* Indicates that a film of this commercial survives.

#SF-61-26 "Quality": Script dated October 16, 1961 *

Kermit is looking for a book in a public library and approaches a librarian (Harry in a wig) to ask for a nonfiction book recommendation. "We have a book entitled *103 Years in the Meat Packing Business* by Schluderberg and Kurdle . . . it's the story of the Esskay Company and its history making quality meat products." Kermit says that it's not what he had in mind. Harry then suggests a new bestseller called *Taste the Difference* and its sequel, *Quality Makes*. Kermit declines and asks the librarian to suggest a novel. "We have the new paperback edition of *Lady Chatterly's Liverwirst* [sic] . . . or *Sonnet to a Sausage* and other hickory-smoked verses by O. B. Smith." Kermit asks if the librarian has any books that aren't about meat products. "Sir," librarian Harry says, "do you know where you are?" The camera zooms wide to reveal a huge sign that reads: Esskay Public Library—Read the Difference Quality Makes.

#SF-61-27 "Pork Sausage": Script dated October 16, 1961

The setting is a cluttered automobile shop with a sign reading Harry's Auto Repairs and Body Shop. Professor Madcliffe visits the auto shop with Kermit, even though he doesn't own a car. "I come in here to buy Esskay Pure Pork Sausage," Madcliffe explains. "Wait a minute," Kermit says. "This is an automobile shop . . . they don't have Esskay Sausage." Madcliffe insists, "Sure, they do. This is a body shop, isn't it? What better way to treat your body than eating Esskay Sausage?" Kermit is confused by Madcliffe's logic, but when proprietor Harry arrives, he gladly fills the Professor's order for several varieties of Esskay Sausage. "Wait a minute . . . hold it!" Kermit says. "This is an automobile shop, isn't it?" "Yeah, man," Harry says. "Well, what are you doing selling Esskay Sausage?" Kermit asks. Harry explains that he sells Esskay Sausage because it's the most delicious sausage made. "And if you're cold and sluggish in the morning, with no get-up-and-go . . . shift to Esskay Sausage and spark your breakfast . . . clutch yourself a bunch of breakfast links for a real smooth start." Harry concludes with the sponsor's slogan, reminding viewers, "You can taste the difference quality makes." Kermit is still perplexed. "Yeah, I know . . . but an auto shop?"

#SF-61-28 "Sausage": Script dated October 16, 1961

Professor Madcliffe is at a lectern in a classroom set. He announces that his lecture for the day will be "the molecule—building block of the universe." Before he can get started, Kermit interrupts. "I brought a little electric frying pan with me today, and I was wondering if you'd mind if I cook a batch of Esskay Pure Pork Sausages while you lecture?" Madcliffe grants permission, adding, "Just don't interrupt me." Madcliffe begins his lecture by announcing that everything in the universe is made of molecules. "Is Esskay Sausage made of molecules?" Kermit asks. "Of course it is," Madcliffe says. "That's funny

". . . I always heard Esskay Sausage is made from pure pork, with no filler added," Kermit says. "That's true," Madcliffe says. "And I've always heard it contains lots of natural protein for your family's good health," Kermit says. "I've never heard about it containing any *molecules*." Madcliffe responds: "*Everything* contains molecules, you clothhead!" Kermit shows Madcliffe the Esskay Sausages cooking in his frying pan and challenges him to show him the molecules. "You can't *see* the molecules!" Madcliffe says. "Oh!" Kermit says. "Then it's sort of like the mouth-watering flavor and aroma . . . they're there, but you can't see 'em." The Professor suggests the sausages be disposed of so Kermit won't interrupt the lecture any more . . . by eating them. "Good idea," Kermit says. "With these Esskay Pure Pork Sausages, we'll taste the molecular difference quality makes."

#SF-61-29 "Bacon": Script dated October 16, 1961 *

We see the backs of Kermit and Harry as they admire an as-yet-unseen piece of art in a museum gallery. "Isn't that beautiful . . . one of the most wonderful things I've seen in my whole life," Kermit says. Harry concurs, "It's a real work of art . . . a priceless masterpiece." Kermit realizes they're blocking the view and step aside so the viewers can see the masterpiece: a package of Esskay Hickory Smoked Bacon. They continue to admire the artistry of the bacon and its package. "I like the way the whole thing is done in orange and blue and white," Kermit says. "Very tasteful," Harry says. "And then up here it says, 'To open, lift here . . . to close, tuck in flap.' Gee, that's thoughtful of them," Kermit adds. Harry compares the eloquence of the name Hickory Smoked Bacon to great verse. "It has a kind of poetic sound to it . . . like . . . 'Four score and seven years ago . . .'" Kermit corrects him on the history of the company, which was founded in 1858, and Harry revises his poem. "Five score and three years ago, our two fathers, William Schluderberg and T. J. Kurdle, brought forth on this continent a new meat-packing plant . . . conceived in Baltimore and dedicated to the proposition that you can taste the difference quality makes." Harry explains that great works of art always move him to speech. "They always move me to the grocery store," Kermit says, "where everyone can buy those Esskay masterpieces and taste the difference quality makes."

#SF-61-30 "Line—Quality": Script dated October 16, 1961

Frank is hosting a quiz show called "Something for Nothing!" and Yorick is the contestant. The first question, worth $5,000, is simple: "Who is the sponsor of this show?" Frank understands Yorick's unintelligible response. "Esskay! You're right!" Frank then asks Yorick the $10,000 question: "What is the slogan of the Esskay Company?" Once again, Frank understands Yorick's response. "You can taste the difference quality makes! That's absolutely correct!" The $50,000 question is seemingly simple, especially for someone who has spent the better part of three years selling Esskay products: "Name five products that Esskay makes." Yorick's guttural sounds rattle off a series of products that Frank has no problem understanding: Esskay Hickory Smoked Bacon, Esskay Pure Pork Sausage, Esskay American Canned Ham, Esskay All-Meat Franks . . . but Yorick doesn't quite nail the fifth one. "Esskay Jellybeans? I'm terribly sorry, sir," Frank says. "Take away all his money. No, Esskay does not make jellybeans, sir. If they did, I'm sure they'd make good ones." Frank wraps up the game show (and commercial) as sore loser Yorick bites Frank and pulls him offscreen.

#SF-61-31 "Franks": Script dated October 16, 1961

In the format of reporting scientific results, unspecified characters (listed in the script as Voice One, Voice Two, Voice Three, and Voice Four—to be assigned and performed by Jim) acting as a research team announce the findings of their tests on Esskay Franks when compared with the other brands. They are proud to announce that the Esskay product does not contain fillers or extenders, but they explain that legal issues prevent them from naming the competing frankfurters that do. When they try to do so, the names of the inferior brands are bleeped on the soundtrack and censored onscreen. In this commercial, they really sock it to the competition, but we never hear exactly who that is. By the end of the spot, it's not just the name of the competing hot dog companies that are censored but the adjectives describing Esskay Franks as well: "When you buy a brand like Esskay, you know you're getting the very finest, because *they* know that *you* know that you can taste the difference quality makes—and believe me, they make a (CENSOR) good hot dog. Oh, come on now! I said they make a dog-goned good hot dog."

#SF-61-34 "Fully Cooked Ham": Script dated October 19, 1961 *

In front of a painted backdrop that features a rendering of a large Esskay Fully Cooked Ham, Professor Madcliffe and a very inexperienced Mildred are preparing to do the commercial. "Now, Mildred, all you need to do is read your part on the cards." Madcliffe points out the offscreen cue card man beside the camera. "I've never done a commercial before," she says. Madcliffe begins the commercial: "Friends, today we'd like to tell you about the wonderful Esskay Fully Cooked Hams. Just open the gold foil wrapper, slice, and serve. Or heat before serving if you prefer." Mildred is having trouble reading the cards: "It's . . . the finest ham . . . I've never tasted." Madcliffe corrects her: "That's 'ever,' Mildred." Mildred continues to mangle the sponsor's message, explaining that the ham is "slowly corked over hickory embers" and comes in a "gold fool wrapper." When she asks if she can go back to her knitting, Madcliffe insists that she does.

#SF-61-35 "Fully Cooked Ham": Script dated October 19, 1961*

In a laboratory full of bubbling test tubes, Professor Madcliffe and Icky Gunk are wearing lab coats; they are playing the roles of two spies, complete with accents, trying to start a company to rival Esskay: the Ajax Cut-Rate Fully Cooked Ham Company. Their experiment is to copy Esskay exactly, and to do so, they sent counterspies over to Esskay to find out how it's done. "Vell, first dey sugar cure zee ham. Unt den zey cook it very slowly over real hickory embers to give it that real old-time country flavor." When Icky suspects that Madcliffe knows a little too much about Esskay Hams, Madcliffe confesses that he is actually a *counterspy* for Esskay. "What! You are too?" asks Icky, who then proudly proclaims, "So am I!" Their bubbling experiments explode and create an escape route to get away from the real bad guys, who have them surrounded.

#SF-61-36 "Skrapple": Script dated October 19, 1961

Mildred is standing in front of the magic mirror and begins the commercial with a direct address to the viewers: "Hi, girls, this is Mildred, your home economist, with a few words about how you can make your husband's eyes light up and his stomach say 'howdy' every time he sits down to breakfast made with Esskay Skrapple." At this point, the sound of a gong accompanies the appearance of the floating face puppet in the magic mirror. "Do not be alarmed as upon me you gaze. / I'm the genie who appears when you say the magic phrase." At first, Mildred is puzzled to learn that "Esskay Skrapple" is the magic phrase that summons the genie, but once he explains, in verse, all the magical goodness of the flavor of Esskay Skrapple, it makes sense. "I must admit that there is something *bewitching* about the way it's made fresh daily from choice combinations of selected meats," she says. The floating face genie concurs:

"For the best-tasting scrapple, where the quality is upper, / Esskay Skrapple for breakfast, lunch, and supper." Mildred says, "Say, you're pretty good with that poetry of yours. Ahem, when I buy scrapple, for goodness' sakes, / I buy Esskay and taste the difference quality makes. How's that—all right?" The genie offers a Señor Wences-inspired "S'all right."

#SF-61-37 "Skrapple": Script dated October 19, 1961

The word "scrapple" is seen written vertically on a blackboard (but spelled with an S-K because, well, you know) as Omar introduces a self-written song entitled "A Song to Skrapple." Accompanied by Kermit on the drums, Omar goes on to passionately sing (to the tune "Mother") a line for each letter in the word "Skrapple." As he sings, he completes the writing of each word beside its corresponding letter on the board, but Omar is not a very good speller. "S stands for I'm certain you will like it . . ." he sings, as he spells the word as "sertain." The rest of the letters in "Skrapple" stand for words like "knice," "phinest," and "phlavor." Not surprisingly, the only letter that comes through unscathed is "E," which, of course, stands for "Esskay." Omar finishes the song and is overcome by emotion. Kermit comforts him and addresses the audience: "I hope you people recognize true devotion."

#SF-61-38 "Quality": Script dated October 19, 1961*

See page 515 for a full description.

#SF-61-39 "Franks": Script dated October 19, 1961

Kermit gathers the cast (and viewers) for a frank talk—a talk about Esskay Hickory Smoked Franks, of course. He talks about going to the grocery store only to find it out of Esskay Franks. Jim added a handwritten gag to the script: "I bet they weren't out of salt"—a reference to the song sometimes used on *Sam and Friends* (see page 89). Harry is downright angry. "Nothing makes me madder than a grocer who doesn't stock those delicious all-meat Esskay Frankfurters. What right does *he* have to deprive *you*, the customer, of buying and enjoying the finest frankfurter made? What right, say I?" Kermit tries to calm him down, but Harry continues with his tirade. "Would you defend this tyranny . . . this oppressive evil force . . . mocking the very face of good . . . of democracy . . . of the right to buy Esskay Hickory Smoked Franks. Sooner would I die than allow the hand of oppression to choke life from the very grocery store I have loved so well!" While Harry accepts the praise of Moldy Hay for his eloquence, Kermit explains that the grocer just brought more Esskay Franks from the refrigerator in the back because the woman in front of Kermit had purchased the last package. "You mean I died in vain?" Harry asks. Kermit assures him that Harry's emotional outburst could still serve as a lesson to some grocer who doesn't stock Esskay, a grocer who is "depriving people of their natural born rights to the pursuit of happiness . . . the happiness of eating Esskay Quality Franks. (An alternate, possibly earlier, draft of the script includes the line, "Sooner would I die than allow Khrushchev to take over this country!" The other draft also has a different end line: After Harry says, "You mean I died in vain?" Kermit simply says, "Yeah, something like that.")

"Esskay Bacon": Undated

Professor Madcliffe and Omar are in front of a backdrop of Washington, D.C.'s Tidal Basin as they admire the cherry blossoms in full bloom. "This is all so unbelievably lovely, it makes me want to do a dance to spring," the Professor says. Omar says he knows how the Professor feels. "Does it make you want to do a dance to spring, too?" Madcliffe asks. "No," Omar says. "It makes me want to do a commercial for Esskay Hickory Smoked Bacon." Madcliffe expresses disbelief. "What?" Omar responds, "Well, this is all so beautiful . . . and it smells so good. . . . And what looks better than the sight of Esskay Bacon in the frying pan . . . and what could smell better than the delicious aroma of its hickory-smoked goodness?" Madcliffe agrees and compares the freshness of the cherry blossoms to the freshness of Esskay Hickory Smoked Bacon, which is made daily. He then points out that Omar hasn't even mentioned the delicious full-bodied flavor. "Just a second," says Omar, who then takes a bite of a cherry blossom. "No, Esskay tastes much better than cherry blossoms." "That's because, with Esskay," Madcliffe says, "you can taste the difference quality makes." Omar quickly points out that "we're not saying that these cherry blossoms are not good quality." "No, no," Madcliffe agrees. "I just wouldn't want to eat them for breakfast."

"Esskay Turkey": Undated

While Kermit tries to conduct a simple commercial to remind viewers that Esskay Turkeys are available at neighborhood stores, Harry pitches his own new product: a do-it-yourself turkey, which is, essentially, an egg. "All I have to do is sit on this egg until it hatches. And there it is. Instant turkey!" Kermit regales Harry with the appealing qualities of Esskay's version. "But our turkeys are big and plump with lots of tender white meat." Harry insists his turkey will be big and plump, too. "I'm gonna feed it French fries and chocolate malts for a couple of weeks and then . . ." Kermit has had it. He launches into a tirade, telling Harry (and the viewers) that "everyone knows that the finest turkeys bear the Esskay label. Even the U.S. government knows. They've certified Esskay Turkeys grade A. Just imagine biting into one of those mouth-watering drumsticks." Harry is undeterred. "It's no use, man. Nothing can stop me from hatching this egg and having a turkey dinner." The commercial's script offers two possible endings. In the first version, the egg, after revealing two eyes and a mouth, tells Harry that he's a turtle egg, not a turkey egg. In the alternate ending, the egg turns out not to be an egg at all but a talking rock. In both endings, the spot ends with Harry, dissuaded from his do-it-yourself turkey scheme and offering a final plug for the sponsor's product: "Buy Esskay Quality Turkeys, folks. It's the only way."

"Esskay Turkey": Undated

Omar is working in a grocery store filled with boxes labeled ESSKAY TURKEYS. He answers the phone, "Omar's Oven Ready Turkey Store, Omar speaking." The lady's voice at the other end of the line asks about ordering a turkey for Thanksgiving. "Okay," Omar says. "Let's talk turkey." The caller asks if Omar sells Esskay Oven Ready Turkeys. Omar addresses the home viewers with his incredulous reaction. "Do we sell Esskay Turkeys? That's like asking if General Motors sells automobiles!" Omar tells the viewers that for the purposes of the commercial he will endeavor to get the caller to elaborate but insists that "you understand, of course, that when *you* order *your* Esskay Turkey for Thanksgiving, *you* won't get this sort of runaround. I mean, the Esskay people, they're nice folks." Omar then plays dumb with the caller. "Now, ma'am, what kind of turkey do you want?" He asks her for more and more information, which sounds an awful lot like advertising copy—which is very handy, as this is a commercial. The caller and Omar become more and more emotional about the wonderful traits of the Esskay Oven Ready Turkey, and the caller finally places an order for a twenty-five-pound bird. "And what is the name please?" Omar asks. "Mrs. Schluderberg," the caller says before hanging up.

"Esskay Turkey": Undated

Sam is dressed as Santa Claus and seated in a department store Santa display. Kermit, dressed as a little girl, asks Santa for a "delicious and easy-to-prepare Esskay Turkey." Santa Sam says, "That's an unusual request for a little girl." She replies, "Not when you consider that an Esskay Turkey comes fully cleaned with the giblets packed separately. Just about all you have to do is pop it into the oven, and soon you have the tenderest, juiciest holiday dinner on earth." Next, Harry dressed as a little boy sits on Santa Sam's lap. He, too, wants an Esskay Turkey, but that's not all. "I thought not," Santa Sam says. "You'd like a sled or an electric train or a—" "No," little Harry says. "I'd like some Esskay Pure Pork Sausage. It makes the most delicious turkey dressing in the world. After all, Mr. Schluderberg and Mr. Kurdle pack nothing but the best." The little ones eventually confess their true identities: Nancy Kurdle and Sammy Schluderberg.

ADDITIONAL
SAM AND FRIENDS MUSIC

The following list of recordings was compiled from Jim Henson's song lists, but since their acetate recordings do not survive and they are not found on the reel-to-reel aircheck tapes, their actual use on *Sam and Friends* could not be confirmed. However, since precise airdates and contents are not known for many episodes, it's comfortable to assume that many of these were indeed used on the show.

In most cases, only the titles are listed, as there were multiple versions of the song and there is no evidence of which recording was in the *Sam and Friends* repertoire.

* Denotes a song later performed on *The Muppet Show* or other Henson production or television appearance

"Ain't a Hankerin'"
"Always"
"The Auctioneer"
"The Babbitt and the Bromide"
"Ballerina"
"Bathtub Admiral" (Danny Kaye)
"The Bird on My Head" (David Seville)
"Blow the Man Down" *
"The Bottle Imp" (Geoffrey Holder)
"Bring Us Together"
"Button Up Your Overcoat" *
"A Capital Ship" (Frankie Laine) *
"Choosing a Career" (Prince Patridge with Monroe Tucker Orchestra)
"Cinderella"

"Classical Audience"
"Concerto for Calliope" (Bernie Green)
"Crazy Mixed Up Song"
"Cruising Down the River"
"Dance School"
"Dance with Me Henry"
"A Dear John and Marsha Letter" (Stan Freberg)
"Dearie"
"Delicious" (Jim Backus)
"The Devil and the Farmer"
"Don't Bug Me Baby"
"Don't Tickle Me" (Danny Kaye)
"Embraceable You"
"Enjoy Yourself"
"Fit as a Fiddle" *
"The General's Horse" (Phil Harris)
"The Girl with the Cigarette Cough" (Sammy Shore)
"Go Tell Your Mother"
"The Golden Goose is Dead" (Jim Lowe)
"Gotta Have Rain"
"Gotta Have Something in the Bank Frank"
"Hallelujah, I'm a Bum"
"Happy Days Are Here Again" *
"He's His Own Grandpa" (Phil Harris) *
"Hernando's Hideaway" (from *The Pajama Game*) *
"Hey, Big Brain" (The Lettermen)
"Hey! Mister Barber" (Jack E. Leonard with Ray Conniff and His Orchestra)
"Hey There" (from *The Pajama Game*)
"His Rocking Horse Ran Away"
"How Come My Dog Don't Bark" (Prince Patridge with Monroe Tucker Orchestra)
"The Honey-Earthers" (Stan Freberg)

"I Made a Fool of Myself Over John Foster Dulles" (Carol Burnett)
"I Never Harmed an Onion" * (Steve Allen)
"I Like It, I Like It" (Jerry Lewis)
"I Like Your Kind of Love"
"I Said My Pajamas (And Put on My Prayers)"
"I Saw Esau"
"I Wish I Was a Car" (Peter Lind Hayes and Mary Healy)
"I Won't Go Hunting with You Jake (But, I'll Go Chasin' Wimmin)" (Jimmy Dean)
"I'd Climb the Highest Mountain"
"I'm Not the Braggin' Kind" (Gene Austin)
"Inka Dinka Doo" (Jimmy Durante)
"I've Got a Wife"
"Is Zat You, Myrtle" (The Carlisles)
"Java Jive"
"Keep Them Cold Icy Fingers Off of Me"
"Lemming" (Ken Nordine)
"Let's Go Fishin'" (Frankie Laine)
"Lil' Darlin'"
"Listen All You Bachelors" (Phil Foster)
"Little Blue Riding Hood" (Stan Freberg)
"Little Darlin'"
"Little Hood Riding Red"
"Make Yourself Comfortable"
"Marian the Librarian" (from The Music Man)
"The Martins and the Coys" *
"Memories Are Made of This"
"The Merry Old Philosopher" (Eddie Lawrence)
"Military Love Song"
"Mule Train"
"Mutual Admiration Society" *
"My Friend the Ghost"
"Never Took a Lesson in My Life"

"The New Philosopher" (Eddie Lawrence)
"The New Face on the Barroom Floor" (Art Carney)
"Nine Pound Hammer"
"Not of This Earth" (*Monster Rally*)
"The Old Philosopher on the Range" (Eddie Lawrence)
"One Suit" (Tennessee Ernie Ford)
"Pal-Yat-Chee"
"Three Little Pigs" ("Pee Little Thrigs")
"Protection"
"The Purple People Eater"
"The Sample Song"
"Save the Bones for Henry Jones"
"Schnitzel Bank"
"Secret Love" *
"Seven and a Half Cents" (from *The Pajama Game*)
"Shadrach"
"Sheesh, What a Grouch!" (Art Carney)
"Silent TV"
"Sloop John B."
"So Long"
"So Long, It's Been Good to Know You"
"Somewhere Over the Rainbow" *
"Southern Fried Boogie" (Phil Harris)
"The Sow Song"
"Stranded in the Jungle"
"Struttin' with Some Barbeque"
"Swingin' Hammer" (The Four Tophatters with Archie Bleyer)
"Take a Letter, Miss Smith" (Tony Martin and Fran Warren)
"Take Me to Your President"
"Take Off the Mask" (from *New Faces of 1952*)
"Tam Pierce" (Burl Ives)
"Tarzan and Jane" (Jack and Jim)
"Temptation" *

"That Holiday Spirit" (Eddie Lawrence)
"That's All Folks"
"That's What I Like About the South" (Phil Harris)
"There's No Piano in This House" (Vaughn Monroe)
"They Didn't Believe Me"
"They Were Doing the Mambo"
"Tombstone"
"The Two Calypsos" (Will Holt)
"Va Va Va Voom" (Art Carney)
"Vagabond Lover"
"The Watermelon Song" (Tennessee Ernie Ford)
"Well Anyway"
"What Do You Hear from the Red Planet Mars" (*Monster Rally*)
"What is a Freem?" (Steve Allen)
"What it Was, Was Football" (Andy Griffith)
"What Shall I Do with the Baby-O?"
"When I Was a Lad" (From *H.M.S. Pinafore*)
"Wherefore Art Thou, Romeo?" (Jill Corey)
"Why Do I Love You?"
"Wringle Wrangle"

LIVE APPEARANCES

In addition to their television broadcasts, Jim and Jane presented live shows throughout the D.C. area. There is little documentation regarding these performances, but we do know that Jim and Jane brought the Muppets to the following events, not including internal promotional appearances for WRC, Esskay, or Wilkins:

August 7, 1956: Lansburgh's Department Store's "Campus Capers" fashion show, Statler Hotel, Washington, D.C., with Paul Arnold and the Muppets

December 18, 1956: Washington Orphan's Christmas Party, U.S. Naval Gun Factory, Washington, D.C.

October 26, 1957: Carnival at the Kate Waller Barrett School in Arlington, Virginia

February 25, 1958: Washington Advertising Club Women's Fashion Show Luncheon, Presidential Arms, Washington, D.C., along with fellow WRC personalities Carl Caudill, Inga Rundvold, Bryson Rash, Jim Simpson, and Tippy Stringer

March 3, 1960: Bolling Officers' Wives Club Luncheon, Bolling Air Force Base Officers' Club, Washington, D.C.

April 29, 1960: Principia Fund Benefit, Woman's Club of Chevy Chase, Maryland

October 7, 1960: United Givers Fund Fundraising Rally, National Institutes of Health, Bethesda, Maryland

October 17, 1961: United Givers Fund Fundraising Rally, National Institutes of Health, Bethesda, Maryland

Kermit, Jane, and Sam greet representatives from the National Institutes of Health. At each of their NIH live fundraising appearances, Jim and Jane not only performed, but also made $100 donations to the organization's patient benefit fund.

Shows were tailored to specific audiences, but they were essentially longer versions of what appeared on WRC, with the Muppets lip-syncing to records and performing comedy sketches.

A script for what appears to be one of these live Muppet performances was located in the Henson archives and is summarized here. Esskay was not an official sponsor of these live performances, but since audiences had become accustomed to funny Muppet commercials, the script included a fictional sponsor.

"Grandma Gertrude's Tippy Top Tunes"

SKETCH: The setting is a television studio. Omar welcomes the audience to this "dress rehearsal" of the show "Grandma Gertrude's Tippy Top Tunes of the Times." Harry and the show's director, Professor Madcliffe, enter, arguing about Harry's request for fifty guitars for the production numbers. "Absolutely not, Harry. . . . You'd overload the circuit and explode us right off the air!" Omar introduces the Professor and Harry to the studio audience. "Why aren't they home watching television?" the Professor asks. Madcliffe instructs announcer Omar to start the rehearsal. "It's 'Tippy Top Tunes of the Times' Time!" Omar says. "Brought to you by Grandma Gertrude's Glorious Pepper-Upper." Icky Gunk interrupts the opening. "As Grandma Gertrude's personal representative, I wish to express my dissatisfaction with Grandma Gertrude's position in the lineup!" Icky insists that Grandma Gertrude's contract states that she gets billed at the top of the show. "Grandma Gertrude will get her bill at the end of the month like everybody else," Madcliffe says. After the billing issue is settled, Icky introduces Grandma Gertrude's nephew (Yorick) and asks that he be given a job on the show. Madcliffe is happy to oblige and asks what Yorick can do. "Yorick can do just about anything," Icky says. "Provided it doesn't require talent . . . ability . . . intelligence . . . or personality." Madcliffe is impressed. "Sounds like he's got the makings of a star." Madcliffe has Omar start the show again, with Grandma Gertrude's name getting top billing. He then introduces Sam and Kermeena to perform.

RECORD: "That Old Black Magic": Performed by Louis Prima and Keely Smith, written by Harold Arlen, Johnny Mercer (see page 142 for a full summary)

SKETCH: "Great number," Madcliffe says. "But we'll have to spice it up a bit." He suggests calling the special effects people to provide "some icy fingers, a spine, one elevator, and some burning desire." Madcliffe then cues Omar to rehearse the commercial for Grandma Gertrude's Pepper-Upper: "Everybody's talking about Grandma Gertrude's Pepper-Upper. . . . The new all-purpose, filter-tipped, candy-coated, vacuum-packed pepper-upper." Omar introduces a testimonial—Moldy Hay as a satisfied customer. "When I used to go to the beach, people would always laugh at me and kick sand in my face. Then I tried Grandma Gertrude's. . . . People don't laugh at me and kick sand in my face anymore. . . . Now they snarl and throw rocks." Omar wraps up the commercial and introduces the next performance.

RECORD: "I've Grown Accustomed to Your Face": Performed by Rosemary Clooney, written by Frederick Loewe and Alan Jay Lerner (see page 308)

SKETCH: Madcliffe decides to take a coffee break and send Moldy out to order some food. "Let's see . . . we want six coffees." Moldy asks, "Wilkins Coffee?" "Of course, dunderhead," Madcliffe says as he gets specific with his order. "Two of those with cream and no sugar, two with sugar and no cream, one with cream and two sugars, one with sugar and two creams . . . then we want four hamburgers with mustard, relish, and no catsup on whole wheat bread . . . two with relish, catsup, and no mustard on white . . . and one hamburger on toasted rye with mustard, relish, catsup, onions, tomatoes, lettuce, and no meat. . . . Better change those two relish, catsup, and no mustard to mustard, catsup, and no relish. . . . Two of the four on white medium rare . . . four of the two on whole wheat medium well . . . and four pounds of raw meat for Yorick. You got that?" Moldy says, "Yeah . . . six coffees." Madcliffe asks, "What about the hamburgers?" Moldy says, "We don't have any." After stopping Yorick from eating the props backstage and another Grandma Gertrude commercial by Omar, the final number is introduced.

RECORD: "The Night Before Christmas": Performed by Stan Freberg with Babette Bain and Billy May's Music, written by Stan Freberg, Jack Brooks (see page 316)

ACKNOWLEDGMENTS

Many people need to be thanked. Just as Sam had all of his Friends, this book has many friends of its own who deserve gratitude.

I want to start with a word of appreciation for Jim and Jane Henson, not just for having such a wonderful story to tell, but for having the presence of mind to save so much of the material that makes it possible to tell it. And I must acknowledge the wonderful Jerry Juhl, whom I had the pleasure to work with. When I began writing for the Muppets, Jerry was a mentor to me, and his lasting words of wisdom continued to guide me through this project.

Next, I extend many, many thanks to Lisa Henson, Cheryl Henson, Brian Henson, Heather Henson, and the entire Henson organization (especially Nicole Goldman) for their support on this project and giving me full access to The Jim Henson Company Archives. Thanks to Cynthia Barron for making it all legal and official.

Speaking of the Henson archives, Karen Falk, Director of The Jim Henson Company Archives, went above and beyond the call of duty (as did her colleague Susie Tofte) to make their collection accessible to me. Special thanks to Carla DellaVedova, Director of The Jim Henson Company Media Archives (and her associate, Shannon Robles), for locating the rare audio recordings and arranging for them to be digitized. Oh, and did I mention Karen Falk? Well, I can't mention her enough.

I would like to acknowledge all the trustees I have served with over the years on the board of The Jim Henson Legacy, with special mention to Bonnie Erickson, Arthur Novell, Al Gottesman, Thea Hambright, Fran Brill, and Rollie Krewson.

Thanks to Frank Oz for graciously agreeing to write the foreword and even more thanks for actually doing it—thus motivating me to finish writing the rest of the book.

Thanks to Bob Payne and Joe Irwin for sharing their stories of Jim, Jane, and the early days of the Muppets. And thank you, Alex Rockwell, for speaking with me about your time working with Jim during the not-so-early days of the Muppets.

Thanks to Leigh Slaughter of The Muppets Studio at The Walt Disney Company, as well as her predecessor, Debbie McClellan, for their support of this project. And thank you Margaret Adamic and Max Raley at Disney for arranging the necessary permissions and paperwork.

A great big thank you to Brian Jay Jones, author of *Jim Henson: The Biography,* for sharing his voluminous research and interview transcripts with me and for taking an advance look at the manuscript, and to Judy Harris for allowing me to use her interview with Jim.

Thanks to Matt Glassman at WRC-TV, who was kind enough to take time from his busy news day to give a tour of the *Sam and Friends* studio.

Thanks to Justin Williams at the Baltimore Museum of Industry, who dug deep into the Esskay collection, and to Maggi Marzolf, who finalized the permissions.

Thanks to Marion Hiller, Elizabeth Hiller, and all of Jack Hiller's family for allowing the use of his amazing photography.

Franchon Priolenau at Hearst was kind enough to arrange permission for photography from the University of Maryland's *Baltimore American* collection, and Lae'l Hughes-Watkins, the Archivist at the University of Maryland, located the wonderful Chris Geraci photos in its Special Collections. And an additional tip of the terrapin topper to Anne S. Turkos and Joni Jones Floyd at UMD for their support.

SAG-AFTRA archivist Valerie Yaros generously supplied the AFTRA directory's Muppets moving ad.

Thanks to Mark Evanier and Pete Kelly for facilitating permission to reprint the lyrics to "Go Go Pogo."

Thanks also go to the nice people at TRO Essex Music (Sarah Smith), Wixen Music Publishing (Michael Agajanian), and Alfred Music (Michael Worden) for arranging to reprint lyrics from their songs.

I wouldn't have learned about Tom Shaw if it wasn't for the folks at the Baseball Games web team—thanks to them.

Thanks to Steve Abrams at the Puppeteers of America for digging around in its archives.

Thanks to Ryan Dillon for being Ryan Dillon and giving such great feedback.

While we're on the subject of Ryans, Ryan Lintelman and his team at the National Museum of American History took us behind the scenes to show us the original *Sam and Friends* puppets. As if it wasn't enough to visit Kermit, Harry, Sam, and the gang, we also got to see Charlie McCarthy, Mr. Moose, and Hawkeye's Hawaiian shirt. Ryan was also kind enough to take an early peek at the manuscript.

Thanks to Joe Hennes and Ryan Roe of toughpigs.com for taking an early look at things, and to Scott Hanson, Danny Horn, and everyone associated with The Muppet Wiki for starting and maintaining such a helpful resource. And thanks to Dave Hulteen for his amazing talent.

Thanks to Greg Ehrbar, Will Friedwald, Randy Skretvedt, Jeff Abraham, Jerry Beck, Will Ryan, Trav S.D., Noah Diamond, Ken Levine, Tom Tierney, and Dr. Demento himself, Barret Hansen, for helping with music identification. And thanks to Chad Bennett and the Barbershop Harmony Society. Also, thank you to Jordan Young, author of *Spike Jones Off the Record: The Man Who Murdered Music,* for checking my Spike Jones facts.

And a great big thank you to Jim Lewis for his all-around help and support.

A slightly less big, but still sizable, thank you to the brilliant Dave Goelz for taking a look at the manuscript and offering support.

Tremendous thanks to my dear friend Kate Larrabee for taking an advance look and offering her terrific insights. And thanks to my just-as-dear friend Tananarive Due for her ongoing support

And let's hear it for my publisher, Ben Ohmart, and his team at BearManor Media.

Many, many thanks to my wonderful sister-in-law, Diana D'Abruzzo, for all of her assistance in the research and copyediting.

Finally, many thanks to my amazing wife (and renowned puppet performer), Stephanie D'Abruzzo, for her valuable assistance throughout this entire project and for being the incredible person she is.

END NOTES/BIBLIOGRAPHY

Part I – The *Sam and Friends* Story

Chapter 1: The History

"**For everybody else in the world**": Orson Welles, *The Orson Welles Show*, 1979.

"**I just heard about a television station**": Jim Henson, *The Orson Welles Show*, 1979.

"**Puppets are very ancient entertainers**": Orson Welles, *Welles.*

"**for my money, the most original thing**": Ibid.

"**Roy Meachum of WTOP-TV has started**": Lawrence Laurent, "Search for Marionetteers; Police Push Safety Drives," *The Washington Post*, May 13, 1954, 47.

"**I absolutely loved television**": Jim Henson, interview by Christopher Finch, March 1982, transcript, The Jim Henson Company Archives.

"**We would go into the school**": Joe Irwin, interview with the author, March 11, 2020.

"**OOPS, SORRY**": Harry MacArthur, "On the Air," *The Evening Star*, June 25, 1954, A-26.

"**They were just too talented**": Bernie Harrison, "On the Air," *The Sunday Star TV Magazine*, February 23, 1969, 53.

Chapter 2: This Is WRC-TV Washington

"**He told me he was up there**": Joe Irwin, interview with the author.

"there wasn't much money": Jim Henson, interview by Judy Harris, September 21, 1982, http://users.bestweb.net/~foosie/henson.htm.

"I was a kid and it was fun": Ibid.

"I'm making GREAT MONEY": Sharon Doran, "Teen Scene," *The Evening Star*, October 28, 1955, B-7.

"For a long time, I would tell people": Jim Henson, Judy Harris interview.

"I think his main craft was jewelry": Jane Henson, interview with the author, February 17, 2009.

"Jim was extremely capable of doing puppets": Ed Longley, *Jane and Friends* panel at the University of Maryland, September 27, 2006.

"They were just doing novelty records": Jim Henson, Judy Harris interview.

Chapter 3: Admiration at First Sight

"It was a senior class": Jane Henson, interview with the author.
"It was admiration": Ibid.
"Jim was great in that class": Ibid.
"a totally natural leader": Ibid.
"He really helped make": Ibid.
"The basic story was good versus evil": Ibid.
"He was working mostly in no color": Ibid.
"It was all planned, and then": Jane Henson, interview by Brian Jay Jones, February 24, 2010.
"a way that one could do entertaining": Jim Henson, Christopher Finch interview.
"We would pick a record": Jane Henson, interview with the author.
"I think one of them had wings": Ibid.
"It was enjoyable": Jane Henson, Brian Jay Jones interview.

"the kid is positively a genius": Lawrence Laurent, "The Straight Man Totes the Load," *The Washington Post and Times–Herald*, May 15, 1955, J3.

"You know, in Washington, D.C.": Jane Henson, interview with the author.

"I think Joe Goodfellow": Ibid.

"In those days, we did a range of things": Jim Henson, Christopher Finch interview.

"We didn't do questionable": Jane Henson, interview with the author.

He insisted it was a short-term arrangement: Ibid.

Harrison proclaimed: Bernie Harrison, "Gobel Persuades Chicago Buddy to Try TV Again," *The Sunday Star,* July 3, 1955, A-9.

"Write an angry letter": Bernie Harrison, "Make That Sad Sam and His Friends . . .," *The Evening Star*, August 19, 1955, A-2.

"Sam came back last night": Bernie Harrison, "WRC Lifts Whammy On Our Sammy," *The Evening Star*, August 31, 1955, A-41.

"Dear Bernie": Ibid.

"I had to make a decision": Jane Henson, Brian Jay Jones interview.

"Mom was a serious artist": Cheryl Henson, correspondence with the author, May 17, 2021.

"next to making Muppets": Ruth Dean, "Student Combines Work and Play," *The Sunday Star,* January 18, 1959, D-8.

She told TV columnist Lawrence Laurent: Lawrence Laurent, "Story Is Next Lad to Accept The 'Challenge,'" *The Washington Post and Times–Herald*, September 2, 1956, G3.

"just a little bit": Ibid.

"One of the brightest": Katherine Elson, "Rollicking Muppets Set a Merry Pace," *The Washington Post and Times–Herald*, February 17, 1957, F15.

"Jane lives in an apartment": Ibid.

"Up every morning": Ibid.

"After the 6:30 p.m. show": Ibid.

He put a lot of mileage: Joe Irwin, interview with the author.

"Many remarks could be made": Mrs. K, comment in Bernie Harrison, "Television and Radio Mailbag," *The Sunday Star*, January 1, 1956, D-6.

Chapter 4: Sam and His Friends

"Most puppeteers at that point": Jim Henson, Christopher Finch interview.

"I think we were one of the first": Ibid.

"immediately started working": Ibid.

". . . it was clearly Jim's vision": Jane Henson, interview with the author.

"Basically, [Jim] would take": Ibid.

"He's easy going": Sheila Gallagher, "Three Years With Muppets," *The Sunday Star TeleVue,* October 14, 1956, 4.

"[Sam] was the only human": Jane Henson, Brian Jay Jones interview.

"I made him originally": Phil Geraci, "Sam's Best Friend," *The Sunday Star Magazine,* December 8, 1957, 2.

Sam was born in October 1954: Bernice Wneck, "Muppet Who's Who," *The Sunday Star TeleVue*, March 29, 1959, 5.

"It was sort of more a turquoise": Jim Henson, Judy Harris interview.

"All the characters in those days were abstract": Ibid.

"If you take a character and you call him a frog": Ibid.

"The nice thing about Kermit": Ibid.

"We didn't know it then": Jane Henson, Brian Jay Jones interview.

"From the very beginning": Ibid.

"Kermit can do everything but talk": Phil Geraci, "Sam's Best Friend," *The Sunday Star Magazine*, December 8, 1957, 2.

Kermit was created: Bernice Wneck, "Muppet Who's Who,"

Born in September 1954: Ibid.
"It's a beautifully made puppet": Jane Henson, Brian Jay Jones interview.
Moldy Hay was created in May 1956: Bernice Wneck, "Muppet Who's Who."
Omar joined the Muppets: Ibid.
The Omar puppet was constructed: Jane Henson, interview by Brian Jay Jones, January 28, 2011.
"Jim liked doing those": Jane Henson, Brian Jay Jones 2010 interview.
Professor Madcliffe made his *Sam and Friends* debut: Bernice Wneck, "New Lineup at WMAL," *The Sunday Star TeleVue*, August 18, 1957, 5.
Yorick was born in June 1954: Bernice Wneck, "Muppet Who's Who."
Jane Henson recalled: Jane Henson, interview with the author.
In a 1957 poll: Bernie Harrison, "Those TV 'Firsts' Are for the Birds," *The Evening Star*, February 21, 1957, D-15.
Mushmellon was born in June 1955: Bernice Wneck, "Muppet Who's Who."
Popular among fans: Bernie Harrison, "Those TV 'Firsts' Are for the Birds,"
Hank and Frank were born in July 1954: Ibid.

Chapter 5: National Exposure

Arnold was, by his own admission: Lawrence Laurent, "Paul Drifted Down the Ohio Into a Career," *The Washington Post and Times-Herald*, June 10, 1956, J1.
"broke, hungry and disgusted": Ibid.
"Kinda had a hankerin'": Ibid.
"The whole *Footlight Theater*": Jane Henson, Brian Jay Jones 2010 interview.

"**I think that** ***Footlight Theater***": B.L.B. letter, Bernie Harrison, "TeleVue Mailbag," *The Sunday Star TeleVue*, July 8, 1956, 7.

"**after howls of protest**": "People and Places," *NBC Chimes*, September–October 1955, 20.

"'**They called us and said**'": Jane Henson, interview with the author.

At the audition: Ibid.

"**The people in Washington**": Ibid.

"**She's singing, and there's a cloth**": Ibid.

"**They certainly did let us know**": Ibid.

"**They were so good**": Bernie Harrison, "Muppets Score on Allen Show," *The Evening Star*, October 12, 1956, A-35.

"**Several years ago**": Steve Allen, *The Steve Allen Show*, NBC, November 4, 1956.

"**The Baird marionettes**": Jack O'Brian, "Elsa's 'Title' All Too True," *New York Journal-American*, December 12, 1957, 22.

She recalled that it was not uncommon: Alex Rockwell, telephone conversation with the author, February 2021.

"**host of this unusual program**": *NBC Spot Sales TeleSpot Flash* press release, 1956.

One of the few surviving visuals: Chuck Knight, "Sam and Friends," *The Old Line*, May 1958, 26.

"**Man of many voices**": WRC *Man of Many Voices* brochure.

"**Paul Arnold's troupe has added**": Bernice Wneck, "New Lineup at WMAL."

"**It occurred to me**": George Kennedy, "The Rambler Learns About Muppetry," *The Evening Star*, August 14, 1958, A-23.

The FCC required broadcasters: *The FCC Rules and Regulations of 1955*, Rule # 3.652.

"**I built Wilkins**": Jane Henson, interview with the author.

"**It was the basic good guy/bad guy**": Ibid.

The Wilkins Company credited: Stacy V. Jones, "Patents Granted For TV Ad Puppets," *The New York Times*, September 19, 1959, 29.

"This is the biggest thing": George Kennedy, "The Rambler Learns About Muppetry."

"Jim was seated right next to him": Jane Henson, interview with the author.

"That was almost some of": Jim Henson, Judy Harris interview.

"Curiously enough, it was": Jane Henson, interview with the author.

"He thought that was a real hoot": Joe Irwin, interview with the author.

"Jim never had me do voices": Jane Henson, interview by Brian Jay Jones, January 28, 2011.

"I'm very ambivalent": Jane Henson, Brian Jay Jones 2010 interview.

Chapter 6: It's Time to Play the Music

"All are either humorous": Phil Geraci, "Sam's Best Friend."

"It was so fun": Jane Henson, interview with the author.

"He knew all of the records": Ibid.

"He would constantly be": Jane Henson, Brian Jay Jones 2010 interview.

"The things that they would": Jane Henson, interview with the author.

"If something worked": Ibid.

"If it didn't look good": Ibid.

"We had this puppet that was made": Jim Henson, Christopher Finch interview.

"If you liked World War II": *Hogan's Heroes*/CBS-TV radio commercial, 1965.

"We used the records": Jane Henson, interview with the author.

"I just remember it was the first": Ibid.

"This is one of the greatest": Stan Freberg telegram, The Jim Henson Company Archives.

"I came down to the show": Stan Freberg, Episode 1 in *GrantCast*, interview by Grant Baciocco, September 24, 2011.

"the Pogo of the group": *Jim Henson, Jim Frank, and Michael Talk About the Muppets*, internal Jim Henson Company video, February 7, 1990.

Chapter 7: 1958: A Very Major Big Year

"It was just stuff that I did as a lark": Jim Henson, Judy Harris interview.

In February of 1958: Chuck Knight, "Sam and Friends."

"NBC had established the color television system": Jim Henson, Judy Harris interview.

"Jim wanted to go": Jane Henson, interview with the author.

"I was an artist" / "The station prevailed upon me": Jim Henson, Judy Harris interview.

"He asked me if I would work": Bob Payne, interview with the author, September 18, 2019.

"Jim was always doing something": Ibid.

"In the afternoon, we'd go to the park": Joe Irwin, interview with the author.

"As we watched the show": Ibid.

"I met a puppeteer in Germany": Jim Henson, Christopher Finch interview.

"He would check in to see": Jane Henson, Brian Jay Jones 2010 interview.

"Salt . . . who needs salt": Jack Adrian (Adrian Greenberg), "Salt," Unique Records, 1956.

"I did a painting of drawers": Bob Payne, interview with the author.

"She was delightful": Ibid.

"We sat and giggled": Ibid.

"Mom had a smart": Cheryl Henson, correspondence.

"I don't think someone would": Jim Henson, *Henson's Place: The Man Behind the Muppets*, Platypus Productions, 1984, Broadcast on PBS, August 1986.

"When I came back from that trip": Jim Henson, Christopher Finch interview.

Incorporated in Washington: Minutes of Muppets Inc. meeting, November 24, 1958, The Jim Henson Company Archives.

"primarily to carry forward": Ibid.

"I think Jim's way of operating": Jane Henson, Brian Jay Jones 2010 interview.

Chapter 8: Jim and Jane Henson

"We just weren't in the same": Jane Henson, Brian Jay Jones 2010 interview.

"We went out on a couple" / "I think we went": Ibid.

You know, we're here: Ibid.

"This is what we're going to do": Ibid.

"Later I heard from people": Ibid.

"I think even Bill and Anne knew": Ibid.

"We were very fond of": Ibid.

"You have to stand there": Jane Henson, interview with the author.

"I was flying in from St. Louis" / "When I landed at National" / "As a best man": Joe Irwin, interview with the author.

"The Muppets are off WRC-TV": Lawrence Laurent, "Rod Serling's Looking At Other Side of Coin," *The Washington Post and Times–Herald*, May 28, 1959, 62.

Jim and Jane were wearing: Isabelle Gournay and Mary Corbin Sies, National Register of Historic Places Multiple Property Documentation Form, June 21, 2004, E-12.

$35,000 price of the house: Ursula Keller, "Muppets Win Way" *Christian Science Monitor*, December 15, 1959, 14.

In anticipation of his graduation: Commonwealth of Virginia Division of Motor Vehicles Temporary Registration Certificate, May 30, 1960.

"mainly for their infant daughter: Bonnie Aikman, "News of D.C. Studios," *The Sunday Star TeleVue*, July 24, 1960, 24.

"Burr was a star": Jane Henson, interview with the author, March 18, 2010.

"The Moppets a sheer delight" / "I'm sure we who": Bill Eubank, "The Moppets—Hensons," *The Puppetry Journal*, September–October 1960, 11–12.

"Jim really was anxious": Jane Henson, interview with the author, March 18, 2010.

"They were having a fundraiser": Ibid.

Chapter 9: Brought to You by Esskay

Esskay had advertised on television before: *Esskay News*, July 1954.

By 1957, Esskay was spreading: *Esskay News*, January–February 1957, 12.

"You and your neighbors": *Esskay News*, December 1958, back cover.

"Of course, the thing that was": Jane Henson, interview with the author, 2009.

"They were great fun": Ibid.

"It was my job": Thomas N. Shaw, *Confessions of an 84 Year Old Teenager*, 2015, 22-24.

"I delivered the commercials": Ibid.

On January 30, 1959: "Into Orbit With the Full Line," *Esskay News*, Winter Issue 1959, 12.

Omar and Harry began: Esskay Sales Meeting Script, Jim Henson Company Archives.

The big news of the 1959 sales meeting: "Into Orbit with the Full Line."

Moldy must have been disappointed: "Load O' Loot Delivered to Winners," *Esskay News*, Summer Issue 1959.

At Esskay's January 29, 1960, annual sales meeting: "Shooting for Super Sales in '60,'" *Esskay News*, Spring Issue 1960, 12.

Kermit as the Esskay Super Salesman: Esskay Sales Meeting Script, Jim Henson Company Archives.

Proudly touted Jim and Jane's Emmy win: "In the News," *Esskay News*, Summer Issue 1959.

The VanSant Dugdale agency turned to: *Tip of the Freberg*, Rhino Entertainment, 2006.

Freberg eventually expanded: Ibid.

Chapter 10: It's Time to Light the Lights

The show's first home was the: Allison DiLiegro, "Washington Marriott Wardman Park: Tales From a Presidential Residence Full of WWII and TV History," February 3, 2019, storiedhotels.com.

"The floor usually could accommodate": Jane Henson, interview with the author, 2009.

"They were five feet, six inches": Ibid.

"Everything was burned into acetate" / "Everything was live": Ibid.

"There was a place in there": Joe Irwin, interview with the author.

At the new building: Bill Reddig, Jr., "Muppets' Managers Merge; Aim is Network Show," *Northern Virginia Sun*, August 15, 1959, 3.

"We had this little cubbyhole at NBC": Bob Payne, interview by Brian Jay Jones, February 27, 2010.

"She could sing": Bob Payne, interview with the author.

"We pre-record the audio": Jim Henson, "Puppetry in Television," *The Puppetry Journal*, September–October 1961, 28–29.
"I think we, as the Muppets, broke new ground": *Jim Henson on Guilty Pleasures*, essay, 1982, Jim Henson Company Archives.
"We play the puppets": Jim Henson, "Puppetry in Television."
"We have found it best": Ibid.
"I started right at the beginning" / "Jim had . . . a machine": Bob Payne, interview by Brian Jay Jones, September 17, 2010.
"I don't remember exactly": Ibid.
"I just was so impressed": Ibid.
"A lot of things that we did": Jane Henson, interview with the author, March 18, 2010.
"On television, you can": Bill Reddig, Jr., "Muppets' Managers Merge; Aim is Network Show," *Northern Virginia Sun,* August 15, 1959, 8.
"We did not work through the monitor": Jane Henson, Brian Jay Jones 2010 interview.
"At that time, it was really a": Ibid.
"We learned very quickly" / "For the most part": Ibid.
"I only did two shows" / "And I thought this": Joe Irwin, interview with the author.
"When we were filming": Del Ankers, *Jane and Friends* panel at the University of Maryland, September 27, 2006.
An engineer named Jim Songer: Peter Glaskowsky, "Video Assist Predates Jerry Lewis 'Patent,'" *CNET*, July 20, 2009.
"Live television calls for": Jane Henson, interview with the author, March 18, 2010.
"That's very like Jim": Ibid.
"quite magical": Jim Henson, *Television Academy Hall of Fame Induction*, November 15, 1987, broadcast on Fox, November 30, 1987.
"These are all things": Jim Henson, "Puppetry in Television."

"**They loved working with Jim**": Jane Henson, interview with the author, 2009.
"***Sam and Friends** was the creative show*": Ibid.
"**They would come up with something**": Ibid.
"**We deliberately had the show**": Ibid.

Chapter 11: The Surviving Shows

"**He started looking for an animation stand**": Jane Henson, interview with the author, March 30, 2010.
"**came off beautifully**": Bernie Harrison, "A Fine Show—But Foreverland?" *The Evening Star*, December 12, 1960, B-14.
All other material from kinescopes of *Sam and Friends,* The Jim Henson Company Archives.

Chapter 12: Jerry

"**Jim felt I was no longer 'dependable'**": Jane Henson, interview with the author, 2009.
"**In 1956, he told a reporter**": Sheila Gallagher, "Three Years With Muppets," *The Sunday Star TeleVue*, October 14, 1956, 4.
"**I was very pregnant with Cheryl**": Jane Henson, interview with the author, March 18, 2010.
"**When we got out to Asilomar**": Ibid.
"**Frank was, I guess, about seventeen**": Ibid.
"**one of those kids who**": Jerry Juhl, interview by Ron Powers, March, 1991, The Jim Henson Company Archives.
"**I had just always been fascinated by it**": Ibid.
"**Of course, we were working for *no* money at all**": Ibid.
"**That was the summer that the**": Ibid.
"**I had been amazed by his work**" / "**For puppeteers, it was just**": Ibid.
"**For many years, Frank told anyone**": Ibid.

"**The first impression that I had**": Jerry Juhl, *Great Performances* interview, PBS, March 1994.
"**Looking back on it, I realize**": Jerry Juhl, Ron Powers interview.
"**Frank was still in high school**": Ibid.
"**I said I'd come for a year**": Ibid.
"**He was in two markets**": Ibid.
"**Jim was living in this big, comfortable**": Ibid.
"**After a few days, I said**": Ibid.
"**really cheap**": Ibid.
"**He said, 'Here, take the Rolls**": Ibid.
"**When I first went to work for Jim**": Jerry Juhl, *Great Performances*.
"**Immediately, when I got there, I started writing**": Ibid.
"**He was performing quite nicely**": Jane Henson, interview with the author, March 18, 2010.
"**I remember going out**": Jerry Juhl, *Great Performances*.

Chapter 13: Five Scripts

All material sourced from The Jim Henson Company Archives.

Chapter 14: I Come for to Sing

"**There will be some long, loud**": Lawrence Laurent, "Susskind Grabs On To 'Smiling' Bear," *The Washington Post and Times-Herald,* December 16, 1961, B6.
"**In this business, we often**": Letter from Robert V. Walsh, October 20, 1961, The Jim Henson Company Archives.
"**This program has been absolute**": Ibid.
"**hope that we will**": Ibid.
"**We at Esskay**": Letter from T. J. Kurdle, December 4, 1961, The Jim Henson Company Archives.
"**didn't really want it to go**": Jane Henson, interview with the author, March 18, 2010.

"It was totally typical": Jerry Juhl, Ron Powers interview.

"Jim said he was going to New York": Bob Payne, interview with the author.

"Puppets do exactly what they're told": Steuart Motor Co. advertisement, *The Evening Star,* April 23, 1963, B-20.

". . . the use of the puppet characters": Letter from Jim Henson to Steuart Motor Company, April 24, 1963, The Jim Henson Company Archives.

"I am not wise in the way of doing things": Letter from Sam Brown to Jim Henson, April 29, 1963, The Jim Henson Company Archives.

"After I got out of the Army": Jerry Nelson, interview by Brian Jay Jones, February 29, 2012.

Jim thought any musical number: Craig Shemin, *The Muppet Show: Music, Mayhem and More* Liner Notes, Rhino 2002.

"People come and they go": Willard Scott, *Sam and Friends* Smithsonian Institution donation ceremony, August 25, 2010.

"I only hope": Walt Disney, *Disneyland,* "The Disneyland Story," ABC, October 27, 1954.

Part II – The Episode Guide

References/Bibliography:

It Only Hurts When I Laugh, Stan Freberg, Times Books, 1988.
The Wacky Top 40, Bruce Nash and Allan Zullo, Bob Adams, Inc, 1993.
Tip of the Freberg, Rhino Entertainment, 2006.
Spike Jones Off the Record: The Man Who Murdered Music, Jordan R. Young, Bear Manor, 2021.

Muppet Wiki

Shazam.com

Discogs.com

ASCAP.com

BMI.com

Index

Numbers in **bold** indicate photographs

"(All of a Sudden) My Heart Sings" 391, 400
"(I've Been So Wrong, For So Long—But) I'm So Right Tonight" 253
"(We're All Invited to) Henrietta's Wedding" 463
"'S Wonderful" 284
13 Clocks, The 20-21

Abbott and Costello 498
"Abe Snake for President" 404
"Abominable Snowman" 294-295, 323, 440
Adams, Don 430
Adams, Edie 158, 391, 395, 408
Adams, Skipper 284, 451
Adler, Richard 239, 301, 449
Adrian, Jack 236, 299, 344, 405
"After the Ball" 261
Afternoon 21-24, **22**, **23**, **24**, 31, **119**, 143, 218, 219, 229, 231, 232, 233
Afternoon with Inga 119, 232
"Ah-1, Ah-2, Ah-Sunset Strip" 475
Ahbez, Eden 348
Aikman, Bonnie 102
"Ain't a Hankerin'" 372, 529
"Ain't Nobody's Business But My Own" 296
Akst, Harry 295, 350, 453

Al Hirt's Fanfare 446
Alexander, Jeff 242
Alexander, Van 235, 294, 303, 414
Alfi and Harry 268, 397, 493
"Alfred in the Circus 461
"Alfred the Airsick Eagle" 272-273
Alfred, Roy 240
"All American Boy" 337, 396
Allen, Robert 510
Allen, Steve 58, 60-61, 65, 68, 76, 162, 179, 214, 245, 251-252, 260, 284, 285, 412, 531, 533
Allen, T. H. 273
Alley Singers, The 484, 485, 488-489, 513
Alley Singers: Side by Side, The 484
Allison, Fran 103, 125
Alstone, Alex 263
Altman, Arthur 372
Alvin and the Chipmunks 81, 266, 268, 319, 346, 387, 414, 423, 504
"Alvin's Harmonica" 346
"Always" 529
"Ambrose (Part Five)" 340, 363
America Song 54
Anderson, Leona 333, 419
Anderson, Leroy 326
Andrews Sisters, The 251, **251**, 368, 440
Andrews, Julie 281, 345, 442

Animal 5, 215
Ankers, Del 45, 134, **135**, 146, 157, 212
Ann, Tex 303, 450
"Any Old Iron" 216
"Anything You Can Do (I Can Do Better)" 291, 327, 456
"Are You Lonesome Tonight?" 486
Arlen, Harold 322, 333, 432, 536
Armstrong, Louis 248, 259, 295, 371, 407, 499, 500
Arnheim, Gus 250
Arnold, Eddy 330
Arnold, Paul 44, 54-55, **55, 56, 57, 58**, 62, **63**, 64, 67, **69**, 125, 229, 230, 271, 283, 285, 286, 534
Arodin, Sidney 259
Art and Paul 509
Arzonia, Joe 237
"As Time Goes By" 448, 480
Astaire, Fred 257-258, 311, 467
At the Drop of a Hat 486
"Atchoo (The Sneezing Record)" 261, 459
Atkins, Chet 153, 497
"Auctioneer, The" 529
Austin, Billy 347, 406
Austin, Gene 531
"Autumn in New York" 402
Averback, Hy 376
Axton, Mae 331, 427
Ayer, Nat D. 489
Ayres, Mitchell 241, 280, 290, 369, 397
Aznavour, Charles **129**, 215, 256

"Babbitt and the Bromide, The" 529
"Baby, It's Cold Outside" 78, 332, 433

Baciocco, Grant 77
Backus, Jim 376, 530
Bagby, Doc 495
Bagdasarian, Ross 81, 266, 268, 319, 324, 326, 346, 414, 451
Bailey, Pearl 245, 415
Bain, Babette 316, 417, 538
Baird, Bil and Cora 12, 17, 61
"Ballad of Roger Boom, The" 276-277
"Ballad of Sir Lancelot, The" 277
"Ballerina" 529
"Banana Boat (Day-O)" 300-301, 311, 383
"Band Played On, The" 273
Barbershop's Best 239
Bare, Bobby 337, 396
Barer, Marshall 466
Bargy, Roy 240
Barker, Jack 415
"Barnacle Bill the Sailor" 263, 342, 405
Barnett, Jack 240
Barnum, Pete 293, 302, 312, 327, 361, 363, 389, 406, 436, 448
Baskerville 210, 264
Bass, Sid 302
"Bathtub Admiral" 529
"Battle of Kookamonga, The" 78, 389
Baxter, Les 158, 253, 343, 357, 398, 419
"Be My Guest" 274
"Bear Chase, The" 495
"Beat Love at First Sight" 382
"Beautiful Day" 47
"Beautiful Dreamer" 341
Bee, Molly 255
"Beep Beep" 310

Belafonte, Harry 75, 95, 278, 287, 291, 301
Benet, Vicki 276
Bennett, Earl *see* Gas, Sir Frederick
Bennett, Roy C. 314, 415
Benny, Jack 82, 244, 247, 248, 269
Benson, Ada 435
Bentley, Jordan 419
Berlin, Irving 239-240, 257-258, 291, 327, 445, 456, 479, 483
Bernard, Felix 479
Berner, Sara 269
Bernice **47**, 47, 50, 70, 158, 195, 385, 399, 401, 407, 416, 441, 446, 447, 477, 481, 484, 488, 499, 502
Bernie Green with the Stereo Mad-Men 461
Bernstein, Leonard 419, 436
Bert & Ernie Sing-Along 353, 472
Bert and Ernie 213, 353, 472
Betti, Henri 330, 399
Bibo, Irving 288
"Big Bad John" 210
Big Bird 213
"Big Rock Candy Mountain" 421
Bikel, Theodore 408, 412
"Bill Bailey, Won't You Please Come Home" 261-262
"Bird in a Gilded Cage, A" 234
"Bird on My Head, The" 529
"Bird on Nellie's Hat, The" 253-254
Birkenfield, Diana 62
Bishop, Henry 395, 432
Blaine, Vivian 326
Blair, Hal 468
Blanc, Mel 75, 239, 265, 292, 299-300, 312, 320-321, 354, 373, 418, 422
Bleyer, Archie 272, 281, 284, 347, 379, 453, 503, 532

Bloch, Ray 236
Bloom, Marty 509
"Blow the Man Down" 529
Bob and Ray 81-82, 159, 413, 440, 474
Bob and Ray on a Platter 159, 440
Bob and Ray Public Radio Show, The 81
Bobo Newsom's Knothole Gang 108
Bolger, Ray 245, 281-282, 398
Bolin, Shannon 301, 449
Bonelli, Lou 72, **72**, 380
Bonfils, Kjeld 499
Bonne, Rose 254, 306
"Bonnie Wee Lassie" 454
"Book Was So Much Better Than the Picture, The" 269-270, 358
Booros, Harry 286
Borel-Clerc, Charles 262
"Bottle Imp, The" 529
"Bowery, The" 253
Braisted, Harry 274
Brand, Oscar 71, 78-79, 442, 446, 468-469, 472
Brandt, Carl E. 460, 475
Brandt, Eddie 294, 316, 371, 396, 402, 403, 460, 475
Brennan, Al *see* Garner, Mousie
Bresslaw, Bernard 343-344, 387
Breuer, Ernest 509
"Bring Us Together" 529
Brinkley, David 52, 121, 139, **142**, 143, 229, 230, 231, 464, 474, 482
"Brooklyn Baseball Fan, A" 364-365, 450, 468
Brooks, Jack 238, 316, 370, 417, 437, 538
Brooks, John 243
Brothers Four, The 497, 498

Brown, Earl 299, 329, 399, 512
Brown, Les 235, 303
Brown, Margaret Wise 466
Brown, Nacio Herb 158, 408
Brown, Sam 212
Bruns, George 287, 330, 338, 399, 510
Bryan, Vincent 239
"Bubble Gum" 321, 447
"Bubbles in the Wine" 391
Bublé, Michael 332
Buchanan, Jack 467
Buffalo Bills, The 239, 244, 297, 362, 405, 434, 439, 444, 448, 480, 489, 490, 493
"Bullwinkle's Corner (Tom, Tom the Piper's Son and Peter Piper)" 500
"Bumble-Ardy" 79
Burke, Johnny 436
Burke, Sonny 239
Burland, Sascha 504
Burnett, Carol 531
Burns, Jethro *see* Homer and Jethro
Burrello, Tony 74, 296, 333, 364, 439, 470
Burtson, Budd 372
Busch, Lou *see* Joe "Fingers" Carr
Butler, Daws 287, 293, 302, 327, 338, 361, 364, 376, 389, 391, 406, 510
"Button Up Your Overcoat" 529
"By the Light of the Silvery Moon" 255
"Bye Bye Blackbird" 434
Bygraves, Max 344

"C'est Si Bon" **150**, 151, 330, 399
Caesar, Sid 272
Cahn, Sammy 269, 274, 288, 317, 479

Calame, Bob 391
"Calico Pie" 277
Calloway, Cab 246
Campbell, Cowboy Joe 17
Campbell, Paul 287, 291
"Can't Stop Talking" 258
Candido, Candy 263, 342, 405
Cannon, Hughie 261
"Capital Ship, A" 529
Carling, Foster 329, 366, 419, 452
Carlisles, The 531
Carlton, Sam 261, 459
Carlyle, Russ 264
Carmichael, Hoagy 248, 259, 345, 410
Carney, Art 240, 268, 272, 305, 532, 533
"Carnival Song, The" 326
"Carol of the Bells" 319
Carr, Joe "Fingers" 254-255
Carrara-Rudolph, Leslie 222
Carroll, David 237
Carroll, Jimmy 272, 275
Carroll, Lewis 40, 386, 388, 496
Carson, Jenny Lou 361-362, 385
Carter, June 78, 332, 433
Carter, Lou 480
Carter, Stanley 274
Caruso, Dee 430
Case, Charley 446
Cates, George 284, 356, 449
Caudill, Carl 534
"Cecilia" 81, 324, 459
"Cement Mixer (Put-ti Put-ti)" 324, 422
Chapin, John 227, 371
Charioteers, The 236, 238, 241, 278, 299, 313, 341, 391, 403, 501
Charlap, Moose 444, 478
"Charles the Poet" 440

Charles, Ray 61-62, 280
Charles, Wolseley 288, 430
Chase, Lincoln 246
Cher 142
Cherry, Don 301
Chevalier, Maurice 262-263
"Chick, The" 349, 450
Chicken Liver **52**, 52-53, **53**, 144, 159, 220, 383, **384**, 509
Chico Hamilton Quintet, The 491
"Chinese Rock and Egg Roll" 450-451
"Chipmunk Song, The" 81, 319, 346, 414-415, 451
"Chloe" 189, 463
"Choosing a Career" 529
Christiné, Henri 263
"Christmas Chopsticks" 265
"Christmas Tree" 320, 416
Christopher, Milbourne 283
Christy, Edwin Pearce 279, 377, 460, 505
Cicchetti, Carl 310
Cinderella
Circle 4 Ranch 17-18, **18**
Cirone, Sylvia 162
"Clammy" 403
Clampett, Bob 75
Claps, Donald 310
Clare, Sidney 356
Clary, Robert 266
"Classical Audience" 530
Clifton, Tony *see* Kaufman, Andy
Clooney, Rosemary 59, 71, 81, 83, 308, 369, 372, 405, 537
"Close the Door" 247-248
Close, Del 168
Coben, Cy 236, 252, 261, 278, 289, 290, 299, 341, 358, 369, 378, 397, 403, 426, 429, 495

"Cocktails for Two" 427, 479
Cohn, Irving 484, 513
Cole, Buddy 265
Cole, Nat King 269, 348, 437
Coleman, Cy 487
Colin, Sid 343, 387
Collins, Al 382
Collins, Judy 254, 353
Colombo, Anthony 286
Colonna, Jerry 250, 266
Comden, Betty 241, 276, 326, 419, 436
Como, Perry 83, 240, 273, 280-281, 290, 348, 369, 397, 426
Comstock, Frank 311
"Concerto for Calliope" 530
Condos, Steve 326
Confederates, The 493
Confrey, Zez 344
Conniff, Ray 301, 530
Conried, Hans 358-359, 365, 374-375, 392
Cook, Barbara 362
Cook, Windy 282
Cookie Monster 213
Coon, Harry 370
"Coplas" 325-326
Corey, Jill 275, 533
Corley, Bob 289-290, 362, 449
"Corn Keeps A-Growin', The" 244
Coslow, Sam 80, 427, 479
Count, The 213
"Country's in the Very Best of Hands, The" 290
"Countryside, The" 74, 425, 434
"Couple of Swells, A" 257-258
Cowan, Stanley 367, 425
Coward, Noël 263
Cox, Wally 245-246, 335, 401, 506
"Crazy Mixed Up Song" 530

Crewe, Bob 289, 366
"Cricket Song, The" 281-282, 398
Cronkite, Walter 12
"Cruising Down the River" 530
"Cry Me a River" 61, 139, 266, 401
Culbertson, Bill 222
Curtis, Sonny 281

D'Andrea, Tom 356, 449
Dacre, Harry 234
"Daisy Bell (A Bicycle Built for Two)" 234
Dale, Alan 274
Daly, Thomas Augustine 488
"Dance of the Hours" 373
"Dance School" 530
"Dance with Me Henry" 530
"Dancing Chandelier" 276
Daniel, Jay 320, 416
"Dante's Inferno" 375
Darin, Bobby 248, 500
Darion, Joe 243
Dark Crystal, The 87
Davie, Bob 277
Davis, Bob 303
"Day I Read a Book, The" 240
Day, Dennis 244
Day, Doris 276
Day, Lazy Jim 496-497
De Luce, Virginia 266
De Paul, Gene 290, 293, 295, 324, 457
De Vol, Frank 276, 480
Dean, Jimmy 61, 78, 210-211, 246, 255, 270, 446, 485, 531
Dean, Ruth 27
"Dear John and Marsha Letter, A" 530
"Dearie" 530

Deep River Boys 236, 278
Degen, Carl **22**, 24, **56**, **57**, 227
Del Monico Four, The 234, 258, 261-262
"Delicious" 530
DellaVedova, Carla 4, 539
Delugg, Milton 268
Denoff, Sam 275-276
DeSylva, Bud 245
"Devil and the Farmer, The" 530
Diamonds, The 286
Dick Cavett Show, The 149, 365
Dietz, Howard 311, 467
"Dig-Dig-Dig Dig for Your Dinner" 249
Diggenhof, Albert 463
"Dinah" 295-296, 350, 453
Dinner Music for People Who Aren't Very Hungry 443
Dixon, Mort 350, 434, 459
"Dizzy Fingers" 344
"Do I Worry?" 367, 425
"Does Your Chewing Gum Lose Its Flavor on the Bedpost Overnight?" 509
"Dollar Down, A" 493-494
Dominguez, Alberto 290
"Don't Bug Me Baby" 530
"Don't Fence Me In" 238-239
"Don't Sing Along (On Top of Old Smokey)" 360-361, 395
"Don't Start Courtin' in a Hot Rod" 255-256
"Don't Sugar Me" 80, 411
"Don't Tickle Me" 530
Donaldson, Walter 405
Donegan, Lonnie 292, 336, 409, 509
"Donkey Tango" 236
Doran, Sharon 15

Dot and the Line, The 148
Dougherty, Dan 261, 459
"Doughnut Song, The" 260
Douglas, Lew 278
"Down by the Old Mill Stream" 310
"Down the Road Apiece" 246
Downs, Hugh 208
Dr. Bunsen Honeydew 215
"Dr. Geek" 242
Dr. Teeth 68, 142, 215, 312
Dragnet 285, 376, 377
"Dragnet Goes to Kindergarten" 284-285
Drake, Ervin 272
Draper, Rusty 237
"Dreamers' Bay" 282
Dresser, Paul 244
Dresslar, Len 370
Dreyer, Dave 324, 459
Driftwood, Jimmie 389
"Drummer and the Cook, The" 287
"Drums West" **147**, 491-492, **492**
Dubey, Matt 305, 330
Dubin, Al 439, 471
"Dufo (What a Crazy Guy)" 245-246, 335, 401, 506
Dunham, By 253
Durante, Jimmy 240-241, 252, 299, 339, 449, 466, 531
Durden, Tommy 331, 427
Dyer-Bennet, Richard 409-410

"Eating Goober Peas" 237
Ebb, Fred 247-248
Ecklund, Les 460, 475
Ed Sullivan Show, The 47, 149, 213, 236, 426
Edens, Roger 241
Edwards, Ad 274

Edwards, Barbara 345, 486
Edwards, Darlene *see* Stafford, Jo
Edwards, Gus 255
Edwards, Jonathan *see* Weston, Paul
Edwards, William 300, 342, 459
"Egghead" 275
"Eggs and Marrowbone" 409-410
Eiseman, Herbert 268, 397, 493
Eisenhower, President Dwight D. 84-85
"El Paso, Numero Dos" 443-444
"Elderly Man River" 293, 327, 389
Electric Mayhem, The 434
"Elements, The" 421
Elliot, Bob *see* Bob and Ray
Elliott, Don 504
Elliott, Jack 276
Elliott, Leonard 468
Elm City Four, The 257
"Eloise" 347, 453, 503
Elson, Katherine 28-29, 31
"Embraceable You" 530
"Empty Saddles" 239
Endor, Chick 500
Englund, Ernie 274, 285, 360
"Enjoy Yourself" 530
Enrohtwah 348
"Erbert" 275-276
Erickson, Bonnie 218, 540
"Etiquette Blues" 235, 294, 414
Eubank, Bill 103
Evans, Dale 239
Evans, Ray 403

Faber, Billy 302
Fabray, Nanette 467
"Face the Funnies" 302, 361, 406
Fain, Sammy 299, 339, 449
Faith, Percy 369

Falk, Karen 2, 4
Fantastic Miss Piggy Show, The 142
Farnum, Dennis 500
Farrar, Walton 248, 345, 410
Fascinato, Jack 260-261, 284, 296
Faye, Joey 261, 459
Feaster, Carl 300, 342, 459
Feaster, Claude 300, 342, 459
Feliciano, José 254
Feller, Sid 240, 305
"Festival of Magic" 283
Fine, Sylvia 265, 269, 279, 283, 286, 328, 360, 371, 407, 427
Fisby 46-47, 406, 412, 413
"Fish" 333
Fisher, Fred 435
Fisher, Marv 242, 277, 320, 418
Fisher, Toni 483
"Fit as a Fiddle" 530
Fitzgerald, Ella 281, 294, 387
"Five Pennies Saints (When the Saints Go Marching In), The" 371, 407
"Five Pound Box of Money" 415
Flanders and Swann 389, 399, 486
Flanders, Michael 389, 399, 486
"Flattery" 444-445
Fletcher Peck Trio 238, 343
Fletcher Rabbit 106
Fletcher, Dusty 238, 313, 391
Flick, Bob 497
"Flight of the Bumblebee" 442-443
Floyd 215
"Flying Home" 510
"Flying Saucer" 374-375
Fogel, Alfie 243
Foley, Dick 497
Footlight Theater 43, 44, 55, **55**, **57**, 62, 229, 271

Foray, June 302, 335, 361, 364, 376, 406, 444
Ford, Joan 326
Ford, Tennessee Ernie 255-256, 260, 284, 296, 532, 533
"Forever Ambrose" 340, 363
"Formula for Love" 499-500
Forrester, Frank 380, 421, 509
Forsyth, Bruce 485
Fort, Hank 296
Foster, Phil 350-351, 364-365, 450, 459, 468, 531
Foster, Stephen 336, 438
"Fountain in the Park, The" 262, 446
Four Tophatters, The 281, 532
"Four-Legged Friend, A" 238-239, 370, 437
Fozzie Bear 216, 245, 277, 313, 374, 485
Freberg, Stan 60, 61, 71, 74, 75-77, **76**, 116-117, 151, 157-158, 249-250, 253, 260, 282-283, 287, 292, 293, 294-295, 300-301, 302, 303, 305, 311, 312, 314, 315, 316, 319, 323, 327, 330, 331, 335, 336-338, 342, 343, 357, 361, 363, 364, 376, 383, 389, 391-392, 398, 399, 404, 406, 409, 415, 417, 419, 422, 423, 427, 432, 436, 438, 440, 444, 447, 448, 457, 459, 460, 472, 483, 485, 499, 510, 530, 531, 538
Fred Katz Group 309, 321, 338, 359, 422, 431, 438, 447, 473, 479
Freed, Arthur 158, 241, 250, 408
Freed, Ralph 235, 299, 339, 449
Freeman, Stan 238, 343
Frees, Paul 145, 269, 391, 400, 402, 403, 471, 500

Frisch, Al 240
"Frog Went a-Courtin'" 497
"Frogg" 497
"Frozen Logger, The" 470
"Fun with Real Audio" 143
Fuzzy Peach Pie and Other Lunacies 468

"G'wan Home, Your Mudder's Callin'" 299, 339, 449
Gade, Jacob 351, 424
Gaillard, Slim 324, 422
Gallop, Sammy 245
Gannaway, Al 248, 345, 410
Gardner, Dave 507
Gardner, Dick 294, 371
Garland, Judy 234, 257-258
Garner, Mousie 441, 484, 485, 488-489, 513
Garroway, Dave 208, 425, 438
Garson, Mort 376
Gas, Sir Frederick 243, 355, 441, 456
Gaunt, Percy 253
Geller, Harvey 498
"General's Horse, The" 530
"George Washington, Abraham Lincoln, Ulysses S. Robert E. Lee" 237
George, Don 260, 272, 305, 406
Gershwin, George 284, 379
Gershwin, Ira 284, 300, 379
Gertz, Linda 340
Gibbons, Jim 230
Gibbs, Georgia 21, 233
Gibson, Bob 154-155, 156, 161, 206, 433, 437, 439, 440, 444, 447, 464, 510, 515
Gifford, Gene 302
Gilbert and Sullivan 420-421

Gilbert, Fred 258
Gilbert, L. Wolfe 443
Gilbert, Mary M. Hadler 266
Gilbert, Ronnie 475
Gilbert, V. C. 266
Gill, Dorothy 296
Gill, Geula 412
Gill, Vince 332
Gillespie, Dizzy 426
Gilroy, John 442
Gimbel, Norman 444
Gimby, Bobby 281, 398
"Girl with the Cigarette Cough, The" 530
"Git Up Off 'n the Floor, Hannah! (A Bitter New Year's Eve)" 329, 419
Give 'Im the Hook! Songs That Killed Vaudeville 79, 469
Glazer, Tom 250, 291, 306, 353, 401
Gleason, Jackie 135
"Glow Worm" 4, **153**, 153, 166, 215, 497
"Gnu, A" 399
"Go Go Pogo" 541
"Go Tell Your Mother" 530
"God Rest Ye Merry Gentlemen" 320
Godfrey, Arthur 61
Goehr, Rudolph 236
Goelz, Dave 215
Goetz, E. Ray 442
Gohman, Don 272
"Going on a Hike" 356, 449
Gold, Louise 254
"Golden Goose is Dead, The" 530
Golly, Jack 316, 396
"Gone" 420
Good Morning 61

Good Morning America 312-313
"Good Ol' Mountain Dew" 270, 342, 409
"Good Old 149" 300, 343
"Good Old Days, The" 349-350, 402
"Good Peanuts" 471-472
"Goodbye My Lover, Goodbye" 273
Goodfellow, Joe 25, 110
Gooding, Cynthia 408
"Goodness Gracious Me" 495-496
"Goodnight Ladies" 279, 377, 460, 505
"Goofus" 254-255
Gordon, Irving 279, 357
Gordon, Mack 249
"Gorilla Walk, The" 504
Gormé, Eydie 436, 444-445
"Gotta Get to Your House" 81, 284, 451
"Gotta Have Rain" 530
"Gotta Have Something in the Bank Frank" 530
Goulding, Ray *see* Bob and Ray
Grade, Lew 214
Graham, Ronny 266, 324-325, 328, 421-422, 427, 430
Grant, John 498
Gray, William B. 259
Grayco, Helen 294, 361, 371
Grayson, Carl 479
Grean, Charles 236, 244, 250, 261, 278, 291, 299, 306, 341, 353, 385, 401, 403, 426, 477
"Great Debate, The" 195-205, **196, 198, 200, 202, 204,** 467
"Great Pretender, The" 60, 337-338, 447
Great Santa Claus Switch, The 240
"Green Christmas" 319

"Green Door" 277
Green, Adolph 241, 276, 326, 419, 436
Green, Bernard 461, 530
Green, Johnny 265, 366, 452
Greenberg, Adrian *see* Adrian, Jack
Greene, Mort 240
"Green-Eyed Dragon, The" 288-289, 430
"Greensleeves" 498
Grey, Clifford 489
Griffith, Andy 272, 289, 290, 301, 345, 366, 401, 414, 486, 512, 533
Grossman, Larry 62, 216
Grover 150, 213, 353
Grubb, Gayle 235, 294, 414
Grump 149
Guard, Dave 325
Gurnee, Hal 61
Gussin, David 320, 418
"Guy with the Voodoo!, The" 238, 343

Hackett, Buddy 274, 450-451
Hagman, Larry 445
Hains, Jack 299, 354
Haley, Ed 262, 446
"Hallelujah, I'm a Bum" 530
Hamblen, Stuart 291
Hamilton, Arthur 266, 401
Hamilton, Chico 491-492
Hammerlee, Patricia 266
Hammerstein II, Oscar 293, 327, 389, 480
Handman, Lou 486
"Handout Song (There's a Handout on Panhandle Hill), The" 257
Hanemann, Felix 255, 414

Hank and Frank **51**, 51-52, **91**, 151, 157, 188-189, **251**, 408, 409, 411, 461, 464-465, 502
Hanley, James F. 336, 396
Hansel and Gretel 91, **92**
Happiness Boys, The 235
"Happy Days Are Here Again" 434, 530
Harbach, William 59, 61
Hare, Ernest *see* Happiness Boys, The
"Harmony" 436-437
Harold, William 254
Harp, Kenneth 276
Harris, Charles K. 261
Harris, Phil 36, 82, 236, 237, 239-240, 243, 244, 245, 247, 248, 249, 250, 252, 253, 254, 257, 259, 289, 291, 306, 336, 354, 358, 361-362, 366, 378, 385, 396, 401, 530, 532, 533
Harrison, Bernie 26-27, 55, 60, 148, 283
Harry the Hipster **40**, 40-41, **41**, **45**, 50, 53, 68, 69-70, 98, 101, 112-113, 115, 116, 130, 137, 139, 142, 144, 145, 148-150, 185-188, 191, 192-195, 206-207, 210, 211, 215, 217, **220**, 220, 222, 283, 296, 307, 308, 309, 313, 314, 315-317, 324, 324-325, 327, 328, 332, 333, 334, 335, 337, 339, 341, 346, 348-349, 350, 351, 352, 354, 355, 356, 359, 363, 365, 367, 368, 369, 370, 371, 372, 374, 375, 376, 377, 378-379, 380, 381-382, 384, 385, 386, 387, 388, 389, 393-394, 395-397, 398, 399, 401, 402, 404-405, 406, 407, 408, 409, 411, 412, 413-414, 415, 416, 417, 418, 419, 420, 421-422, 424, 425-426, 427, 428-429, 432, 433, 434-435, 436, 437, 438, 439, 440, 441, 442, 445, 446, 448, 450, 451, 453, 454-456, 457-459, 461, 462, 466, 468, 471, 472, 473, 474, 475, 476, 477-478, 480, 481, 482-484, 485-486, 487, 489-490, 491-492, 493, 494, 497, 498, 499, 501, 502, 503, 504, 505, 508-509, 511, 513, 515, 518-519, 520-521, 525, 526-527, 528, 536, 541
Hart, Lorenz 294, 387
Hartmann, Maurie 302
"Hat I Got for Christmas Is Too Beeg, The" 320-321, 418
Hatch, Earl 393
Hawes, Bess 280, 322, 388
Hayes, Clancy 237
Hayes, Peter Lind 292, 357, 455, 531
Haynes, Homer *see* Homer and Jethro
Hazlewood, Lee 367
"Hazy Yon, The" 410
"He's a Tramp" 239
"He's His Own Grandpa" 530
Healy, Mary 531
"Heartbreak Hotel" 74, 331, 427, 499
Heath, Hy 259
Heatherton, Joey 273
Heatherton, Ray 272-273
Hector 49, 284, 379
Heider, Fred 265
Heidt, Horace 323, 395, 456
Helian, Jacques 263
Hemion, Dwight 59, 61, 62
Henderson, Luther 416
Henderson, Ray 350, 434, 459

Hendry, Hubie 257
Henning, Doug 288
Hensley, Harold 303, 450
Henson, Betty **80**
Henson, Brian 214, 222-223
Henson, Cheryl 27, 90, 160, 214
Henson, Heather 214
Henson, Jane xii, 3, 4, 5, 16, 20-21, 23, **23**, 24-25, 26, 27-28, **28**, 29-30, 31, **33**, 33-34, 35, 39, **41**, 43, 44-45, 47, 48, 51, 52, **53**, 55, **57**, **58**, 59-60, 61, 65, **66**, 66, 67, 68, **69**, 70, 71-73, **72**, 75-76, 84, 85, 86, 87, **87**, 89, **90**, 90, **91**, 92, 93, **94**, 94, 95-98, **97**, **98**, 99, **100**, 101, **101**, 102, 103-106, **104**, **106**, 108, 110, 116, 118, 119, **120**, 120, **121**, 121, **122**, 122, **123**, **126**, 126, 130-131, 132, 133, **134**, 134, **135**, 136, 137, 139, 140, 142, 143, 146, 160, 161, 163, 164, **165**, 166, **167**, 184, 195, 207, 208, 210, 213, 214, 216, 217, 218, **218**, 219, 223, 227, 229, 230, 231, 233, 234, 245, 371, 377, 416, 446, 456, 534, **535**
Henson, Jim xi-xii, xiii, **xiii**, 1-7, 11-14, 15-18, **19**, 20-21, 23-27, **28**, 29-30, **29**, 31, 32-34, **33**, 35, 36-38, 39-41, 42, 43, 45, **46**, 47, 48, 49, 52, **56**, **57**, **58**, 59-60, 61-62, 64-65, 66-68, **66**, **69**, 70, 71-74, 75, 76, 77, 78, 79-80, **80**, 81, 82, 83, 84-94, **85**, 95-107, **97**, **98**, **100**, **101**, **102**, **104**, **106**, 108, 110, 113, 116, 118, 120-121, **121**, 122, **123**, 124, 125-126, **126**, 128, 130, 131, 132-133, **134**, 134, **135**, 135-136, 137-140, **140**, 141, 142, 143, 145-148, **147**, 149, 150, 151-152, 155, **156**, 160-161, 162, 163, 164, 165, **165**, 166, **167**, 168, **169**, **170**, 170, 171, 172, **172**, 173, 184, 188, 191, 195, 206, 207, 208, 210-211, 212, 213-214, 215, 216-218, 220, 222-223, 227, 228, 229, 230, 231, 233, 234, 238, 240, 244, 245, 257, 259, 260, 262, 271, 273, 278, 280, 282, 290, 292, 296, 298, 303, 304, 309, 318, 321, 338-339, 344, 345, 352, 354, 365, 371, 374, 377, 381, 383, 385, 388, **390**, 391, 392, 400, 419, 424-425, 426-427, 429, 433, 434, 435, 437, 450, 451, 454, 456, 464, 474, 479, 482, 483, 485, 488, 491-492, **492**, 493, 506, 507, **507**, **508**, 510, 512, **513**, 514, 518, 521-522, 524-525, 529, 534, **535**
Henson, John 214
Henson, Lisa Marie 101, **101**, 102-103, 106, 120, **121**, 160-161, 195, 214, 231, 456
Henson, Paul 37, **80**
Herman Finnius Madcliffe *see* Professor Orin E. Madcliffe
Herman Horne on Hi-Fi 312, 363, 436, 448
"Hernando's Hideaway" 530
Herpin, Henri 391, 400
Herron, Joel 355, 358, 365, 374, 403
Hertz, Fred 355, 358, 365, 374, 403
"Hey There" 530
"Hey! Mister Barber" 530
"Hey, Big Brain" 530

"Hey, Boy! Hey, Girl!" 366
"Hey, Look Me Over!" 487
Heyman, Edward 366, 452
Hibbert, Geoffrey 345, 413
Hill, Billy 239
Hilliard, Bob 276-277, 278, 307, 376, 458
Hilliard, Jerry 356, 449
Hills, William H. 252
Hi-Lo's, The 311-312
"His Rocking Horse Ran Away" 530
Hoffman, Al 242, 275, 379
Hogan's Heroes 75, 266
"Hold 'em Joe" 278
Holder, Geoffrey 529
"Hole in My Soul" 504
Hollywood Palace, The 61
Holmes, LeRoy 275, 277
Holt, David 493
Holt, Will 280, 322, 388, 533
"Home Sweet Home" 432-433
Homer and Jethro 78, 264, 266-267, 270, 279, 297-298, 308, 332, 357, 360-361, 389, 395, 416, 420, 429, 433, 443-444, 447, 460, 468, 478, 486, 495
Honey Dreamers, The 303
"Honey-Earthers, The" 530
Honeymooners, The 135, 240
Hood, Anne Marie 95
Hooper, Larry 277, 278, 307, 458
Hope, Bob 62, **63**, 238-239, 250, 266, 285, 370, 372, 437
Hornez, Andre 330, 399
"Horse Named Bill" **154**, 154-155, 156, 440
"Hot Dog Polka" 370
Houdini, Wilmoth 281
"House, The" 281

Houston, Cisco 493
"How Come My Dog Don't Bark" 530
"How Deep Is the Ocean?" 483
"How Do'ye Do and Shake Hands" 252, 289, 358, 378
"How High the Fidelity" 469
Howdy Doody 104, 124
Howell, Don 238, 313, 391
Hoyt, Charles H. 253
Huckleberry Hound for President 193-194, 504
Huddleston, Floyd 247, 249, 268, 397, 493
Hugo and Luigi 379-380
"Hunger Is From" 49, **156**, 157, 338, 422
"Hunting Song, The" 308, 386
Huntley, Chet 52, 122, **142**, 143, 230, 464, 474, 482
Huntley-Brinkley Report, The 121, 139, **142**, 143, 229, 230, 231
Hupfeld, Herman 448, 480
Husky, Ferlin 420
Hutton, Betty 250, 252, 256, 258, 289, 290, 291, 306, 358, 369, 378, 397, 401

"I Ain't Gonna Give Nobody None O' This Jelly Roll" 248
"I Am the Very Model of a Modern Major-General" 421
"I Can't Carry a Tune" 253
"I Come for to Sing" 206, 437, 515
"I Cried for You" 250
"I Dreamed" 278-279
"I Dream of Jeannie" 336
"I Found My Mamma" 369
"I Got a Wife" 334

"I Got the Shiniest Mouth in Town" 303
"I Just Goofed" 274-275, 285-286, 360
"I Keep Her Picture Hanging Upside Down" 393
"I Know an Old Lady" 254, 306
"I Like It, I Like It" 531
"I Like People (The Friendly Song)" 466
"I Like Your Kind of Love" 531
"I Love Me (I'm Wild About Myself)" 299-300, 354, 355
"I Love Paris" 489
"I Love Your Pizza" 495
"I Made a Fool of Myself Over John Foster Dulles" 531
"I Need a Vacation" 376
"I Never Harmed an Onion" 531
"I Only Have Eyes for You" 471
"I Said My Pajamas (And Put on My Prayers)" 531
"I Saw Esau" 531
"I Search for Golden Adventure (In My Seven Leaky Boots)" 460
"I Tant Wait Till Quithmuth" 265
"I Went to Your Wedding" 243, 355, 456
"I Wish I Was a Car" 531
"I Won't Dance" 256
"I Won't Go Hunting with You Jake (But, I'll Go Chasin' Wimmin)" 531
"I Wonder When I Shall Be Married" 471
"I'd Climb the Highest Mountain" 531
"I'll Pay as I Go" 242
I'll Remember 235
"I'm a Little Busybody" 250
"I'm a Lonely Little Petunia (in an Onion Patch)" **302**, 302
"I'm Five" 357, 424
"I'm Not the Braggin' Kind" 531
"I'm Popeye the Sailor Man" 282
"I've Got a Wife" 531
"I've Got My Love to Keep Me Warm" 479
"I've Got You Under My Skin" 71, **157**, 157-158, 253, 351, 357, 398, 455
"I've Gotta Crow" 478
"I've Grown Accustomed to Your Face" 59-60, 71, 83, 103, 125, 214, 222, 308, 405, 537
Icky Gunk **49**, 49, 51, 157, 220, 379, 380, 384, 386, 387, 392, 393, 395, 398, 404, 411, 415, 420, 431, 439, 443, 452, 461, 471, 493, 502, 503, 512, 523, 536
"If 'n" 330
"If You Felt Like I Did When We Said Goodbye" 488-489
"If You Were the Only Girl in the World" 489
Improvisations to Music 352, 386
In Our Town 232, 233, 305
"Inchworm" 82, 128, **129**, 215, 256, 307, 377, 410, 438
"Income Tax" 289-290, 362, 449
Ingle, Red 77, 318, 329, 348, 366, 419, 431, 452, 463, 501
Ink Spots, The 367, 425
"Inka Dinka Doo" 531
"Interview with Shorty Petterstein" 270-271, 373
"Invisible Man, The" 355, 403
Irwin, Joe 13, 15, 30, 68, 86, 87-88, **88**, 98, 121, 133, 150, 168, **170**, 540

Irwin, Roy 343, 387
"Is Zat You, Myrtle" 531
"It's a Quiet Town" 251, **251**, 368, 440
"It's a Sin to Tell a Lie" 246
"It's Magic" 288, 317
"It's Never Too Late to Fall in Love" 345, 413
"Itsy Bitsy Teenie Weenie Yellow Polka Dot Bikini" 304, 349
Ives, Burl 247, 260, 352-353, 408, 421, 454, 532
"Ivy League" 284

"Jabberwocky" 388
Jack and Jim 532
"Jack and the Beanstalk (Bebop's Fable)" 251-252
Jack Benny's Quartet *see* Sportsmen, The
Jacobs, Dick 274, 279, 364, 412, 413, 450
Jacobs, Henry 270-271, 373
Jacobson, Sidney 363
"Jalousie" 351, 424
Jamblan 391, 400
Jameson, Joyce 460
Janney, Leon 236
"Java" 215
"Java Jive" 531
Jeff Alexander Quartet 242
Jim Henson Hour, The 374
Jimmy Dean Show, The 61, 78, 210-211, 246, 255, 270, 446, 485
Jimmy Joyce Singers, The 331
"Jingle Bells" 319, 417, 481
"John Henry" 291
Johnson, Betty 278-279
Johnson, Lynn 460

Johnston, Arthur 427, 479
Jones, Biff 507
Jones, Billy *see* Happiness Boys, The
Jones, Brian Jay 21, 23, 70, 94, 95, 122, 213, 228
Jones, Chuck 148
Jones, Spike 71, 77, 145, 189, 243, 255, 264, 269, 276, 282, 287-288, 294, 316, 318, 355, 360, 361, 371, 373, 391, 396, 400, 402, 403, 414, 441-442, 443, 456, 460, 463, 469, 471, 475, 479-480, 484, 542
Jordan, Louis 281, 419
Joy Boys, The 72
Joyce, Jimmy 331, 388
"Jubilation T. Cornpone" 293, 324, 457
Jud Conlon Choir 269
Jud Conlon Singers 269, 457
Juhl, Jerry xii, **xiii**, 3, 152, 161-166, **165**, **168**, 168, **169**, **170**, 170, 172, 208, 212, 213, 214, 227, 507, **507**, 509, 512, **513**, 514-515
Julie on Sesame Street 281
"June in January" 479
Jung, Chick 437, 515
Junior Morning Show, The 12, 13-14, 17, 18
Jurist, Irma 468
"Just a Bum (Ma Pomme)" 262
Juster, Norton 148

Kahn, Gus 254, 405
Kamano, Johnny 302
Kaplan, Dave 235
Karin, Fia 407, 411, 424
Karr, Harold 305, 330
Katz, Fred 309, 321, 338, 359, 422, 431, 438, 447, 473, 479

Katz, William 267
Kaufman, Andy 142
Kaye, Barry 286
Kaye, Danny 64, 82, 128, 129, 215, 241, 251, 252, 256, 257, 263, 264-265, 267, 269, 279, 283, 286, 295-296, 300, 307, 313, 319, 328, 343, 349, 350, 357, 360, 368, 371, 377, 380, 407, 410, 415, 420, 423, 424, 427, 440, 453, 457, 490, 529, 530
Kaye, Stubby 290, 293, 324, 457
"Keep Them Cold Icy Fingers Off of Me" 531
Keep U.S. Beautiful 487
Kelly, Gene 158, 249
Kelly, Red 83, 506
Kelly, Walt 36, 80, **80**, 194, 407-408, 410, 411, 424, 465
Kennedy, Jacqueline 93
Kennedy, John F. 195, 197, 467, 474, 502
Kenney, Ed 416
Kenton Live from the Las Vegas Tropicana 83, 506
Kenton, Stan 83, 506
Kermeena 38, **39**, 59, 71, 83, 139, 142, 214, 266, 308, **353**, 418, 453, 454-455, 503, 536
Kermit xii-xiii, 30, 34, **36**, 36-40, **38**, **39**, 42-43, 45, **45**, 46, 48, **56**, **57**, **58**, 59, 68-69, **68**, **69**, 70, 77, 80, **87**, **97**, 103, 106, **109**, 111-112, 115, 125, 129, **129**, 136-137, 138, **138**, 142, 143, 144, 148-149, **149**, 150, 151, **153**, 153, **154**, 154, 157, **159**, 159, 173, 175, 177, 179, 181, 183, 184, 186, 187, 188-190, 191-195, 197, 199, 201, 203, 205-207, 210, 211, 212, 213, 215, 217, 218, **220**, 220, 222, **251**, 260, 262, 266, 271, 283, 286, 288, 291, 296, 298, 298, 306, 307, 308, 309, 310, 311, 313, 317, 318, 319, 321-322, 325, 329, 329-330, 332, 333, 343, 344, 352, 357, 358, 365, 370-371, 378-379, 380-381, 382, 383, 384-385, 387, 388, 389, 390, 392, 393-394, 395-396, 397, **397**, 398, 399-400, 401, 404, 406, 412-413, 415, 417, 419-420, 421, 422, 424, 425, 426, 428, 429, 430, 431, 432, 434-436, 437, 438-439, 441, 442, 446, 448-449, 453-454, 459, 460, 461-462, 463, 464-465, 466, 467-468, 470, 471, 472, 473, 474, 475, 476, 477, 478, 481, 482-483, 485, 487, 488, 489-490, 491-492, 493, 494-495, 496, 497, 498, 499, 501, 503, 505, 506, 509, 511, 512, 514, 515, 516, 517, 518, 519-520, 521, 524, 525, 526, 527, **535**, 541
Kern, Jerome 293, 327, 389, 480
Kerr, Walter and Jean 326
Keyes, James 300, 342, 459
"Kids on the Corner, The" 350, 459
"King of Eight, The" 303
King Sisters, The 275
King, Wayne 254
"King's New Clothes, The" 267, 368, 457
Kingdom of Eddie Lawrence, The 458
Kingston Trio, The 95, 325-326
Kirby Stone Four, The 284, 379
Kirkland, Mike 497
Kitt, Eartha 151

Klavan, Eugene 275-276
Klein, Lew 235
Klein, Paul 247
Kovach, Jim 14, 15
Kovacs, Ernie 158, 333, 395
Kraft Music Hall 426
Kretzmer, Herbert 495-496
Kukla, Fran and Ollie 103, 124, 125, 260
Kurdle, Thomas J. 108
Kurdle, Tom 108, 110, 112, 114, 116, 188, 207, 518, 520-521, 528

"La Plume de Ma Tante" 379-380
Labyrinth 238, 352
Laine, Cleo 446
Laine, Frankie 488, 529, 531
Lamb, Arthur J. 234, 253
Lane, Burton 235
Lane, Ken 80
Lange, Johnny 259
Lasky, Paul S. 264
"Last Time I Saw Paris, The" 480
Latshaw, George 104
Laurent, Lawrence 12, 25, 27, 54, 99, 207
Laurie, Linda *see* Gertz, Linda
Lawrence, Eddie 252, 315, 341-342, 349-350, 402, 409, 452, 458, 531, 532, 533
Lawrence, Steve 279-280, 436-437, 444-445
"Lay Somethin' on the Bar (Besides Your Elbows)" 347, 406
Lay, Dilys 345, 413
"Lazy Jim Day's News" 496-497
"Lazy River" 259
"Leather-Winged Bat" 352-353
LeBaron, Eddie 110-111

Lee and Paul 349, 450
Lee, Alfred 287, 360, 414
Lee, Bill 320, 416
Lee, David 495
Lee, Peggy 71, 239, 455
Leeds, Milton 290
Leeds, Peter 292, 300, 302, 311, 336, 361, 383, 406, 409
"Leetla Giorgio Washeenton (Little George Washington)" 488
Lehrer, Tom 308, 386, 421
Leigh, Carolyn 478, 487
Leighton Bros. 273
Leithner, Frank 443
"Lemming" 531
Lemon Sisters, The 391
Leonard, Jack E. 530
Lerner, Alan Jay 308, 405, 537
Lerner, Sammy 244, 282
Les Paul and Mary Ford Show, The 31
"Let it Snow! Let it Snow! Let it Snow!" 479
"Let Me Call You Sweetheart" 458
"Let Me In" 318, 431, 501
"Let's Go Fishin'" 488, 531
Letterman, David 61
Lettermen, The 530
Leven, Mel 269, 358
Levene, Gus 372, 479
Levine, Bill 430
Lewis, Jerry 77, 242, 249, 250, 253, 269-270, 274, 311, 347, 358, 393, 406, 531
Lewis, Patti and Jerry 242
Lewis, Sam M. 295, 350, 453
Leybourne, George 287, 360, 414
Leyden, Norman 247, 260
"Lida Rose" 362

Liebert, Billy 391
Life Can Be Miserable 429
"Life Gits Tee-Jus, Don't It?" 292, 357, 455
"Lil' Darlin'" 531
Limbo 166, **167**
Limeliters, The 493-494, 495
Lincke, Paul 497
"Lines Upon a Tranquil Brow" 410, 465
Link Hogthrob 444
Lippman, Sidney 269
"Listen All You Bachelors" 531
"Listen to the Gooney Bird" 270, 478
Liszt, Franz 361
"Little Beauty, A" 268
"Little Blue Riding Hood" 531
"Little Brass Band" 81, 326
"Little Darlin'" 531
"Little Fiddle (Symphony for Unstrung Tongue), The" 265
"Little Hood Riding Red" 531
"Little Man You've Had a Busy Day" 242
Livingston, Alan 292, 373
Livingston, Jay 403
"Lo, Hear the Gentle Lark" 395
Locklear, Heather 262
Locklin, Hank 468
Loden, Dan 112
Loesser, Frank 78, 82, 245, 256, 256, 258, 267, 272, 307, 332, 349, 368, 377, 391, 401, 410, 418, 423, 433, 457
Loewe, Frederick 308, 405, 537
Lomax, Alan 277
Lombardo, Carmen 241
Lombardo, Guy 241, 376

London, Julie 83, 266, 401
"Lone Psychiatrist, The" 364
Longley, Ed 16, 20
Lonnie Donegan and His Skiffle Group 292, 509
"Looking at Numbers" 309, 431, 438
Loren, Sophia 495-496
"Louise" 391
"Love Poems: To the Lovely Juanita Beasley" 414
"Love Poems: Togetherness" 345, 486
Lowe, Jim 247, 277, 530
Lubbock Lou and His Jughuggers 156
"Lucky Pierre" 266
"Lullaby of Bird Dog" 297-298, 308
Luther, Frank 263, 342, 405
Lyman, Abe 250

"M.T.A. (The Boston Subway Song)" 280, 322, 388
"Ma Says, Pa Says" 496
MacDonald, Ballard 336, 396
"Mad Dogs and Englishmen" 263-264
Madden, Edward 255
"Maggie" 315, 432
Maggio, Jack 21
Magoon, Jr., Eaton 416
"Mahna Mahna" 215
Mahoney, Will 299, 354
"Make Yourself Comfortable" 531
"Maladjusted Jester, The" 279, 283, 286, 360
"Mama from the Train (Throw Mama Down the Stairs Her Hat of Blue)" 279, 357
"Man on the Flying Trapeze, The" 287-288, 360, 414

"Man Who Broke the Bank at Monte Carlo, The" 258
Man, The 163
Mancini, Henry 325, 395, 408, 452
Mann, Herbie 510
Manning, Dick 275, 379
Manson, Eddy 369
"Many Harry Returns" 424
Marais and Miranda 463, 471, 496
Marais, Josef *see* Marais and Miranda
March, Hal 356
"Marian the Librarian" 531
Marion, Jr., George 301
Mark IV, The 334, 375
Marks, Franklin 239, 253
Marks, Sammy 302
Martin, Dean 80, 242, 270, 347, 479
Martin, Mary 445, 478
Martin, Skip 254, 306
Martin, Tony 250, 252, 289, 291, 306, 358, 378, 401, 532
"Martins and the Coys, The" 531
Marvin Suggs and his Muppaphone 81
"Mary Had a Little Lamb" 181, 369, 482
Mascari, Edward 334, 375
Mason, John 238, 313, 391
"Matador, The" 374, 440
Matthews, Gerry 430
May, Billy 249-250, 260, 289, 292, 300, 305, 311, 312, 314, 316, 335, 336, 337, 342, 345, 364, 366, 373, 383, 391, 404, 406, 414, 415, 417, 422, 423, 438, 444, 447, 457, 459, 486, 538
May, Elaine 351-352, 386, 424
Mayhew, Billy 246

McAdory, Patrick 267, 447
McConnell, George 282
McGarry, Mac 21
McGrath, Bob 511
McHugh, Jimmy 256
McIntyre, Mark 268, 282, 397, 493
McKenzie, Pat 210
McKinley, Ray 243, 246, 302
McLollie, Oscar 366
McRae, Floyd F. 300, 342, 459
McVea, Jack 238, 313, 391
McWain, Wes 340
Meachum, Roy 12, 14
"Meet Me in St. Louis" 234
Meet Roy Meachum 12
"Meet the Johnson Boys" 474-475
Mel Clement Quartet 22
Mellomen, The *see* Pound Hounds, The
"Memories Are Made of This" 531
Mercer, Johnny 248, 250, 290, 293, 295, 322, 324, 333, 432, 437, 457, 497, 500, 536
Merman, Ethel 291, 327, 330, 445-446, 456
Merrill, Bob 260, 318, 381, 431
Merry Mutes, The 77
"Merry Old Philosopher, The" 342, 531
Meyer, Chuck 507
Middleton, Ray 291, 327, 456
Mike Douglas Show, The 149, 152, 312, 510
"Military Love Song" 531
Miller, Bob 235
Miller, Mitch 466, 510, 511
Mills, Alan 254, 306
Mills, Kerry 234
"Minnie the Mermaid" 245

"Miss Cone" 4, **146**, 146-148, 479
Miss Piggy 5, 142, 239, 254, 288, 332, 349, 374, 444
"Miss Piggy's Hollywood" 374
"Mobile" 493
"Moe Zart's Turkey Trot" 329
Moldy Hay **42**, 42-43, 61, 113-114, 151, 186, 189, 190, 211, **298**, 305, 306, 307, 311, 312, 314, 315, 318, 319, 325, 330, 340, 348, 352, 354, 365, 367, 368, 369, 372, 373, 375, 381, 382, 383, 385, 387, 389, 390, 395, 407, 411, 413-414, 422, 424, 425, 428, 435, 445, 463, 465, 468, 471, 473, 475, 476, 481, 499, 502, 506, 525, 537
Mommy, Gimme a Drinka Water 357
Monath, Norman 407, 410, 411, 424, 465
"Money" 312-313, 422
"Money Is King" 437
Monroe, Vaughn 533
Monster Rally 354, 355, 358-359, 365, 374-375, 392, 532, 533
Monty Python 21
Moore, Clement 316
Moore, Marvin 277, 278
Morgan, Freddy 316, 361, 396, 441, 484, 485, 488-489, 513
Morgan, Jaye P. 83, 142, 233-234, 330
Morning Show, The 12, 17
"Morris" 239
Morris, Howard 272
"Moses Supposes" 241
Most, Sam 510
"Mostly Ghostly" 365
"Mrs. Murphy's Chowder" 468-469

"Mule Train" 531
Mullikin, Bill 266
Muppet Beach Party 349
Muppet Country Trio, The 433
Muppet Family Christmas, A 417
Muppet Movie, The 11, 135
"Muppet News" 184
Muppet Show, The 53, 61-62, 74, 78, 80, 81, 82-83, 87, **129**, 139, 142, 153, 156, 158, 184, 214, 215-217, 234, 239, 245, 248, 254, 256, 264, 276, 277, 278, 288, 291, 292, 299, 301, 312-313, 330, 332, 345, 353, 357, 388, 399, 411, 426, 433, 434, 435, 438, 444, 446, 455, 463, 470, 484, 485, 497, 506, 509, 512, 514, 517, 529-533
Muppet Show: Sex and Violence, The 214
Muppets on Puppets, The 365
Muppets Present . . . Great Moments in American History, The 255
Muppets Take Manhattan, The 240
Muppets Tonight 262
Muppets Valentine Show, The 214, 303, 497
Muppets: A Celebration of 30 Years, The 217
"Murder He Says" 256
Murphy, Chuck 406
Murray, Tom 296, 333, 364, 439, 470
Murrow, Edward R. 77, 145, 287
Mushmellon 48, **50**, 50-51, **58**, 220, 286, 312, 329, 420, 422, 437, 462, 489
Musically Mad 461
"Musicians, The" 250, 252, 278, 291, 306, 401

"Muskrat" 303, 450
"Mutual Admiration Society" 531
"My Baby" 359-360, 438
"My Baby Just Cares for Me" 405
"My Friend the Ghost" 531
"My Future Just Passed" 301
"My Gal Sal" 244
"My Name Is John Wellington Wells" 420
"Myrtle" 325, 452
Mysels, Sammy 257
"Mysterioso" 386

"Natives Are Restless Tonight, The" 243
Naturals, The 275, 277
Nazarro, Cliff 235-236, 240
Nebel, Jane *see* Henson, Jane
Nelson, Jerry 212-213, 215, 239, 433
"Never Hit Your Grandma with a Shovel (Use an Ax Instead)" 255, 414
"Never Took a Lesson in My Life" 531
"Never Trust a Woman" 361-362, 385
"New Face on the Barroom Floor, The" 532
"New Philosopher, The" 532
Newman, Greatrex 288, 430
"News of the World" 236
Newsom, Bobo 108
Nichols, Mike 351-352, 386, 424
"Night Before Christmas, The" 316, 417, 538
"Night Heat" 430
Nina & Frederik 499-500
"Nine Pound Hammer" 532
Nixon, Richard 96-97, **97**, 195, 197, 467, 474, 502

"No Ring on Her Finger" 258
Nolan, Kathy 478
Noland, Kenneth 27
"None But the Lonely Heart" 294, 371-372
Nordine, Ken 79, 147-148, 157, 267, 309, 321, 338, 352, 359-360, 422, 431, 438, 447, 473, 479, 531
Norman Luboff Choir, The 479
Norman, Loulie Jean 325, 391, 400, 403, 452, 471
Norworth, Jack 364, 450
"Not of This Earth" 532
"Nowhere" 366, 452
"Numba One Day of Christmas (The Twelve Days of Christmas)" 416
Nureyev, Rudolf 332
"Nuttin' for Christmas" 314, 415
Nutty Squirrels, The 504

O'Brian, Jack 61
O'Reilly, Rosemary 266
Oakland, Ben 244
"Oh Boy! (Ain't It Great to Be Crazy)" 272
"Oh That's Terrible" 429
"Oh, Don't Go Near Them Lion's Cage Tonight (Don't Go in the Lion's Cage Tonight)" 442
"Oh, Happy Day" 295
Ol' Brown Ears Is Back 506
"Old Chimney, The" 264
"Old Grey Mare, The" 511
"Old King Cole" 280
"Old MacDonald Had a Farm" 268, 271-272
"Old Man Atom" 288
"Old Man River" 293

"Old Payola Roll Blues (Like the Beginning), The" 423
"Old Philosopher on the Range, The" 532
"Old Philosopher, The" 252, 341-342, 350, 452, 458
"Old Piano Roll Blues, The" 423
"Old, Old Vienna" 252, 315, 409
Oliver, Sy 246, 257, 281, 398
Olsen, Dorothy 277
Omar **43**, 43-44, 109, 111-112, **123**, 130, **151**, 151-152, 166, **168**, 173, 175, 177, 179, 181, 183, 201, 220, **221**, 306, 307, 308, 309-310, 313, 315, 318-319, 320, 321, 322, 323, 333, 343, 344, 346-347, 348-349, 350, 354, 355-356, 358, 361, 364, 365, 367, 368, 369-370, 372, 374, 375, 376, 379, 380, 381, 382, 394, 399, 412-414, 417, 421, 422, 438-439, 442, 447, 448, 449, 452, 453, 461-462 464, 481, 496, 502, 513, 524, 525-526, 527, 536-537
Omnibust 460
"On the Good Ship Lollipop" 282, **356**, 356-357
"On Top of Old Smokey" 157, 353, 360-361, 395
"Once in Love with Amy" 245, 282
"One Hundred Easy Ways" 436
"One Suit" 532
"Oooh Looka There, Ain't She Pretty?" 241
"Open the Door, Richard" 238, 313, 391, 501
Oscar the Grouch 79, 213, 220
Osser, Glenn 272, 401
Oswalt, Patton 237

"Outer Space" 352
"Outfox the Fox" 269
Oz, Frank xi-xiii, **xiii**, 11, 106-107, 161, 162, 163, 210, 212, 213, 214, 215, 433
Oznowicz, Mike and Frances 107, 161, 163

Paar, Jack 61, 318, 502, 516
"Pachalafaka" 80, **298**, 299, 329, 399, 512
Paganini, Niccolò 250
Page, Patti 243
Paine, John 497
Pal, George 104
Palmer, John 273
"Pal-Yat-Chee" 532
Paone, Nicola 248-249
"Pardners" 274
Parker, Charlie 511
Parks and Recreation 237
Parnell, Jack 216
Parnes, Paul 500
Partlow, Vern 288
Partridge Family, The 162
"Party Political Speech" 470
"Party, The" 136
"Party's Over, The" 276
"Pass the Football" 419
Patience and Prudence 282
Patridge, Prince 529, 530
Patterson, Ruth 466
Paul Arnold Show, The 54
Payne, Bob 1, 47, 70, 86, 87, **87**, **91**, 92, 96, **97**, **122**, 122, 126, 126, 128-129, 158, 160, 208, 214, 371, 416
Payne, John Howard 432
"Peanuts" 472

Pearce, Alice 353-354, 355, 358-359, 365, 385, 392, 403, 477
Peck, Fletcher 238, 343
"Peony Bush, The" 295, 313, 380
"Perfidia" 290
Perito, Nick 252, 315, 409
Perry Como Winter Show, The 240, 273
"Person to Pearson" 287, 338, 510
Person to Person 77, 145, 287
Pete Seeger & Brother Kirk Visit Sesame Street 254
Peterson, Marie 243
Phelps, Gordon N. 416
Pierre the French Rat 12, 15-16, **32**, 32, 220
"Pig & the Inebriate, The" 444
Piller, Gene 267
"Place Pigalle" 263
Platters, The 337
Playmates, The 310
"Please" 391
"Please Help Me, I'm Falling" 468
"Please Pass the Biscuits" 340
"Ploop de Ma Tante, La" 468
Pober, Leon 249, 250
"Pocketbook Song, The" 367
Pockriss, Lee 303, 349, 450
Podell, Art *see* Art and Paul
"Poison to Poison" 77, **145**, 145-146
Ponchielli, Amilcare 373
Porter, Bob 17
Porter, Cole 71, 157, 253, 351, 357, 398, 444, 455, 489
"Possibilities" 249
Potash, Paul *see* Art and Paul
Pound Hounds, The 432-433
Prairie Dawn 47, 213
"Preacher and the Bear, The" 237

Presley, Elvis 74, 112, 246, 331, 337, 426, 427, 432, 486, 499, 506
Preston, Robert 297
Prima, Louis 71, 142, 259, 322, 333, 351, 366, 432, 536
Producers' Showcase 283
Professor Orin E. Madcliffe **44,** 44-47, **45, 46,** 52, 64, 67-68, 111-112, 114, **125,** 171, 184, 185, 187, 201, 203, 213, 215, 220, 285, 286, 298, 305, 306, 308, 309, 313, 314, 316, 317, 318, 319, 323, 328, 330, 333, 339, 346, 348, 352, 355, 365, 367, 368, 369-370, 372, 373, 375, 376, 377, 378-379, 380, 382, 383, 385, 386, 387, 389, 390, **390,** 392, 393, 394, 395, 398, 400, 402, 404, 406, 407, 408, 411, 412, 417, 419, 421, 425, 428, 432, 433, 434, 443, 447, 448, 449, 452, 455, 456, 457-458, **469,** 469-470, 472, 477-478, 485, 487, 501, 502, 506, 511, 519-520, 522, 523, 525-526, 536-537
"Professor, The" 458
"Protection" 532
"Proud New Father" 101, 323, 395, 456
Pryor, Ainslie 289, 366
Pryor, Joe 325, 452
"Pum-Pa-Lum (The Bad Donkey)" 279-280
"Punsmoke (Powderburn)" **144,** 144-145, 387
Puppet Up! 223
"Purple People Eater, The" 532

Quadling, Lew 276
Quenzer, Arthur 253, 393

"Quest for Bridey Hammerschlaugen, The" 335, 444

Radio Programme No. 1 Audio Collage: Henry Jacobs' Music and Folklore 270
"Rain No More" 303
Rainger, Ralph 391, 479
Ram, Buck 337, 447
"Ramona" 443
Randall, Tony 437-438
Randolph Singers, The 319, 320
Randolph, David 319, 320
Randy Van Horne Swing Choir 310
Raposo, Joe 83
Rash, Bryson 229, 230, 534
Raskin, Ruby 312, 404, 422
Ravenscroft, Thurl 242, 264, 433, 442
Rawls, Lou 434
Ray Charles Singers, The 280
Raye, Don 246
"Real Gone Galoot" 411
Red Ingle and The Natural Seven 318, 329, 366, 419, 452
Red Ingle and The Unnatural Seven 348
Redman, Don 245
Reed, Robin 161
Reep, Philip 257
Reese, Claude 257
Reiner, Carl 272
Reisman, Joe 280, 303
"Reluctant Cannibal, The" 486
René, Henri 244, 250, 252, 262, 263, 289, 291, 306, 358, 378, 401
Revel, Harry 240
Reynolds, J. J. 389
"Rhapsody from Hunger(y)" 361
Ricardo, Don 265
Ridgely, Lois Jean 265
Rimsky-Korsakov, Nikolai 443
Rinker, Al 247, 249
Robbins, Marty 443-444
Roberts, Kenny 270, 342, 409
Roberts, Ruth 267
Robertson, Don 468
Robin 357
"Robin, He Married" 408
Robin, Leo 391, 479
Robin, Sid 320, 416
Robinson, Carson 357
Robinson, Jessie Mae 243, 355, 456
Robison, Carson 263, 292, 342, 405, 455
"Rock Around Stephen Foster" 336-337, 438
"Rock Island Line" 292, 336, 409
Rock, George 264, 316, 396, 402, 403
Rockwell, Alex 62, 540
Rocky & His Friends 500
Rodgers, Richard 294, 387
"Roger Boom" 277, 278, 307, 458, 503
Roger Roger 452
Rogers, Jr., Will 61
Rogers, Roy 238-239, 497
Rogers, Smokey 420
Roland, Fritz 45
Rome, Harold 391, 400
Rose, Billy 350, 459, 509
Rose, David 513
Rose, Rufus and Margo 104
Ross, Jerry 239, 301, 449
"Round and Round" 280-281
Rowlf the Dog 2, 83, 210-211, 215, 222, 246, 255, 264, 270, 485, 506

Rubinstein, Marty 351, 386, 424
Ruby, Herman 324, 459
Rugolo. Pete 256
Rundvold, Inga 22, **22**, 119, 232, 534
Russell, Bob 251, 368, 440
Russell, Rosalind 436

"Sad Cowboy, The" 248, 345, 410
"Sadder-But-Wiser Girl, The" 297
Sadoff, Bob 264
Sahlin, Don 104, 106, 210, 212
Salaway, Lowell 272
"Salt" 89, **90**, 236, 299, 344, 405
Sam **24**, 26-27, **29**, 29, 31, 33, **33**, 34-36, **34**, **35**, 37, 64, 68, **68**, 82, **91**, **97**, **109**, **127**, **141**, 142, 187, 188, 189, 191-193, 211, **219**, **220**, 220, 222, 283, 285, 302, 307, 312, 337, 359, 372, 377, **378**, 378, 385, 396, 399, 427, 434, 436, 446, 461, 465-466, 468, 499, 504, 506, 517, 527-528, **535**, 536
Sam Butera and The Witnesses 366
Sam the Eagle 276
"Sam, Don't Slam the Door!" 302
"Sam's Song (The Happy Tune)" 276
"Sample Song, The" 532
Sanford, Dick 257
"Santa Brought Me Choo Choo Trains (But Daddy's Having Fun)" 264
"Santa Claus Looks Like My Daddy" 264-265
"Santy's Movin' On" 264, 416
Sarnoff, David 84
Saturday Night Live 143
"Save the Bones for Henry Jones" 532

"Say 'Skada Wada Do" 480
Schafer, Milton 357, 424
Scharf, Walter 247, 249
Schell, Bob 281
Schlinger, Sol 382
Schluderberg, William 108, 110, 116, 188, 418, 518, 520-521, 528
Schmittmann, Bill 95
"Schnitzel Bank" 532
Schoen, Vic 251, 368, 440
Schrouder, Chuck 391
Schubert, Lettie 162
Schumann, Walter 276-277, 284, 320
Schwartz, Arthur 311, 467
Scoop and Skip 184
Scott, Bill 500
Scott, Willard 21, 70, 72, 218, **218**, 219
Scott, Winfield 233
Scourby, Alexander 488
Season's Greetings: A Christmas Festival of Stars! 416
"Secret Love" 532
Seeger, Pete 157, 254, 291, 498
Seelen, Jerry 330, 399
Segal, Jack 277
Sellers, Peter 470, 495-496
"Serutan Yob (A Song for Backward Boys and Girls Under 40)" 348
Sesame Street 2, 47, 79, 87, 139, 150, 184, 213, 215, 246, 250, 254, 261, 280, 281, 291, 303, 349, 353, 354, 383, 464, 472, 511
"Seven and a Half Cents" 532
Severson, Paul 370
Seville, David *see* Bagdasarian, Ross
"Shadrach" 532
Shand, Terry 253

Shapiro, Joe 280
Shaw, Tom 110-111
"Sh-Boom" 300, 342, 459
"She Is More to Be Pitied Than Censured" 259
"She May Have Seen Better Days" 254
"She Never Left the Table" 240
"She's a Lady" 290, 369, 397
Shearing, George 297-298, 308
"Sheesh, What a Grouch!" 532
Sherman, Allan 255
Sherwin, Manning 258
Shields, Brooke 388
Shields, Ren 273
"Shine on Your Shoes, A" 311-312
Shirl, Jimmy 272
Shore, Dinah 250, 252, 289, 291, 306, 358, 378, 401, 426
Shore, Sammy 374, 440, 530
"Side by Side" 485
Siegmeister, Elie 421
"Sifting, Whimpering Sands" 266-267
Sigler, Maurice 242
"Silas Lee" 259
"Silent TV" 532
"Silhouettes" 289, 366
"Silly Signs Song" 272
Silver, Frank 484, 513
Simpson, Jim 534
Sinatra, Frank 74
Sinatra, Nancy 331, 367
"Sincere" 297, 405
"Singin' in the Rain" **158**, 158, 408
"Sipping Cider Through a Straw" 257
"Six Months Out of Every Year" 301, 449
"Sixteen Tons" 260-261

Skin, Sammy 491
Slatkin, Felix 266, 401
Slay, Jr., Frank C. 289, 366
"Sloop John B." 532
Smigel, Robert 143
Smiley, Guy 45, 68, 213
Smith Bros., The 302
Smith, Beasley 243
Smith, Dick 479
Smith, Gary 61, 62
Smith, Keely 71, 142, 322, 333, 351, 366, 432, 536
Smith, Landrew 367
Smith, Sheldon 347, 406
"Smoke! Smoke! Smoke! (That Cigarette)" 257
"Sneezin' Bee, The" 443
Snow, Hank 264, 416
"So Long" 532
"So Long, It's Been Good to Know You" 532
Solman, Alfred 253
"Somebody Else, Not Me" 336, 396
Somethin' Smith and the Redheads 246
"Somewhere Over the Rainbow" 532
Son of Word Jazz 352
"Song of Reproduction" 389
"Song of the Sewer" 305
Songer, Jim 136
Songs of Earth and Sky 510
Songs of the Pogo **80**, 80, 194, 408, 410, 411, 424, 465
Sons of the Pioneers 239, 288, 441
Sons of the Sons of the Pioneers 441
Sorcerer, The 420
"Sortileges" 452
Sousa, John Philip 510

"Southern Fried Boogie" 532
"Sow Song, The" 532
Spike Jones in Hi-Fi: A Spooktacular in Screaming Sound 77, 145, 391, 402, 403, 471
Spina, Harold 251, 282, 368, 440
Sportsmen Quartet, The 247, 248, 268, 271, 279, 345, 377, 410, 460, 505
Springer, Philip 276
Sprung, Lou 340
"Squirrel, The" 439
"S-S-S'Wonderful (Hector the Nearsighted Rattlesnake)" 49, 284, 379
"St. George and the Dragonet" 376-377
Stabile, Dick 242, 269, 347, 358, 393
Stafford, Jo 288, 317, 402-403, 427, 479, 480, 489
Stallman, Lou 280, 363
Stan Freberg Show, The 75
"Standing on the Corner" 272, 401
Standley, Johnny 101, 323, 395, 456
Stanley, Ray 275
Starlighters, The 479
"Stars and Stripes Forever, The" 461, 482, 510
"Steamboat Bill" 273
Steiner, Jacqueline 280, 322, 388
"Stereo Demonstration" 437-438
Sterling, Andrew B. 234, 259
Stern, Phil *see* Morgan, Freddy
Steve Allen Show, The 65, 68, 76, 179, 260
Stevens, James 470
Stewart, Harry 411
Stewart, Mike 407, 410
Stoller, Alvin 260, 305, 406

"Stone Cold Dead in the Market (He Had It Coming)" 281
Stone, Butch 235, 294, 303, 414
Stone, Cliffie 255, 315, 432
Stone, George 237
Stone, Jon 79
Stone, Wilson 274
Story, Milt 275
"Stranded in the Jungle" 532
Stringer, Tippy 22, **22**, 121, 122, 143, 230, 380, 534
Stritch, Elaine 326
"Struttin' with Some Barbeque" 532
Stuffed and Unstrung 222-223
Styne, Jule 260, 276, 288, 317, 326, 479
"Such a Night" 246
Sullivan, Ed 47, 60, 149, 213, 236, 426, 502
Sullivan, Gene 340
Sully, Lew 433
"Sunday Driving" 249-250
"Sunshine Girl" 381
"Sur La Route" 408
Sutton, Art 264
Svengoolie 392
"Swan Lake" 301
Swann, Donald 389, 399, 486
Swedish Chef, The 43, 44, 151, 152, 446, 484
"Sweet Violets" 426
Sweetums 142
"Swingin' Hammer" 532
Swope, Mel 162
Sylvie and Pup 161, 162
Syms, Sylvia 276

"Take a Letter, Miss Smith" 532
"Take Me Out to the Ball Game" 364, 450

"Take Me to Your President" 532
"Take Off the Mask" 532
"Tam Pierce" 532
"Tammy" 403
"Tango" 351-352, 424
"Tarzan and Jane" 532
Taylor, Irving 79-80, 296, 299, 325, 329, 331, 388, 399, 452, 512
Taylor, Peggy 391
Taylor, Tell 310
Tchaikovsky, Peter 294, 371
"Tea for Two" 514
Tedder, Karen 348
"Telephone No Ring, The" 248-249
Temple, Shirley 356-357
"Temptation" 532
"Tennessee Hillbilly Ghost" 243
Tepper, Sid 314, 415
Terribly Sophisticated Songs: A Collection of Unpopular Songs for Popular People 79, 299, 325, 331
Terry, Percy 367
Tetley, Walter 500
Textor, Keith 303
"That Holiday Spirit" 533
"That Old Black Magic" 34, 103, **141**, 142, 166, 322, 333, 372, 432, 536
"That Old Gang of Mine" 350, 459
"That's All Folks" 533
"That's My Boy" 343, 419
"That's What I Like About the South" 82, 366, 533
Theodore Bikel and Geula Gill Sing Folk Songs from Just About Everywhere 412
"There Is a Tavern in the Town" 252
"There Once Was a Poor Young Girl" 446
"There's a Hole in the Bucket" 464, 509
"There's a New Sound" 74, 296-297, 364, 439, 470
"There's No Piano in This House" 533
"They Call the Wind Maria" 357
"They Didn't Believe Me" 533
"They Laid Him in the Ground" 267, 447
"They Were Doing the Mambo" 533
"Thing, The" 236, 244, 278, **353**, 353-354, 385, 477
"Thirty Days" 365
"This is a Wife? (What is a Wife?)" 267
"This is Your Death / Two Heads Are Better Than One" 402
"This Ole World" 291
Thomas, Harry 278
Thomas, Jimmie 366
Thomas, John Charles 288-289, 430
Thomas, Millard 291
Thompson, Kay 347, 453, 503
Thornton, James 254
"Three Blind Mice" 280
Three Haircuts, The 271-272
"Three Little Pigs (Pee Little Thrigs)" 532
Thurber, James 20
"Tick-Tock Sick" 74, 425, 434, 435
Tillstrom, Burr 103, 104, **105**, 106, 124, 131, 208, 260
Time for Beany 75
Time Piece 148, 435
"To Keep My Love Alive" 294, 387
"To Morrow" 156, 433
Toads, The 300, 337, 342, 423, 447, 459

Today 12, 53, 148, 149, 162, 165, 208, 210, 425, 438, 484, 492, 498
Todd, Clarence 241
"Tombstone" 533
"Tongue Twisters" 241
Tonight Show, The 25, 58-61, 142, 149, 214, 244, 245, 312, 318
"Too Young" 269
Tormé, Mel 487
Travis, Merle 257, 260, 303, 450
"Triplets" 467
"Trouble with Harry, The" 81, 268, 397, 493
"True Love" 444
"Tschaikowsky (And Other Russians)" 300, 319, 415
Tucker, Monroe 529, 530
Turk, Roy 486
"Tweedle Dee" 21, 23, 215, 233
"Twelve Days of Christmas, The" 416
Twiggy 345
"Two Calypsos, The" 533

"Ugly Chile (You're Some Pretty Doll)" 250-251
"Ugly Duckling, The" 256, 349, 423

"Va Va Va Voom" 533
"Vagabond Lover" 533
Vagabonds, The 89, 236, 299, 344, 405
"Valentine" 263
Van Dyke, Dick 77, 250, 276
Van Dyke, Leroy 367
Van Heusen, James 274, 436
Van Pallandt, Frederik and Nina 499
Vance, Paul 303, 349, 450
Vanoff, Nick 59, 61

"Variation on an Old English Theme" 498
Vera, Ricky 284-285
VerStandig, M. Belmont and Helen 65, 66
"Very Square Dance" 412
Virginia, Mary 282
"Visit to the Spirit of the Crystal Ball, A" 438
"Viva Jujuy" 412
"Voice Coach, The" 81-82, 413
Voices of Walter Schumann, The 276-277, 320, 416
Von Blitzstein, Count 290
Von Tilzer, Albert 234, 364, 450
Von Tilzer, Harry 234, 259

"Wait 'till the Sun Shines, Nellie" 259
Wakely, Jimmy 238, 370, 437
Walker, Eddie 72
Wall, Russell
Wallace, Oliver 252, 289, 358, 378
Waller, Fats 435
Walsh, Robert V. 207
Walters, Barbara 208
"Waltz of the Bubbles" 513
Ward, Charles 273
Ward, Jay 359, 500
Warren, Fran 532
Warren, Harry 249, 439, 471
Washburne, Country 366, 452
Washburne, Joe 329, 419
"Watermelon Song, The" 533
"Wayfaring Stranger" 247, 352
Wayne, David 326
Wayne, Johnny 281, 398
Wayne, Mabel 242, 443
"We Wish You a Merry Christmas" 417

"Weather Warehouse" 4, **149**, 150, 508-509
Weaver, Doodles 77, 287, 360, 373, 414
Weavers, The 157, 291, 353, 417, 470, 474-475, 498
Webb, Jack 285, 376, 413
Weber, Edwin J. 299, 354
Weidler, George 264
Weidler, Walter 264
Weidler, Warner 264
Weil, Robert 236
Weill, Kurt 300
Weismantel, Fred 281
Welk, Lawrence 277, 278, 307, 376, 391-392, 458, 475, 503
"Well Anyway" 533
Welles, Orson 11-12
Wells, Robert 347, 453, 493, 503
Wenzlaff, Erwin 334, 375
"Westerners (Two Face West), The" 81, **159**, 159, 474
Weston, Paul 250, 288, 317, 344, 402, 427, 479, 480, 489
"What Are Folks Made Of?" 447
"What Are You Doing New Year's Eve?" 418
"What Did He Say? (The Mumble Song)" 236, 278, 299, 303, 304, 341, 403
"What Do You Hear from the Red Planet Mars?" 392, 533
"What Happened to the Hair (On the Head of the Man I Love?)" 245
"What is a Freem?" 533
"What it Was, Was Football" 533
"What Shall I Do with the Baby-O?" 533

"What'd He Say?" 303-304
"When I Was a Lad" 533
"When the Crabgrass Blooms Again" 331, 388
"When You See a Pretty Girl" 266
"When You Wish Upon a Star" 375
"Whence That Wince" 407-408
"Where Did You Get That Name?" 235
"Where is the Beast in You?" 326
"Wherefore Art Thou, Romeo?" 533
"While the Lights are Low" 275
White, Jesse 117, 423
Whiting, Margaret 418, 487
Whiting, Richard 301, 356, 391
"Who Takes Care of the Caretaker's Daughter" 500
"Who's on First?" 498
"Why Do I Love You?" 533
"Wild Bill Hiccup" 316, 396
Wilder Brothers, The 264
Wilkins xi, 65, 66, 67, **104**
Wilkins, Jr., John H. 65, 66-67, 424
Will I Ever Tell You 362
Willemetz, Albert 263
Williams, Clarence 248, 250-251
Williams, Pat 504
Williams, Spencer 248
Williams, Tex 257
Willson, Meredith 279, 295, 297, 313, 362, 380, 405, 457
Wilson, John N. 264
Wilson, Sandy 345, 413
"Winter Wonderland" 479
Winterhalter, Hugo 278
"Witch Doctor" 81, 326
"With Plenty of Money and You" 439
Wontkins xi, 65, 66, 67, **104**

Wood, Al 279
"Woodman, Woodman, Spare That Tree" 239-240
Woodrow, Professor Leaf 270, 373
Woods, Harry 485
Woodyard, Darrel 257
"Woolie Boogie Bee" 247
Worth, Bobby 367, 425
Wright, William 437, 515
"Wringle Wrangle" 533
"Wun'erful, Wun'erful!" 391-392
"Wyatt Earp Makes Me Burp" 441-442

"Ya Got Trouble" 457
"Yaller Rose of Texas You-All" 460
"Yankee Doodle" 423-424, 436
"Yellow Rose of Texas, The" 61, 260, 305, 338, 406
"Yes! We Have No Bananas" 53, 484, 513
"Yon-u-ary" 328, 427
Yorgesson, Yogi 411
Yorick 33, 43, **48**, 48-49, 59-60, 79, **87**, **91**, 114, 144, 157, 171, 187, 205, 211, 213, 214, 215, 217, 220, **302**, 308, 315, 320, 321, 322, 333, 342, 351, 354, 364, 369, 370-371, 376, 377, 384-385, 396, 398, 399, 407, 418, 425, 430, 434, 441, 447, 450, 454, 458, 461-462, 464, 465, 466, 467, 482, 490-491, 521, 536, 537
"Yosemite Sam" 292, 373
"You and I and George" 83, 506
"You Are My Love" 507
"You Are So Rare to Me" 271-272
"You Can't Do Wrong Doin' Right" 247
"You Can't Hurt Me Now Cuz I'm Daid" 296
"You Go Your Way (And I'll Go Crazy)" 240
"You Laughed When I Cried Over You (The Laughing Record)" 261
"You Need Feet" 343-344, 387
"You Need Hands" 344
"You're Just in Love" 445-446
"You're Not the Only Pebble on the Beach" 274
"You're the Top" 291
Young Man and a Maid: Love Songs of Many Lands 408
Young, Jim 65
Young, Joe 295, 350, 453
Young, Ralph 261
"Your Feet's Too Big" 435

"Zip Zip" 286
Zoocus 214

About the Author

Craig Shemin is a freelance writer/producer/director and President of The Jim Henson Legacy, a nonprofit organization dedicated to preserving and celebrating the work of Jim Henson. He began his career at The Jim Henson Company—then known as Henson Associates—where he wrote television scripts, books, computer games, trading cards, and lots of other stuff. His television work includes *Clifford the Big Red Dog*, *Courage the Cowardly Dog*, *Jim Henson's Dog City*, as well as shows that have nothing to do with dogs, including *Dora and Friends: Into the City*, *Lou and Lou: Safety Patrol*, and *Telling Stories with Tomie DePaola*. Shemin received a Writers Guild Award nomination for his work on *The Wubbulous World of Dr. Seuss* and an Emmy nomination for Disney's *Tasty Time with ZeFronk*. He co-produced and directed the *Spookley Holiday Show* series of holiday specials, and he writes and directs the long-running live concert series *LOS Kids* for New York City's Little Orchestra Society.

Shemin produced and directed *Behind the Scenes in Frogtown Hollow*, an award-winning documentary about *Emmet Otter's Jug-Band Christmas,* and wrote the sold-out live Jim Henson tribute concerts at Carnegie Hall in New York and the Fowler Centre in Wellington, New Zealand. He is the author of *The Muppets Character Encyclopedia*.

Craig Shemin lives in New York City with his wife, Tony-nominated actor and Muppet performer Stephanie D'Abruzzo.

CPSIA information can be obtained
at www.ICGtesting.com
Printed in the USA
LVHW080758080323
741127LV00001B/5